THE ULTIMATE
Anti-Inflammatory Diet
COOKBOOK

800 Healthy and Delicious Recipes to Reduce Inflammation, Boost Autoimmune System and Strengthen Overall Health| 28-day meal plan with daily anti-inflammation tips and motivational quotes

Doreen J. Murphy

TABLE OF CONTENTS

CHAPTER 4: SOUPS AND SALADS

CHAPTER 5: VEGETARIAN MAINS

CHAPTER 6: FISH AND SEAFOOD

CHAPTER 7: POULTRY AND MEATS

CHAPTER 8: SAUCES, CONDIMENTS AND DRESSINGS

CHAPTER 9: SMOOTHIES AND DRINKS

CHAPTER 10: SNACKS, SIDES AND APPETIZERS

CHAPTER 11: DESSERTS

Introduction

If you've picked up this book, inflammation must be on your mind—fighting it, preventing it, and staying healthy every day. You've come to the right cookbook! For many of us, inflammation can cause problems and symptoms that may be uncomfortable, painful or even unbearable. You are not alone in experiencing the symptoms of inflammation or perhaps knowing somebody who does. Inflammation is a normal part of the body's response system but what happens when you experience extreme pain and further conditions? That's when the inflammation process has gone wrong; inflammation has been linked to various symptoms and pain in the joints, as well as many other life-changing diseases such as diabetes and even cancer.

I'll teach you how to fight inflammation using recipes with minimal prep work and simple ingredients. They also taste amazing so you won't get bored. The Ultimate Anti-Inflammatory Diet Cookbook is not a radical new 'fad' diet; it does not encourage you to live on bland and uninspiring foods; it does not recommend unrealistically small portion sizes, nor does it suggest that you need to stick to crazy 'one day off' and 'one day on' eating regimes. The recipes you will find in this cookbook do not require you to remain stuck at the stove for ages, preparing everyone else a lovely dinner, whilst you're cooking up an entirely separate dish for yourself.

Instead, the anti-inflammatory diet values fresh, inflammation reducing foods that are easy to prepare and delicious to eat! With this cookbook, you can continue to enjoy delicious meals with your loved one, family and friends, whilst at the same time reducing inflammation, becoming pain free and improving your overall health. There are 800 scrumptious meal and drink ideas for you to try as well as an overview of what inflammation is, the symptoms and diseases linked to inflammation, and useful information about the types of foods that should be avoided as well as those you can continue to indulge in!

The 28-day meal plan will help you get started immediately and are designed for you to continue cooking the meals you love, without worrying whether the ingredients are going to flare up your symptoms and make you feel even worse.

Each of the recipes in this cookbook are made with easy to find fresh ingredients, are simple to prepare, and are either quick to bake, steam or saute, or they make use of a slow cooker, giving you more time to get on with your busy life whilst dinner's cooking!

Our philosophy is that if you take the time to understand which foods make you feel great and which flare up your symptoms, only cook with those that make you feel better and stick to fresh and healthy options, then you won't need to worry about weight and your symptoms and inflammation will in time start to reduce.

This will make you feel amazing and get you back on track with enjoying life rather than feeling pain.

Happy cooking and good luck on your anti-inflammatory journey!

CHAPTER 1:
UNDERSTANDING INFLAMMATION

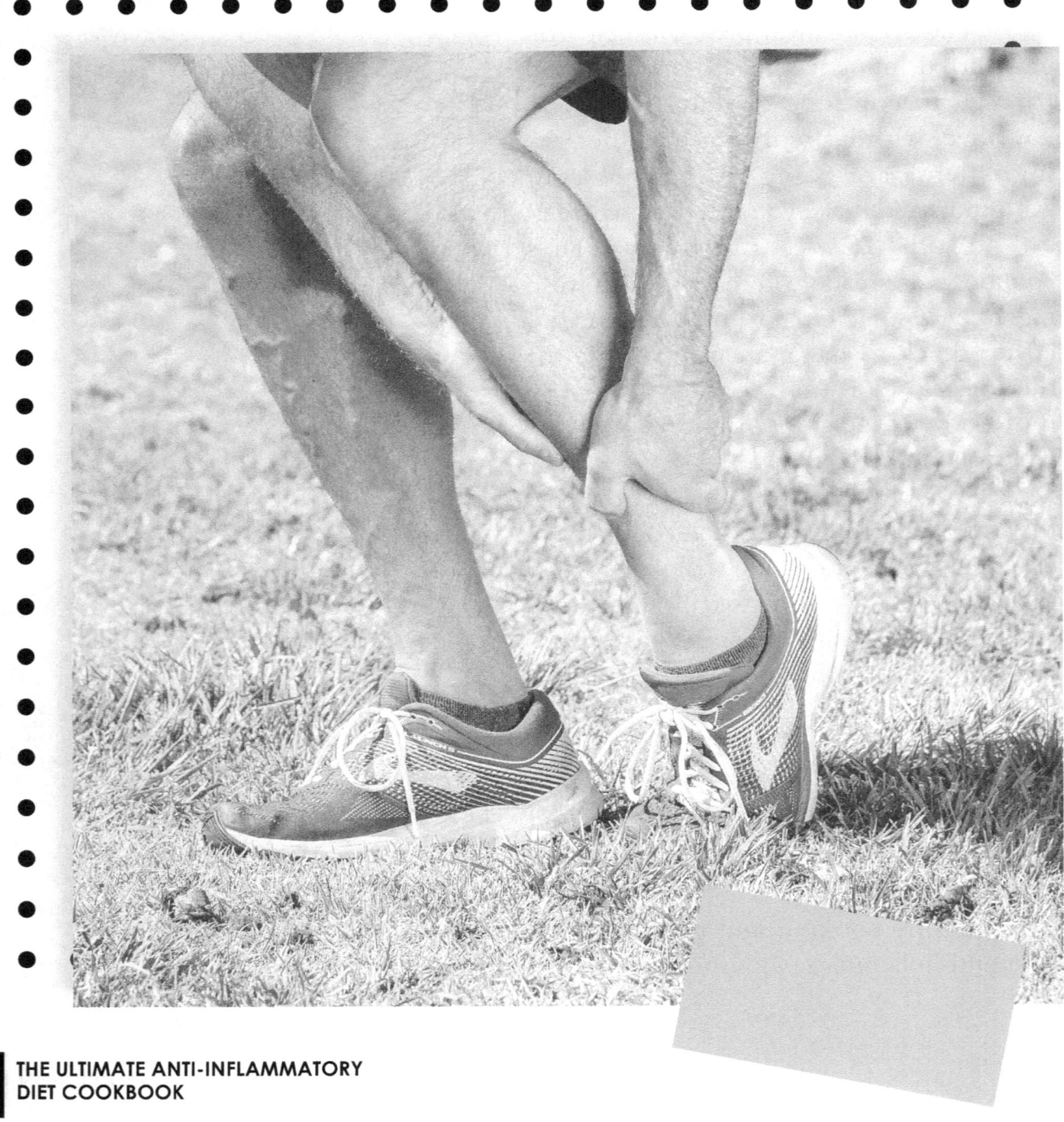

**THE ULTIMATE ANTI-INFLAMMATORY
DIET COOKBOOK**

What Exactly Is Inflammation?

If you've ever had a cold, a cut, a rash, or a bruise, then you've experienced inflammation. In urgent situations, inflammation is incredibly useful—similar to when emergency personnel are dispatched to help accident victims. It activates our immune system, destroys pathogens, and delivers needed oxygen and nutrients to affected areas. However, if inflammation becomes chronic, or one's immune system fails to work properly, a person can develop a host of diseases that can impact all aspects of day-to-day existence.

Inflammation—which is a growing problem worldwide—can be caused by such things as poor nutrition, environmental toxins, genetics, reliance on medication, stress, and limited physical activity. However, when educated and prepared, you can take control of your health, both preventing inflammation from happening or managing it when it occurs.

Inflammation is a normal, healthy response to an injury or infection. It's a protective measure, designed to sweep out harmful invaders so we can repair and heal. Without inflammation, a simple cut from slicing vegetables or a bruise from banging your elbow could become quite dangerous.

Acute inflammation is short-lived, allowing us to repair and move on with our lives. Chronic inflammation occurs when we are unable to quash the original injury, the irritant continues to enter the body, or, as is the case with autoimmune diseases, the body begins to attack healthy tissues.

The Root of Many Health Problems

Inflammation is at the root of many diseases and conditions. Any condition that ends with "itis" involves inflammation: arthritis, colitis, endocarditis, bronchitis, appendicitis, laryngitis, just to name a few. Everyone is susceptible to inflammation, though people with weakened immune systems—children, the elderly, those with autoimmune conditions—can be at an increased risk.

Health conditions linked to inflammation include:

Inflammatory Bowel Disease (IBD).

This includes Crohn's disease and colitis, which occur when the digestive tract becomes inflamed, leading to poor digestion and absorption of nutrients. According to the Centers for Disease Control and Prevention (CDC) and Crohn's and Colitis Canada, more than 1 million people in the United States have IBD, and one in 150 Canadians live with the disease—the highest of any country in the world.

Heart Disease.

This is a broad term for a wide range of conditions that impact the cardiovascular system. The Centers for Disease Control and Prevention (CDC) report that heart disease is the leading cause of death in the United States for both men and women, killing 610,000 people every year.

Obesity.

Excess weight is a worldwide problem. According to the World Health Organization (WHO), obesity rates have doubled since 1980, and 1.9 billion people around the world are obese.

Rheumatoid Arthritis and Osteoarthritis.

Rheumatoid arthritis occurs when the body attacks its own tissues, causing inflammation in the joints. Osteoarthritis also involves inflammation, but its cause is wear and tear in the joints over time. In the United States, 52.5 million people suffer from arthritis and CDC experts predict this number will grow to 67 million by 2030.

Allergies.

Food, drugs, animals, plants, mold, latex, or other toxins can cause the immune system to overreact, leading to a host of uncomfortable symptoms. The American College of Allergy, Asthma & Immunology estimates that more than 50 million Americans suffer from allergies.

Asthma.

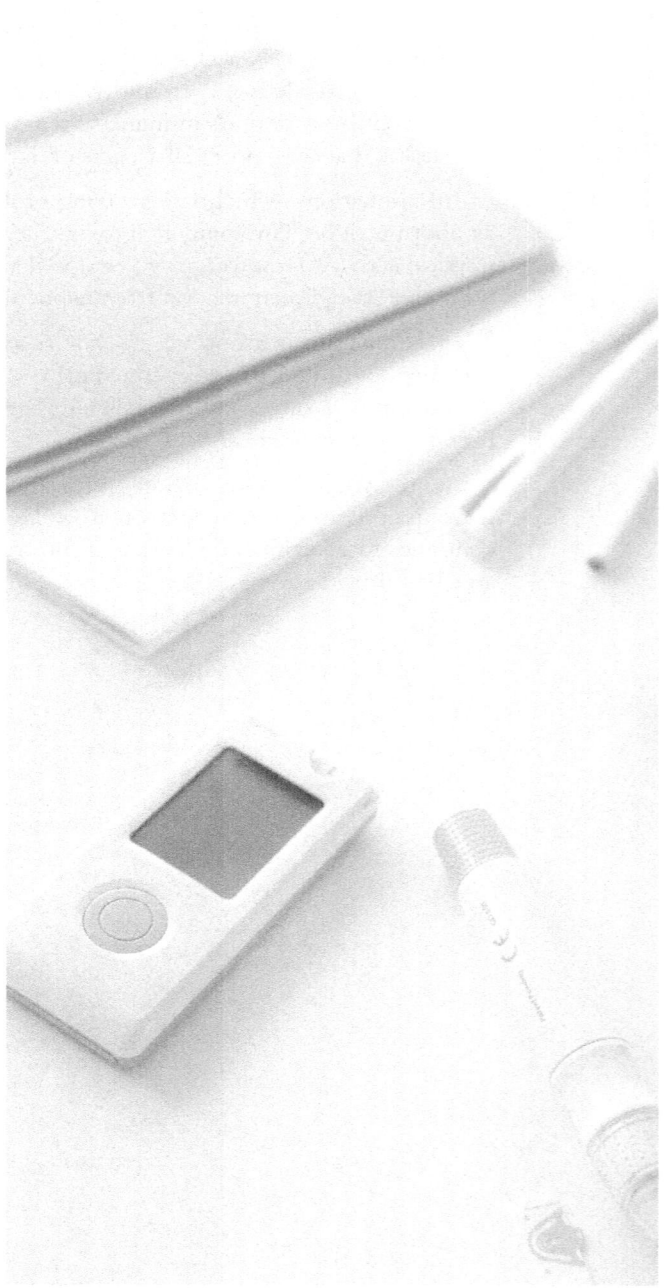

THE ULTIMATE ANTI-INFLAMMATORY DIET COOKBOOK

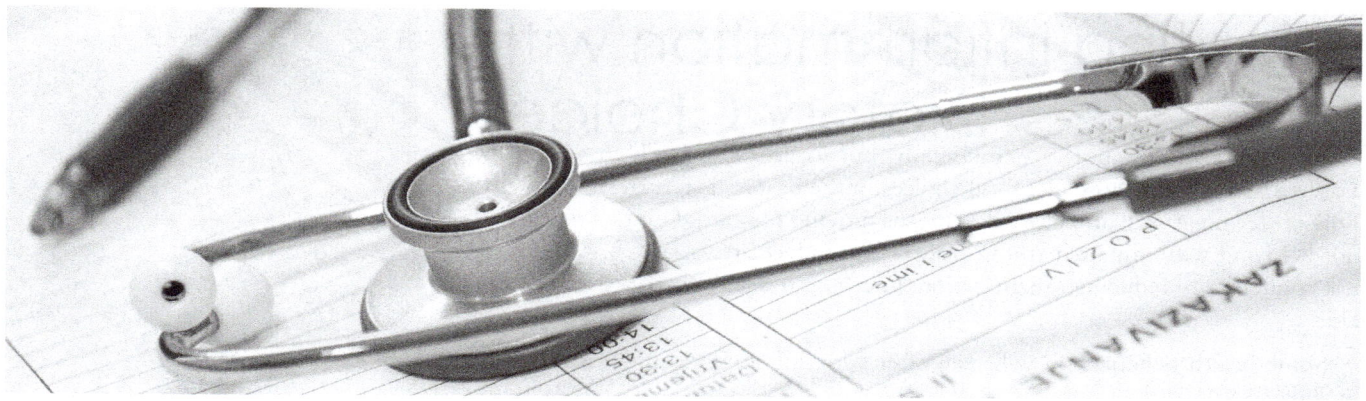

This disease of the lungs involves coughing, shortness of breath, and chest tightness. The National Heart, Lung, and Blood Institute says that 25 million adults and seven million children live with this condition.

Lupus.

This autoimmune disease involves the body attacking its own tissues, leading to inflammation in many parts of the body. The Lupus Foundation of America indicates it mostly affects young women, and about 1.5 million people in the United States have forms of lupus; a 2002 CDC report noted that African American women are three times more likely to get lupus than women of other ethnicities.

Hashimoto's Disease.

This is an autoimmune disease in which the immune system attacks and damages the thyroid, which can lead to swelling of the thyroid (called a goiter), among other symptoms. The journal Thyroid Research reports that Hashimoto's is the most common hypothyroid condition in the United States.

Diabetes.

This occurs when the body doesn't produce enough insulin, or can't effectively use the insulin it creates. Many complications from diabetes involve inflammation, such as obesity, atherosclerosis, and foot ulcers. In the United States, 20.9 million people have been diagnosed with type 2 diabetes—a number that has tripled since 1980, according to the CDC.

Cancer.

This happens when abnormal cells grow, invade different parts of the body, and hijack healthy cells. It is the leading cause of death worldwide. According to the World Health Organization (WHO), 14 million cancer cases are diagnosed each year and that number is expected to rise by a whopping 70 percent in the next two decades.

Celiac Disease.

Having this autoimmune disease means the body can't process gluten, leading to damage in the small intestine. According to the National Foundation for Celiac Awareness, approximately one in 133 Americans have celiac disease, though many people go undiagnosed. Untreated celiac disease can lead to other conditions like diabetes and dermatitis herpetiformis, an uncomfortable skin condition.

Multiple Sclerosis (MS).

This autoimmune disease of the nervous system results in the protective coatings on nerve cells—called myelin sheaths—being attacked and damaged. This can cause vision problems, disrupted motor function, dizziness, and muscle weakness. The National Multiple Sclerosis Society estimates that 400,000 Americans suffer from MS.

Skin Diseases.

Inflammatory skin conditions such as eczema, acne, rosacea, and psoriasis can lead to redness, itchiness, dry skin, skin bumps, and pimples. The Encyclopedia of Natural Medicine says that eczema affects two to seven percent of the population, while two to four percent have psoriasis. According to the National Rosacea Society, 16 million Americans suffer from that condition.

Headaches.

Tension headaches usually involve a steady, dull pain or pressure, while migraines tend to have a throbbing or pounding quality. The WHO says nearly half of adults worldwide experience at least one headache a year; according to the Migraine Research Foundation, 36 million Americans are affected by migraines.

Brain Disorders.

Neurologist David Perlmutter, MD, author of Grain Brain, links inflammation and the consumption of sugar and carbs to a variety of brain disorders, including dementia, ADHD, anxiety, depression, and epilepsy.

Fighting Inflammation with Dietary Choices

We all make bad choices occasionally, but we learn from them and grow. Forgive yourself for those bad food choices in the past and start fresh—literally! Following an anti-inflammatory diet means moving forward. Guilt or regret will not help and will only hold you in place—and induce stress, which we know is not conducive to reducing inflammation. Focus on the good—no, great—things ahead.

Some health benefits you will reap after adopting an anti-inflammatory diet include:

Reduction in symptoms. As you consistently choose to fill your plate with soothing, anti-inflammatory food, you'll likely notice your symptoms diminish. If your symptoms are especially cumbersome and intrusive, this will be a great relief!

More energy. When you fuel your body with the variety of macro- and micronutrients it needs, you'll feel more energized and ready to tackle daily activities.

Improved digestion. Good health begins with good digestion. Since the recipes in this book all have minimal ingredients, the result is less work for your body to process them. You may notice fewer digestive problems, such as acid reflux, bloating, cramping, or gas, while on an anti-inflammatory diet. Also, 70 percent of the immune system is located in and around the digestive tract. A healthy digestive tract means a healthy immune system, too!

Increased focus. You may feel more clear-headed, more attentive, and sharper—always a good thing.

Fewer aches and pains. Our immune response naturally produces redness, swelling, or pain so the chemical messengers can sweep away the injury and heal the body. An anti-inflammatory diet can lead to fewer aches and pains, as that redness or swelling won't happen in the first place.

A strengthened immune system. Widespread inflammation means your body is on high alert, sending out inflammatory messengers on a regular basis. Without the constant fire of inflammation to douse, your immune system will work more efficiently.

Great for gluten free. For many people who have a gluten allergy, this book can also help you. A lot of the time people may not recognize gluten as a problem until they're on this diet or a gluten-free diet. The anti-inflammatory nature of this diet can actually help relieve the symptoms experienced by those who are intolerant to gluten.

Improve your skin. Alongside all of these benefits, the diet can also greatly improve skin. Sometimes, inflammation can cause dry and ageing skin and you might also have noticed redness, and even problems such as rosacea of the skin, all of which which can be caused by inflammation. This diet can help improve your skin's appearance, meaning you'll feel and look younger!

Be the happiest and healthiest version of yourself. Making your own well-informed choices can change your life for the better. Try this diet and you will soon realize the potential that your body and mind have, and what you've been missing out on all this time. Don't let your health get in the way of feeling happy – eat well, live well and be well!

Empowered Eating for Healthy Living

Food plays a key role in the inflammatory response. Our food choices can soothe, or worsen, inflammation. First, let's look at foods to eat on an anti-inflammatory diet. The following foods and food groups are packed with nutrients that prevent or reduce inflammation. So eat up!

Foods Worth Embracing

Allium vegetables. ✓

Onions, garlic, leeks, shallots, scallions, ramps, and chives offer a host of benefits. Onions are a rich source of vitamin C and quercetin (which helps relieve allergy symptoms). Onions also contain onionin A—a molecule that targets the immune system to prevent unwanted inflammation. Garlic is no slouch either; it contains a range of sulfurous compounds that reduce inflammation throughout the body, plus it has antiviral and antibacterial properties.

Apple cider vinegar. ✓

Made from fermented apples, apple cider vinegar is a good source of probiotics and can help boost stomach acid levels. Apple cider vinegar has long been used to address a wide variety of inflammatory conditions, including Crohn's disease, colitis, arthritis, diabetes, colds, and flu. Be sure to select raw, unpasteurized apple cider vinegar to maximize its health benefits.

Basil. ✓

Eugenol, a volatile oil found in basil, inhibits the enzymes that produce inflammation (and actually affects the same enzymes targeted by NSAIDs).

Berries. ✓

Blueberries, raspberries, blackberries, and strawberries are potent sources of antioxidants that combat cellular damage and inhibit the enzymes that promote inflammation.

Berries are also high in fiber, which benefits the digestive tract, cardiovascular system, and blood sugar levels.

Bone broth. ✓

Bone broth, prepared with organic animal bones, simmered for at least several hours, contains the amino acids glycine, proline, and arginine. It helps support the digestive tract by bringing digestive juices to the gut, and reduces joint pain.

Coconut oil and extra-virgin olive oil. ✓

Coconut oil is a healthy saturated fat that is especially high in lauric acid, which enriches brain function and the immune system. It is easily digested and used immediately by the body for energy rather than being stored as fat.

Extra-virgin olive oil contains numerous polyphenols that reduce the chemical messengers and enzymes that lead to inflammation.

Dark leafy greens. ✓

Dark leafy greens contain the antioxidant vitamins A, C, E, and K, which combat cellular damage that can contribute to inflammation. They're also great sources of anti-inflammatory omega-3 fatty acids and B vitamins, which help manage stress and nourish the nervous system.

Dill.

This herb helps neutralize carcinogens and is used for digestive problems like gas, indigestion, and constipation.

Fennel.

This sweet vegetable contains a number of anti-inflammatory phytonutrients, but it is especially high in a compound called anethole. It has anti-inflammatory and anti-cancer properties, and helps shut down the signaling process that triggers inflammation. Fennel also contains antioxidants and immune-boosting nutrients.

Fish.

Wild salmon, sardines, anchovies, mackerel, and halibut are wonderful sources of omega-3 fatty acids—the healthy fats. Salmon, in particular, is high in two omega-3s called EPA and DHA, which help produce anti-inflammatory molecules.

Ginger.

This root contains anti-inflammatory compounds called gingerols, which inhibit pro-inflammatory molecules. Ginger is used to treat a wide variety of conditions, including digestive issues, nausea, motion sickness, arthritis, headaches, colds, and flu.

Gluten-free grains.

Quinoa and brown rice are used throughout the anti-inflammatory recipes here, and for good reason.

Quinoa is a complete plant-based source of protein, which means it has the same amino acids found in animal products. Sufficient protein is key to healing inflammation. It's also a rich source of magnesium, a relaxant mineral that reduces inflammation and contains vitamin E.

Brown rice is also high in magnesium as well as selenium, which helps with detoxification and protects cells from damage.

Natural sweeteners.

While refined white sugars are inflammatory, there are some natural sweeteners that can be used in an anti-inflammatory diet. Raw honey is rich in healing amino acids, digestive enzymes, and antiviral constituents—helping to enhance the immune system. Maple syrup is rich in antioxidants, plus it's high in zinc—another important nutrient for the immune system. Of course, using natural sugars is completely optional. Omit them if you prefer to avoid sweeteners completely.

Nuts and seeds.

Walnuts, almonds, cashews, hemp seeds, chia seeds, flaxseed, and more contain a wide range of healthy fats, protein, and fiber. Walnuts, hemp seed, chia seeds, and flaxseed are particularly high in omega-3 fatty acids.

Pineapple.

The core and stem of this tropical fruit contains bromelain, which reduces inflammation and helps protein digestion.

Root vegetables.

Carrots, sweet potatoes, parsnips, turnips, celery root, rutabaga, and beets are anti-inflammatory and antioxidant powerhouses.

Carrots and sweet potatoes are rich sources of vitamin A, which helps nourish the mucosal cells in the digestive tract, aids vision, boosts the immune system, and keeps skin healthy.

Sweet potatoes contain anthocyanin pigments and beets are full of compounds called betalains, both of which reduce the production of inflammatory enzymes.

Sustainable, organic meat.

Lamb, chicken, and turkey are high in protein, which is essential for healing and repairing inflammation. They are also rich in B vitamins, particularly B12—a key nutrient for the nervous system rarely present in plants.

Turmeric.

Turmeric's anti-inflammatory power stems from curcumin. It can help reduce inflammation associated with inflammatory bowel disease, arthritis, cystic fibrosis, and cancer.

Winter squashes.

Similar to root vegetables, winter squashes contain high amounts of vitamins C and A. They also contain special compounds called cucurbitacins that inhibit the enzymes that lead to inflammation.

THE ULTIMATE ANTI-INFLAMMATORY DIET COOKBOOK

Foods to Avoid or Cut Down:

After reading about which foods to eat, Let's look at foods to avoid on an anti-inflammatory diet, as well as unexpected or hidden sources for these inflammation-inducing foods.

Gluten

Gluten is a protein found in wheat, wheat germ, barley, rye, spelt, kamut, farro, bulgur, semolina, farina, and triticale. People with celiac disease mount an immune response to a specific protein in gluten called gliadin. As a result, the immune cells destroy the microvilli in the small intestine, which are responsible for absorbing nutrients.

For people without celiac, gluten can still be incredibly hard to process, and can aggravate most inflammatory conditions. Some effects of consuming gluten include digestive upset, brain fog, sinus problems, joint pain, blood sugar imbalances, hormonal imbalances, and skin conditions.

Dairy

Most people don't produce the lactase enzyme required to digest the lactose sugars in cow's milk, leading to bloating, gas, and diarrhea.

Milk is a mucus-forming food and, when that mucus coats the digestive tract, it prevents nutrients from being absorbed. Dairy cows raised for conventional milk products are fed growth hormones and antibiotics, which can interfere with a person's hormonal balance and/or lead to inflammation. Finally, conventional dairy products are often loaded with sugar and preservatives (especially the low-fat ones) and this can further contribute to the inflammatory processes.

Corn

Corn is a common allergen, and it is also often genetically modified—about 90 percent of corn in the United States is genetically engineered, according to the GMO Compass website. Genetically modified organisms, or GMOs, are relatively new to our food system and can potentially pose serious risks to health. For example, they can suppress the immune system and encourage inflammation. Corn is ubiquitous in processed foods, as well—so if you're eating those foods, you're eating corn.

Soy

Similar to corn, this controversial bean is a common allergen, and GMO Compass reports that 93 percent of soy grown in the United States is genetically modified. In addition to the genetic modification, soy is high in goitrogens, compounds that can suppress thyroid function. Soy also contains antinutrients, such as phytates and oxalates, which interfere with our digestion and disrupt the endocrine system.

Peanuts

Another common allergen, peanuts contain a carcinogenic mold called aflatoxin, which can affect those with liver conditions or candida. Peanut crops are heavily treated with pesticides and this can lead to further inflammation or allergic reactions. They are also high in omega-6 fatty acids, a pro-inflammatory fat, and conventional peanut butters are often loaded with added sugar and trans fats.

Caffeine

Coffee propels the stomach to release its contents prematurely, injecting undigested food into the small intestine where it can aggravate the digestive tract. Caffeine can send blood sugar soaring, raise blood pressure and heart rate, suppress appetite, and disrupt sleep. Coffee also stresses the nervous system, which can interfere with the production of the anti-inflammatory hormone cortisol.

Alcohol

While the occasional glass of wine offers a hit of antioxidants, overall, excess alcohol consumption can increase the production of C-reactive protein (CRP), a marker of inflammation in the blood.

Many alcoholic beverages are chock-full of sugar, which can wreak havoc on our blood sugar levels, cause headaches, and suppress the immune system. Alcohol also destroys gut flora, an integral part of the digestive system. Poor intestinal flora can lead to a leaky gut, where particles of food break through the intestinal barrier and activate the immune system, inducing further inflammation and allergies.

Citrus Foods

Most citrus foods are acidic and can provoke inflammation in people with a variety of conditions such as gastroesophageal reflux disease (GERD), arthritis, and citrus sensitivities. To buffer their acidity in the body, we pull from our body's pool of soothing alkaline minerals such as calcium, magnesium, and potassium. An acidic environment can place undue stress on the body, leaving a person susceptible to disease.

However, lemons or limes can be a handy addition to an anti-inflammatory diet. They kick-start digestion, enhance liver detoxification, and once metabolized by the body, they leave alkaline minerals behind. Overall, though, avoid citrus.

Feedlot Animal Products

Conventional animal products induce inflammation for a variety of reasons. Animals are fed hormones and antibiotics. This not only contributes to inflammation but also

to the growing worldwide problem of antibiotic resistance.

Feedlot animals are often fed fare that is different from their natural diet—mostly grains like wheat, GMO corn, and GMO soy. We know these are inflammatory. Grain-fed animals also yield meat that is higher in inflammatory omega-6 fatty acids.
You don't need to avoid meat entirely. Instead, choose organic products from animals that were raised without hormones or antibiotics, had outdoor access, and were fed a mix of grass and grain. If you don't have access to organic meat, check with your local farmer. Sometimes farms follow organic practices but cannot afford to become "certified organic" which is expensive; talk to the farmer about their practices if you don't see this label.

Sugar

There's no sugarcoating the truth: White, refined sugar is harmful to health: It spikes blood sugar, which can increase production of inflammatory cytokines (the chemical messengers involved in our immune response). Sugar produces advanced glycation end products (AGEs), substances that cause damage to cells and play a role in aging and disease. Adding to that, sugar damages teeth, robs bodies of vitamins and minerals, causes mood swings, and inhibits the immune system.

Artificial or Processed Foods

Processed foods contain many ingredients that contribute to inflammation. These include chemicals, preservatives, unhealthy fats, excess sugars, additives, artificial food dyes, refined carbohydrates, and synthetic vitamins and minerals bodies can't absorb—and more.

Eggs

According to Health Canada, eggs are a top allergen in North America and can be difficult to digest; many people are sensitive or intolerant to their protein. For people with this allergy, eggs are particularly high in inflammatory nutrients, such as omega-6 fatty acids.

Nightshade Vegetables

This family of vegetables includes tomatoes, white potatoes, eggplant, tobacco, and peppers. While many nightshades can be nutritious, they contain substances called alkaloids, which can cause gastrointestinal upset and aggravate inflammation in some people, particularly those who suffer from rheumatoid arthritis and osteoarthritis, headaches, lupus, kidney disease, gout, hypertension, and cancer. Nightshade foods may also leach calcium from bones and redistribute it to places where it shouldn't be, like joints, kidneys, and arteries.

Tips and Tricks to Make Your Day Easier

Prepare vegetables in advance. Chopping ingredients can be a chore. Spend a few hours each week washing, chopping, and storing all the ingredients you need for each week's recipes.

Batch cook on weekends. Anti-inflammatory eating is even easier when you've got a few premade meals in the refrigerator or freezer. Make a large batch of soup, cook a large pot of grains you can pair with meals throughout the week, and throw a batch of chili in the slow cooker. If you love smoothies in the morning, prepare a week's worth of smoothie kits; simply split your greens, fruit, and nuts or seeds into individual portions, then freeze them in jars. Then, in the morning, all you'll have to do is toss your ingredients into a blender, along with the liquid, and breakfast is served.

Buy supermarket shortcuts. It's not always realistic to prepare every ingredient from scratch. Buy organic, prewashed salad greens, purchase precut fresh veggies, or buy premade guacamole or hummus. The prepared options are often more expensive, but if they help you stick to your anti-inflammatory goals, then it's money well spent.

Use leftovers. There's no need to prepare a new recipe for every meal—that takes a lot of time and effort, and can lead to food waste. Consume meals repeatedly throughout the week, or double favorite recipes and freeze for another time. If you become bored, think of creative ways to repurpose food: for example, take last night's burger, crumble it up, and transform it into a taco salad for lunch.

Get the whole family involved. If you live with other people, ask them to help with preparing ingredients and cooking meals. This will speed the process and make it more enjoyable. Throw on some tunes to raise the fun factor!

CHAPTER 2:
THE ANTI-INFLAMMATORY ACTION PLAN

The Anti-Inflammatory Pantry

A well-stocked pantry is part of organizing your kitchen and easing meal preparation. Keep the following items in stock, as you'll use them regularly in cooking the recipes in this book.

Dried Herbs and Spices

Cardamom, ground

Chipotle powder

Cinnamon, ground

Coriander, ground

Cumin, ground

Curry powder

Garlic powder

Ginger, ground

Mustard powder

Nutmeg, ground

Onion powder

Oregano

Peppercorns, black and white

Rosemary

Sage

Sea salt

Sumac

Turmeric

Gluten-Free Flours

Almond meal or flour

Coconut flour

Brown rice or white rice flour

Oil, Vinegar, and Condiments

Aminos, coconut

Mustard, Dijon (no added sugar)

Oil, coconut

Oil, extra-virgin olive

Vinegar, apple cider

Vinegar, balsamic

Canned and Jarred Foods

Chicken broth, low-sodium

Coconut milk, full-fat

Vegetable broth

Nondairy Milk

Almond milk, unsweetened

Coconut milk, unsweetened

Rice milk, unsweetened

28-Day Meal Plan
with Motivational Quotes

The 4-week meal plan includes motivational quotes for breakfast, lunch, dinner, and snacks. Each uses affordable, easy-to-find ingredients, and most recipes require about 30 minutes of active preparation time.
To set yourself up for success, follow the meal plan to make it work for you.

	Breakfast	Lunch	Dinner	Snacks /Desserts	Motivational Quotes
1	Millet-Blueberry Bake with Applesauce	Tomato-Basil Pasta with Garlic	Chicken, Butternut Squash and Hazelnut	Vegetable Crackers with Flaxseed	A journey of a thousand miles begins with a single step.
2	Anti-Inflammatory Oatmeal	Bell Pepper and Sweet Potato Hash	Portuguese Cod Casserole	Turmeric Bars	Healthy eating isn't about counting fat grams, dieting, cleanses and antioxidants; it's about eating food untouched from the way we find it in nature in a balanced way.
3	Anti-Inflammatory Blueberry Smoothie	Spinach and Quinoa Florentine	Easy Stir-Fried Chicken	Anti-Inflammatory Turmeric Gummies	Take care of your body. It's the only place you have to live.
4	Anti-Inflammatory Porridge	Kale Frittata with Sunflower Seeds	Chicken Burger with Brussel Sprouts Slaw	Ginger Spiced Mixed Nuts	By choosing healthy over skinny, you are choosing self-love over self-judgment.
5	Quinoa and Asparagus Mushroom Frittata	Asparagus and Tomato Frittata	Buckwheat Pasta With Basil Pesto	Spicy Kale Chips	Health is like money. we never have a true idea of its value until we lose it.
6	Anti-Inflammatory Cherry Spinach Smoothie	Tomato and Black Bean Chili with Garlic	Chickpea Curry with Raisins	Turmeric Nuggets	Eating healthy food fills your body with energy and nutrients. Imagine your cells smiling back at you and saying: 'thank you!
7	Golden Milk Chia Pudding	Whitefish and Broccoli Curry	Salmon with Dried Tomatoes	White Beans Hummus	Fight back against the damaging effects of inflammation with these super-healthy foods.
8	No-Bake Turmeric Protein Donuts	Poached Halibut and Mushrooms	Island Style Sardines	Salted Raw Caramel Dip	What doesn't kill you makes you stronger.
9	Choco-Nana Pancakes	Halibut Stir Fry	Chicken Breasts with Stuffing	Simple Guacamole	Nobody can take away your pain, but don't let pain take away your happiness.

10	Sweet Potato Cranberry Breakfast bars	Steamed Garlic-Dill Halibut	Chicken and Avocado Lettuce Wraps	Cumin Cauliflower Bites	I'm thankful for my struggle because without it, I wouldn't have stumbled across my strength.
11	Savory Breakfast Pancakes	Italian Halibut Chowder	Roasted Chicken	Vinegary Honey Two-Bean Dip	The hard days are what make you stronger.
12	Raspberry Grapefruit Smoothie	Molasses Glazed Salmon	Sweet Potato, Kale and Chicken Patties	Baked Beets in Cider Vinegar	Your body is not a temple, it's an amusement park. Enjoy the ride.
13	Breakfast Burgers with Avocado Buns	Thai Cod Curry	Honey Chicken Tagine	Zucchini Fries	A year from now, you will wish you started today.
14	Spinach Breakfast	Salmon with Lemon	Brussels Sprouts and Chicken Thighs	Honey Granola Trail Mix	Quit slacking and make shit happen.
15	Breakfast Chocolate Donuts	Salmon in Parchment	Greek Chicken Stew	Almond Butter Chocolate Cups	Success is the sum of small efforts, repeated day in and day out.
16	Baked Eggs with Portobello Mushrooms	Sesame Chicken Lettuce Wraps	Minted Salmon	Vanilla Cookies with Chocolate Chips	To ensure good health: eat lightly, breathe deeply, live moderately, cultivate cheerfulness and maintain an interest in life.
17	Spinach Mushroom Tomato Fry Up	Rosemary Grilled Chicken	Coconut-Garlic Lentils	Avocado-Chocolate Mousse	I try to stay out of the mindset of needing to fix myself. I do whatever seems fun to me.
18	Sweet Cherry Almond Chia Pudding	Curried Coconut Chicken	African Chicken Stew	Almond-Cherry Chocolate Clusters	Exercise is king. nutrition is queen. put them together and you've got a kingdom
19	Pineapple Ginger Smoothie	Curried Chicken, Chickpeas	Avocado Baked Salmon	Vanilla Coconut Ice Cream Sandwiches	Proper nutrition is the difference between feeling exhausted and getting the most out of a workout.
20	Beet and Cherry Smoothie	Balsamic Vinaigrette on Chicken	Multi-Spice Cod Curry	Blueberry and Fig Pie	Eat breakfast like a king, lunch like a prince and dinner like a pauper.
21	Spicy Pineapple Smoothie	Chicken Pasta Parmesan	Chicken-Bell Pepper Sauté	Vanilla Coconut Yogurt	Your diet is a bank account. good food choices are good investments.
22	Breakfast Cherry Muffins	Chicken and White Bean	Avocado-Orange Grilled Chicken	Cinnamon-Nutmeg Pecans	You may have to fight a battle more than once to win it.
23	Breakfast Shakshuka	Chicken Pad Thai	Avocado-Veggie Spring Rolls	Berry Pops	Moderation. small helpings. sample a little bit of everything. these are the secrets of happiness and good health.
24	Anti-Inflammatory Crepes	Chicken Thighs with Butternut Squash	Steamed Lemon Pepper Salmon	Hot Coconut Chocolate	To keep the body in good health is a duty, otherwise we shall not be able to keep our mind strong and clear.
25	Chickpea Scramble with Kale	Cajun Rice & Chicken	Asian Poached Cod	Blueberry and Peach Cobbler	Let food be thy medicine, thy medicine shall be thy food.
26	Creamy Whole Grain Porridge	Vegetable Lover's Chicken Soup	Baked Spicy Cod	Ritzy Compote	Sorry, there's no magic bullet. You got to eat healthy and live healthy to be healthy and look healthy. End of story.
27	Omega-3 Chocolate Chia Hemp Pudding	Herbed Chicken Salad	Sesame Cauliflower Rice with Peas	Blueberry Muffins	If you keep good food in your fridge, you will eat good food.
28	No Bake Granola Breakfast Bars	Chicken in Pita Bread	Tofu Sloppy Joes with Cider Vinegar	Banana Missouri Cookies	It is health that is real wealth and not pieces of gold and silver.

Kitchen Essential Equipment

In addition to a well-stocked pantry, you'll want to have the right equipment to prepare your meals. The good news is these recipes can be prepared with equipment you likely have and use regularly; no specialized equipment is needed. Anything you don't have is available for affordable prices and will be a great investment as you'll use it again and again to prepare delicious anti-inflammatory meals.

Good Knives

A good knife makes all the difference when preparing meals. It's great to have a chef's knife, a paring knife, and a serrated knife on hand. The best knife to buy is the knife that fits you. Pick up the knife and feel the weight; notice how the length of the blade works for you. The right knife should feel good in your hand and be easy to manipulate. It's worth it to purchase a sharpener, or to make a commitment to regularly get your knives professionally sharpened. Always keep your fingers tucked in when chopping.

Pots and Pans

You can do little wrong with a large cast-iron pan. Once seasoned, it requires very little oil to cook with, and browns food beautifully. Even old, rusty pans can be resurrected with some steel wool and elbow grease, followed by a a good seasoning. When shopping for non-stick pans, look for ceramic ones; avoid traditional nonstick pans, as there is some evidence that the chemical coating can flake into food. Finally, an omelet pan is great for rounding out your collection.

Slow Cooker

A slow cooker is a true time-saver; for instance, you can prepare your ingredients before work, throw them in your slow cooker, and dinner is waiting when you get home. Or fill it with steel-cut oats or other grains before bedtime and wake up to a hearty breakfast. The size of the slow cooker you purchase should correspond with the volume of food you cook regularly. Make sure it has low, medium, and high settings, or a high setting with a four- and six-hour option, and a low setting with an eight- and twelve-hour option. A slow cooker is also perfect for doubling or tripling recipes and freezing the extras.

Food Processors and Blenders

A food processor is indispensable for puréeing, slicing, chopping, and shredding. For smoothies, a blender is the best tool for pulverizing fruits, vegetables, and ice.

Now that you're armed with anti-inflammatory information, determined your best meal plan, stocked your pantry, and gathered your equipment, it's time to get cooking.

CHAPTER 3:
BREAKFASTS

**THE ULTIMATE ANTI-INFLAMMATORY
DIET COOKBOOK**

Millet-Blueberry Bake with Applesauce

Prep time: 5 minutes | Cook time: 11 minutes | Serves 8

2 cups millet, soaked in water overnight
2 cups fresh or frozen blueberries
1¾ cups unsweetened applesauce
⅓ cup coconut oil, melted
2 teaspoons grated fresh ginger
1½ teaspoons ground cinnamon

1. Preheat the oven to 350°F (180°C).
2. In a fine-mesh sieve, drain and rinse the millet for 1 to 2 minutes. Transfer to a large bowl.
3. Gently fold in the blueberries, applesauce, coconut oil, ginger, and cinnamon.
4. Pour the mixture into a 9-inch by 9-inch casserole dish. Cover with aluminum foil.
5. Place the dish in the preheated oven and bake for 40 minutes. Remove the foil and bake for 10 to 15 minutes more, or until lightly crisp on top.

Per Serving
calories: 323 | fat: 13g | protein: 6g | carbs: 48g | fiber: 6g | sugar: 9g | sodium: 4mg

Anti-Inflammatory Oatmeal

Prep time: 10 minutes | Cook time: 3 minutes | Serves 1

⅔ cup unsweetened coconut milk
1 egg white, pasture-raised
½ cup gluten-free quick cooking oats
½ teaspoon turmeric powder
½ teaspoon cinnamon
¼ teaspoon ginger

1. Place the non-dairy milk in a saucepan and heat over medium flame.
2. Stir in the egg white and continue whisking until the mixture becomes smooth.
3. Add in the rest of the ingredients and cook for another 3 minutes.

Per Serving
calories: 395 | fat: 34g | protein: 10g | carbs: 19g| fiber: 3g | sugar: 2g | sodium: 76mg

Anti-Inflammatory Porridge

Prep time: 10 minutes | Cook time: 0 minutes | Serves 1

6 tablespoons organic cottage cheese
3 tablespoons flax seed
3 tablespoons flax oil
2 tablespoons unsweetened almond milk
1 tablespoon organic coconut meat
1 tablespoon raw honey
¼ cup water

1. Combine all ingredients in a bowl. Mix until well combined.
2. Place in a bowl and chill before serving.
Per Serving
calories: 632 | fat: 49g | protein: 23g | carbs: 32g | fiber: 6g | sugar: 22g | sodium: 265mg

Anti-Inflammatory Blueberry Smoothie

Prep time: 10 minutes | Cook time: 0 minutes | Serves 1

17 tablespoons unsweetened almond milk
1 frozen banana
1 cup frozen blueberries
2 handfuls spinach
¼ teaspoon cinnamon
¼ teaspoon cayenne pepper
1 teaspoon maca powder

1. Combine all ingredients in a blender and pulse until well combined.
2. Serve immediately.

Per Serving
calories: 431 | fat: 21g | protein: 10g | carbs: 56g | fiber: 8g | sugar: 38g | sodium: 201mg

Anti-Inflammatory Cherry Spinach Smoothie

Prep time: 10 minutes | Cook time: 0 minutes | Serves 1

1 cup plain kefir
1 cup frozen cherries, pitted
½ cup baby spinach leaves
¼ cup mashed ripe avocado
1 tablespoon unsweetened almond milk
1-piece peeled ginger (½-inch)
1 teaspoon chia seeds

1. Place all ingredients in a blender.
2. Pulse until smooth.
3. Allow to chill in the fridge before serving.

Per Serving
calories: 410 | fat: 20g | protein: 17g | carbs: 47g | fiber: 10g | sugar: 33g | sodium: 169mg

Anti-Inflammatory Blueberry Smoothie

Prep time: 10 minutes | Cook time: 0 minutes | Serves 1

17 tablespoons unsweetened almond milk
1 frozen banana
1 cup frozen blueberries
2 handfuls spinach
¼ teaspoon cinnamon
¼ teaspoon cayenne pepper
1 teaspoon maca powder

1. Combine all ingredients in a blender and pulse until well combined.
2. Serve immediately.

Per Serving
calories: 431 | fat: 21g | protein: 10g | carbs: 56g | fiber: 8g | sugar: 38g | sodium: 201mg

Anti-Inflammatory Porridge

Prep time: 10 minutes | Cook time: 0 minutes | Serves 1

6 tablespoons organic cottage cheese
3 tablespoons flax seed
3 tablespoons flax oil
2 tablespoons unsweetened almond milk
1 tablespoon organic coconut meat
1 tablespoon raw honey
¼ cup water

1. Combine all ingredients in a bowl. Mix until well combined.
2. Place in a bowl and chill before serving.

Per Serving
calories: 632 | fat: 49g | protein: 23g | carbs: 32g | fiber: 6g | sugar: 22g | sodium: 265mg

Quinoa and Asparagus Mushroom Frittata

Prep time: 10 minutes | Cook time: 30 minutes | Serves 3

2 tablespoons olive oil
1 cup sliced mushrooms
1 cup asparagus, cut into 1-inch pieces
½ cup chopped tomato
6 large eggs, pasture-raised
2 large egg whites, pasture-raised
¼ cup non-dairy milk
1 cup quinoa, cooked according to packaged instructions
3 tablespoons chopped basil
1 tablespoon chopped parsley, garnish
Salt and pepper, to taste

1. Preheat the oven to 350ºF (180ºC).
2. In a skillet, heat the olive oil over medium flame.
3. Stir in the mushrooms and asparagus. Season with salt and pepper to taste. Sauté for 7 minutes or until the mushrooms and asparagus have browned. Add the tomatoes and cook for another 3 minutes. Set aside.
4. Meanwhile, mix the eggs, egg white, and milk in a mixing bowl. Set aside.
5. Place in a baking dish the quinoa and top with the vegetable mixture. Pour in the egg mixture.
6. Place in the oven and bake for 20 minutes or until the eggs have set.

Per Serving
calories: 450 | fat: 37g | protein: 12g | carbs: 17g | fiber: 3g | sugar: 2g | sodium: 60mg

Quinoa and Asparagus Mushroom Frittata

Prep time: 10 minutes | Cook time: 30 minutes | Serves 3

2 tablespoons olive oil
1 cup sliced mushrooms
1 cup asparagus, cut into 1-inch pieces
½ cup chopped tomato
6 large eggs, pasture-raised
2 large egg whites, pasture-raised
¼ cup non-dairy milk
1 cup quinoa, cooked according to packaged instructions
3 tablespoons chopped basil
1 tablespoon chopped parsley, garnish
Salt and pepper, to taste

1. Preheat the oven to 350ºF (180ºC).
2. In a skillet, heat the olive oil over medium flame.
3. Stir in the mushrooms and asparagus. Season with salt and pepper to taste. Sauté for 7 minutes or until the mushrooms and asparagus have browned. Add the tomatoes and cook for another 3 minutes. Set aside.
4. Meanwhile, mix the eggs, egg white, and milk in a mixing bowl. Set aside.
5. Place in a baking dish the quinoa and top with the vegetable mixture. Pour in the egg mixture.
6. Place in the oven and bake for 20 minutes or until the eggs have set.

Per Serving
calories: 450 | fat: 37g | protein: 12g | carbs: 17g | fiber: 3g | sugar: 2g | sodium: 60mg

Golden Milk Chia Pudding

Prep time: 10 minutes | Cook time: 0 minutes | Serves 4

4 cups unsweetened coconut milk
3 tablespoons honey
1 teaspoon vanilla extract
1 teaspoon ground turmeric
½ teaspoon ground cinnamon
½ teaspoon ground ginger
¾ cup coconut yogurt
½ cup chia seeds
1 cup fresh mixed berry
¼ cup toasted coconut chips

1. In a mixing bowl, combine the coconut milk, honey, vanilla extract, turmeric, cinnamon, and ginger. Add in the coconut yogurt.
2. In bowls, place chia seeds, berries, and coconut chips.
3. Pour in the milk mixture.
4. Allow to chill in the fridge to set for 6 hours.

Per Serving

calories: 337 | fat: 11g | protein: 10g | carbs: 51g | fiber: 2g | sugar: 29g | sodium: 262mg

No-Bake Turmeric Protein Donuts

Prep time: 10 minutes | Cook time: 0 minutes | Serves 8

1½ cups raw cashews
½ cup medjool dates, pitted
1 tablespoon vanilla protein powder
½ cup shredded coconut
2 tablespoons pure maple syrup
¼ teaspoon vanilla extract
1 teaspoon turmeric powder
¼ cup dark chocolate

1. Combine all ingredients except for the chocolate in a food processor.
2. Pulse until smooth.
3. Roll batter into 8 balls and press into a silicone donut mold.
4. Place in the freezer for 30 minutes to set.
5. Meanwhile, make the chocolate topping by melting the chocolate in a double boiler.
6. Once the donuts have set, remove the donuts from the mold and drizzle with chocolate.

Per Serving

calories: 320 | fat: 26g | protein: 7g | carbs: 20g | fiber: 2g | sugar: 9g | sodium: 163mg

Raspberry Grapefruit Smoothie

Prep time: 5 minutes | Cook time: 0 minutes | Serves 1

Juice from 1 grapefruit, freshly squeezed
1 banana, peeled and sliced
1 cup raspberries

1. Place all ingredients in a blender and pulse until smooth.
2. Chill before serving.

Per Serving

calories: 381 | fat: 0.8g | protein: 4g | carbs: 96g | fiber: 11g | sugar: 2g | sodium: 11mg

Choco-Nana Pancakes

Prep time: 10 minutes | Cook time: 6 minutes | Serves 2

2 large bananas, peeled and mashed
2 large eggs, pasture-raised
3 tablespoons cacao powder
2 tablespoons unsweetened almond milk
1 teaspoon pure vanilla extract
⅛ teaspoon salt
Coconut oil for greasing

1. Preheat a skillet on medium low heat and grease the pan with coconut oil.
2. Place all ingredients in a food processor and pulse until smooth.
3. Pour a batter (about ¼ cup) onto the skillet and form a pancake.
4. Cook for 3 minutes on each side.

Per Serving

calories: 303 | fat: 17g | protein: 5g | carbs: 36g | fiber: 5g | sugar: 15g | sodium: 108mg

Sweet Potato Cranberry Breakfast bars

Prep time: 10 minutes | Cook time: 40 minutes | Serves 8

1 ½ cups sweet potato puree
2 tablespoons coconut oil, melted
2 tablespoons pure maple syrup
2 eggs, pasture-raised
1 cup almond meal
1/3 cup coconut flour
1 ½ teaspoon baking soda
1 cup fresh cranberry, pitted and chopped
¼ cup water

1. Preheat the oven to 350°F (180°C).
2. Grease a 9-inch baking pan with coconut oil. Set aside.
3. In a mixing bowl. Combine the sweet potato puree, water, coconut oil, maple syrup, and eggs.
4. In another bowl, sift the almond flour, coconut flour, and baking soda.
5. Gradually add the dry ingredients to the wet ingredients. Use a spatula to fold and mix all ingredients.
6. Pour into the prepared baking pan and press the cranberries on top.
7. Place in the oven and bake for 40 minutes or until a toothpick inserted in the middle comes out clean.
8. Allow to rest or cool before removing from the pan.

Per Serving

calories: 98 | fat: 6g | protein: 3g | carbs: 9g | fiber: 0.5g | sugar: 7g | sodium: 113mg

Savory Breakfast Pancakes

Prep time: 10 minutes | Cook time: 6 minutes | Serves 4

½ cup almond flour
½ cup tapioca flour
1 cup unsweetened coconut milk
½ teaspoon chili powder
¼ teaspoon turmeric powder
½ red onion, chopped
1 handful cilantro leaves, chopped
½ inch ginger, grated
1 teaspoon salt
¼ teaspoon ground black pepper

1. In a mixing bowl, mix all ingredients until well combined.
2. Heat a pan on low medium heat and grease with oil.
3. Pour ¼ cup of batter onto the pan and spread the mixture to create a pancake.
4. Fry for 3 minutes per side.
5. Repeat until the batter is done.

Per Serving

calories: 108 | fat: 2g | protein: 2g | carbs: 20g | fiber: 0.5g | sugar: 4g | sodium: 37mg

Breakfast Burgers with Avocado Buns

Prep time: 10 minutes | Cook time: 5 minutes | Serves 1

1 ripe avocado
1 egg, pasture-raised
1 red onion slice
1 tomato slice
1 lettuce leaf
Sesame seed for garnish
Salt, to taste

1. Peel the avocado and remove the seed. Slice the avocado into half. This will serve as the bun. Set aside.
2. Grease a skillet over medium flame and fry the egg sunny side up for 5 minutes or until set.
3. Assemble the breakfast burger by placing on top of one avocado half with the egg, red onion, tomato, and lettuce leaf. Top with the remaining avocado bun.
4. Garnish with sesame seeds on top and season with salt to taste.

Per Serving

calories: 458 | fat: 39g | protein: 13g | carbs: 20g | fiber: 14g | sugar: 61g | sodium: 118mg

Chia Pudding with Cashews and Cherries

Prep time: 10 minutes | Cook time: 0 minutes | Serves 4

2 cups almond milk
½ cup chia seeds
1 teaspoon vanilla extract
¼ cup pure maple syrup
½ cup chopped cashews, divided
1 cup frozen no-added-sugar pitted cherries, thawed, juice reserved, divided

1. Combine the almond milk, chia seeds, vanilla, and maple syrup in a bowl. Stir to mix well. Refrigerate overnight.
2. Divide the almond milk mixture in four bowls, then serve with cashews and cherries on top.

Per Serving

calories: 271 | fat: 14g | protein: 7g | carbs: 38g | fiber: 6g | sugar: 25g | sodium: 83mg

Breakfast Chocolate Donuts

Prep time: 10 minutes | Cook time: 15 minutes | Serves 12

1 cup coconut flour
¼ cup raw cacao powder
½ teaspoon baking soda
4 eggs, pasture-raised
¼ cup coconut oil, melted
¼ cup unsweetened applesauce
1 teaspoon vanilla
¼ cup honey
¼ teaspoon salt

1. Preheat the oven to 350°F (180°C).
2. In a mixing bowl, mix the coconut flour, cacao, baking soda, and salt. Set aside.
3. In another bowl, mix the eggs, coconut oil, and applesauce. Stir in the vanilla and honey.
4. Fold the dry ingredients gradually into the wet ingredients until well combined.
5. Grease the donut pan with coconut oil.
6. Press down the dough into the pan.
7. Bake for 15 minutes or until the dough is cooked through.
8. Remove from the oven and allow to cool before removing from the donut pan.

Per Serving

calories: 115 | fat: 8g | protein: 4g | carbs: 9g | fiber: 0g | sugar: 7g | sodium: 108mg

Baked Eggs with Portobello Mushrooms

Prep time: 5 minutes | Cook time: 20 minutes | Serves 4

4 portobello mushroom caps
1 cup arugula
1 medium tomato, chopped
4 large eggs, pasture-raised
Salt and pepper, to taste

1. Preheat the oven to 350°F (180°C) and line a baking sheet with parchment paper.
2. Scoop out the gills from the mushrooms using a spoon. Discard the gills and set aside.
3. Place the mushrooms on the baking sheet inverted (gill side up) and fill each cap with arugula and tomato.
4. Carefully crack an egg on each mushroom cap.
5. Bake in the oven for 20 minutes or until the eggs have set.

Per Serving
calories: 80 | fat: 5g | protein: 5g | carbs: 5g | fiber: 2g | sugar: 3g | sodium: 19mg

Spinach Mushroom Tomato Fry Up

Prep time: 5 minutes | Cook time: 5 minutes | Serves 2

1 teaspoon olive oil
1 red onion, sliced
6 button mushrooms, sliced
½ cup cherry tomatoes, halved
½ teaspoon diced lemon rind
3 large handful baby spinach
Salt and pepper, to taste

1. Heat oil in a skillet over medium low heat.
2. Sauté the onion until fragrant.
3. Add in the mushrooms and tomatoes. Season with lemon rind, salt and pepper. Cook for another 5 minutes.
4. Stir in the baby spinach until wilted.

Per Serving
calories: 38 | fat: 3g | protein: 2g | carbs: 3g | fiber: 1.5g | sugar: 1g | sodium: 37mg

Pineapple Ginger Smoothie

Prep time: 5 minutes | Cook time: 0 minutes | Serves 1

1 cup pineapple slice
½ inch thick ginger, sliced
1 cup unsweetened coconut milk

1. Place all ingredients in a blender.
2. Pulse until smooth.
3. Chill before serving.

Per Serving
calories: 299 | fat: 8g | protein: 9g | carbs: 51g | fiber: 2g | sugar: 48g | sodium: 108mg

Sweet Cherry Almond Chia Pudding

Prep time: 10 minutes | Cook time: 0 minutes | Serves 4

2 cups whole sweet cherries, pitted
2 cups unsweetened coconut milk
¼ cup pure maple syrup
1 teaspoon vanilla extract
¾ cup chia seeds
½ cup hemp seeds
⅛ teaspoon salt

1. In the blender, combine the cherries, coconut milk, maple syrup, and vanilla extract. Season with salt. Pulse until smooth.
2. Distribute the chia seeds and hemp seeds in four glasses and pour in the cherry and milk mixture.
3. Allow to chill in the fridge for 3 hours before serving.

Nutrition Facts Per Serving
calories: 302 | fat: 17g | protein: 10g | carbs: 29g | fiber: 7g | sugar: 20g | sodium: 59mg

Beet and Cherry Smoothie

Prep time: 5 minutes | Cook time: 0 minutes | Serves 4

10-ounce (283-g) unsweetened almond milk
2 small beets, peeled and cut into quarters
½ cup frozen cherries, pitted
½ teaspoon frozen banana

1. Add all ingredients in a blender.
2. Blend until smooth.

Per Serving
calories: 470 | fat: 38g | protein: 16g | carbs: 24g | fiber: 10g | sugar: 10g | sodium: 67mg

Spicy Pineapple Smoothie

Prep time: 10 minutes | Cook time: 0 minutes | Serves 1

1½ cups frozen pineapple chunks
1 orange, peeled
1 cup coconut water
1 tablespoon chia seeds
1 teaspoon ground turmeric
1 teaspoon black pepper powder

1. Place all ingredients in a blender.
2. Pulse until smooth.
3. Serve chilled.

Per Serving
calories: 378 | fat: 10g | protein: 9g | carbs: 73g | fiber: 20g | sugar: 42g | sodium: 261mg

Breakfast Cherry Muffins

Prep time: 10 minutes | Cook time: 30 minutes | Serves 6

1½ cups almond flour
¼ cup arrowroot flour
¼ cup coconut oil
¼ cup pure maple syrup
3 whole eggs
2 teaspoons vanilla extract
1½ teaspoons almond extract
1 teaspoon baking powder
1 cup fresh cherry, pitted and chopped
¼ teaspoon salt

1. Preheat the oven to 350°F (180°C).
2. In a mixing bowl, combine all ingredients except for the cherries. Mix until well combined.
3. Add the cherries last.
4. Fill muffin liners with the batter and bake for 30 minutes or until a toothpick inserted comes out clean.

Per Serving

calories: 528 | fat: 39g | protein: 13g | carbs: 36g | fiber: 7g | sugar: 15g | sodium: 177mg

Breakfast Shakshuka

Prep time: 10 minutes | Cook time: 5½ minutes | Serves 8

1 tablespoon olive oil
½ onion, chopped
1 garlic cloves, minced
1 red bell pepper, seeded and chopped
4 cups tomatoes, diced
1 teaspoon chili powder
1 teaspoon paprika
6 eggs, pasture-raised
½ tablespoon fresh parsley, chopped
Salt and pepper, to taste

1. Heat oil in a skillet over medium flame.
2. Sauté the onion and garlic for 30 seconds or until fragrant.
3. Add in the red bell pepper and tomatoes. Season with salt and pepper to taste. Stir in the chili powder and paprika. Allow to simmer until the tomatoes are soft.
4. Reduce the heat and create 6 wells in the skillet.
5. Crack in one egg in each well and increase the heat.
6. Cover and allow to simmer for 5 minutes.
7. Garnish with parsley last.

Per Serving

calories: 177 | fat: 12g | protein: 10g | carbs: 7g | fiber: 2g | sugar: 4g | sodium: 109mg

Anti-Inflammatory Crepes

Prep time: 10 minutes | Cook time: 4 minutes | Serves 4

2 tablespoons coconut flour
4 large eggs, pasture-raised
1 tablespoon coconut oil
1 cup hazelnuts, soaked in water overnight
⅔ cup dark chocolates
½ teaspoon vanilla extract
2 tablespoons pure maple syrup
½ cup water

1. Preheat the oven to 350°F (180°C).
2. In a bowl, mix the coconut flour, eggs, and water until well combined.
3. Heat oil in a skillet over medium flame and grease the skillet with coconut oil.
4. Scoop ☐ cup of the crepe mixture into the skillet and cook for 4 minutes while flipping halfway through the cooking time.
5. Repeat until all batter is made into crepes.
6. Make the hazelnut sauce by combining the hazelnuts, dark chocolates, vanilla extract, and maple syrup in a blender.
7. Pulse until smooth.
8. Spread the Nutella sauce over the crepes before serving.

Per Serving

calories: 465 | fat: 29g | protein: 9g | carbs: 46g | fiber: 5g | sugar: 32g | sodium: 53mg

Chickpea Scramble with Kale

Prep time: 10 minutes | Cook time: 3½ minutes | Serves 2

1 cup chickpea flour
1 teaspoon turmeric powder
1 tablespoon nutritional yeast
1 tablespoon olive oil
½ small onion, diced
4 garlic cloves, minced
1 bunch kale, torn into small pieces
½ cup water
½ teaspoon salt

1. Mix the chickpea flour and water until well combined. Season with salt, turmeric powder, and nutritional yeast.
2. Heat oil in a skillet over medium flame.
3. Sauté the onion and garlic until fragrant.
4. Stir in the kale for 30 seconds.
5. Pour in the chickpea mixture and continue mixing for 3 minutes or until the chickpea eggs have set.

Per Serving

calories: 279 | fat: 10g | protein: 14g | carbs: 34g | fiber: 7g | sugar: 6g | sodium: 301mg

Creamy Whole Grain Porridge

Prep time: 5 minutes | Cook time: 0 minutes | Serves 2

½ cup cooked quinoa
¼ cup sunflower seeds
¼ cup raw walnuts
2 tablespoons chopped dates
1 teaspoon cinnamon
¼ cup unsweetened almond milk
1 tablespoon raw honey
½ diced apple
1 tablespoon chia seeds

1. In a saucepan, add the quinoa, sunflower seeds, walnuts, dates, cinnamon, milk, and raw honey.
2. Heat over medium flame. Add more water or water to achieve a porridge consistency.
3. Before serving, stir in apple and chia seeds last.

Per Serving

calories: 317 | fat: 17g | protein: 8g | carbs: 39g | fiber: 6g | sugar: 22g | sodium: 27mg

Omega-3 Chocolate Chia Hemp Pudding

Prep time: 10 minutes | Cook time: 0 minutes | Serves 1

2 tablespoons chia seeds
2 tablespoons hemp seeds
1 tablespoon cacao powder
6 small pitted dates, chopped
½ cup unsweetened almond milk
½ teaspoon pure vanilla extract
1 tablespoon chocolate protein powder
¼ teaspoon salt

1. Add all ingredients in a blender and pulse until smooth.
2. Pour into individual containers and place inside the fridge for at least 2 hours before serving.

Per Serving

calories: 367 | fat: 13g | protein: 12g | carbs: 55g | fiber: 8g | sugar: 39g | sodium: 129mg

No Bake Granola Breakfast Bars

Prep time: 10 minutes | Cook time: 0 minutes | Serves 6

2 cups raisins, soaked in water then drained
3 tablespoons pure maple syrup
½ cup tahini or almond milk
2 cups oats
1 cup raw sunflower seeds
½ cup cacao nibs

1. Mix all ingredients in mixing bowl until well combined.
2. Press firmly into a parchment-lined baking pan.
3. Allow to set in the fridge for two hours.
4. Remove from the pan once set and slice into bars.

Per Serving

calories: 372 | fat: 26g | protein: 15g | carbs: 36g | fiber: 9g | sugar: 9g | sodium: 52mg

Anti-Inflammatory Energy Bars

Prep time: 5 minutes | Cook time: 0 minutes | Serves 5

1¼ cup packed dates, pitted and chopped
1 cup unsweetened fine coconut meat
1 cup hemp seeds
⅔ cup cashew nuts, toasted and chopped
2 tablespoons coconut oil

1. Place all ingredients in a food processor until well combined.
2. Line a baking dish with parchment paper and press the dough into the pan.
3. Place in the fridge for an hour to set.
4. Once frozen, lift the bars out of the pan and cut into 10 squares.

Per Serving

calories: 471 | fat: 34g | protein: 10g | carbs: 41g | fiber: 7g | sugar: 26g | sodium: 60mg

No-Bake Chocolate Chia Energy Bars

Prep time: 10 minutes | Cook time: 0 minutes | Serves 5

1½ cups pitted dates, chopped
1/3 cup cacao powder
½ cup whole chia seeds
½ cup shredded coconut
1 cup raw walnut, chopped
½ cup dark chocolate bar, chopped
½ cup oats
½ teaspoon vanilla extract
¼ teaspoon salt

1. Place all ingredients in a food processor and pulse until a thick dough is formed.
2. Line a baking pan with parchment paper.
3. Press the dough into the pan.
4. Place inside the fridge to allow to set for at least 2 hours.
5. Once hardened, slice into 10 bars.

Per Serving

calories: 284 | fat: 12g | protein: 5g | carbs: 45g | fiber: 6g | sugar: 32g | sodium: 40mg

Breakfast Oatmeal Raisin Bars

Prep time: 5 minutes | Cook time: 0 minutes | Serves 8

3 cups dates, pitted and chopped
2 cups oats
½ cup chocolate chips, organic
½ cup raisins
½ teaspoon salt

1. Place all ingredients in a food processor and pulse until a thick dough is formed.
2. Line a baking pan with parchment paper.
3. Press the dough into the pan.
4. Place inside the fridge to allow to set for at least 2 hours.
5. Once hardened, slice into 16 bars.

Per Serving

calories: 235 | fat: 3g | protein: 6g | carbs: 59g | fiber: 8g | sugar: 36g | sodium: 3mg

Quinoa Breakfast Bowl

Prep time: 15 minutes | Cook time: 12 minutes | Serves 1

¼ cup quinoa, rinsed
2 tablespoons dried goji berries
1 small banana, peeled and sliced
¼ cup fresh blueberries
1 tablespoon chopped walnuts
1 tablespoon slivered almonds
1 tablespoon pumpkin seeds, hulled
¼ cup unsweetened almond milk
1 tablespoon pure maple syrup
⅛ teaspoon ground cinnamon
⅛ teaspoon vanilla extract
¾ cup water

1. Bring water to a boil in a small pot and add quinoa. Cook for 12 to 15 minutes then drain.
2. Allow the quinoa to cool. Fluff it and place in a bowl.
3. Top with goji berries, banana, blueberries, walnuts, almond, and pumpkin seed.
4. Pour over almond milk and maple syrup.
5. Dust with cinnamon and flavor with vanilla extract.

Per Serving

calories: 516 | fat: 13g | protein: 13g | carbs: 94g | fiber: 9g | sugar: 47g | sodium: 70mg

Quinoa Bowls Avocado Egg

Prep time: 10 minutes | Cook time: 6 minutes | Serves 1

2 teaspoons extra-virgin olive oil
2 large eggs, pasture-raised
1 cup grape tomatoes, halve
1 teaspoon red wine vinegar
1 cup cooked quinoa
½ cup black beans, cooked
2 tablespoons chopped cilantro
½ ripe avocado, sliced
¼ teaspoon salt

1. Heat oil in a skillet over medium flame.
2. Fry the eggs for 3 minutes. Set aside.
3. Using the same skillet, sauté the tomatoes for 3 minutes until wilted.
4. Add in the red wine vinegar and season with salt and pepper to taste. Set aside.
5. Assemble the bowl by putting the quinoa in a bowl and top with beans and tomatoes. Add in the eggs and avocado.
6. Garnish with avocado slices.

Per Serving

calories: 343 | fat: 16g | protein: 15g | carbs: 35g | fiber: 9g | sugar: 3g | sodium: 332mg

Ginger Turmeric Oatmeal

Prep time: 10 minutes | Cook time: 0 minutes | Serves 2

1 cup rolled oats
2 tablespoons pure maple syrup
¼ teaspoon ground turmeric
¼ teaspoon ground ginger
1 cup frozen assorted berries
½ cup water
1 pinch of black of pepper

1. Mix the oats with water, maple, turmeric, black pepper, and ginger until well combined.
2. Add in the berries.
3. Allow to sit in the fridge overnight.

Per Serving

calories: 280 | fat: 6g | protein: 11g | carbs: 64g | fiber: 7g | sugar: 30g | sodium: 59mg

Tropical Chia Seed Oats

Prep time: 10 minutes | Cook time: 0 minutes | Serves 1

½ cup quick oats
1 cup diced fresh pineapples
1 tablespoon chia seeds
1 cup unsweetened almond milk
½ teaspoon pure vanilla extract
1 sliced banana
2 tablespoons toasted coconut

1. In a container, place the oats, pineapples, chia seeds, almond milk, and vanilla. Stir to combine everything.
2. Place inside the fridge for at least 2 hours.
3. Once ready, top with banana and toasted coconut.

Per Serving

calories: 535 | fat: 14g | protein: 17g | carbs: 89g | fiber: 13g | sugar: 42g | sodium: 142mg

Vanilla Cherry Quinoa

Prep time: 5 minutes | Cook time: 15 minutes | Serves 2

½ cup quinoa
½ cup unsweetened fresh cherries
1 cup water
¼ teaspoon ground nutmeg
½ teaspoon vanilla extract

1. Get a pan and combine all the ingredients, cooking over medium-high heat until boiling.
2. Once boiling, cover and simmer for 15 minutes or until the quinoa is soft, and the liquid has been absorbed.
3. Pour into serving bowls and enjoy.

Per Serving

calories: 179 | fat: 3g | protein: 6g | carbs: 32g | fiber: 3g | sugar: 3g | sodium: 6mg

Tahini Oatmeal with Maple Syrup

Prep time: 5 minutes | Cook time: 13 minutes | Serves 2

2 cups water
1 cup gluten-free rolled oats
⅛ teaspoon salt
⅓ cup tahini
2 tablespoons pure maple syrup, divided

1. In a medium pot set over medium-high heat, stir together the water, oats, and salt. Bring to a boil. Reduce the heat to low and cover. Simmer for about 10 minutes, stirring occasionally, and checking for tenderness.
2. Stir in the tahini, letting it melt into the oatmeal. Cook for 3 to 4 minutes more, or until the oatmeal is cooked through.
3. Divide the oatmeal between two bowls. Drizzle each with 1 tablespoon of maple syrup.

Per Serving
calories: 500 | fat: 28g | protein: 15g | carbs: 55g | fiber: 12g | sugar: 9g | sodium: 131mg

Avocado Toast with Kale

Prep time: 5 minutes | Cook time: 3 minutes | Serves 1

2 slices gluten-free bread
1 ripe avocado, halved and pitted
1½ tablespoons freshly squeezed lemon juice, plus additional as needed
⅛ teaspoon salt, plus additional as needed
2 cups lightly packed spinach leaves

1. Toast the bread.
2. Fill a medium pot with 2 inches of water and insert a steamer basket. Bring the water to a boil over high heat.
3. Into a small bowl, scoop the avocado flesh from the peel with a spoon.
4. Add the lemon juice and salt. Mash together with a fork. Taste, and adjust the seasoning with more lemon juice or salt, if necessary.
5. When the water boils, add the spinach to the steamer basket. Cover and steam for 3 to 4 minutes, or until wilted.
6. Divide the avocado mixture between the two pieces of toast. Top each with half of the wilted greens.

Per Serving
calories: 589 | fat: 44g | protein: 6g | carbs: 46g | fiber: 2g | sugar: 18g | sodium: 219mg

Kale and Cauliflower Bowl

Prep time: 5 minutes | Cook time: 5 minutes | Serves 1

4 kale leaves, thoroughly washed and chopped
1½ cups cauliflower florets
½ avocado, chopped
1 teaspoon freshly squeezed lemon juice
1 teaspoon extra-virgin olive oil
Pinch salt

1. Fill a medium pot with 2 inches of water and insert a steamer basket. Bring to a boil over high heat.
2. Add the kale and cauliflower to the basket. Cover and steam for 5 minutes.
3. Transfer the vegetables to a medium bowl. Toss with the avocado, lemon juice, olive oil, and salt.

Per Serving
calories: 317 | fat: 25g | protein: 7g | carbs: 24g | fiber: 12g | sugar: 4g | sodium: 236mg

Carrot and Quinoa Stew with Dill

Prep time: 5 minutes | Cook time: 15 minutes | Serves 1

¼ cup quinoa
¾ cup water, plus additional as needed
½ small broccoli head, finely chopped
1 carrot, grated
¼ teaspoon salt
1 tablespoon chopped fresh dill

1. In a fine-mesh strainer, rinse the quinoa well.
2. In a small pot set over high heat, stir together the quinoa and water. Bring to a boil. Reduce the heat to low. Cover and cook for 5 minutes.
3. Add the broccoli, carrot, and salt. Cook for 10 to 12 minutes more, or until the quinoa is fully cooked and tender. If the stew gets too dry, add more water. This should be on the liquid side, as opposed to the drier consistency of a pilaf.
4. Fold in the dill and serve.

Per Serving
calories: 220 | fat: 3g | protein: 10g | carbs: 41g | fiber: 7g | sugar: 5g | sodium: 667mg

Chia Pudding with Cranberries

Prep time: 5 minutes | Cook time: 0 minutes | Serves 4

¾ cup chia seeds
½ cup hemp seeds
2¼ cups unsweetened coconut milk
½ cup dried cranberries
¼ cup pure maple syrup

1. In a medium bowl, stir together the chia seeds, hemp seeds, coconut milk, cranberries, and maple syrup, ensuring that the chia is completely mixed with the milk.
2. Cover the bowl and refrigerate overnight.
3. In the morning, stir and serve.

Per Serving
calories: 483 | fat: 41g | protein: 9g | carbs: 25g | fiber: 6g | sugar: 17g | sodium: 22mg

Cinnamon Granola with Sunflower Seeds

Prep time: 5 minutes | Cook time: 35 minutes | Serves 8 to 10

4 cups gluten-free rolled oats
1½ cups sunflower seeds
½ cup pure maple syrup
½ cup coconut oil
1½ teaspoons ground cinnamon

1. Preheat the oven to 325°F (163°C).
2. Line two baking sheets with parchment paper.
3. In a large bowl, stir together the oats, sunflower seeds, maple syrup, coconut oil, and cinnamon. Stir well so the oats and seeds are evenly coated with the syrup, oil, and cinnamon.
4. Divide the granola mixture evenly between the two sheets.
5. Place the sheets in the preheated oven and bake for 35 to 40 minutes, stirring every 10 minutes so everything browns evenly.
6. Cool completely, then store in large glass jars with tight-fitting lids.

Per Serving

calories: 400 | fat: 22g | protein: 9g | carbs: 47g | fiber: 6g | sugar: 12g | sodium: 3mg

Parmesan Spinach Frittata

Prep time: 10 minutes | Cook time: 11 minutes | Serves 4

2 tablespoons extra-virgin olive oil
2 cups fresh baby spinach
8 eggs, beaten
1 teaspoon garlic powder
½ teaspoon sea salt
⅛ teaspoon freshly ground black pepper
2 tablespoons grated Parmesan Cheese

1. Preheat the broiler to high.
2. In a large oven-proof skillet (well-seasoned cast iron works well) over medium-high heat, heat the olive oil until it shimmers.
3. Add the spinach and cook for about 3 minutes, stirring occasionally.
4. In a medium bowl, whisk the eggs, garlic powder, salt, and pepper. Carefully pour the egg mixture over the spinach and cook the eggs for about 3 minutes until they begin to set around the edges.
5. Using a rubber spatula, gently pull the eggs away from the edges of the pan. Tilt the pan to let the uncooked egg flow into the edges. Cook for 2 to 3 minutes until the edges set.
6. Sprinkle with the Parmesan Cheese and put the skillet under the broiler. Broil for about 3 minutes until the top puffs.
7. Cut into wedges to serve.

Per Serving

calories: 203 | fat: 17g | protein: 13g | carbs: 2g | fiber: 0g | sugar: 0g | sodium: 402mg

Oregano Scramble with Cherry Tomatoes

Prep time: 5 minutes | Cook time: 2 minutes | Serves 2

4 eggs
2 teaspoons chopped fresh oregano
1 tablespoon extra-virgin olive oil
1 cup halved cherry tomatoes
½ garlic clove, sliced
½ avocado, sliced

1. In a medium bowl, beat the eggs until well combined; whisk in the oregano.
2. Place a large skillet over medium heat. Once the pan is hot, add the olive oil.
3. Pour the eggs into the skillet and use either a heat-resistant spatula or wooden spoon to scramble the eggs. Transfer the eggs to a serving dish.
4. Add the cherry tomatoes and garlic to the pan and sauté for about 2 minutes. Spoon the tomatoes over the eggs and top the dish with the avocado slices.

Per Serving

calories: 310 | fat: 26g | protein: 13g | carbs: 10g | fiber: 5g | sugar: 3g | sodium: 131mg

Mushroom Omelet with Bell Pepper

Prep time: 5 minutes | Cook time: 9 minutes | Serves 2

2 tablespoons extra-virgin olive oil
1 red bell pepper, sliced
1 cup sliced mushrooms
6 eggs, beaten
½ teaspoon sea salt
⅛ teaspoon freshly ground black pepper

1. In a large nonstick skillet over medium-high heat, heat the olive oil until it shimmers.
2. Add the red bell pepper and mushrooms. Cook for about 4 minutes, stirring occasionally, until soft.
3. In a medium bowl, whisk the eggs, salt, and pepper. Pour the eggs over the vegetables and cook for about 3 minutes without stirring until the eggs begin to set around the edges.
4. Using a rubber spatula, gently pull the eggs away from the edges of the pan. Tilt the pan so the uncooked egg can flow to the edges. Cook for 2 to 3 minutes until the eggs are set at the edges and the center.
5. Using a spatula, fold the omelet in half. Cut into wedges to serve.

Per Serving

calories: 336 | fat: 27g | protein: 18g | carbs: 7g | fiber: 1g | sugar: 5g | sodium: 656mg

Scrambled Eggs with Smoked Salmon

Prep time: 5 minutes | Cook time: 8 minutes | Serves 4

2 tablespoons extra-virgin olive oil
6 ounces (170 g) smoked salmon, flaked
8 eggs, beaten
¼ teaspoon freshly ground black pepper

1. In a large nonstick skillet over medium-high heat, heat the olive oil until it shimmers.
2. Add the salmon and cook for 3 minutes, stirring.
3. In a medium bowl, whisk the eggs and pepper. Add them to the skillet and cook for about 5 minutes, stirring gently, until done.

Per Serving

calories: 236 | fat: 18g | protein: 19g | carbs: 0g | fiber: 0g | sugar: 0g | sodium: 974mg

Turmeric Mushroom Frittata

Prep time: 10 minutes | Cook time: 29 minutes | Serves 6

1½ cups chickpea flour
1½ cups water
1 teaspoon salt
2 tablespoons extra-virgin olive oil
1 small red onion, diced
2 pints sliced mushrooms
1 teaspoon ground turmeric
½ teaspoon ground cumin
1 teaspoon salt
½ teaspoon freshly ground black pepper
2 tablespoons chopped fresh parsley

1. Preheat the oven to 350°F (180°C).
2. In a small bowl, slowly whisk the water into the chickpea flour; add the salt and set aside.
3. In a large cast iron or oven-safe skillet over high heat, add the olive oil. When the oil is hot, add the onion.
4. Sauté for 3 to 5 minutes, until onion is softened and slightly translucent. Add the mushrooms and sauté for 5 minutes more. Add the turmeric, cumin, salt, and pepper, and sauté for 1 minute.
5. Pour the batter over the vegetables and sprinkle with the parsley. Place the skillet in the preheated oven and bake for 20 to 25 minutes.
6. Serve warm or at room temperature.

Per Serving

calories: 240 | fat: 8g | protein: 11g | carbs: 34g | fiber: 10g | sugar: 7g | sodium: 792mg

Mushroom and Sweet Potato Hash

Prep time: 15 minutes | Cook time: 13 minutes | Serves 4

2 tablespoons coconut oil
½ onion, thinly sliced
1 cup sliced mushrooms
1 garlic clove, thinly sliced
2 large sweet potatoes, cooked and cut into ½-inch cubes
1 cup finely chopped Swiss chard
½ cup vegetable broth
1 teaspoon salt
¼ teaspoon freshly ground pepper
1 tablespoon chopped fresh thyme
1 tablespoon chopped fresh sage

1. In a large skillet over high heat, melt the coconut oil.
2. Add the onion, mushrooms, and garlic. Sauté for about 8 minutes, or until the onions and mushrooms are tender.
3. Add the sweet potatoes, Swiss chard, and vegetable broth. Cook for 5 minutes.
4. Stir in the salt, pepper, thyme, and sage.

Per Serving

calories: 323 | fat: 7g | protein: 30g | carbs: 35g | fiber: 6g | sugar: 2g | sodium: 708mg

Chia-Coconut Oatmeal Bowl

Prep time: 10 minutes | Cook time: 5 minutes | Serves 2

2 cups wholemeal oats
1 tablespoon milled chia seeds
3 cups unsweetened coconut milk
3 teaspoons raw cacao (optional)
½ teaspoon stevia
1 teaspoon coconut shavings
6 fresh cherries

1. In a pan, mix the oats, cacao, stevia and coconut milk. Heat over medium heat and then simmer until the oats are fully cooked through, 5 to 10 minutes.
2. Pour into your favorite breakfast bowl and sprinkle the coconut shavings, cherries, and milled chia seeds on top.
3. If you've got a sweet tooth or fancy an extra treat, try adding cacao or a drizzle of honey to serve.

Per Serving

calories: 653 | fat: 21g | protein: 29g | carbs: 87g | fiber: 17g | sugar: 23g | sodium: 162mg

Cinnamon Gingerbread Oatmeal

Prep time: 10 minutes | Cook time: 5 minutes | Serves 2

3 cups water or soy milk
2 cups steel-cut or wholemeal oats
1 tablespoon ground cinnamon
1 teaspoon ground cloves
¼ teaspoon grated fresh ginger
¼ teaspoon ground allspice
¼ teaspoon nutmeg
¼ teaspoon cardamom
1 teaspoon honey

1. Mix the oats and water in a saucepan and gently heat over medium heat for 5 to 8 minutes or until cooked through.
2. Whilst cooking, stir in the spices.
3. When cooked and hot through, pour into your bowl.
4. Drizzle honey over the top if desired.

Per Serving

calories: 390 | fat: 6g | protein: 16g | carbs: 68g | fiber: 16g | sugar: 4g | sodium: 12mg

---

Ginger-Rhubarb Muffins

Prep time: 15 minutes | Cook time: 20 minutes | Serves 2

1 cup almond meal
3 teaspoons stevia
2 tablespoons chopped crystalized ginger
1 tablespoon ground linseed meal
½ cup buckwheat flour
¼ cup brown rice flour
2 tablespoons organic corn flour
2 teaspoons gluten-free baking powder
½ teaspoon ground cinnamon
1 cup sliced rhubarb
1 apple, peeled and diced
⅓ cup unsweetened almond milk
¼ cup extra-virgin olive oil
1 free-range egg
1 teaspoon vanilla extract

1. Preheat the oven to 350°F (180°C). Coat muffin tins with coconut or olive oil using a baking brush. Put the almond meal, stevia, ginger, and the linseed into a bowl.
2. Sieve the flours over the mix along with the baking powder and spices, then stir. Add the rhubarb and the apple into the flour mixture.
3. In a separate bowl, beat the egg, vanilla, milk, and oil until combined. Fold the wet ingredients into the dry ingredients until smooth.
4. Pour batter into the muffin tin, leaving a 1 cm gap at the top so that the muffin can rise and then bake for 20 minutes or until risen and golden.
5. Remove and place on a cooling rack before serving.

Per Serving

calories: 689 | fat: 33g | protein: 8g | carbs: 90g | fiber: 9g | sugar: 54g | sodium: 103mg

---

Buckwheat-Apple Oatmeal

Prep time: 10 minutes | Cook time: 1 hour | Serves 2

1 cup wholemeal or steel-cut oats
⅓ cup buckwheat
2 cups water
⅓ cup sunflower seeds
⅓ cup pumpkin seeds
⅓ cup chopped strawberries or raspberries
½ cup peeled and finely chopped apples
5 tablespoons coconut oil
4 tablespoons cacao powder

1. Preheat the oven to 350°F (180°C).
2. Meanwhile, mix the oats, buckwheat, and seeds into a bowl.
3. Put the berries, apples, coconut oil and water in a pan, cover and simmer for 10 to 15 minutes over medium-high heat until the fruits are soft to touch. Then stir in the ginger.
4. Add the fruit mixture to a blender with the cacao and blend until smooth. Mix the fruits with the buckwheat.
5. Grease a baking tray with coconut oil and then spread the granola mixture on top using a knife or spatula to create a thin layer. Bake for 45 minutes.
6. Stir the mixture every 15 minutes so it doesn't burn. When crispy all over, remove the tray and allow to cool.

Per Serving

calories: 854 | fat: 58g | protein: 22g | carbs: 61g | fiber: 14g | sugar: 5g | sodium: 11mg

---

Scotch Eggs with Ground Turkey

Prep time: 10 minutes | Cook time: 25 minutes | Serves 2

16 ounces (454 g) lean ground turkey
½ teaspoon black pepper
½ teaspoon nutmeg
½ teaspoon cinnamon
½ teaspoon cloves
½ teaspoon dried tarragon
½ cup finely chopped fresh parsley
½ tablespoon dried chives
1 garlic clove, finely chopped
4 free-range eggs, boiled and peeled

1. Preheat the oven to 375°F (190°C).
2. Cover a baking sheet with parchment paper.
3. Combine the turkey with the cinnamon, nutmeg, pepper, cloves, tarragon, chives, parsley and garlic in a mixing bowl and mix with your hands until thoroughly mixed.
4. Divide the mixture into 4 circular shapes with the palms of your hands.
5. Flatten each one into a pancake shape using the backs of your hands or a rolling pin.
6. Wrap the meat pancake around 1 egg, until it's covered. (You can moisten the meat with water first to help prevent it from sticking to your hands).
7. Bake in the oven for 25 minutes or until brown and crisp. Serve.

Per Serving

calories: 502 | fat: 30g | protein: 55g | carbs: 3g | fiber: 1g | sugar: 1g | sodium: 290mg

Maple-Vanilla Crepes

Prep time: 10 minutes | Cook time: 4 minutes | Serves 2

2 free-range eggs
1 teaspoon vanilla
½ cup nut milk of your choice
½ cup water
1 teaspoon pure maple syrup
1 cup gluten-free all-purpose flour
3 tablespoons coconut oil

1. In a medium bowl add the eggs, vanilla, nut milk, water, and syrup together until combined. Add the flour to the mix and whisk to combine to a smooth paste.
2. Take 2 tablespoons of the coconut oil and melt in a pan over medium heat.
3. Add ½ crepe mixture and tilt and swirl the pan to form a round crepe shape.
4. Cook for about 2 minutes until the bottom is light brown and comes away from the pan with the spatula.
5. Flip it and cook for a further 2 minutes.
6. Serve and repeat with the rest of the mixture!

Per Serving

calories: 615 | fat: 39g | protein: 13g | carbs: 53g | fiber: 3g | sugar: 4g | sodium: 75mg

Zucchini and Sweet Potato Frittata

Prep time: 5 minutes | Cook time: 23 minutes | Serves 2

1 tablespoon coconut or extra-virgin olive oil
4 free-range eggs
1 sweet potato, peeled and sliced
1 zucchini, peeled and sliced
2 teaspoons parsley
1 teaspoon cracked black pepper

1. Preheat the broiler to medium heat.
2. Heat the oil in a skillet under the broiler until hot.
3. Spread the potato slices across the skillet and cook for 8 to 10 minutes or until soft.
4. Add the zucchini to the skillet and cook for a further 5 minutes.
5. Meanwhile, whisk the eggs and parsley in a separate bowl, and season to taste before pouring mixture over the veggies in the skillet.
6. Cook for 10 minutes over low heat until golden.
7. Remove and turn over onto a plate or serving board.

Per Serving

calories: 239 | fat: 15g | protein: 12g | carbs: 14g | fiber: 2g | sugar: 3g | sodium: 162mg

Almond Yogurt, Berry, and Walnut Parfait

Prep time: 5 minutes | Cook time: 0 minutes | Serves 2

2 cups plain unsweetened almond yogurt
2 tablespoons honey
1 cup fresh raspberries
1 cup fresh blueberries
½ cup walnut pieces

1. Combine the yogurt and honey in a bowl. Stir to mix well, then pour half of the honey-yogurt in a large glass.
2. Top the honey-yogurt with berries, then top the berries with remaining honey-yogurt.
3. Spread the walnut pieces on top and serve immediately.

Per Serving

calories: 504 | fat: 22g | protein: 23g | carbs: 56g | fiber: 8g | sugar: 45g | sodium: 175mg

Coconut Rice with Dates, Almonds, and Blueberries

Prep time: 10 minutes | Cook time: 30 minutes | Serves 4

1 cup brown basmati rice
2 dates, pitted and chopped
1 cup coconut milk
1 teaspoon sea salt
1 cup water
¼ cup toasted slivered almonds, divided
½ cup shaved coconut, divided
1 cup fresh blueberries, divided

1. Combine the basmati rice, dates, coconut milk, salt, and water in a saucepan. Stir to mix well. Bring to a boil.
2. Reduce the heat to low, then simmer for 30 minutes or until the rice is soft.
3. Divide them into four bowls and serve with almonds, coconut, and blueberries on top.

Per Serving

calories: 280 | fat: 8g | protein: 6g | carbs: 49g | fiber: 5g | sugar: 7g | sodium: 621mg

Apple Muesli

Prep time: 10 minutes | Cook time: 0 minutes | Serves 4 to 6

2 cups gluten-free rolled oats
¼ cup no-added-sugar apple juice
1¾ cups coconut milk
1 tablespoon apple cider vinegar
1 apple, cored and chopped
Dash ground cinnamon

1. Combine the oats, apple juice, coconut milk, and apple cider vinegar in a bowl. Stir to mix well. Wrap the bowl in plastic and refrigerate overnight.
2. Remove the bowl from the refrigerator. Top with apple and sprinkle with cinnamon, then serve.

Per Serving

calories: 212 | fat: 4g | protein: 6g | carbs: 39g | fiber: 6g | sugar: 10g | sodium: 73mg

Buckwheat Waffles

Prep time: 15 minutes | Cook time: 12 minutes per waffle | Serves 4

1½ cups buckwheat flour
½ cup brown rice flour
1 teaspoon baking soda
2 teaspoons baking powder
½ teaspoon sea salt
1 egg
2 teaspoons vanilla extract
1 tablespoon pure maple syrup
1½ cups almond milk
1 cup water
Coconut oil, for greasing the waffle iron

1. Combine the flours, baking soda, baking powder, and salt in a bowl. Stir to mix well.
2. Whisk together the egg, vanilla, maple syrup, almond milk, and water in a separate bowl.
3. Pour the egg mixture into the flour mixture and keep stirring until a smooth batter forms. Let the batter stand for 10 minutes.
4. Preheat the waffle iron and grease with coconut oil.
5. Pour the batter in the waffle iron to cover ¾ of the bottom. Cook for 10 to 12 minutes or until golden brown and crispy. Flip the waffle halfway through the cooking time. The cooking time will vary depending on the waffle iron you use.
6. Serve the waffles immediately.

Per Serving

calories: 281 | fat: 4g | protein: 9g | carbs: 55g | fiber: 6g | sugar: 7g | sodium: 691mg

Berry and Chia Yogurt

Prep time: 10 minutes | Cook time: 3 minutes | Serves 4

1 (10-ounce / 284-g) package frozen mixed berries, thawed
2 tablespoons freshly squeezed lemon juice
½ vanilla bean, halved lengthwise
2 tablespoons pure maple syrup
1 tablespoon chia seeds
4 cups unsweetened almond yogurt

1. Combine the mixed berries, lemon juice, vanilla bean, and maple syrup in a saucepan. Bring to a boil over medium-high heat. Stir constantly.
2. Reduce the heat to low and simmer for 3 minutes.
3. Turn off the heat, then discard the vanilla bean. Mix in the chia seeds, then let sit for 10 minutes or until the seeds are thickened.
4. Divide them into four serving bowls, then pour 1 cup of yogurt in each bowl. Serve immediately.

Per Serving

calories: 245 | fat: 10g | protein: 5g | carbs: 35g | fiber: 5g | sugar: 21g | sodium: 3mg

Quinoa with Seeds, Hazelnuts, and Raspberries

Prep time: 10 minutes | Cook time: 20 minutes | Serves 4

1 cup quinoa, rinsed well
2 cups water
¼ cup hemp seeds
½ cup shredded coconut
1 teaspoon ground cinnamon
2 tablespoons flaxseeds
1 teaspoon vanilla extract
Pinch sea salt
¼ cup chopped hazelnuts
1 cup fresh raspberries

1. Pour the quinoa and water in a saucepan. Bring to a boil over high heat. Reduce the heat to low and simmer for 20 minutes or until soft.
2. When the simmering is complete, mix in the hemp seeds, coconut, cinnamon, flaxseeds, vanilla, and salt.
3. Serve the quinoa with hazelnuts and raspberries on top.

Per Serving

calories: 285 | fat: 13g | protein: 10g | carbs: 32g | fiber: 6g | sugar: 1g | sodium: 45mg

Simple Coconut Pancakes

Prep time: 10 minutes | Cook time: 5 minutes per pancake | Serves 8 pancakes

4 eggs
1 cup coconut milk, plus additional as needed
1 tablespoon pure maple syrup
1 teaspoon vanilla extract
1 tablespoon melted coconut oil, plus additional for greasing the pan
½ cup coconut flour
1 teaspoon baking soda
½ teaspoon sea salt

1. Whisk together the eggs, coconut milk, maple syrup, vanilla, and coconut oil in a large bowl. Stir to mix well.
2. Combine the coconut flour, baking soda, and salt in a separate bowl. Stir to mix well.
3. Make a well in the middle of the coconut flour mixture, then pour the egg mixture in the well. Stir to mix well until smooth and no lump.
4. Grease a nonstick skillet with coconut oil, then heat over medium-high heat until shimmering.
5. Divide the batter and pour ½ cup of batter in the skillet and cook for 5 minutes or until lightly browned. Flip halfway through the cooking time. Repeat with the remaining batter.
6. Transfer the pancakes to four plates and serve immediately.

Per Serving

calories: 192 | fat: 11g | protein: 9g | carbs: 15g | fiber: 7g | sugar: 6g | sodium: 736mg

Mini Spinach Muffins

Prep time: 15 minutes | Cook time: 15 minutes | Makes 12 muffins

2 cups packed spinach
¼ cup raw honey
1 teaspoon vanilla extract
3 tablespoons extra-virgin olive oil
2 eggs
1 cup almond flour
1 cup oat flour
1 teaspoon baking soda
2 teaspoons baking powder
½ teaspoon salt
Pinch freshly ground black pepper

1. Preheat the oven to 350°F (180°C). Line a 12-cup muffin pan with paper muffin cups.
2. Put the spinach, honey, vanilla, and olive oil in a food processor, then break the eggs into it. Pulse to mix well until creamy and smooth.
3. Combine the flours, baking soda, baking powder, salt, and black pepper in a large bowl. Stir to mix well.
4. Make a well in the center of the flour mixture, then pour the spinach mixture into the well. Stir to mix well.
5. Divide the batter into muffin cups, then arrange the muffin pan in the preheated oven and bake for 15 minutes or until a toothpick inserted in the center comes out clean.
6. Remove the pan from the oven. Allow to cool for 10 minutes, then serve immediately.

Per Serving

calories: 107 | fat: 6g | protein: 3g | carbs: 12g | fiber: 1g | sugar: 6g | sodium: 216mg

Spinach Breakfast

Prep time: 10 minutes | Cook time: 30½ minutes | Serves 4

2 sweet potatoes, peeled and diced
2 tablespoons olive oil
½ teaspoon onion powder
½ teaspoon garlic powder
¼ teaspoon paprika
4 eggs, pasture-raised
½ onion, sliced
½ cup mushrooms, sliced
2 cups fresh baby spinach
Salt and pepper, to taste
Coconut oil for greasing

1. Preheat the oven to 425°F (220°C).
2. Place the potatoes in a baking dish and drizzle with olive oil. Season with onion powder, garlic powder, paprika, salt, and pepper to taste. Once cooked, set aside.
3. Bake in the oven for 30 minutes while turning the sweet potatoes halfway through the cooking time.
4. Heat skillet and grease with coconut oil.
5. Sauté the onion for 30 seconds until fragrant.
6. Add in the mushrooms and egg. Season with salt and pepper to taste.
7. Scramble the eggs.
8. Before the eggs have set, stir in the baby spinach until wilted.
9. Plate the potatoes and top with the egg mixture.

Per Serving
calories: 252 | fat: 17g | protein: 11g | carbs: 15g | fiber: 2g | sugar: 4g | sodium: 151mg

CHAPTER 4:
SOUPS AND SALADS

Sesame Noodle Soup with Scallion

Prep time: 15 minutes | Cook time: 0 minutes | Serves 4

8 ounces (227 g) buckwheat noodles or rice noodles, cooked
2 tablespoons sesame seeds
¼ cup thinly sliced cucumber
¼ cup sliced scallion
¼ cup chopped fresh cilantro
2 tablespoons sesame oil
2 tablespoons rice vinegar
1 tablespoon grated peeled fresh ginger
1 tablespoon coconut aminos
1 tablespoon raw honey
1 tablespoon freshly squeezed lime juice
1 teaspoon chili powder

1. In a large serving bowl, thoroughly mix the noodles, sesame seeds, cucumber, scallion, cilantro, sesame oil, vinegar, ginger, coconut aminos, honey, lime juice, and chili powder.
2. Divide among 4 soup bowls and serve at room temperature.

Per Serving
calories: 169 | fat: 9g | protein: 2g | carbs: 20g | fiber: 1g | sugar: 4g | sodium: 38mg

Nutty and Fruity Garden Salad

Prep time: 10 minutes | Cook time: 0 minutes | Serves 2

6 cups baby spinach
½ cup chopped walnuts, toasted
1 ripe red pear, sliced
1 ripe persimmon, sliced
1 teaspoon garlic minced
1 shallot, minced
3 tablespoons extra-virgin olive oil
2 tablespoons fresh lemon juice
1 teaspoon whole grain mustard

1. Mix well garlic, shallot, oil, lemon juice and mustard in a large salad bowl.
2. Add spinach, pear and persimmon. Toss to coat well.
3. To serve, garnish with chopped pecans.

Per Serving
calories: 354 | fat: 22g | protein: 6.8g | carbs: 37g | fiber: 9g | sugar: 20g | sodium: 225mg

Salad Greens with Pear and

Persimmon

Prep time: 10 minutes | Cook time: 0 minutes | Serves 2

6 cups baby spinach
½ cup chopped pecans, toasted
1 ripe red pear, sliced
1 ripe persimmon, sliced
1 teaspoon minced garlic
1 shallot, minced
3 tablespoons extra-virgin olive oil
2 tablespoons fresh lemon juice
1 teaspoon whole grain mustard

1. In a big mixing bowl, mix garlic, olive oil, lemon juice and mustard.
2. Once thoroughly mixed, add remaining ingredients.
3. Toss to coat.
4. Equally divide into two bowls, serve and enjoy.

Per Serving
calories: 220 | fat: 16g | protein: 7g | carbs: 12g | fiber: 5g | sugar: 2g | sodium: 368mg

Herbed Kale and Flaxseed Salad

Prep time: 10 minutes | Cook time: 5 minutes | Serves 4

¼ cup Kalamata olives
1 garlic clove, minced
1 small cucumber, sliced thinly
2 tablespoons green onion, chopped
2 tablespoons red onion, minced
1½ tablespoons flaxseeds
1 tablespoon extra-virgin olive oil
1 pinch of salt
1 pinch of dried basil
½ of a lemon
6 cups dinosaur kale, chopped

1. Bring a medium pot, half-filled with water to a boil.
2. Rinse kale and cut into small strips. Place in a steamer and put on top of boiling water and steam for 5 to 7 minutes.
3. Transfer steamed kale to a salad bowl.
4. Season kale with oil, salt, basil and lemon. Toss to coat well.
5. Add remaining ingredients into salad bowl, toss to mix.
6. Serve and enjoy.

Per Serving
calories: 90 | fat: 5g | protein: 3g | carbs: 11.7g | fiber: 4g | sugar: 5g | sodium: 149mg

Cucumber and Tomato Salad

Prep time: 10 minutes | Cook time: 0 minutes | Serves 4

Ground pepper, to taste
Salt, to taste
1 tablespoon fresh lemon juice
1 onion, chopped
1 cucumber, peeled and diced
2 tomatoes, chopped
4 cups spinach

1. In a salad bowl, mix onions, cucumbers and tomatoes.
2. Season with pepper and salt, to taste.
3. Add lemon juice and mix well.
4. Add spinach, toss to coat, serve and enjoy.

Per Serving

calories: 41 | fat: 0g | protein: 2g | carbs: 9g | fiber: 2g | sugar: 4g | sodium: 29mg

Ginger Yogurt Dressed Citrus Salad

Prep time: 10 minutes | Cook time: 0 minutes | Serves 6

⅔ cup minced crystallized ginger
1 (16-oouce / 454-g) Greek yogurt
¼ teaspoon ground cinnamon
2 tablespoons honey
½ cup dried cranberries
3 navel oranges
2 large tangerines, peeled
1 pink grapefruit, peeled

1. Into sections, break tangerines and grapefruit.
2. Cut tangerine sections into half.
3. Into thirds, slice grapefruit sections.
4. Cut orange pith and peel in half and slice oranges into ¼ inch thick rounds, then quartered.
5. In a medium bowl, mix oranges, grapefruit, tangerines and its juices.
6. Add cinnamon, honey and ½ cup of cranberries.
7. Cover and place in the ref for an hour.
8. In a small bowl, mix ginger and yogurt.
9. To serve, add a dollop of yogurt dressing onto a serving of fruit and sprinkle with cranberries.

Per Serving

calories: 155 | fat: 1g | protein: 9g | carbs: 31g | fiber: 3g | sugar: 24g | sodium: 31mg

Goat Cheese 'n Red Beans on Salad

Prep time: 10 minutes | Cook time: 0 minutes | Serves 6

1½ cups red grape tomatoes, halved
1 bunch parsley, chopped
½ teaspoon salt
½ teaspoon white pepper
2 cans of Red Kidney Beans, drained and rinsed well
3 garlic cloves, minced
3 tablespoons lemon juice
3 tablespoons olive oil
6 ounces (170 g) goat cheese, crumbled
Water or vegetable broth to cover beans

1. In a large bowl, combine beans, parsley, tomatoes and garlic.
2. Add olive oil, lemon juice, salt and pepper.
3. Mix well and refrigerate until ready to serve.
4. Spoon into individual dishes top with crumbled goat cheese.

Per Serving

calories: 262 | fat: 20g | protein: 11g | carbs: 12g | fiber: 1g | sugar: 7g | sodium: 414mg

Grilled Eggplant Caprese

Prep time: 5 minutes | Cook time: 6 minutes | Serves 4

1 eggplant aubergine, small/medium
1 tomato large
2 basil leaves or a little more as needed
4 ounces (113 g) mozzarella
Good quality olive oil
Pepper and salt, to taste

1. Cut the ends of the eggplant and then cut it lengthwise into ¼-inch thick slices. Discard the smaller pieces that's mostly skin and short.
2. Slice the tomatoes and mozzarella into thin slices just like the eggplant.
3. On medium-high the fire, place a griddle and let it heat up.
4. Brush eggplant slices with olive oil and place on grill. Grill for 3 minutes. Turnover and grill for 1 minute. Add a slice of cheese on one side and tomato on the other side. Continue cooking for another 2 minutes.
5. Sprinkle with basil leaves. Season with pepper and salt.
6. Fold eggplant in half and skewer with a cocktail stick.
7. Serve and enjoy.

Per Serving

calories: 82 | fat: 0g | protein: 11g | carbs: 11g | fiber: 5g | sugar: 7g | sodium: 216mg

Caesar Salad Supreme

Prep time: 10 minutes | Cook time: 0 minutes | Serves 2

1 head romaine lettuce, torn into bite sized pieces
Ground black pepper, to taste
Salt, to taste
1 tablespoon lemon juice
1 teaspoon Dijon mustard
1 teaspoon Worcestershire sauce
6 tablespoons low-fat Parmesan Cheese, grated and divided
5 anchovy filets, minced
½ cup low-fat mayonnaise
3 garlic cloves, peeled and minced

1. In a small bowl, whisk well lemon juice, mustard, Worcestershire sauce, 2 tablespoons Parmesan Cheese, anchovies, mayonnaise, and minced garlic. Season with pepper and salt to taste. Set aside in the ref.
2. In large bowl, place lettuce and pour in dressing. Toss well to coat. Top with remaining Parmesan Cheese.
3. Serve, and enjoy.

Per Serving

calories: 199 | fat: 9g | protein: 17g | carbs: 15g | fiber: 7g | sugar: 6g | sodium: 708mg

Spinach and Cranberry Salad

Prep time: 10 minutes | Cook time: 3 minutes | Serves 2

½ cup olive oil
¼ cup cider vinegar
¼ cup white wine vinegar
¼ teaspoon paprika
2 teaspoons minced onion
¼ cup honey
1 cup dried cranberries
1 pound (454 g) spinach, rinsed and torn into bite sized pieces
½ cup pumpkin seeds

1. Toast pumpkin seeds by placing in a nonstick saucepan on medium fire. Stir frequently and toast for at least 3 to 5 minutes. Remove from fire and set aside.
2. In a medium bowl, mix well olive oil, cider vinegar, white wine vinegar, paprika, onion, and honey. Whisk well until mixture is uniform.
3. In a large salad bowl, add torn spinach.
4. Drizzle with dressing and toss well to coat.
5. Garnish with cooled and toasted pumpkin seeds and dried cranberries.
6. Serve and enjoy.

Per Serving

calories: 508 | fat: 35g | protein: 9g | carbs: 45g | fiber: 5g | sugar: 34g | sodium: 145mg

Fresh Carrot Salad

Prep time: 10 minutes | Cook time: 0 minutes | Serves 4

1 large avocado, diced
1 cup cherry tomatoes, halved
1 bunch scallions, sliced
4 cups carrots, spiralized
Salt, to taste
¼ teaspoon chipotle powder
1 tablespoon chili powder
2 tablespoons olive oil
1 tablespoon lemon juice
3 tablespoons lime juice

1. In a salad bowl, mix and arrange avocado, cherry tomatoes, scallions and spiralized carrots. Set aside.
2. In a small bowl, whisk salt, chipotle powder, chili powder, olive oil, lemon juice and lime juice thoroughly.
3. Pour dressing over noodle salad. Toss to coat well.
4. Serve and enjoy at room temperature.

Per Serving

calories: 25 | fat: 8g | protein: 3g | carbs: 25g | fiber: 8g | sugar: 11g | sodium: 142mg

Winter Persimmon Salad

Prep time: 10 minutes | Cook time: 0 minutes | Serves 2

½ cup sweet potato, spiralized
2 fuyu persimmon, sliced
1 red bell pepper, julienned
4 cups mixed greens
Salt, to taste
3 tablespoons lime juice
1 pinch of chipotle powder
1 tablespoon chili powder
1 ripe fuyu persimmon, diced
1 red bell pepper, diced
½ cup coarsely chopped pistachio

1. In a salad bowl, mix and arrange persimmons, bell pepper and sweet potatoes. Set aside.
2. In a food processor, puree salt, lime juice, chipotle powder, chili powder, diced persimmon and diced bell pepper until smooth and creamy.
3. Pour over salad, toss to mix.
4. Serve and enjoy.

Per Serving

calories: 346 | fat: 15g | protein: 11g | carbs: 52g | fiber: 15g | sugar: 27g | sodium: 293mg

Arugula Garden Salad

Prep time: 10 minutes | Cook time: 0 minutes | Serves 2

1 large avocado, sliced into ½ inch cubes
¼ cup grated Parmesan Cheese
Black pepper, freshly ground
Salt, to taste
1 tablespoon rice vinegar
2 tablespoons olive oil or grapeseed oil
¼ cup pine nuts
1 cup cherry tomatoes, halved
4 cups young arugula leaves, rinsed and dried

1. Get a bowl with cover, big enough to hold the salad and mix together the Parmesan Cheese, vinegar, oil, pine nuts, cherry tomatoes and arugula.
2. Season with pepper and salt according to how you like it. Place the lid and jiggle the covered bowl to combine the salad.
3. Serve the salad topped with sliced avocadoes.

Per Serving
calories: 375 | fat: 30g | protein: 9g | carbs: 24g | fiber: 9g | sugar: 11g | sodium: 242mg

Grilled Vegetable Salad

Prep time: 10 minutes | Cook time: 5 minutes | Serves 3

Ingredients:
¼ cup feta cheese
¼ cup fresh basil leaves
Pepper and salt, to taste
¼ cup extra-virgin olive oil, for brushing
1 red bell pepper, quartered, seeds and ribs removed
1 yellow bell pepper, quartered, seeds and ribs removed
1 medium onion, cut into ½ inch rings
1-pint cherry tomatoes
½ bunch asparagus, trimmed and cut into bite-size pieces

1. Toss olive oil and vegetables in a big bowl. Season with salt and pepper.
2. Frill vegetables in a preheated griller for 5 to 7 minutes or until charred and tender.
3. Transfer veggies to a platter, add feta and basil.
4. In a separate small bowl, mix olive oil, balsamic vinegar, garlic seasoned with pepper and salt.
5. Drizzle dressing over vegetables and serve.

Per Serving
calories: 231 | fat: 21g | protein: 4g | carbs: 9g | fiber: 2g | sugar: 3g | sodium: 119mg

Fennel and Pears Salad

Prep time: 10 minutes | Cook time: 0 minutes | Serves 6

2 tablespoons olive oil
3 tablespoons fresh lime juice
¼ cup chopped pistachios
¼ cup green onions, sliced
1 cup red bell pepper, diced
2 cups medium sized fennel bulb, thinly sliced
1 bunch watercress, trimmed
3 cups Asian pears, cut into matchstick size

1. In a large salad bowl, mix pistachios, green onions, bell pepper, fennel, watercress and pears.
2. In a small bowl, mix vegetable oil and lime juice. Season with pepper and salt to taste.
3. Pour dressing to salad and gently mix before serving.

Per Serving
calories: 199 | fat: 7g | protein: 3g | carbs: 34g | fiber: 6g | sugar: 25g | sodium: 49mg

Fruity Salmon-Spinach Salad

Prep time: 10 minutes | Cook time: 14 minutes | Serves 2

2 teaspoons avocado oil
6 ounces (170 g) wild caught salmon fillet with skin
1/3 cup raw pecans
½ cup cherry tomatoes
½ ripe nectarine
½ avocado
2 cups baby spinach leaves
Vinaigrette Ingredients:
Freshly ground black pepper, to taste
¼ teaspoon Paleo Dijon style mustard
3 teaspoons walnut oil
2 teaspoons fresh lemon juice

1. Place a cast iron pan on medium high fire and melt avocado oil. Preheat oven to 400°F (205°C).
2. Once oil is hat sear salmon on both sides for 2 minutes per side. Pop in oven and bake for 10 minutes.
3. In a small bowl whisk all vinaigrette ingredients until emulsified. Season with pepper to taste and set aside.
4. Chop pecans into small pieces. Chop avocado, tomatoes, and nectarines into bite-sized pieces and place in a large salad bowl.
5. Add spinach and chopped pecans in bowl. Pour dressing and toss to coat well.
6. Serve salad with roasted salmon on top.

Per Serving
calories: 305 | fat: 24g | protein: 4g | carbs: 23g | fiber: 8g | sugar: 13g | sodium: 29mg

Tuna Salad Mediterranean Style

Prep time: 10 minutes | Cook time: 0 minutes | Serves 3

1 head lettuce
1 tablespoon small capers, rinsed and drained
2 green onions, sliced
¼ cup drained and chopped roasted red peppers
¼ cup chopped pitted ripe olives
¼ cup Mayonnaise dressing with olive oil
2 (6 ounces / 170 g) cans of tuna, drained and flaked

1. With the exception of salad greens or bread, mix together all of the ingredients in a bowl. If desired, you can arrange it on top of salad greens.

Per Serving

calories: 110 | fat: 9g | protein: 5g | carbs: 3g | fiber: 1g | sugar: 1g | sodium: 354mg

Oregano Dressing on Salad Greens

Prep time: 10 minutes | Cook time: 0 minutes | Serves 4

1/3 cup chopped red onion
¾ cup crumbled soft fresh goat cheese
1½ cups diced celery
1½ large red bell peppers, diced
4 cups baby spinach leaves, coarsely chopped
1 tablespoon chopped fresh oregano
2 tablespoons fresh lemon juice
2 tablespoons extra-virgin olive oil

1. In a large salad bowl, mix oregano, lemon juice and oil.
2. Add pepper and salt, to taste.
3. Mix in red onion, goat cheese, celery, bell peppers and spinach.
4. Toss to coat well, serve and enjoy.

Per Serving

calories:91 | fat: 4g | protein: 6g | carbs: 11g | fiber: 6g | sugar: 3g | sodium: 207mg

Arugula-Craisins Salad

Prep time: 5 minutes | Cook time: 0 minutes | Serves 1

1 cup baby arugula
1 cup spinach
1 tablespoon craisins
1 tablespoon almonds, shaved or chopped
1 tablespoon balsamic vinegar
½ tablespoon extra-virgin olive oil

1. In a plate, mix arugula and spinach.
2. Top with craisins and almonds.
3. Drizzle olive oil and balsamic vinegar.
4. Serve and enjoy.

Per Serving

calories: 83 | fat: 4g | protein: 2g | carbs: 11g | fiber: 2g | sugar: 8g | sodium: 93mg

Ginger-Broccoli Salad

Prep time: 10 minutes | Cook time: 30 minutes | Serves 3

¼ teaspoon sea salt
¼ teaspoon ground cinnamon
½ teaspoon ground turmeric
¾ teaspoon ground ginger
½ tablespoon extra-virgin olive oil
½ tablespoon apple cider vinegar
2 tablespoons chopped green onion
1/3 cup coconut cream
½ cup carrots, shredded
1 small head of broccoli, chopped

1. In a large salad bowl, mix well salt, cinnamon, turmeric, ginger, olive oil, and vinegar.
2. Add remaining ingredients, tossing well to coat.
3. Pop in the ref for at least 30 to 60 minutes before serving.

Per Serving

calories: 113 | fat: 10g | protein: 2g | carbs: 5g | fiber: 2g | sugar: 1g | sodium: 233mg

Summer Jicama & Cabbage Slaw

Prep time: 10 minutes | Cook time: 1 minutes | Serves 2

1 handful parsley, finely chopped
½ pound (227 g) jicama, peeled, and sliced
½ red onion, sliced thinly
Salt, to taste
½ head green cabbage, shredded
½ head purple cabbage, shredded
Dressing Ingredients:
¼ teaspoon salt
½ lemon, juiced
2 tablespoons apple cider vinegar
1/3 cup extra-virgin olive oil
½ cup warm filtered water
½ cup coconut concentrate warmed in a bowl of hot water

1. In blender, add all dressing ingredients except for warm water. Puree until smooth and creamy. Add warm water by teaspoonful to reach desired consistency.
2. In a large salad bowl, add shredded cabbages and add salt. Massage for 1 minute or two to soften some tough fibers.
3. Add parsley, jicama, and red onion into bowl. Pour dressing and toss well to combine.
4. Serve and enjoy.

Per Serving

calories: 143 | fat: 1g | protein: 6g | carbs: 33g | fiber: 13g | sugar: 13g | sodium: 98mg

Quinoa Minestrone Soup

Prep time: 20 minutes | Cook time: 20 minutes | Serves 6

1 tablespoon ghee
2 garlic cloves, minced
1 medium white onion, diced
2 carrots, chopped
2 celery stalks, diced
1 small zucchini, diced
½ red bell pepper, diced
5 cups vegetable broth
1 (14-ounce / 397-g) can diced tomatoes with their juice
1 (14-ounce / 397-g) can cannellini beans, drained and rinsed well
1 cup packed kale, stemmed and thoroughly washed
½ cup quinoa, rinsed well
1 tablespoon freshly squeezed lemon juice
2 teaspoons dried rosemary
2 teaspoons dried thyme
1 bay leaf
½ teaspoon salt
Freshly ground black pepper, to taste

1. In a large soup pot over medium heat, add the ghee, garlic, onion, carrots, and celery, and sauté for 3 minutes.
2. Add the zucchini and red bell pepper, and sauté for 2 minutes.
3. Stir in the broth, tomatoes, beans, kale, quinoa, lemon juice, rosemary, thyme, bay leaf, and salt, and season with black pepper. Bring to a simmer, reduce the heat to low, cover, and cook for 15 minutes, or until the quinoa is cooked. Remove the bay leaf and discard. Serve hot.

Per Serving

calories: 319 | fat: 5g | protein: 18g | carbs: 42g | fiber: 9g | sugar: 10g | sodium: 1007mg

Broccoli, Carrot and Celery Soup

Prep time: 10 minutes | Cook time: 17 minutes | Serves 4

1 tablespoon ghee
1 medium white onion, diced
3 garlic cloves, minced
1 head broccoli, roughly chopped
1 carrot, chopped
1 celery stalk, diced
3 cups vegetable broth
½ teaspoon salt
½ teaspoon freshly squeezed lemon juice
½ teaspoon lemon zest
Freshly ground black pepper, to taste

1. In a large soup pot over medium heat, melt the ghee.
2. Add the onion and garlic, and sauté for 5 minutes.
3. Add the broccoli, carrot, and celery, and sauté for 2 minutes.
4. Stir in the broth, salt, lemon juice, and lemon zest, and season with pepper. Bring to a simmer and cook for about 10 minutes. Serve immediately.

Per Serving

calories: 80 | fat: 4g | protein: 2g | carbs: 10g | fiber: 3g | sugar: 4g | sodium: 726mg

Salad Greens with Roasted Beets

Prep time: 10 minutes | Cook time: 1 hour | Serves 4

½ cup chopped walnuts
4 cups baby spinach
½ teaspoon Dijon mustard
1 tablespoon minced red onions
2 tablespoons sherry vinegar
¼ cup extra-virgin olive oil
3 medium beets, washed and trimmed
1 tablespoon dried cranberries, chopped roughly

1. In foil, wrap beets and bake in a preheated 400°F (205°C) oven. Bake until beets are tender, around 1 hour. Once done, open foil and allow to cool. When cool to touch, peel beets and dice.
2. Mix well mustard, red onions, vinegar, and olive oil. Mix in spinach, beets and cranberries. Toss to coat well.

Per Serving

calories: 130 | fat: 13g | protein: 3g | carbs: 3g | fiber: 1g | sugar: 1g | sodium: 147mg

Oregano-Basil Tomato Soup

Prep time: 15 minutes | Cook time: 11 minutes | Serves 6

1 tablespoon ghee
1 small onion, chopped
3 garlic cloves, chopped
1 teaspoon dried basil
1 teaspoon dried oregano
½ teaspoon salt
¼ teaspoon chili powder
⅛ teaspoon freshly ground black pepper
⅛ teaspoon dried thyme
2 (14-ounce / 397-g) cans diced tomatoes with their juice
2 cups vegetable broth
¼ cup tomato paste
½ cup plain whole-milk yogurt

1. In a large soup pot over medium heat, melt the ghee.
2. Add the onion and garlic, and sauté for 5 minutes.
3. Stir in the basil, oregano, salt, chili powder, pepper, and thyme.
4. Add the tomatoes, broth, and tomato paste, and stir to combine. Bring to a simmer, turn the heat to low, and cook for 5 to 10 minutes. Remove the pot from the heat. With an immersion blender (or in batches in a standard blender), purée the mixture in the pot until you have the desired consistency.
5. Add the yogurt. Blend for 1 minute more. Serve immediately.

Per Serving

calories: 75 | fat: 3g | protein: 2g | carbs: 10g | fiber: 3g | sugar: 7g | sodium: 411mg

Nutty Brussels Sprouts Salad

Prep time: 5 minutes | Cook time: 9 minutes | Serves 4

1½ tablespoons toasted walnuts, finely chopped
⅛ teaspoon black pepper
¼ teaspoon salt
¾ pound Brussels sprouts
1/3 cup fresh breadcrumbs
1 garlic clove, minced
1½ teaspoons olive oil, divided

1. Slice Brussels sprouts in half then separate the leaves from the cores. Cut the cores in quarters and set aside.
2. On medium fire, place a large nonstick saucepan and heat 1 teaspoon oil. Sauté garlic for 1 minute.
3. Add breadcrumbs and sauté for another minute or until lightly browned. Transfer to a bowl.
4. In same pan, add remaining oil and cook Brussels sprouts until crisp tender around 8 minutes.
5. Transfer to serving bowl, pour in breadcrumb mixture and toss to mix.
6. Garnish with nuts before serving

Per Serving

calories: 71 | fat: 4g | protein: 4g | carbs: 8g | fiber: 4g | sugar: 2g | sodium: 167mg

Garlic Cauliflower Soup

Prep time: 10 minutes | Cook time: 20 minutes | Serves 6

1 tablespoon avocado oil
1 small white onion, diced
3 garlic cloves, minced
1 small celery root, trimmed, peeled, and cut into 1-inch pieces
1 head cauliflower, roughly chopped into 1-inch pieces
4 cups vegetable broth
2 tablespoons ghee
2 scallions, sliced

1. In a large soup pot over medium heat, heat the avocado oil.
2. Add the onion and garlic, and sauté for 5 minutes.
3. Add the celery root and cauliflower. Increase the heat to medium-high and continue to sauté for 5 minutes, or until the cauliflower begins to brown and caramelize on the edges.
4. Stir in the broth and ghee and bring to a boil. Reduce the heat to medium-low and simmer for 10 minutes. Remove the pot from the heat.
5. With an immersion blender, or in batches in a standard blender, purée the soup until creamy. Serve immediately, sprinkled with the scallions.

Per Serving

calories: 183 | fat: 8g | protein: 9g | carbs: 10g | fiber: 3g | sugar: 4g | sodium: 400mg

Miso Mushroom Soup with Spinach

Prep time: 10 minutes | Cook time: 0 minutes | Serves 4

3 cups filtered water
3 cups vegetable broth
1 cup sliced mushrooms
½ teaspoon fish sauce
3 tablespoons miso paste
1 cup fresh baby spinach, thoroughly washed
4 scallions, sliced

1. In a large soup pot over high heat, add the water, broth, mushrooms, and fish sauce, and bring to a boil. Remove from the heat.
2. In a small bowl, mix the miso paste with ½ cup of heated broth mixture to dissolve the miso. Stir the miso mixture back into the soup.
3. Stir in the spinach and scallions. Serve immediately.

Per Serving

calories: 44 | fat: 0g | protein: 2g | carbs: 8g | fiber: 1g | sugar: 3g | sodium: 1152mg

Red Lentil Dal with Tomato

Prep time: 15 minutes | Cook time: 27 minutes | Serves 6

3 cups vegetable broth
1 cup red dried lentils, sorted and rinsed well
1 bay leaf
1 medium white onion, diced
2 garlic cloves, minced
1 tablespoon coconut oil
1 medium tomato, diced
1 teaspoon sesame seeds
1 teaspoon ground ginger
1 teaspoon ground cumin
1 teaspoon ground turmeric
1 teaspoon mustard seeds
½ teaspoon salt
Dash ground cinnamon
1 (14-ounce / 397-g) can unsweetened coconut milk
2 tablespoons chopped fresh cilantro leaves

1. In a large soup pot over high heat, mix the broth, lentils, and bay leaf, and bring to a boil. Reduce the heat to medium-low and simmer for 20 minutes, or until the lentils are cooked.
2. Meanwhile, in a medium saucepan over medium heat, sauté the onion and garlic in the coconut oil for 2 minutes.
3. Add the tomato, sesame seeds, ginger, cumin, turmeric, mustard seeds, salt, and cinnamon. Cook, stirring frequently, for 5 minutes.
4. Stir in the coconut milk and bring to a simmer.
5. Remove and discard the bay leaf. Add the coconut milk mixture to the lentils along with the cilantro and stir to combine. Serve alone or over rice if desired.

Per Serving

calories: 283 | fat: 6g | protein: 14g | carbs: 32g | fiber: 5g | sugar: 4g | sodium: 548mg

Dijon Turkey Meatball Veggie Soup

Prep time: 15 minutes | Cook time: 21 minutes | Serves 6

Meatballs:
1 pound (454 g) ground turkey
1 tablespoon Dijon mustard
1 teaspoon dried basil
1 teaspoon garlic powder
½ teaspoon dried oregano
½ teaspoon salt
¼ teaspoon red pepper flakes
Freshly ground black pepper, to taste
1 tablespoon ghee
Soup:
1 medium white onion, diced
2 carrots, diced
2 garlic cloves, minced
½ teaspoon dried thyme
6 cups vegetable broth
2 cups shredded kale leaves, stemmed and thoroughly washed
1 bay leaf

Make the Meatballs
1. In a medium bowl, put the turkey, mustard, basil, garlic power, oregano, salt, and red pepper flakes, and season with pepper. With your hands, mix the ingredients until they are well combined.
2. Add the ghee to a stockpot over medium-high heat. Roll the meat mixture into 1-inch balls and layer across the bottom of the pot. Cook for about 2 minutes per side, until almost cooked through. Transfer the meatballs to a plate.
Make the Soup
3. To the stockpot, add the onion, carrots, garlic, and thyme. Cook for about 2 minutes, gently stirring, until the onions are translucent.
4. Add the broth, kale, bay leaf, and meatballs. Bring to a simmer, reduce the heat to medium-low, and simmer for about 15 minutes until the meatballs are cooked through and the kale has softened. Remove and discard the bay leaf. Serve hot.

Per Serving
calories: 259 | fat: 14g | protein: 26g | carbs: 9g | fiber: 2g | sugar: 4g | sodium: 832mg

Coconut Veggie Soup with Cashews

Prep time: 15 minutes | Cook time: 26 minutes | Serves 6

2 tablespoons coconut oil
¾ cup toasted cashews
2 red chili peppers, seeded and diced
3 garlic cloves, peeled and minced
1 white onion, diced
1½ tablespoons peeled and minced fresh ginger
2 carrots, peeled and chopped
1 small butternut squash, halved, peeled, and diced
1 small Napa cabbage, roughly shredded
2 cups trimmed green beans
3 cups vegetable broth
1 (14-ounce / 397-g) can full-fat coconut milk
½ teaspoon salt
Freshly ground black pepper, to taste
1 cup mung bean sprouts
4 tablespoons toasted coconut shavings

1. In a large soup pot over medium heat, melt the coconut oil. Add the cashews and sauté for 2 minutes. Remove them from the pan and set aside.
2. Add the peppers, garlic, and onion, and sauté for 6 minutes. Then add the ginger and carrots, and sauté for about 3 minutes, or until the carrots and squash begin to soften.
3. Stir in the cabbage, green beans, broth, coconut milk, and salt. Season with pepper. Simmer for 15 minutes. Turn off the heat and stir in the bean sprouts and coconut shavings.
4. Pour into soup bowls and serve immediately.

Per Serving
calories: 340 | fat: 25g | protein: 7g | carbs: 23g | fiber: 5g | sugar: 10g | sodium: 591mg

Kale and Broccoli Soup

Prep time: 10 minutes | Cook time: 15 minutes | Serves 4

2 tablespoons extra-virgin olive oil, plus extra for garnish (optional)
1 onion, finely chopped
4 cups kale
1 cup broccoli florets
6 cups no-salt-added vegetable broth
1 teaspoon garlic powder
½ teaspoon sea salt
¼ teaspoon freshly ground black pepper
Micro-greens (optional)
Coconut milk (optional)

1. In a large pot over medium-high heat, heat the olive oil until it shimmers.
2. Add the onion and cook about 5 minutes, stirring occasionally, until it is soft.
3. Add the kale, broccoli, vegetable broth, garlic powder, salt, and pepper. Bring to a boil and reduce the heat to medium-low. Simmer 10 to 15 minutes, until the vegetables are soft.
4. Carefully transfer to a blender and blend until smooth. Serve hot with the additional oil, micro-greens, and coconut milk, if using.

Per Serving
calories: 129 | fat: 7g | protein: 3g | carbs: 16g | fiber: 2g | sugar: 6g | sodium: 302mg

Lime Chicken and Tomato Soup

Prep time: 15 minutes | Cook time: 15 minutes | Serves 6

1 tablespoon avocado oil
3 garlic cloves, minced
1 medium white onion, diced
1 jalapeño pepper, seeded and minced
6 cups chicken broth or vegetable broth
1 pound (454 g) shredded cooked chicken
1 (14-ounce / 397-g) can diced tomatoes with their juice
1 (4-ounce / 113-g) can diced green chiles
3 tablespoons freshly squeezed lime juice
1 teaspoon chili powder
1 teaspoon ground cumin
½ teaspoon salt
¼ teaspoon cayenne pepper
Freshly ground black pepper, to taste
1 avocado, sliced
Fresh cilantro, for garnish

1. In a large soup pot over medium heat, heat the avocado oil.
2. Add the garlic, onion, and jalapeño pepper, and sauté for 5 minutes.
3. Stir in the broth, chicken, tomatoes, green chiles, lime juice, chili powder, cumin, salt, and cayenne pepper, and season with black pepper. Bring to a simmer and cook for 10 minutes.
4. Serve hot, topped with slices of avocado and garnished with cilantro.

Per Serving
calories: 283 | fat: 7g | protein: 29g | carbs: 12g | fiber: 3g | sugar: 4g | sodium: 1085mg

Sweet Potato Soup with Leek

Prep time: 10 minutes | Cook time: 4 hours | Serves 4 to 6

5 medium sweet potatoes, peeled and chopped
1 leek, washed and sliced
1½ teaspoons garlic powder
1 teaspoon sea salt
½ teaspoon ground turmeric
¼ teaspoon ground cumin
4 cups vegetable broth
Freshly ground black pepper, to taste

1. In your slow cooker, combine the sweet potatoes, leek, garlic powder, salt, turmeric, cumin, and broth, and season with pepper.
2. Cover the cooker and set to low. Cook for 4 to 5 hours.
3. Using an immersion blender, purée the soup until smooth and serve.

Per Serving
calories: 200 | fat: 1g | protein: 3g | carbs: 46g | fiber: 6g | sugar: 10g | sodium: 1137mg

Carrot and Split Pea Soup

Prep time: 10 minutes | Cook time: 7 hours | Serves 4 to 6

2 cups dried split peas, soaked in water overnight, drained, and rinsed well
3 carrots, chopped
1 celery stalk, diced
½ medium onion, diced
1 tablespoon extra-virgin olive oil
1 tablespoon freshly squeezed lemon juice
2 teaspoons dried thyme leaves
1 teaspoon garlic powder
½ teaspoon dried oregano
2 bay leaves
8 cups broth of choice

1. In your slow cooker, combine the split peas, carrots, celery, onion, olive oil, lemon juice, thyme, garlic powder, oregano, bay leaves, and broth.
2. Cover the cooker and set to low. Cook for 7 to 8 hours.
3. Remove and discard the bay leaves. For a smoother soup, blend with an immersion blender and serve.

Per Serving
calories: 306 | fat: 4g | protein: 23g | carbs: 66g | fiber: 26g | sugar: 9g | sodium: 1156mg

Onion and White Bean Soup

Prep time: 10 minutes | Cook time: 7 hours | Serves 4 to 6

2 large onions, thinly sliced
¼ cup extra-virgin olive oil
¾ teaspoon sea salt
2 (14-ounce / 397-g) cans cannellini beans, rinsed and drained well
4 cups vegetable broth
½ teaspoon garlic powder
½ teaspoon dried thyme leaves
1 bay leaf
Freshly ground black pepper, to taste

1. In your slow cooker, combine the onions, olive oil, and salt.
2. Cover the cooker and set to high. Cook for 3 hours, allowing the onions to caramelize.
3. Stir the onions well and add the beans, broth, garlic powder, thyme, and bay leaf, and season with pepper.
4. Cover the cooker and set to low. Cook for 4 hours.
5. Remove and discard the bay leaf before serving.

Per Serving
calories: 328 | fat: 14g | protein: 11g | carbs: 39g | fiber: 10g | sugar: 7g | sodium: 968mg

Sweet Potato and Tomato Soup

Prep time: 15 minutes | Cook time: 6 hours | Serves 4 to 6

4 cups vegetable broth, plus more as needed
1 (15-ounce / 425-g) can diced tomatoes
2 medium sweet potatoes, peeled and diced
1 medium onion, diced
1 jalapeño pepper, seeded and diced
½ cup unsalted almond butter
½ teaspoon sea salt
½ teaspoon garlic powder
½ teaspoon ground turmeric
½ teaspoon ground ginger
¼ teaspoon ground cinnamon
Pinch ground nutmeg
½ cup full-fat coconut milk

1. In your slow cooker, combine the broth, tomatoes, sweet potatoes, onion, jalapeño, almond butter, salt, garlic powder, turmeric, ginger, cinnamon, and nutmeg.
2. Cover the cooker and set to low. Cook for 6 to 8 hours.
3. Stir in the coconut milk after cooking.
4. Using an immersion blender, purée the soup until smooth and serve.

Per Serving

calories: 358 | fat: 23g | protein: 7g | carbs: 34g | fiber: 7g | sugar: 11g | sodium: 1066mg

Mixed Berry Salad with Orange

Prep time: 5 minutes | Cook time: 0 minutes | Serves 4

1 cup fresh blueberries
1 cup fresh raspberries
1 cup fresh strawberries
1 tablespoon grated fresh ginger
Zest of 1 orange
Juice of 1 orange

1. In a medium bowl, stir together the blueberries, raspberries, strawberries, ginger, orange zest, and orange juice to mix well.

Per Serving

calories: 75 | fat:1 g | protein: 1g | carbs: 18g | fiber: 5g | sugar: 11g | sodium: 1mg

Turmeric Carrot and Lentil Soup

Prep time: 15 minutes | Cook time: 6 hours | Serves 4 to 6

1 cup dried yellow lentils, soaked in water overnight, drained, and rinsed well
4 cups vegetable broth
1 small onion, diced
1 carrot, diced
1 celery stalk, minced
2 teaspoons ground turmeric
1 teaspoon garlic powder
½ teaspoon sea salt
½ teaspoon ground ginger
½ teaspoon ground cumin
½ teaspoon dried thyme leaves
¼ teaspoon ground cinnamon
2 cups full-fat coconut milk

1. In your slow cooker, combine the lentils, broth, onion, carrot, celery, turmeric, garlic, salt, ginger, cumin, thyme, and cinnamon.
2. Cover the cooker and set to low. Cook for 6 to 8 hours.
3. Stir in the coconut milk and serve.

Per Serving

calories: 328 | fat: 21g | protein: 12g | carbs: 32g | fiber: 13g | sugar: 7g | sodium: 876mg

Ginger-Garlic Egg Soup

Prep time: 10 minutes | Cook time: 20 minutes | Serves 4

2 tablespoons toasted sesame oil
1 (2-inch) piece fresh ginger, peeled
4 garlic cloves, peeled
4 cups bone broth
1 tablespoon coconut aminos
1 tablespoon fish sauce
Pinch of fine Himalayan salt
4 large eggs, whisked
2 green onions, sliced, for garnish
4 sprigs fresh cilantro, minced, for garnish

1. In a pot, heat the sesame oil over medium heat. Add the ginger and garlic and stir until lightly browned.
2. Add the broth, coconut aminos, fish sauce, and salt. Bring to a low simmer, reduce the heat to low, cover, and cook for 20 minutes.
3. Slowly drizzle in the eggs while stirring the soup so the eggs cook instantly in ribbons as they hit the broth.
4. Garnish with the green onions and cilantro and serve hot. Store leftovers in an airtight container in the fridge for up to 5 days. I don't recommend freezing this soup.

Per Serving

calories: 185 | fat: 12g | protein: 16g | carbs: 4g | fiber: 0g | sugar: 0g | sodium: 1043mg

Snow Pea and Watermelon Salad

Prep time: 10 minutes | Cook time: 0 minutes | Serves 4

Dressing:
½ cup olive oil
¼ cup apple cider vinegar
2 tablespoons raw honey
1 teaspoon freshly grated lemon zest (optional)
Pinch sea salt
Salad:
4 cups (½-inch) watermelon cubes
1 English cucumber, cut into ½-inch cubes
1 cup halved snow peas
1 scallion, white and green parts, chopped
2 cups shredded kale
1 tablespoon chopped fresh cilantro

Make the Dressing
1. In a small bowl, whisk the olive oil, cider vinegar, honey, and lemon zest (if using). Season with sea salt and set it aside.
Make the Salad
2. In a large bowl, toss together the watermelon, cucumber, snow peas, scallion, and dressing.
3. Divide the kale among four plates and top with the watermelon mixture.
4. Serve garnished with the cilantro.

Per Serving
calories: 353 | fat: 26g | protein: 4g | carbs: 30g | fiber: 3g | sugar: 20g | sodium: 8mg

Greens and Fruit Salad with Coconut

Prep time: 10 minutes | Cook time: 0 minutes | Serves 4

Dressing:
¾ cup canned lite coconut milk
2 tablespoons almond butter
2 tablespoons freshly squeezed lime juice
Salad:
6 cups mixed greens
½ pineapple, peeled, cored, and diced, or 3 cups pre-cut packaged pineapple
1 mango, peeled, pitted, and diced, or 2 cups frozen chunks, thawed
1 cup quartered fresh strawberries
1 cup (1-inch) green bean pieces
½ cup shredded unsweetened coconut
1 tablespoon chopped fresh basil

Make the Dressing
1. In a small bowl, whisk the coconut milk, almond butter, and lime juice until smooth. Set it aside.
Make the Salad
2. In a large bowl, toss the mixed greens with three-fourths of the dressing. Arrange the salad on four plates.
3. In the same bowl, toss the pineapple, mango, strawberries, and green beans with the remaining fourth of the dressing.
4. Top each salad with the fruit and vegetable mixture and serve garnished with the coconut and basil.

Per Serving
calories: 311 | fat: 19g | protein: 5g | carbs: 36g | fiber: 7g | sugar: 26g | sodium: 140mg

Swiss Chard and Egg Salad

Prep time: 10 minutes | Cook time: 4 minutes | Serves 4

Dressing:
¼ cup olive oil
3 tablespoons freshly squeezed lemon juice
2 teaspoons raw honey
1 teaspoon Dijon mustard
Sea salt, to taste
Salad:
5 cups chopped Swiss chard
3 large hard-boiled eggs, peeled and chopped
1 English cucumber, diced
½ cup sliced radishes
½ cup chopped pecans

For the Dressing
1. In a small bowl, whisk the olive oil, lemon juice, honey, and mustard. Season with salt and set it aside.
For the Salad
2. In a large bowl, toss the Swiss chard and dressing together for about 4 minutes, or until the greens start to soften. Divide the greens evenly among four plates.
3. Top each salad with egg, cucumber, radishes, and pecans.

Per Serving
calories: 241 | fat: 21g | protein: 7g | carbs: 9g | fiber: 2g | sugar: 5g | sodium: 163mg

Spinach and Grapefruit Salad

Prep time: 10 minutes | Cook time: 0 minutes | Serves 4

Dressing:
½ avocado, peeled and pitted
¼ cup freshly squeezed lemon juice
2 tablespoons raw honey
Pinch sea salt
Water, for thinning the dressing
Salad:
4 cups fresh spinach
1 Ruby Red grapefruit, peeled, sectioned, and cut into chunks
¼ cup sliced radishes
¼ cup roasted sunflower seeds
¼ cup dried cranberries

Make the Dressing
1. In a blender, combine the avocado, lemon juice, honey, and sea salt. Pulse until very smooth.
2. Add enough water to reach your desired consistency and set the dressing aside.
Make the Salad
3. In a large bowl, toss the spinach with half the dressing. Divide the dressed spinach among four plates.
4. Top each with grapefruit, radishes, sunflower seeds, and cranberries.
5. Drizzle the remaining half of the dressing over the salads and serve.

Per Serving
calories: 126 | fat: 7g | protein: 2g | carbs: 16g | fiber: 3g | sugar: 13g | sodium: 30mg

Broccoli Salad with Cherry Dressing

Prep time: 10 minutes | Cook time: 0 minutes | Serves 4

Dressing:
½ cup pitted Rainier cherries
¼ cup olive oil
2 tablespoons freshly squeezed lemon juice
2 tablespoons raw honey
1 teaspoon chopped fresh basil
Pinch sea salt
Salad:
4 cups lightly blanched broccoli florets
2 cups mixed greens
1 cup snow peas
½ English cucumber, quartered lengthwise and sliced
½ red onion, thinly sliced

Make the Dressing
1. In a blender, combine the cherries, olive oil, lemon juice, honey, and basil. Pulse until smooth. Season with sea salt and set it aside.
Make the Salad
2. In a large bowl, toss the broccoli, greens, snow peas, cucumber, and red onion with the dressing to coat.

Per Serving
calories: 189 | fat: 13g | protein: 3g | carbs: 18g | fiber: 3g | sugar: 12g | sodium: 59mg

Root Vegetable Salad with Maple Dressing

Prep time: 10 minutes | Cook time: 0 minutes | Serves 4

Dressing:
¼ cup olive oil
3 tablespoons pure maple syrup
2 tablespoons apple cider vinegar
1 teaspoon grated fresh ginger
Sea salt, to taste
Slaw:
1 jicama, or 2 parsnips, peeled and shredded
2 carrots, shredded
½ celeriac, peeled and shredded
¼ fennel bulb, shredded
5 radishes, shredded
2 scallions, white and green parts, peeled and thinly sliced
½ cup roasted pumpkin seeds

Make the Dressing
1. In a small bowl, whisk the olive oil, maple syrup, cider vinegar, and ginger until well blended. Season with sea salt and set it aside.
Make the Slaw
2. In a large bowl, toss together the jicama, carrots, celeriac, fennel, radishes, and scallions.
3. Add the dressing and toss to coat.
4. Top the slaw with the pumpkin seeds and serve.

Per Serving
calories: 343 | fat: 21g | protein: 7g | carbs: 36g | fiber: 11g | sugar: 14g | sodium: 46mg

Balsamic Pear Salad with Walnuts

Prep time: 5 minutes | Cook time: 0 minutes | Serves 4

4 pears, peeled, cored, and chopped
¼ cup chopped walnuts
2 tablespoons honey
2 tablespoons balsamic vinegar
2 tablespoons extra-virgin olive oil

1. In a medium bowl, combine the pears and walnuts.
2. In a small bowl, whisk the honey, balsamic vinegar, and olive oil. Toss with the pears and walnuts.

Per Serving
calories: 263 | fat: 12g | protein: 3g | carbs: 41g | fiber: 7g | sugar: 29g | sodium: 3mg

Turkey and Green Salad with Pecans

Prep time: 10 minutes | Cook time: 0 minutes | Serves 4

Dressing:
¼ cup olive oil
2 tablespoons balsamic vinegar
2 teaspoons whole-grain Dijon mustard
1 teaspoon chopped fresh thyme
Sea salt, to taste
Salad:
4 cups mixed greens
1 cup arugula
½ red onion, thinly sliced
16 ounces (454 g) cooked turkey breast, chopped
3 apricots, pitted and each fruit cut into 8 pieces
½ cup chopped pecans

Make the Dressing
1. In a small bowl, whisk the olive oil, balsamic vinegar, mustard, and thyme. Season with sea salt and set it aside.
Make the Salad
2. In a large bowl, toss together the mixed greens, arugula, and red onion with ¾ of the dressing. Arrange the dressed salad on a serving platter.
3. Top the greens with the turkey, apricots, and pecans.
4. Drizzle with the remaining fourth of the dressing and serve.

Per Serving
calories: 305 | fat: 20g | protein: 21g | carbs: 12g | fiber: 2g | sugar: 4g | sodium: 482mg

THE ULTIMATE ANTI-INFLAMMATORY DIET COOKBOOK

Honeydew Salad with Mint
Prep time: 10 minutes | Cook time: 0 minutes | Serves 4

Dressing:
3 tablespoons olive oil
2 tablespoons red wine vinegar
Sea salt, to taste
Salad:
1 honeydew melon, rind removed, flesh cut into 1-inch cubes
½ cantaloupe, rind removed, flesh cut into 1-inch cubes
3 stalks celery, sliced
½ red onion, thinly sliced
¼ cup chopped fresh mint

Make the Dressing
1. In a small bowl, whisk the olive oil and red wine vinegar. Season with sea salt and set it aside.
Make the Salad
2. In a large bowl, combine the honeydew, cantaloupe, celery, red onion, and mint.
3. Add the dressing and toss to combine.

Per Serving
calories: 223 | fat: 11g | protein: 2g | carbs: 32g | fiber: 4g | sugar: 27g | sodium: 80mg

Mackerel and Beetroot Salad with Dill
Prep time: 10 minutes | Cook time: 15 minutes | Serves 2

1 cup peeled sweet potatoes
12 ounces (340 g) smoked mackerel fillets, skin removed
2 green onions, finely sliced
1 cup cooked beetroot, sliced into wedges
2 tablespoons finely chopped dill
2 tablespoons olive oil
Juice of 1 lemon, zest of half
1 teaspoon crushed caraway seeds

1. Place the potatoes in a small saucepan of boiling water and simmer for 15 minutes over medium-high heat or until fork-tender.
2. Cool and cut into thick slices.
3. Flake the mackerel into a bowl and add the cooled potatoes, green onions, beetroot and dill.
4. In a separate bowl, whisk together the olive oil, lemon juice, caraway seeds and black pepper.
5. Pour over the salad and toss well to coat.
6. Scatter over the lemon zest.
7. Pack into plastic containers and chill for later, or enjoy straight away.

Per Serving
calories: 530 | fat: 38g | protein: 34g | carbs: 13g | fiber: 4g | sugar: 5g | sodium: 209mg

Cranberry, Orange and Spinach Salad
Prep time: 10 minutes | Cook time: 0 minutes | Serves 1

1 cup fresh spinach, leaves trimmed and coarsely chopped
1 orange, peeled and sliced
1 cup chopped fresh cranberries
2 tablespoons red wine vinegar
4 teaspoons olive oil
2 teaspoons peeled and grated ginger
1 pinch of black pepper

1. Grab a salad bowl and mix the vinegar and olive oil until blended and then add in the cranberries and ginger, adding pepper to taste.
2. Add the spinach and orange slices to the dressing and then toss to coat.
3. Chill before serving.

Per Serving
calories: 298 | fat: 18g | protein: 2g | carbs: 32g | fiber: 8g | sugar: 16g | sodium: 31mg

Chicken and Carrot Salad
Prep time: 10 minutes | Cook time: 15 minutes | Serves 2

1 tablespoon extra-virgin olive oil
2 skinless chicken breasts, chopped
2 carrots, sliced
½ large onion, chopped
2 teaspoons cumin seeds
½ avocado, chopped
1 lime, juiced
½ cucumber, chopped
½ cup fresh spinach
1 mason jar

1. In a skillet, heat the oil over medium heat and then cook the chicken for 10 to 15 minutes until browned and cooked through.
2. Remove and place to one side to cool.
3. Add the carrots and onion and continue to cook for 5 to 10 minutes or until soft.
4. Add the cumin seeds in a separate pan over high heat and toast until they're brown before crushing them in a pestle and mortar or blender.
5. Put them into the pan with the veggies and turn off the heat.
6. Add the avocado and lime juice into a food processor and blend until creamy.
7. Layer the jar with half of the avocado and lime mixture, then the cumin roasted veggies, and then the chicken, packing it all in.
8. Top with the tomatoes, cucumbers, and the cilantro and spinach, refrigerating for 20 minutes before serving.

Per Serving
calories: 522 | fat: 22g | protein: 64g | carbs: 17g | fiber: 6g | sugar: 6g | sodium: 181mg

Artichoke and Kale Salad with Quinoa

Prep time: 10 minutes | Cook time: 0 minutes | Serves 4

2 cups cooked quinoa
2 (15-ounce / 425-g) cans water-packed artichoke hearts, drained
1 cup chopped kale
½ cup chopped red onion
½ cup chopped almonds
3 tablespoons finely chopped fresh parsley
Juice of 1 lemon (or 3 tablespoons)
Zest of 1 lemon (optional)
2 tablespoons olive oil
1 tablespoon balsamic vinegar
1 teaspoon bottled minced garlic
Sea salt, to taste

1. In a large bowl, toss together the quinoa, artichoke hearts, kale, red onion, almonds, parsley, lemon juice, lemon zest (if using), olive oil, balsamic vinegar, and garlic until well mixed.
2. Season with sea salt and serve.

Per Serving

calories: 402 | fat: 16g | protein: 16g | carbs: 56g | fiber: 17g | sugar: 3g | sodium: 595mg

Salmon and Veggie Salad with Thyme

Prep time: 10 minutes | Cook time: 14 minutes | Serves 2

2 skinless salmon fillets
2 cups seasonal greens
½ cup sliced zucchini
1 tablespoon balsamic vinegar
2 tablespoons extra-virgin olive oil
2 sprigs thyme, torn from the stem
1 lemon, juiced

1. Preheat the broiler to medium-high heat.
2. Broil the salmon in parchment paper with some oil, lemon and pepper for 10 minutes.
3. Slice the zucchini and sauté for 4 to 5 minutes with the oil in a pan over medium heat.
4. Build the salad by creating a bed of zucchini and topping with flaked salmon.
5. Drizzle with balsamic vinegar and sprinkle with thyme.

Per Serving

calories: 531 | fat: 27g | protein: 67g | carbs: 5g | fiber: 1g | sugar: 2g | sodium: 248mg

Cabbage Slaw with Cashew Dressing

Prep time: 5 minutes | Cook time: 0 minutes | Serves 6

Salad:
2 carrots, grated
1 large head green or red cabbage, sliced thin
Dressing:
1 cup cashews, soaked in water for at least 4 hours, drained
¼ cup freshly squeezed lemon juice
¾ teaspoon sea salt
½ cup water

1. Combine the carrots and cabbage in a large serving bowl. Toss to combine well.
2. Put the ingredients for the dressing in a food processor, then pulse until creamy and smooth.
3. Dress the salad, then refrigerate for at least 1 hour before serving.

Per Serving

calories: 208 | fat: 11g | protein: 7g | carbs: 25g | fiber: 8g | sugars: 4g | sodium: 394mg

Carrot and Ginger Soup

Prep time: 5 minutes | Cook time: 28 minutes | Serves 6 to 8

4½ cups plus 2 tablespoons water, divided
1 large onion, peeled and roughly chopped
8 carrots, peeled and roughly chopped
1½-inch piece fresh ginger, sliced thin
1¼ teaspoons sea salt
2 cups unsweetened coconut milk

1. Add 2 tablespoons of water to a large pot, then add the onion and sauté over medium heat for 4 minutes or until translucent.
2. Add the carrots, ginger, salt, and remaining water to the pot. Bring to a boil, then reduce the heat to low. Cover and simmer for 20 minutes.
3. When the simmering is over, open the lid, then mix in the coconut milk and cook for 4 more minutes.
4. Pour the soup in a blender, then pulse to purée until creamy and smooth. Serve the soup in a large bowl immediately.

Per Serving

calories: 228 | fat: 19g | protein: 3g | carbs: 15g | fiber: 4g | sugars: 8g | sodium: 554mg

Creamy Broccoli and Cashew Soup

Prep time: 10 minutes | Cook time: 25 minutes | Serves 6

5 cups plus 2 tablespoons water, divided
1 onion, finely chopped
4 garlic cloves, finely chopped
4 broccoli heads with stalks, heads cut into florets and stalks roughly chopped
1½ teaspoons sea salt, plus additional as needed
1 cup cashews, soaked in water for at least 4 hours, drained

1. Add 2 tablespoons of water to a large pot, then add the onion and garlic and sauté over medium heat for 5 minutes or until the onion is translucent.
2. Add the broccoli, salt, and remaining water. Bring to a boil, then reduce the heat to low. Cover and simmer for 20 minutes.
3. Pour the soup in a blender, then add the cashews. Pulse to purée until creamy and smooth.
4. Pour the soup in a large bowl and serve immediately.

Per Serving

calories: 224 | fat: 11g | protein: 11g | carbs: 26g | fiber: 7g | sugars: 6g | sodium: 85mg

Pumpkin Soup with Crispy Sage

Prep time: 10 minutes | Cook time: 11 minutes | Serves 4

2 tablespoons extra-virgin olive oil
1 onion, chopped
2 garlic cloves, cut into ⅛-inch-thick slices
1 (15-ounce / 425-g) can pumpkin purée
4 cups low-sodium vegetable broth
2 teaspoons chipotle powder
1 teaspoon sea salt
½ teaspoon freshly ground black pepper
2 tablespoons coconut oil
12 sage leaves, stemmed

1. Heat the olive oil in a large pot over high heat until shimmering.
2. Add the onion and garlic and sauté for 5 minutes or until the onion browns.
3. Pour in the pumpkin purée and vegetable broth, then sprinkle with chipotle powder, salt, and ground black pepper. Stir to mix well.
4. Bring to a boil. Reduce the heat to low and simmer for 5 minutes.
5. Meanwhile, heat the coconut oil in a nonstick skillet over high heat.
6. Add the sage leaves to the skillet and cook for 1 minute or until crispy.
7. When the simmering is complete, divide the soup in four serving bowls, then garnish each bowl with 3 crispy sage leaves and serve.

Per Serving

calories: 380 | fat: 20g | protein: 10g | carbs: 45g | fiber: 18g | sugar: 17g | sodium: 1364mg

Super Greens Soup

Prep time: 10 minutes | Cook time: 15 minutes | Serves 4 to 6

2 cups unsweetened coconut milk
3 cups water
1½ teaspoons sea salt, or to taste
1 bunch fresh parsley, rinsed, stemmed and roughly chopped
4 cups tightly packed kale, rinsed, stemmed, and roughly chopped
4 cups tightly packed spinach, rinsed, stemmed and roughly chopped
4 cups tightly packed collard greens, rinsed, stemmed and roughly chopped

1. Pour the coconut milk and water in a large pot, then sprinkle with salt. Bring to a boil over high heat. Reduce the heat to low.
2. Add 1 cup of each greens to the pot and cook for 5 minutes or until wilted. Repeat with the remaining greens.
3. When all the greens are wilted, simmer for 10 minutes.
4. Pour the soup in a blender, then pulse until creamy and smooth.
5. Pour the soup in a large bowl and serve immediately.

Per Serving

calories: 334 | fat: 29g | protein: 7g | carbs: 18g | fiber: 6g | sugars: 4g | sodium: 959mg

Massaged Kale and Crispy Chickpea Salad

Prep time: 5 minutes | Cook time: 20 minutes | Serves 4 to 6

1 large bunch kale, rinsed, stemmed, and cut into thin strips
2 teaspoons freshly squeezed lemon juice
2 tablespoons extra-virgin olive oil, divided
¾ teaspoon sea salt, divided
1 (14-ounce / 397-g) can cooked chickpeas
1 teaspoon sweet paprika
1 avocado, chopped

1. Put the kale in a large bowl, then drizzle with 1 tablespoon of olive oil and lemon juice. Sprinkle with ¼ teaspoon of salt.
2. Gently knead the kale leaves in the bowl for 5 minutes or until wilted and bright. Rip the leafy part of the kale off the stem, then discard the stem.
3. Heat the remaining olive oil in a nonstick skillet over medium-low heat until shimmering.
4. Add the chickpeas, paprika, and remaining salt, then cook for 15 minutes or until the chickpeas are crispy.
5. Transfer the kale to a large serving bowl, then top with chickpeas and avocado. Toss to combine well and serve.

Per Serving

calories: 359 | fat: 20g | protein: 13g | carbs: 35g | fiber: 10g | sugars: 1g | sodium: 497mg

Glorious Vegetable, Pear, and Cashew Soup

Prep time: 10 minutes | Cook time: 13 minutes | Serves 4 to 6

2 tablespoons extra-virgin olive oil
1 fennel bulb, cut into ¼-inch-thick slices
2 leeks, white part only, sliced
2 pears, peeled, cored, and cut into ½-inch cubes
1 teaspoon sea salt
¼ teaspoon freshly ground black pepper
½ cup cashews
3 cups low-sodium vegetable broth
2 cups packed spinach

1. Heat the olive oil in a large pot over high heat until shimmering.
2. Add the fennel and leeks and sauté for 5 minutes or until tender.
3. Add the pears and sprinkle with salt and pepper. Sauté for another 3 minutes.
4. Add the cashews and vegetable broth. Bring to a boil. Reduce the heat to low. Cover and simmer for 5 minutes.
5. Pour the soup in a blender and add the spinach. Pulse until creamy and smooth.
6. Pour the soup in a large serving bowl and serve immediately.

Per Serving

calories: 266 | fat: 15g | protein: 5g | carbs: 33g | fiber: 7g | sugar: 13g | sodium: 626mg

Sumptuous Mediterranean Salad

Prep time: 15 minutes | Cook time: 0 minutes | Serves 4

1 bunch radishes, sliced thin
1 English cucumber, peeled and diced
2 cups packed spinach
3 large tomatoes, diced
1 tablespoon chopped fresh mint
1 tablespoon chopped fresh parsley
2 scallions, sliced
2 garlic cloves, minced
1 cup unsweetened plain almond yogurt
1 tablespoon apple cider vinegar
3 tablespoons freshly squeezed lemon juice
1 tablespoon sumac
2 tablespoons extra-virgin olive oil
1 teaspoon sea salt
¼ teaspoon freshly ground black pepper

1. Combine all the ingredients in a large salad bowl. Toss to mix well, then serve immediately.

Per Serving

calories: 195 | fat: 14g | protein: 4g | carbs: 15g | fiber: 5g | sugar: 7g | sodium: 660mg

Butternut Squash, Carrot, and Celery Soup

Prep time: 5 minutes | Cook time: 30 minutes | Serves 6

4½ cups plus 2 tablespoons water, divided
1 onion, roughly chopped
1 large butternut squash, washed, peeled, ends trimmed, halved, seeded, and cut into ½-inch chunks
3 carrots, peeled and roughly chopped
2 celery stalks, roughly chopped
1 teaspoon sea salt, or to taste

1. Add 2 tablespoons of water to a large pot, then add the onion and sauté over medium heat for 5 minutes or until tender.
2. Add the butternut squash, carrots, celery, salt, and remaining water. Bring to a boil. Reduce the heat to low, then simmer for 25 minutes or until the squash is soft.
3. Pour the soup in a food processor, then pulse to purée until creamy and smooth.
4. Pour the soup in a large bowl and serve immediately.

Per Serving

calories: 104 | fat: 0g | protein: 2g | carbs: 27g | fiber: 5g | sugars: 6g | sodium: 417mg

Ritzy Green Bean and Papaya Salad

Prep time: 10 minutes | Cook time: 2 minutes | Serves 4

Salad:
8 ounces (227 g) green beans, trimmed
2 (12-ounce /340-g) green papayas, peeled, deseeded, and julienned
½ cup chopped mint
½ cup chopped cilantro
½ cup coarsely chopped Marcona almonds
2 cups cherry tomatoes, halved
Dressing:
3 tablespoons sugar-free fish sauce
2 tablespoons raw honey
2 red Thai chiles, deseeded and thinly sliced
½ cup lime juice

1. Prepare a bowl of ice water.
2. Bring a pot of salted water to a boil, then add the green beans and cook for 2 minutes. Transfer the cooked beans in the bowl of ice water to cool.
3. Pat the green beans dry and slice in half crosswise.
4. Combine the ingredients for the dressing in a small bowl. Stir to mix well.
5. Combine the green beans with remaining ingredients in a large serving bowl. Drizzle with the dressing, then toss to combine well.
6. Serve immediately.

Per Serving

calories: 154 | fat: 1g | protein: 4g | carbs: 38g | fiber: 6g | sugars: 27g | sodium: 1084mg

Spinach Salad with Lemony Dressing

Prep time: 5 minutes | Cook time: 0 minutes | Serves 4

2 tablespoons freshly squeezed lemon juice
¼ cup Dijon mustard
1½ tablespoons maple syrup
2 tablespoons extra-virgin olive oil
¼ teaspoon sea salt, or to taste
6 cups baby spinach leaves

1. Make the lemon dressing: Combine all the ingredients, except for the spinach, in a small bowl. Stir to mix well.
2. Put the spinach in a large serving bowl, the drizzle with the lemon dressing. Toss to combine well. Serve immediately.

Per Serving

calories: 150 | fat: 14g | protein: 2g | carbs: 8g | fiber: 2g | sugars: 5g | sodium: 362mg

Luxurious Fruit and Vegetable Salad

Prep time: 10 minutes | Cook time: 0 minutes | Serves 4

Salad:
4 cups spinach
2 celery stalks, sliced thin
2 green apples, cored and quartered, sliced
2 small beets, peeled and quartered, sliced
½ cup shredded carrots
½ red onion, sliced thin
¼ cup pumpkin seeds
Dressing:
1 tablespoon raw honey
1 tablespoon apple cider vinegar
2 tablespoons extra-virgin olive oil
Sea salt and freshly ground black pepper, to taste

1. Combine the ingredients for the salad in a large serving bowl, then toss to combine well.
2. Combine the ingredients for the dressing in a small bowl. Stir to mix well.
3. Dressing the salad, then toss to combine well. Serve immediately.

Per Serving

calories: 238 | fat: 15g | protein: 4g | carbs: 27g | fiber: 5g | sugar: 18g | sodium: 120mg

Tomato Salad with Basil

Prep time: 5 minutes | Cook time: 0 minutes | Serves 4

4 large heirloom tomatoes, chopped
¼ cup torn fresh basil leaves
2 garlic cloves, finely minced
¼ cup extra-virgin olive oil
½ teaspoon sea salt
¼ teaspoon freshly ground black pepper

1. In a medium bowl, gently mix together the tomatoes, basil, garlic, olive oil, salt, and pepper.

Per Serving

calories: 140 | fat: 14g | protein: 1g | carbs: 4g | fiber: 1g | sugar: 3g | sodium: 239mg

Chicken and Bell Pepper Soup

Prep time: 10 minutes | Cook time: 10 minutes | Serves 4

2 tablespoons extra-virgin olive oil
1 onion, chopped
2 red bell peppers, chopped
1 tablespoon grated fresh ginger
3 cups shredded rotisserie chicken, skin removed
8 cups no-salt-added chicken broth
½ teaspoon sea salt
⅛ teaspoon freshly ground black pepper

1. In a large pot over medium-high heat, heat the olive oil until it shimmers.
2. Add the onion, red bell peppers, and ginger. Cook for about 5 minutes, stirring occasionally, until the vegetables are soft.
3. Stir in the chicken, chicken broth, salt, and pepper. Bring to a simmer. Reduce the heat to medium-low and simmer for 5 minutes.

Per Serving

calories: 341 | fat: 15g | protein: 40g | carbs: 11g | fiber: 1g | sugar: 8g | sodium: 577mg

CHAPTER 5:
VEGETARIAN MAIN

Tomato-Basil Pasta with Garlic

Prep time: 10 minutes | Cook time: 10½ minutes | Serves 4

2 tablespoons extra-virgin olive oil
1 onion, minced
6 garlic cloves, minced
2 (28-ounce / 794-g) cans crushed tomatoes, undrained
½ teaspoon sea salt
¼ teaspoon freshly ground black pepper
¼ cup chopped basil leaves
1 (8-ounce / 227-g) package whole-wheat pasta

1. In a large pot over medium-high heat, heat the olive oil until it shimmers.
2. Add the onion. Cook for about 5 minutes, stirring occasionally, until soft.
3. Add the garlic. Cook for 30 seconds, stirring constantly.
4. Stir in the tomatoes, salt, and pepper. Bring to a simmer. Reduce the heat to medium and cook for 5 minutes, stirring occasionally.
5. Remove from the heat and stir in the basil. Toss with the pasta.

Per Serving

calories: 330 | fat: 8g | protein: 14g | carbs: 56g | fiber: 17g | sugar: 24g | sodium: 1000mg

Bell Pepper and Sweet Potato Hash

Prep time: 5 minutes | Cook time: 19 minutes | Serves 4

4 tablespoons extra-virgin olive oil, divided
1 onion, chopped
1 red bell pepper, chopped
4 cups cubed, peeled sweet potato
1 teaspoon sea salt, divided
⅛ teaspoon freshly ground black pepper
4 eggs

1. In a large nonstick skillet over medium-high heat, heat 2 tablespoons of the olive oil until it shimmers.
2. Add the onion, red bell pepper, and sweet potato. Season with ½ teaspoon of the salt and the pepper. Cook for 15 to 20 minutes, stirring occasionally, until the sweet potatoes are soft and browned. Divide the potatoes among 4 plates.
3. Return the skillet to the heat, reduce the heat to medium-low, and heat the remaining 2 tablespoons of olive oil, swirling to coat the bottom of the pan.
4. Carefully crack the eggs into the pan and sprinkle with the remaining ½ teaspoon of salt. Cook for 3 to 4 minutes until the whites are set. Gently flip the eggs and turn off the heat. Let the eggs sit in the hot pan for 1 minute. Place 1 egg on top of each serving of hash.

Per Serving

calories: 384 | fat: 19g | protein: 10g | carbs: 47g | fiber: 8g | sugar: 16g | sodium: 603mg

Spinach and Quinoa Florentine

Prep time: 10 minutes | Cook time: 18½ minutes | Serves 4

2 tablespoons extra-virgin olive oil
1 onion, chopped
3 cups fresh baby spinach
3 garlic cloves, minced
2 cups quinoa, rinsed well
4 cups no-salt-added vegetable broth
½ teaspoon sea salt
⅛ teaspoon freshly ground black pepper

1. In a large pot over medium-high heat, heat the olive oil until it shimmers.
2. Add the onion and spinach. Cook for 3 minutes, stirring occasionally.
3. Add the garlic and cook for 30 seconds, stirring constantly.
4. Stir in the quinoa, vegetable broth, salt, and pepper. Bring to a boil and reduce the heat to low. Cover and simmer for 15 to 20 minutes, until the liquid is absorbed. Fluff with a fork.

Per Serving

calories: 403 | fat: 12g | protein: 13g | carbs: 62g | fiber: 7g | sugar: 4g | sodium: 278mg

Kale Frittata with Sunflower Seeds

Prep time: 5 minutes | Cook time: 14½ minutes | Serves 4

2 tablespoons extra-virgin olive oil
4 cups stemmed and chopped kale
3 garlic cloves, minced
8 eggs
½ teaspoon sea salt
¼ teaspoon freshly ground black pepper
2 tablespoons sunflower seeds

1. Preheat the broiler to high.
2. In a large oven-proof skillet over medium-high heat, heat the olive oil until it shimmers.
3. Add the kale. Cook for about 5 minutes, stirring, until soft.
4. Add the garlic. Cook for 30 seconds, stirring constantly.
5. In a medium bowl, beat the eggs, salt, and pepper. Carefully pour them over the kale. Reduce the heat to medium. Cook the eggs for about 3 minutes until set around the edges. Using a rubber spatula, carefully pull the eggs away from the edges of the skillet and tilt the pan to let the uncooked eggs run into the edges. Cook for about 3 minutes, until the edges set again.
6. Sprinkle with the sunflower seeds. Transfer the pan to the broiler and cook for 3 to 5 minutes until puffed and brown. Cut into wedges to serve.

Per Serving

calories: 231 | fat: 17g | protein: 14g | carbs: 9g | fiber: 1g | sugar: 1g | sodium: 387mg

Asparagus and Tomato Frittata

Prep time: 10 minutes | Cook time: 17 minutes | Serves 4

2 tablespoons extra-virgin olive oil
10 asparagus spears, trimmed
10 cherry tomatoes
6 eggs
1 tablespoon chopped fresh thyme
½ teaspoon sea salt
⅛ teaspoon freshly ground black pepper

1. Preheat the broiler to high.
2. In a large oven-proof skillet over medium-high heat, heat the olive oil until it shimmers.
3. Add the asparagus. Cook for 5 minutes, stirring occasionally.
4. Add the tomatoes. Cook 3 minutes, stirring occasionally.
5. In a medium bowl, whisk together the eggs, thyme, salt, and pepper. Carefully pour over the asparagus and tomatoes, moving the vegetables around so they are evenly spread in the pan.
6. Reduce the heat to medium. Cook the eggs for about 3 minutes until set around the edges. Using a rubber spatula, carefully pull the eggs away from the edges of the skillet and tilt the pan to let the uncooked eggs run into the edges. Cook for about 3 minutes, until the edges set again.
7. Carefully transfer the pan to the broiler and cook for 3 to 5 minutes until puffed and brown. Cut into wedges to serve.

Per Serving
calories: 224 | fat: 14g | protein: 12g | carbs: 15g | fiber: 5g | sugar: 10g | sodium: 343mg

Tomato and Black Bean Chili with Garlic

Prep time: 10 minutes | Cook time: 20 minutes | Serves 4

2 tablespoons extra-virgin olive oil
1 onion, chopped
2 (28-ounce / 794-g) cans chopped tomatoes, undrained
2 (14-ounce / 397-g) cans black beans, drained
1 tablespoon chili powder
1 teaspoon garlic powder
½ teaspoon sea salt

1. In a large pot over medium-high heat, heat the olive oil until it shimmers.
2. Add the onion. Cook for about 5 minutes, stirring occasionally, until soft.
3. Stir in the tomatoes, black beans, chili powder, garlic powder, and salt. Bring to a simmer. Reduce the heat to medium and cook for 15 minutes, stirring occasionally.

Per Serving
calories: 481 | fat: 10g | protein: 25g | carbs: 80g | fiber: 21g | sugar: 14g | sodium: 278mg

Tofu Sloppy Joes with Cider Vinegar

Prep time: 10 minutes | Cook time: 15 minutes | Serves 4

2 tablespoons extra-virgin olive oil
1 onion, chopped
10 ounces (283 g) tofu, chopped
2 (14-ounce / 397-g) cans crushed tomatoes, 1 drained and 1 undrained
¼ cup apple cider vinegar
1 tablespoon chili powder
1 teaspoon garlic powder
½ teaspoon sea salt
⅛ teaspoon freshly ground black pepper

1. In a large pot over medium-high heat, heat the olive oil until it shimmers.
2. Add the onion and tofu. Cook for about 5 minutes, stirring occasionally, until the onion is soft.
3. Stir in the tomatoes, cider vinegar, chili powder, garlic powder, salt, and pepper. Simmer for 10 minutes to let the flavors blend, stirring occasionally.

Per Serving
calories: 209 | fat: 10g | protein: 11g | carbs: 21g | fiber: 8g | sugar: 13g | sodium: 644mg

Egg and Broccoli "Muffins"

Prep time: 10 minutes | Cook time: 18 minutes | Serves 4

Nonstick cooking spray
2 tablespoons extra-virgin olive oil
1 onion, chopped
1 cup chopped broccoli florets
8 eggs, beaten
1 teaspoon garlic powder
½ teaspoon sea salt
¼ teaspoon freshly ground black pepper

1. Preheat the oven to 350°F (180°C).
2. Spray a muffin tin with nonstick cooking spray.
3. In a large nonstick skillet over medium-high heat, heat the olive oil until it shimmers.
4. Add the onion and broccoli. Cook for 3 minutes. Spoon the vegetables evenly into 4 muffin cups.
5. In a medium bowl, beat the eggs, garlic powder, salt, and pepper. Pour them over the vegetables in the muffin cups.
6. Bake for 15 to 17 minutes until the eggs set.

Per Serving
calories: 207 | fat: 16g | protein: 12g | carbs: 5g | fiber: 1g | sugar: 2g | sodium: 366mg

Coconut-Garlic Lentils

Prep time: 15 minutes | Cook time: 20 minutes | Serves 4

1 tablespoon avocado oil
1 small white onion, diced
2 garlic cloves, minced
2 cups vegetable broth
1 cup dried lentils, sorted and rinsed
3 tablespoons coconut aminos
2 tablespoons coconut sugar
1 tablespoon rice vinegar
1 teaspoon sesame oil
½ teaspoon ground ginger
¼ teaspoon red pepper flakes
1 tablespoon sesame seeds (optional)
2 scallions, sliced (optional)

1. To a stockpot over medium heat, add the avocado oil, onion, and garlic. Sauté for 5 minutes, or until the onion is translucent.
2. Stir in the broth, lentils, coconut aminos, coconut sugar, vinegar, sesame oil, ginger, and red pepper flakes. Increase the heat to medium-high and bring to a simmer.
3. Reduce the heat to low, cover, and cook for 15 minutes, or until the lentils are cooked.
4. Garnish with the sesame seeds and scallions (if using).

Per Serving

calories: 281 | fat: 5g | protein: 14g | carbs: 45g | fiber: 10g | sugar: 7g | sodium: 293mg

Sesame Cauliflower Rice with Peas

Prep time: 10 minutes | Cook time: 16 minutes | Serves 4

1 head cauliflower, cored and florets broken into chunks
1 tablespoon sesame oil
½ cup diced onion
2 garlic cloves, minced
2 scallions, sliced
1 carrot, minced
¼ cup peas
2 eggs, whisked
¼ teaspoon red pepper flakes
Coconut aminos (optional)

1. In a food processor (or blender), cautiously pulse the cauliflower until it breaks down into small pieces the size of rice grains.
2. In a large skillet or sauté pan over medium heat, heat the sesame oil.
3. Add the onion and garlic. Cook for 2 to 3 minutes until the onion is translucent.
4. Stir in the scallions, carrot, and peas, and cook for 5 minutes, stirring frequently.
5. Add the cauliflower rice and cook for 5 to 7 minutes, stirring, until the cauliflower is crispy on the outside but cooked on the inside.
6. With the back of a spoon, make a well in the middle of the vegetable mixture. Add the eggs in the well and stir slowly for about 4 minutes until softly cooked.
7. Incorporate the cooked eggs into the vegetable mixture. Stir in the red pepper flakes. Serve immediately, sprinkled with coconut aminos (if using).

Per Serving

calories: 128 | fat: 6g | protein: 7g | carbs: 13g | fiber: 4g | sugar: 2g | sodium: 37mg

Buckwheat Pasta With Basil Pesto

Prep time: 10 minutes | Cook time: 0 minutes | Serves 4

Pesto:
1 cup tightly packed fresh basil leaves
1 cup chopped zucchini
¼ cup shelled sunflower seeds, plus more for garnish
2 garlic cloves
½ cup extra-virgin olive oil, divided
¼ cup shredded Parmesan Cheese
1 teaspoon freshly squeezed lemon juice
¼ teaspoon salt
Freshly ground black pepper, to taste
Pasta:
8 ounces (227 g) buckwheat pasta
Filtered water, for cooking the pasta

Make the Pesto
1. In a food processor (or blender), combine the basil, zucchini, sunflower seeds, garlic, and ¼ cup of olive oil. Blend for 15 seconds.
2. Add the Parmesan Cheese, lemon juice, and salt, and season with pepper. Pulse to combine.
3. With the food processor (or blender) running, slowly pour in the remaining ¼ cup of olive oil until all ingredients are well combined.
Make the Pasta
4. Cook the pasta according to the package instructions.
5. Pour the desired amount of pesto over the pasta, garnish with sunflower seeds, and serve.

Per Serving

calories: 548 | fat: 35g | protein: 10g | carbs: 45g | fiber: 3g | sugar: 0g | sodium: 262mg

Chickpea Curry with Raisins

Prep time: 15 minutes | Cook time: 12 minutes | Serves 4

2 small white onions, diced
2 garlic cloves, minced
2 tablespoons avocado oil
1 red bell pepper, chopped
1½ cups vegetable broth
1 tablespoon curry powder
½ teaspoon salt
2 cups cooked chickpeas, rinsed and drained
1 medium apple, diced
½ cup golden raisins
½ cup cashews, roughly chopped
½ cup plain whole-milk yogurt (optional)

1. In a large skillet over medium heat, sauté the onions and garlic in the avocado oil for 2 to 3 minutes until translucent.
2. Add the red bell pepper, and sauté for 5 minutes.
3. Stir in the broth, curry powder, and salt, and bring to a simmer.
4. Add the chickpeas, apple, and raisins, and cook for 5 minutes.
5. Just before turning off the heat, stir in the cashews. Serve hot, topped with yogurt (if using) to soften the heat of the spices.

Per Serving

calories: 422 | fat: 18g | protein: 11g | carbs: 55g | fiber: 11g | sugar: 26g | sodium: 525mg

Avocado-Veggie Spring Rolls

Prep time: 20 minutes | Cook time: 0 minutes | Makes 10 rolls

Sauce:
½ cup almond butter
1 tablespoon coconut aminos
1 tablespoon coconut sugar
1 tablespoon freshly squeezed lime juice
¼ teaspoon garlic powder
¼ teaspoon red pepper flakes
Dash ground ginger
Filtered water, to thin
Rolls:
10 rice paper wrappers
1 large avocado, thinly sliced
1 red bell pepper, very thinly sliced
½ cup shredded carrots
½ cup julienned cucumber
½ cup shredded cabbage
¼ cup sliced scallion
¼ cup fresh cilantro leaves

Make the Sauce
1. In a small bowl, whisk the almond butter, coconut aminos, coconut sugar, lime juice, garlic powder, red pepper flakes, and ginger. If needed, add a little of the water to thin.
Make the Rolls
2. Prepare the rice paper wrappers according to the package instructions.
3. In a large bowl, gently combine the avocado, red bell pepper, carrots, cucumber, cabbage, scallion, and cilantro. On a clean work surface, divide the vegetables into 10 portions.
4. On a large plastic cutting board, lay out one wrapper and smooth any wrinkles.
5. Place 1 portion of veggies on the bottom third of the wrapper. Beginning at the bottom edge, roll it like a burrito until about three-fourths of the way to the top. Fold the side edges in and continue to roll toward the top of the wrapper.
6. Repeat steps 3 and 4 with the remaining ingredients.
7. Serve the rolls with the dipping sauce alongside.

Per Serving
calories: 176 | fat: 10g | protein: 5g | carbs: 21g | fiber: 3g | sugar: 5g | sodium: 150mg

Bean-Stuffed Sweet Potatoes

Prep time: 10 minutes | Cook time: 37 minutes | Serves 4

4 medium sweet potatoes
1 tablespoon avocado oil
1 small white onion, thinly sliced
2 garlic cloves, minced
1 (14-ounce / 397-g) can black beans, drained and rinsed well
12 cherry tomatoes, chopped
½ teaspoon chili powder
¼ teaspoon red pepper flakes
¼ teaspoon salt
1 large avocado, sliced
Juice of 1 lime

1. Preheat the oven to 400°F (205°C).
2. With a fork, poke holes 5 to 6 times into each sweet potato. Loosely wrap each sweet potato in aluminum foil, place them on a baking sheet, and bake for 25 minutes, or until cooked.
3. Meanwhile, in a large skillet or sauté pan over medium heat, heat the avocado oil. Add the onion and garlic, and sauté for 5 minutes.
4. Stir in the beans, tomatoes, chili powder, red pepper flakes, and salt. Cook for about 7 minutes. Remove from the heat.
5. When the sweet potatoes are cooked, remove them from the oven and carefully unwrap the foil. Slice each potato lengthwise, almost through to the bottom. Open the potatoes to create room for the filling, and spoon equal amounts of filling into each.
6. Top with avocado slices and a drizzle of lime juice.

Per Serving
calories: 326 | fat: 10g | protein: 10g | carbs: 51g | fiber: 13g | sugar: 8g | sodium: 235mg

Lentil and Carrot Sloppy Joes

Prep time: 15 minutes | Cook time: 20 minutes | Serves 4

2 tablespoons avocado oil, divided
1 small white onion, chopped
1 celery stalk, finely chopped
1 carrot, minced
2 garlic cloves, minced
1 pound (454 g) cooked lentils
½ red bell pepper, finely chopped
7 tablespoons tomato paste
2 tablespoons apple cider vinegar
1 tablespoon pure maple syrup
1 teaspoon Dijon mustard
1 teaspoon chili powder
½ teaspoon dried oregano

1. In a large pan over medium-high heat, heat 1 tablespoon of avocado oil.
2. Add the onion, celery, carrot, and garlic, and sauté for about 3 minutes, or until the onion is translucent.
3. Add the lentils and the remaining 1 tablespoon of avocado oil, and sauté for about 5 minutes.
4. Add the red bell pepper, and sauté for 2 minutes.
5. Stir in the tomato paste, vinegar, maple syrup, mustard, chili powder, and oregano. Reduce the heat to medium-low and cook for about 10 minutes, stirring occasionally.
6. Serve over rice or on gluten-free bread, if desired.

Per Serving
calories: 277 | fat: 7g | protein: 14g | carbs: 29g | fiber: 12g | sugar: 10g | sodium: 68mg

Poached Eggs Verdes with Arugula

Prep time: 15 minutes | Cook time: 6 minutes | Serves 2

Dressing:
¼ cup extra-virgin olive oil
2 tablespoons white wine vinegar
1 teaspoon Dijon mustard
¼ teaspoon freshly ground black pepper
¼ teaspoon salt
¼ teaspoon dried basil
Few drops raw honey
Eggs Verdes:
2 cups packed baby arugula
½ cup organic whole corn kernels
6 cherry tomatoes, halved
Filtered water, for cooking the asparagus and eggs
6 asparagus spears, tough ends trimmed
1 tablespoon distilled white vinegar
4 eggs

Make the Dressing
1. In a small bowl, whisk the olive oil, vinegar, mustard, pepper, salt, basil, and honey until emulsified. Set aside.
Make the Eggs Verdes
2. Place 1 cup of arugula on each of the two plates. Top each with ¼ cup of corn and 6 of the cherry tomato halves.
3. Bring a medium saucepan two-thirds full of water to a boil. Add the asparagus and cook for 2 minutes. With a slotted spoon, remove the asparagus and run it under cool water to stop the cooking. Divide the asparagus between the plates.
4. Lower the heat under the saucepan so the water barely simmers (only small bubbles coming to the surface). Add the vinegar.
5. Crack 1 egg into a measuring cup with a handle to ease the transfer. Carefully lower the cup into the water and slowly tip it until the egg is submerged in the water. Set a timer to 4 minutes for a runny yolk, or longer to suit your preference.
6. With a slotted spoon, remove the egg and place it on the arugula on one plate. Repeat with the remaining eggs, serving two to a plate.
7. Drizzle with the dressing and serve immediately.

Per Serving

calories: 515 | fat: 38g | protein: 18g | carbs: 28g | fiber: 6g | sugar: 3g | sodium: 471mg

Oat and Root Vegetable Loaf

Prep time: 10 minutes | Cook time: 57 minutes | Serves 6 to 8

1 onion, finely chopped
2 tablespoons water
2 cups grated carrots
1½ cups grated sweet potatoes
1½ cups gluten-free rolled oats
¾ cup butternut squash purée
1 teaspoon salt

1. Preheat the oven to 350°F (180°C).
2. Line a loaf pan with parchment paper.
3. In a large pot set over medium heat, sauté the onion in the water for about 5 minutes, or until soft.
4. Add the carrots and sweet potatoes. Cook for 2 minutes. Remove the pot from the heat.
5. Stir in the oats, butternut squash purée, and salt. Mix well.
6. Transfer the mixture to the prepared loaf pan, pressing down evenly.
7. Place the pan in the preheated oven and bake for 50 to 55 minutes, uncovered, or until the loaf is firm and golden.
8. Cool for 10 minutes before slicing.

Per Serving

calories: 169 | fat: 2g | protein: 5g | carbs: 34g | fiber: 6g | sugar: 3g | sodium: 442mg

Veggie-Stuffed Portobellos

Prep time: 10 minutes | Cook time: 16 minutes | Serves 4

8 portobello mushrooms, stems removed and gently cleaned
2 tablespoons avocado oil, divided
1 small white onion, diced
2 garlic cloves, minced
½ teaspoon salt
¼ teaspoon freshly ground black pepper
1 teaspoon dried basil
1 small zucchini, diced
1 red bell pepper, diced

1. Preheat the broiler.
2. Line a baking sheet with aluminum foil.
3. Pat each mushroom cap dry and rub them with 1 tablespoon of avocado oil. Place them in the prepared pan and broil for 6 minutes, turning them halfway through so both sides cook evenly.
4. Meanwhile, in a large skillet over medium heat, heat the remaining 1 tablespoon of avocado oil.
5. Add the onion, garlic, salt, pepper, and basil, and sauté for 5 minutes.
6. Stir in the zucchini and red bell pepper, and sauté for about 5 minutes until everything is cooked.
7. Scoop equal portions of the vegetable mixture into each mushroom cap and serve warm.

Per Serving

calories: 131 | fat: 7g | protein: 5g | carbs: 13g | fiber: 5g | sugar: 2g | sodium: 295mg

Tahini Chickpea Falafel

Prep time: 10 minutes | Cook time: 30 minutes | Serves 6 to 8

3 cups cooked chickpeas
⅓ cup tahini
1 tablespoon ground cumin
4 garlic cloves
½ teaspoon salt
1 small bunch fresh basil, stemmed and torn into pieces
Water, for thinning

1. Preheat the oven to 350°F (180°C).
2. Line a baking sheet with parchment paper.
3. In a food processor, combine the chickpeas, tahini, cumin, garlic, and salt. Process until mostly smooth.
4. Add the basil. Pulse until incorporated.
5. If necessary, add 1 or 2 tablespoons of water to help the ingredients form a ball, being careful not to add too much. The mixture should not be wet and pasty.
6. Measure 2 tablespoons of dough and roll it into a ball. Place it on the baking sheet. With the bottom of a glass or your hand, press the ball into a patty about 1 inch thick. Repeat with the remaining chickpea mixture; it should yield about 24 patties.
7. Place the patties in the preheated oven and bake for 30 minutes. The falafels will be quite soft when straight out of the oven, but they firm as they cool.

Per Serving

calories: 242 | fat: 12g | protein: 12g | carbs: 24g | fiber: 7g | sugar: 1g | sodium: 225mg

Navy Bean and Yam Burgers

Prep time: 5 minutes | Cook time: 35 minutes | Serves 4 to 6

1 cup gluten-free rolled oats
3 cups cooked navy beans (1½ cups dried)
2 cups yam or sweet potato purée (about 2 yams or sweet potatoes, steamed and mashed)
½ cup sunflower seed butter or tahini
1 tablespoon grated fresh ginger
½ teaspoon salt

1. In a food processor, pulse the oats a few times until a rough meal forms.
2. Add the beans, yam purée, sunflower seed butter, ginger, and salt. Blend until well mixed. You can make this completely smooth, or leave slightly chunky.
3. Refrigerate the mixture for 30 minutes to firm.
4. Preheat the oven to 350°F (180°C).
5. Line a baking sheet with parchment paper.
6. Using a ¼-cup or ½-cup measure, scoop the mixture onto the prepared sheet. (The scoop size depends on how large you want the burgers to be.) Gently pat the mixture down so the patties are 1 inch thick. Makes about 12 patties.
7. Place the sheet in the preheated oven and bake for 35 minutes. Flip the burgers halfway through the cooking time.

Per Serving

calories: 581 | fat: 19g | protein: 27g | carbs: 81g | fiber: 26g | sugar: 6g | sodium: 355mg

Lush Veggie Brown Rice Bibimbap

Prep time: 10 minutes | Cook time: 13 minutes | Serves 2

2 cups cooked brown rice, divided
1 head baby bok choy, shredded
2 teaspoons sesame oil, divided
2 garlic cloves, minced
1 cup packed fresh baby spinach, thoroughly washed
2 teaspoons avocado oil, divided
½ cup shredded carrots
1 cup sliced mushrooms
1 cup cooked chickpeas, drained and rinsed well
2 eggs
1 tablespoon toasted sesame seeds
Dash salt

1. Divide the 2 cups of rice evenly between two bowls, with 1 cup in each.
2. In a large skillet or sauté pan over medium heat, sauté the bok choy with 1 teaspoon of sesame oil for 1 to 2 minutes until it begins to wilt. Remove from the heat. Top the rice in each bowl with half of the bok choy.
3. Add the remaining 1 teaspoon of sesame oil to the skillet along with the garlic and spinach, and sauté for 1 to 2 minutes until wilted. Remove from the heat and arrange half in each bowl over the bok choy.
4. Add 1 teaspoon of avocado oil to the skillet along with the carrots, and sauté for 5 minutes, or until tender. Remove from the heat and arrange half in each bowl over the spinach.
5. Add the remaining 1 teaspoon of avocado oil to the skillet along with the mushrooms, and sauté for 5 minutes, or until their liquid has evaporated. Remove from the heat and arrange half in each bowl over the carrots.
6. Divide the chickpeas between the two bowls.
7. Crack the eggs one at a time into the skillet and fry for 1 to 2 minutes, depending on how runny you prefer the yolk. Add 1 egg to each bowl. Sprinkle with the sesame seeds and the salt.

Per Serving

calories: 593 | fat: 21g | protein: 22g | carbs: 76g | fiber: 12g | sugar: 6g | sodium: 133mg

Tahini Kale Spaghetti with Parsley

Prep time: 10 minutes | Cook time: 0 minutes | Serves 4

8 ounces (227 g) brown rice spaghetti, or buckwheat noodles
4 cups lightly packed kale
½ cup tahini
¾ cup hot water, plus additional as needed
¼ teaspoon salt, plus additional as needed
½ cup chopped fresh parsley

1. Cook the noodles according to the package instructions. During the last 30 seconds of cook time, toss in the kale. In a colander, drain the noodles and kale. Transfer to a large bowl.
2. In a medium bowl, stir together the tahini, hot water, and salt. If you'd like a thinner sauce, add more water.
3. Add the parsley and sauce to the noodles. Toss to coat. Taste and adjust the seasoning if necessary.
4. Serve hot or cold.

Per Serving

calories: 404 | fat: 18g | protein: 15g | carbs: 54g | fiber: 10g | sugar: 2g | sodium: 223mg

Sweet Potato Shepherd's Pie

Prep time: 10 minutes | Cook time: 45 minutes | Serves 4 to 6

3 sweet potatoes, cubed
2 tablespoons coconut oil
1 teaspoon salt, divided
1 onion, chopped
2 tablespoons water, plus additional for cooking
3 carrots, grated
2 cups cooked black beans, or 1 (14-ounce / 397-g) can

1. Preheat the oven to 350ºF (180ºC).
2. Fill a large pot with 2 inches of water and insert a steamer basket. Bring to a boil over high heat.
3. Add the sweet potatoes. Cover and steam for 10 to 12 minutes, or until tender. Drain off any remaining liquid.
4. Add the coconut oil and ½ teaspoon of salt. Mash the sweet potatoes and set aside.
5. In a large skillet over medium heat, sauté the onion in 2 tablespoons of water for about 5 minutes, or until softened.
6. Add the carrots. Cook for 5 minutes. Remove from the heat.
7. Stir in the black beans and remaining ½ teaspoon of salt. Transfer the mixture to a 9-inch by 9-inch baking dish.
8. Top with the mashed sweet potatoes.
9. Place the dish in the preheated oven and bake for 30 minutes.
10. Cool for a few minutes before serving.

Per Serving

calories: 431 | fat: 8g | protein: 14g | carbs: 79g | fiber: 15g | sugar: 5g | sodium: 630mg

Spinach Fritters with Chia Seeds

Prep time: 5 minutes | Cook time: 10 minutes | Makes 12 fritters

2 cups chickpea flour
1½ cups water
2 tablespoons ground chia seeds
½ teaspoon salt
3 cups lightly packed spinach leaves, finely chopped
1 tablespoon coconut oil, or extra-virgin olive oil

1. In a medium bowl, whisk together the chickpea flour, water, chia seeds, and salt. Mix well to ensure there are no lumps.
2. Fold in the spinach.
3. In a nonstick skillet set over medium-low heat, melt the coconut oil.
4. Working in batches, use a ¼-cup measure to drop the batter into the pan. Flatten the fritters to about ½ inch thick. Don't crowd the pan.
5. Cook for 5 to 6 minutes. Flip the fritters and cook for 5 minutes more.
6. Transfer to a serving plate.

Per Serving (2 fritters)

calories: 318 | fat: 10g | protein: 15g | carbs: 45g | fiber: 15g | sugar: 7g | sodium: 222mg

Avocado Quinoa Sushi

Prep time: 10 minutes | Cook time: 15 minutes | Serves 4

1½ cups dry quinoa
3 cups water, plus additional for rolling
½ teaspoon salt
6 nori sheets
3 avocados, halved, pitted, and thinly sliced, divided
1 small cucumber, halved, seeded, and cut into matchsticks, divided
Coconut aminos, for dipping (optional)

1. Rinse the quinoa in a fine-mesh sieve.
2. In a medium pot set over high heat, combine the rinsed quinoa, water, and salt. Bring to a boil. Reduce the heat to low. Cover and simmer for 15 minutes. Fluff the quinoa with a fork.
3. On a cutting board, lay out 1 nori sheet. Spread ½ cup of quinoa over the sheet, leaving 2 to 3 inches uncovered at the top.
4. Place 5 or 6 avocado slices across the bottom of the nori sheet (the side closest to you) in a row. Add 5 or 6 cucumber matchsticks on top.
5. Starting at the bottom, tightly roll up the nori sheet. Dab the uncovered top with water to seal the roll.
6. Slice the sushi roll into 6 pieces.
7. Repeat with the remaining 5 nori sheets, quinoa, and vegetables.
8. Serve with the coconut aminos (if using).

Per Serving

calories: 557 | fat: 33g | protein: 13g | carbs: 57g | fiber: 15g | sugar: 2g | sodium: 309mg

Broccoli and Bean Casserole with Walnuts

Prep time: 5 minutes | Cook time: 31 minutes | Serves 4

¾ cup vegetable broth, or water
2 broccoli heads, crowns and stalks finely chopped
1 teaspoon salt
2 cups cooked pinto or navy beans, or 1 (14-ounce / 397-g) can
1 to 2 tablespoons brown rice flour, or arrowroot flour
1 cup chopped walnuts

1. Preheat the oven to 350ºF (180ºC).
2. In a large oven-proof pot over medium heat, warm the broth.
3. Add the broccoli and salt. Cook for 6 to 8 minutes, or until the broccoli is bright green.
4. Stir in the pinto beans and brown rice flour. Cook for 5 minutes more, or until the liquid thickens slightly.
5. Sprinkle the walnuts over the top.
6. Place the pot in the preheated oven and bake for 20 to 25 minutes. The walnuts should be toasted.

Per Serving

calories: 410 | fat: 20g | protein: 22g | carbs: 43g | fiber: 13g | sugar: 4g | sodium: 635mg

Kale Pasta with Cashew-Carrot Marinara

Prep time: 10 minutes | Cook time: 5 minutes | Serves 6

1¼ cups cashews, soaked in water for at least 4 hours
5 large carrots, peeled and roughly chopped
1½ to 2 cups water
1 tablespoon finely chopped fresh basil
1 teaspoon salt
1 (12-ounce / 340-g) package brown rice spaghetti
1 bunch kale, thoroughly washed, stemmed, and chopped into 1-inch pieces

1. Drain and rinse the cashews.
2. In a medium pot set over high heat, combine the carrots with 1½ cups of water. Bring to a boil. Reduce the heat to low and simmer for 5 to 8 minutes, or until tender. Drain the carrots and reserve the cooking water.
3. In a blender, combine the cashews, basil, and salt. Add the cooked carrots and reserved cooking water. Blend until smooth, taking care with the hot liquid. If the sauce is too thick, thin with more water.
4. Bring a large pot of water to a boil over high heat. Add the pasta and cook according to the package directions.
5. During the last minute of cook time, toss in the kale and let it wilt. Drain the pasta and return it to the pot. Toss with the carrot marinara. You may not need to use all the sauce. Leftover sauce will keep refrigerated for 3 to 4 days, and freezes well.

Per Serving

calories: 408 | fat: 14g | protein: 10g | carbs: 65g | fiber: 4g | sugar: 4g | sodium: 460mg

Brussels Sprout and Lentil Stew

Prep time: 15 minutes | Cook time: 12 minutes | Serves 4 to 6

1 tablespoon extra-virgin olive oil
1 onion, chopped
3 carrots, peeled and sliced
8 Brussels sprouts, halved
1 large turnip, peeled, quartered, and sliced
1 garlic clove, sliced
6 cups vegetable broth
1 (15-ounce / 425-g) can lentils, drained and rinsed
1 cup frozen corn
1 teaspoon salt
¼ teaspoon freshly ground black pepper
1 tablespoon chopped fresh parsley

1. In a Dutch oven, heat the oil over high heat.
2. Add the onion and sauté until softened, about 3 minutes.
3. Add the carrots, Brussels sprouts, turnip, and garlic and sauté for an additional 3 minutes.
4. Add the broth and bring to a boil. Reduce to a simmer and cook until the vegetables are tender, about 5 minutes.
5. Add the lentils, corn, salt, pepper, and parsley and cook for an additional minute to heat the lentils and corn. Serve hot.

Per Serving

calories: 240 | fat: 4g | protein: 10g | carbs: 42g | fiber: 12g | sugar: 11g | sodium: 870mg

Garlic Sautéd Veggies with Quinoa

Prep time: 10 minutes | Cook time: 10 minutes | Serves 4 to 6

3 tablespoons extra-virgin olive oil
1½ cups quartered Brussels sprouts
1 large zucchini, chopped
1 onion, chopped
3 garlic cloves, sliced
2½ cups cooked quinoa
1 cup vegetable broth or tomato sauce
1 tablespoon fresh lemon juice
1 teaspoon dried oregano
1 teaspoon salt
¼ teaspoon freshly ground black pepper

1. In a large skillet, heat the oil over high heat.
2. Add the Brussels sprouts, zucchini, onion, and garlic and sauté until the vegetables are tender, 5 to 7 minutes.
3. Add the quinoa and broth, cover, and cook for an additional 5 minutes.
4. Add the lemon juice, oregano, salt, and pepper and stir to fluff the quinoa.
5. Serve warm or at room temperature.

Per Serving

calories: 270 | fat: 13g | protein: 8g | carbs: 34g | fiber: 8g | sugar: 5g | sodium: 640mg

Swiss Chard Penne with White Beans

Prep time: 10 minutes | Cook time: 3 minutes | Serves 4 to 6

1 (12-ounce / 340-g) package whole-wheat penne
2 tablespoons extra-virgin olive oil
1 bunch Swiss chard, cut into thin ribbons
1 garlic clove, sliced
1 teaspoon salt
⅛ teaspoon red pepper flakes
1 (15-ounce / 425-g) can white beans, drained and rinsed
¼ cup chopped toasted walnuts (optional)

1. Cook the penne in a large pot of boiling water according to the package directions, then drain.
2. While the pasta is cooking, in a large skillet, heat the oil over high heat.
3. Add the chard, garlic, salt, and red pepper flakes and cook until the chard has wilted, about 3 minutes. Stir in the white beans until warm.
4. In a large serving bowl, toss together the penne and chard-bean mixture, mixing well. Sprinkle with the walnuts and serve.

Per Serving

calories: 620 | fat: 14g | protein: 25g | carbs: 101g | fiber: 17g | sugar: 5g | sodium: 660mg

Spinach and Tofu Scramble

Prep time: 10 minutes | Cook time: 6 minutes | Serves 2

1 package extra-firm tofu, pressed and crumbled
1 tablespoon extra-virgin olive oil
2 spring onions, finely chopped
1 cup spinach leaves
½ cup quartered cherry tomatoes (optional)
1 garlic clove, finely chopped
1 teaspoon lemon juice
1 teaspoon black pepper

1. Heat olive oil in a skillet over medium heat.
2. Add the spring onion, tomatoes and garlic and sauté for 3 to 4 minutes.
3. Lower the heat and add the tofu, lemon juice, and pepper.
4. Sauté for 3 to 5 minutes.
5. Turn the heat off and add the spinach, stirring until spinach is wilted.
6. Transfer to a serving dish and enjoy.

Per Serving

calories: 273 | fat: 17g | protein: 21g | carbs: 9g | fiber: 4g | sugar: 2g | sodium: 25mg

Black Bean Stew with Olives

Prep time: 10 minutes | Cook time: 32 minutes | Serves 4

1 cup cooked brown rice
1 cup cooked quinoa
½ cup halved black olives
½ cup cooked black beans
1 avocado, sliced
2 tablespoons plain non-fat Greek yogurt
1 beef tomato, finely chopped (optional)
½ red onion, finely chopped
2 limes, 1 juiced and 1 cut into wedges
1 tablespoon finely chopped fresh cilantro

1. Heat a pan of water over high heat and add brown rice, allowing to cook for 15 minutes.
2. Heat a separate pan of water over high heat and add quinoa, allowing to cook for 15 minutes.
3. Add the black beans to the pan of rice to cook along with the rice.
4. Check most of the water in each pan has been absorbed, drain and cover on the heat for 2 minutes. Turn off heat.
5. Grab a large serving bowl and mix rice, quinoa, beans, olives, red onion, tomato and lime juice together.
6. In a separate bowl, crush the avocado into the yogurt with a fork and squeeze any remaining lime juice into the dip.
7. Enjoy your authentic Mexican meal, topped with cilantro, the avocado dip, and the lime wedges to serve.

Per Serving

calories: 266 | fat: 10g | protein: 7g | carbs: 37g | fiber: 9g | sugar: 3g | sodium: 139mg

Veggie-Tofu Lasagna

Prep time: 15 minutes | Cook time: 1 hour | Serves 1

½ package soft tofu
½ package firm tofu
Whole-grain lasagna sheets (½ box)
1 cup baby spinach
1 cup unsweetened almond milk
¼ teaspoon garlic powder
Juice of half a lemon
1½ tablespoons chopped fresh basil
1 can chopped tomatoes
1 pinch of black pepper
1 zucchini, diced
1 red pepper, diced (optional)

1. Preheat the oven to 325°F (163°C).
2. In a blender, process the soft and firm tofu, garlic powder, almond milk, basil, lemon juice and pepper until smooth.
3. Toss in the spinach and zucchini for the last 30 seconds.
4. Put about $^1/_3$ of the chopped tomatoes at the bottom of an oven dish.
5. Top the sauce with ⅓ of the lasagna sheets and then $^1/_3$ of the tofu mixture.
6. Repeat the layers finishing with the chopped tomatoes on top.
7. Cook for around 1 hour or until the pasta sheets are soft.
8. Serve with a lovely side salad and enjoy.

Per Serving

calories: 610 | fat: 30g | protein: 50g | carbs: 35g | fiber: 8g | sugar: 21g | sodium: 177mg

Spinach and Tempeh Burgers

Prep time: 10 minutes | Cook time: 13 minutes | Serves 2

1 package extra-firm tempeh
1 teaspoon red chili flakes
1 red pepper, diced (optional)
½ red onion, diced
½ cup baby spinach
1 tablespoon olive oil
2 100% whole-grain buns (optional)

1. Preheat the broiler to medium-high heat.
2. Marinate the tempeh in oil and red chilli flakes.
3. Heat a little olive oil in a skillet over medium heat.
4. Sauté the onion in the skillet for 6 to 7 minutes or until caramelized.
5. Stir in the pepper and baby spinach for a further 3 to 4 minutes.
6. Broil the tempeh for around 4 minutes on each side.
7. Lay down the tempeh in the buns and then add the caramelized onion, spinach and diced peppers.
8. Serve immediately while hot with a side of arugula.

Per Serving

calories: 440 | fat: 28g | protein: 11g | carbs: 36g | fiber: 2g | sugar: 1g | sodium: 211mg

Spaghetti Squash Bake with Tempeh

Prep time: 10 minutes | Cook time: 57 minutes | Serves 2

1 package tempeh, drained and cubed
1 spaghetti squash or pumpkin, halved and seeded
3 tablespoons tamari or low-sodium soy sauce
1 can chopped tomatoes
1 tablespoon extra-virgin olive oil
2 garlic cloves, chopped finely
1 cup small broccoli florets
½ cup baby spinach

1. Preheat the oven to 375°F (190°C). Get a medium-sized bowl and toss together the tamari, tempeh, garlic.
2. Marinate and set aside for at least 30 minutes and overnight if possible. Grab a large baking dish and arrange the squash halves with the cut side down.
3. Pour half a cup of water into the dish. Bake for around 45 minutes or until tender and remove the dish out of the oven. Turn the squash over and allow to slightly cool.
4. Get a large skillet and heat oil over medium heat.
5. Add tempeh and cook for 7 to 8 minutes until golden brown, occasionally stirring.
6. Remove the tempeh and keep warm on a plate.
7. In a medium-sized pot, heat chopped tomatoes over medium heat, and then add the broccoli and allow to cook until tender (around 5 minutes.) Stir the spinach in and remove from heat.
8. Use a fork to scrape off spaghetti squash strands onto a platter. Spoon broccoli and hot chopped tomatoes over the dish.
9. Top with the tempeh to serve.

Per Serving

calories: 553 | fat: 21g | protein: 25g | carbs: 66g | fiber: 16g | sugar: 27g | sodium: 851mg

Garlic Kidney Bean and Quinoa

Prep time: 10 minutes | Cook time: 15 minutes | Serves 2

½ cup kidney beans
½ cup uncooked quinoa
2 cups low-sodium vegetable broth
3 green onion stalks, diced
4 garlic cloves, minced
¼ teaspoon black pepper
1 tablespoon extra-virgin olive oil

1. Sauté garlic and onion in olive oil, in a large pan over medium heat until onions soften.
2. Lower heat. Add the quinoa, kidney beans and vegetable broth.
3. Cover the pan and simmer for around 15 to 20 minutes or until quinoa is soft and liquid is absorbed.
4. Serve with the diced green onion scattered over the quinoa and a little black pepper to taste.

Per Serving

calories: 389 | fat: 9g | protein: 16g | carbs: 61g | fiber: 10g | sugar: 3g | sodium: 561mg

Mozzarella Tomato Pasta with Walnuts

Prep time: 10 minutes | Cook time: 0 minutes | Serves 2

1 cup 100% whole-grain pasta
1 garlic clove, minced
¼ cup coarsely chopped walnuts
½ cup chopped sun-dried tomatoes (optional)
2 tablespoons extra-virgin olive oil
1 bunch fresh basil, chopped
3½ ounces (99 g) low-fat Mozzarella cheese
Pinch of black pepper

1. Boil a large saucepan of water over high heat.
2. Add the pasta and cook following directions on the package.
3. While the pasta is cooking, prepare the sauce:
4. Put minced garlic in a bowl. Add sun-dried tomatoes, walnuts, basil, Mozzarella and oil.
5. Once the pasta is cooked, drain and add to the sauce.
6. Toss through until the pasta is well coated.
7. Transfer the dish onto a serving plate.

Per Serving

calories: 500 | fat: 32g | protein: 21g | carbs: 32g | fiber: 6g | sugar: 9g | sodium: 357mg

Broccoli Rabe and Cauliflower Stir-Fry

Prep time: 15 minutes | Cook time: 24 minutes | Serves 4

12 bunch broccoli rabe
½ cauliflower, cut into florets
1 onion, diced
1 thumb sized piece of ginger, minced
4 garlic cloves, minced
1 teaspoon black mustard seeds
1 teaspoon cumin seeds
½ teaspoon turmeric
1 teaspoon cumin powder
½ teaspoon coriander powder
½ teaspoon red chili flakes
1 pinch of black pepper
2 tablespoons coconut oil
1 tablespoon chopped fresh cilantro, for garnish

1. In a skillet over medium heat, add the oil.
2. Add the black mustard seeds, cumin seeds, and the spices and stir for 4 to 5 minutes.
3. Add the onions and stir for a further 5 minutes or until softened.
4. Add the ginger, garlic and red chili flakes, stirring for a further 5 minutes and then add in the rest of the spices.
5. Let the spices sink in for 5 minutes and then add in the broccoli rabe and cauliflower.
6. Stir until the greens are covered in the spices and then reduce the heat and sauté for about 5 to 6 minutes.
7. Garnish with cilantro and add pepper to taste and serve.

Per Serving

calories: 119 | fat: 7g | protein: 4g | carbs: 10g | fiber: 4g | sugar: 3g | sodium: 55mg

Roasted Rainbow Cauliflower
Prep time: 5 minutes | Cook time: 20 minutes | Serves 4 to 6

1½ cups white cauliflower florets
1½ cups yellow cauliflower florets
1½ cups purple cauliflower florets
¼ cup fresh lemon juice
3 tablespoons extra-virgin olive oil
1 teaspoon sea salt
¼ teaspoon freshly ground black pepper

1. Preheat the oven to 400°F (205°C).
2. Add the cauliflower, lemon juice, and olive oil to a large bowl, and toss to combine.
3. Spread out the coated cauliflower on a rimmed baking sheet and season with salt and pepper.
4. Wrap in aluminum foil and bake in the preheated oven for 15 minutes. Remove the foil and bake for an additional 5 minutes, or until the tips and edges of the cauliflower are beginning to brown.
5. Let the cauliflower cool for 5 minutes before serving.

Per Serving
calories: 121 | fat: 11g | protein: 3g | carbs: 8g | fiber: 2g | sugar: 3g | sodium: 621mg

Lentils Stew with Tomatoes
Prep time: 10 minutes | Cook time: 10 minutes | Serves 4

2 tablespoons extra-virgin olive oil, plus more for garnish
1 tablespoon ground turmeric
1 onion, finely chopped
1 (14-ounce / 397-g) can lentils, drained
1 (14-ounce / 397-g) can chopped tomatoes, drained
1 teaspoon garlic powder
½ teaspoon sea salt
¼ teaspoon freshly ground black pepper

1. Heat the olive oil in a large skillet over medium-high heat until shimmering.
2. Toss in the turmeric and onion and sauté for about 5 minutes, stirring occasionally, or until the onion is translucent.
3. Add the lentils, tomatoes, garlic powder, salt, and pepper and mix well. Continue cooking for 5 minutes until heated through.
4. Remove from the heat to a plate and garnish with additional olive oil, if desired.

Per Serving
calories: 247 | fat: 8g | protein: 12g | carbs: 34g | fiber: 16g | sugar: 5g | sodium: 242mg

Sweet Potato and Spinach
Prep time: 10 minutes | Cook time: 20 minutes | Serves 4

2 tablespoons extra-virgin olive oil
1 onion, chopped
4 cups fresh baby spinach
4 cups cubed, peeled sweet potato
3 cups no-salt-added vegetable broth
1 cup unsweetened coconut milk
2 tablespoons curry powder
½ teaspoon sea salt
⅛ teaspoon freshly ground black pepper

1. Heat the olive oil in a large skillet over medium-high heat until shimmering.
2. Add the onion and cook for about 5 minutes, stirring occasionally, or until the onion is tender.
3. Stir in the spinach, sweet potatoes, vegetable broth, coconut milk, curry powder, salt, and pepper, and bring to a boil.
4. Reduce the heat to medium and bring to a simmer for about 15 minutes, stirring occasionally, or until the vegetables are softened.
5. Remove from the heat and serve on a plate.

Per Serving
calories: 315 | fat: 11g | protein: 8g | carbs: 51g | fiber: 10g | sugar: 14g | sodium: 401mg

Baby Bok Choy Stir-Fry
Prep time: 10 minutes | Cook time: 11 minutes | Serves 6

2 tablespoons coconut oil
1 large onion, finely diced
2 teaspoons ground cumin
1-inch piece fresh ginger, grated
1 teaspoon ground turmeric
½ teaspoon sea salt
12 baby bok choy heads, ends trimmed and sliced lengthwise
3 cups cooked brown rice

1. Heat the coconut oil in a large skillet over medium heat.
2. Add the onion and sauté for 5 minutes, stirring occasionally.
3. Fold in the cumin, ginger, turmeric, and salt, and stir until the onion is coated in the spices.
4. Add the bok choy and stir-fry for about 6 to 7 minutes, or until the bok choy is tender but still crisp.
5. Remove from the heat to a plate and serve with cooked brown rice.

Per Serving
calories: 443 | fat: 9g | protein: 30g | carbs: 76g | fiber: 19g | sugar: 21g | sodium: 1290mg

Sweet Potato and Butternut Squash Curry

Prep time: 10 minutes | Cook time: 11 minutes | Serves 4 to 6

1 tablespoon coconut oil
1 onion, chopped
1 large sweet potato, peeled and cut into ½-inch cubes
2 cups (½-inch) butternut squash cubes
2 garlic cloves, sliced
2 cups no-salt-added vegetable broth
1 (13.5-ounce / 383-g) can coconut milk
2 teaspoons curry powder
1 teaspoon sea salt
2 tablespoons chopped fresh cilantro

1. Heat the coconut oil in a Dutch oven over high heat.
2. Add the onion and sauté for about 3 minutes until softened.
3. Stir in the sweet potato, butternut squash, and garlic and sauté for 3 minutes more.
4. Add the vegetable broth, coconut milk, curry powder, and salt to the vegetables, and bring to a boil.
5. Reduce the heat and bring to a simmer and continue cooking for about 5 minutes, or until the vegetables are fork-tender.
6. Sprinkle the cilantro on top for garnish and serve.

Per Serving

calories: 122 | fat: 5g | protein: 2g | carbs: 20g | fiber: 3g | sugar: 4g | sodium: 671mg

Ritzy Wild Rice Stuffed Sweet Potatoes

Prep time: 10 minutes | Cook time: 20 minutes | Serves 4

2 cups cooked wild rice
½ cup chopped hazelnuts
½ cup dried blueberries
1 teaspoon chopped fresh thyme
½ cup shredded Swiss chard
1 scallion, white and green parts, peeled and thinly sliced
Sea salt and freshly ground black pepper, to taste
4 sweet potatoes, baked in the skin until tender, cut the top third off lengthwise, hollowed

1. Preheat the oven to 400°F (205°C).
2. Combine the wild rice, hazelnuts, blueberries, thyme, Swiss chard, and scallion in a large bowl. Sprinkle with salt and pepper. Stir to mix well.
3. Fill the hollowed sweet potatoes with the wild rice mixture, then arrange the stuffed sweet potato on a parchment paper lined baking sheet.
4. Bake in the preheated oven for 20 minutes or until the skin of the sweet potato is lightly charred.
5. Remove the stuffed sweet potato from the oven and serve on a large plate.

Per Serving

calories: 316 | fat: 11g | protein: 8g | carbs: 50g | fiber: 8g | sugar: 12g | sodium: 54mg

Sweet Potatoes and Pea Hash

Prep time: 15 minutes | Cook time: 7 minutes | Serves 4

2 tablespoons coconut oil
3 garlic cloves, minced
4 scallions, sliced
2 teaspoons minced fresh ginger
1 teaspoon curry powder
½ teaspoon ground turmeric
1 teaspoon sea salt
2 medium sweet potatoes, roasted in their skins, peeled, and chopped
2 cups cooked brown rice
1 cup frozen peas
1 tablespoon coconut aminos
¼ cup chopped fresh cilantro, for garnish
½ cup chopped cashews, for garnish

1. In a large skillet, melt the coconut oil over medium-high heat.
2. Add the garlic, scallions, ginger, curry powder, turmeric, and salt, and stir well. Sauté for 2 minutes until fragrant.
3. Fold in the sweet potatoes, brown rice, peas, and coconut aminos, and sauté for 5 minutes, stirring occasionally.
4. Sprinkle the cilantro and cashews on top for garnish and serve warm.

Per Serving

calories: 510 | fat: 17g | protein: 11g | carbs: 83g | fiber: 10g | sugar: 4g | sodium: 634mg

Sautéed Tofu and Spinach

Prep time: 10 minutes | Cook time: 7½ minutes | Serves 4

2 tablespoons extra-virgin olive oil
1 onion, chopped
8 ounces (227 g) tofu
4 cups fresh baby spinach
3 garlic cloves, minced
Juice and zest of 1 orange
½ teaspoon sea salt
⅛ teaspoon freshly ground black pepper

1. Heat the olive oil in a large skillet over medium-high heat until shimmering.
2. Add the onion, tofu, and spinach and mix well. Cook for about 4 to 5 minutes, stirring occasionally, or until the onion is softened.
3. Stir in the garlic and cook for 30 seconds until fragrant.
4. Add the lemon juice and zest, salt, and pepper. Stir to combine and continue cooking for 3 minutes until heated through.
5. Remove from the heat and serve on a plate.

Per Serving

calories: 127 | fat: 10g | protein: 6g | carbs: 7g | fiber: 2g | sugar: 3g | sodium: 265mg

THE ULTIMATE ANTI-INFLAMMATORY DIET COOKBOOK

Braised Bok Choy with Mushrooms

Prep time: 10 minutes | Cook time: 5 minutes | Serves 4

1 tablespoon coconut oil
8 baby bok choy, halved lengthwise
1 cup shiitake mushrooms, stemmed and thinly sliced
½ cup water
1 tablespoon coconut aminos
Sea salt and freshly ground black pepper, to taste
1 scallion, sliced thin
1 tablespoon toasted sesame seeds

1. Melt the coconut oil in a large skillet over high heat.
2. Add the bok choy, mushrooms, water, and coconut aminos to the skillet. Braise the vegetables for about 5 to 10 minutes, covered, or until the bok choy is softened.
3. Remove from the heat and sprinkle the salt and pepper to season.
4. Divide the bok choy and mushrooms among plates. Scatter each plate evenly with the scallions and sesame seeds.
5. Serve immediately.

Per Serving

calories: 286 | fat: 8g | protein: 26g | carbs: 43g | fiber: 18g | sugar: 21g | sodium: 1184mg

Zucchini Spaghetti with Almonds and Peas

Prep time: 10 minutes | Cook time: 0 minutes | Serves 4

1 cup packed fresh oregano leaves
½ cup almonds
Juice and zest of 1 lemon
1 cup packed fresh basil leaves, plus more for garnish
2 teaspoons minced garlic
Sea salt and freshly ground black pepper, to taste
2 tablespoons extra-virgin olive oil
1 cup fresh peas
2 large green zucchini, julienned or spiralized

1. Put the oregano, almonds, lemon juice and zest, basil, garlic, salt, and ground black pepper in a food processor. Pulse to combine well until smooth.
2. While the food processor is processing, gently mix the olive oil in the mixture until the mixture performs a thick consistency.
3. Combine the peas and spiralized zucchini in a large bowl, then pour in the mixture. Toss to coat well.
4. Garnish with more fresh basil leaves and serve immediately.

Per Serving

calories: 356 | fat: 19g | protein: 12g | carbs: 51g | fiber: 29g | sugar: 8g | sodium: 29mg

Broccolini and Quinoa Sauté

Prep time: 10 minutes | Cook time: 9 minutes | Serves 4

1 tablespoon coconut oil
2 garlic cloves, chopped
2 leeks, white part only, sliced
4 cups chopped broccolini
½ cup no-salt-added vegetable broth
2 cups cooked quinoa
1 tablespoon coconut aminos
1 teaspoon curry powder

1. In a large skillet, melt the coconut oil over high heat.
2. Stir in the garlic and leeks and sauté for 2 minutes until fragrant.
3. Add the broccolini and vegetable broth. Cover and cook for 5 minutes until the broccolini softens.
4. Add the cooked quinoa, coconut aminos, and curry powder and stir to incorporate. Cook uncovered for 2 to 3 minutes until warmed through, stirring occasionally.
5. Divide the mixture among four plates and serve warm.

Per Serving

calories: 274 | fat: 6g | protein: 11g | carbs: 44g | fiber: 6g | sugar: 5g | sodium: 55mg

Buddha Bowl

Prep time: 15 minutes | Cook time: 33½ minutes | Serves 4

2 tablespoons coconut oil, divided
1 cup brown basmati rice
2 cups low-sodium vegetable broth
2 teaspoons sea salt, divided
2 cups sliced mushrooms
4 ounces (113 g) fresh snow peas, strings removed
2 carrots, sliced thin
2 garlic cloves, sliced thin
½ cup frozen peas, thawed
3 tablespoons chopped fresh cilantro
2 scallions, sliced thin
½ teaspoon red pepper flakes
3 tablespoons freshly squeezed lime juice
1 tablespoon coconut aminos
1 tablespoon extra-virgin olive oil

1. Heat the coconut oil in a saucepan over high heat until melted.
2. Add the basmati rice, vegetable broth, and 1 teaspoon of salt to the saucepan. Bring to a boil.
3. Reduce the heat to low. Cover and simmer for 25 minutes or until the rice is tender. Transfer the cooked rice in a large serving bowl.
4. Meanwhile, Heat the remaining coconut oil in a nonstick skillet over high heat until melted.
5. Add the mushrooms and sauté for 5 minutes or until lightly browned.
6. Add the snow peas, carrots, and garlic to the skillet and sauté for an additional 3 minutes, then add the peas and cover to cook for 30 seconds until the peas are warmed through.
7. Transfer the sautéed vegetables to the bowl of rice, then stir to combine well. Sprinkle them with cilantro, scallions, red pepper flakes, and remaining teaspoon of salt, then drizzle with lime juice, coconut aminos, and olive oil. Toss to combine well.
8. Serve warm.

Per Serving

calories: 370 | fat: 15g | protein: 9g | carbs: 51g | fiber: 4g | sugar: 5g | sodium: 1592mg

Spinach, Butternut Squash, and Lentils Gratin

Prep time: 15 minutes | Cook time: 21 minutes | Serves 4 to 6

1 tablespoon coconut oil
2 garlic cloves, minced
1 onion, peeled and chopped
4 cups packed spinach
1 small butternut squash, peeled, deseeded, and cut into ½-inch cubes
1 teaspoon sea salt
½ teaspoon freshly ground black pepper
1 (13.5-ounce / 383-g) can coconut milk
1½ or 2 cups low-sodium vegetable broth
¼ cup chopped fresh parsley
1 (15-ounce / 425-g) can lentils, drained and rinsed
2 tablespoons chopped fresh sage
½ cup chopped toasted walnuts

1. Preheat the oven to 375°F (190°C).
2. Heat the coconut oil in an oven-safe skillet over high heat until melted.
3. Add the garlic and onion to the skillet and sauté for 3 minutes or until fragrant and the onion is translucent.
4. Add the spinach, butternut squash, salt, and ground black pepper to the skillet and sauté for an additional 3 minutes or until the spinach is lightly wilted.
5. Pour in the coconut milk and enough vegetable broth to cover the butternut squash. Bring to a boil.
6. Then add the parsley, lentils, and sage. Stir to combine well.
7. Arrange the skillet in the preheated oven and bake for 15 minutes or until the butternut squash is soft.
8. Remove the skillet from the oven and transfer them on a large plate. Garnish with walnuts and serving immediately.

Per Serving
calories: 503 | fat: 37g | protein: 20g | carbs: 47g | fiber: 16g | sugar: 9g | sodium: 1162mg

Roasted Broccoli and Cashews

Prep time: 5 minutes | Cook time: 15 minutes | Serves 4

6 cups broccoli florets
2 tablespoons extra-virgin olive oil
1 teaspoon sea salt
½ cup toasted cashews
1 tablespoon coconut aminos

1. Preheat the oven to 375°F (190°C).
2. Combine the broccoli, olive oil, and salt in a large bowl, and toss until the broccoli is coated well.
3. Spread out the broccoli on a baking sheet in a single layer.
4. Roast in the preheated oven for 15 to 20 minutes, or until the broccoli is crisp-tender and slightly browned around the edges.
5. Transfer the roasted broccoli to a serving bowl. Allow it rest for a few minutes until cooled slightly.
6. Add the cashews and coconut aminos to the bowl of broccoli and toss to coat well. Serve immediately.

Per Serving
calories: 210 | fat: 15g | protein: 6g | carbs: 15g | fiber: 4g | sugar: 3g | sodium: 634mg

Sumptuous Vegetable Cabbage Cups

Prep time: 15 minutes | Cook time: 13 minutes | Serves 4

1 tablespoon extra-virgin olive oil
1 sweet onion, chopped
1 teaspoon grated fresh ginger
1 teaspoon minced garlic
1 cup shredded sweet potato
2 cups shredded broccoli stalks
1 carrot, shredded
2 cups finely chopped cauliflower
1 cup chopped fresh spinach
1 cup fresh peas
1 teaspoon ground cumin
½ teaspoon ground coriander
2 tablespoons apple cider vinegar
¼ cup dried cherries
¼ cup pumpkin seeds
4 large cabbage leaves

1. Heat the olive oil in a nonstick skillet over medium-high heat until shimmering.
2. Add the onion, ginger, and garlic to the skillet and sauté for 3 minutes or until fragrant and the onion is translucent.
3. Add the sweet potato, broccoli, carrot, and cauliflower to the skillet and sauté for 8 minutes or until soft.
4. Add the spinach, peas, cumin, coriander, and cider vinegar to the skillet and sauté for an additional 2 minutes or until the spinach is wilted.
5. Turn off the heat and fold in the cherries and pumpkin seeds.
6. Unfold the cabbage leaves on four serving plates, then divide the mixture over the leaves and serve warm.

Per Serving
calories: 191 | fat: 8g | protein: 9g | carbs: 25g | fiber: 6g | sugar: 10g | sodium: 93mg

Corn Tostadas with Black Beans

Prep time: 15 minutes | Cook time: 0 minutes | Serves 6

1 (15-ounce / 425-g) can black beans, drained and rinsed well
½ teaspoon ground cumin
½ teaspoon salt
½ teaspoon garlic powder
¼ teaspoon red pepper flakes
Dash freshly ground black pepper
1 tablespoon avocado oil
6 sprouted corn tortillas
1 red bell pepper, thinly sliced
½ red onion, thinly sliced
1 large avocado, sliced
½ cup sliced radishes
Lime wedges, for garnish

1. In a small saucepan over medium heat, warm the black beans, lightly mashing some of them to make them more spreadable.
2. Stir in the cumin, salt, garlic powder, red pepper flakes, and black pepper.
3. In a large skillet over medium heat, heat the avocado oil. One at a time, add the tortillas and cook on both sides until warmed through and as crispy as you like. Transfer to a work surface.
4. Spread some of the bean mixture over each tortilla. Top each with slices of red bell pepper, onion, avocado, and radish.
5. Sprinkle with lime juice and serve.

Per Serving

calories: 196 | fat: 7g | protein: 6g | carbs: 28g | fiber: 7g | sugar: 2g | sodium: 213mg

Cumin Baby Bok Choy Stir-Fry

Prep time: 10 minutes | Cook time: 10 minutes | Serves 6

2 tablespoons coconut oil
1 large onion, finely diced
1-inch piece fresh ginger, grated
2 teaspoons ground cumin
1 teaspoon ground turmeric
½ teaspoon salt
12 baby bok choy heads, ends trimmed and sliced lengthwise
Water, as needed for cooking
3 cups cooked brown rice

1. In a large pan set over medium heat, heat the coconut oil.
2. Add the onion and cook for 5 minutes.
3. Add the ginger, cumin, turmeric, and salt. Stir to coat the onion with the spices.
4. Add the bok choy. Stir-fry for 5 to 8 minutes, or until the bok choy is crisp-tender. If the pan gets dry, add 1 tablespoon of water at a time until done.
5. Serve with the brown rice.

Per Serving

calories: 444 | fat: 9g | protein: 30g | carbs: 76g | fiber: 19g | sugar: 21g | sodium: 1290mg

Tahini Brown Rice Spaghetti with Kale

Prep time: 10 minutes | Cook time: 10 minutes | Serves 4

12 cups water
1¼ teaspoons sea salt, divided
8 ounces (227 g) brown rice spaghetti
4 cups packed kale
½ cup tahini
¾ cup hot water
½ cup chopped fresh parsley

1. Bring 12 cups of water to a boil, sprinkle with 1 teaspoon of salt, then add the brown rice spaghetti.
2. Cook for 10 minutes or until the pasta is al dente. Keep stirring during the cooking time.
3. During the last minute of the cooking time, add the kale to blanch.
4. When the cooking is complete, transfer the pasta and kale in a colander to drain, then put them in a large bowl. Set aside.
5. Combine the tahini, remaining salt, and hot water in a small bowl. Stir to mix well.
6. Add the tahini sauce with parsley to the pasta. Toss to coat well. Serve warm.

Per Serving

calories: 403 | fat: 18g | protein: 15g | carbs: 54g | fiber: 10g | sugar: 2g | sodium: 224mg

CHAPTER 6:
FISH AND SEAFOOD

Grilled Salmon Teriyaki

Prep time: 5 minutes | Cook time: 6 minutes | Serves 2

½ teaspoon coarsely ground black pepper
2 tablespoons teriyaki sauce
2 (8 ounces / 227 g) Salmon fillets

1. In a shallow dish, place salmon.
2. Add teriyaki sauce and marinate in room temperature for 10 minutes.
3. Preheat grill to medium high fire and grease grate.
4. Rub pepper on fleshy part of salmon and place on grate skin part touching grate.
5. Grill for 4 minutes. Turnover and grill for another 2 minutes or until salmon is cooked to desired doneness.
6. Serve and enjoy.

Per Serving

calories: 365 | fat: 16g | protein: 48g | carbs: 3g | fiber: 0.2g | sugar: 48g | sodium: 1302mg

Salmon with Tangerine-Jicama Relish

Prep time: 10 minutes | Cook time: 15 minutes | Serves 4

Relish:
4 tangerines, peeled, segmented, and chopped
½ cup chopped jicama
1 scallion, white and green parts, chopped
2 tablespoons chopped fresh cilantro
1 teaspoon lemon zest (optional)
Pinch sea salt
Fish:
1 teaspoon ground cumin
1 teaspoon ground coriander
4 (6-ounce / 170-g) skin-on salmon fillets, patted dry
1 teaspoon olive oil

Make the Relish
1. In a small bowl, stir together the tangerines, jicama, scallion, cilantro, and lemon zest (if using). Season with sea salt and set it aside.
Make the Fish
2. Preheat the oven to 425°F (220°C).
3. In a small bowl, stir together the cumin and coriander.
4. Rub the flesh side of the fillets with the spice mixture. Arrange the salmon in a baking dish in a single layer, skin-side up. Brush with the olive oil.
5. Bake for about 15 minutes, or until just cooked through and lightly golden.
6. Serve the fish with the salsa.

Per Serving

calories: 290 | fat: 12g | protein: 34g | carbs: 14g | fiber: 2g | sugar: 10g | sodium: 171mg

Whitefish and Broccoli Curry

Prep time: 15 minutes | Cook time: 12 minutes | Serves 4 to 6

2 tablespoons coconut oil
1 onion, chopped
2 garlic cloves, minced
1 tablespoon minced fresh ginger
2 teaspoons curry powder
1 teaspoon salt
¼ teaspoon freshly ground black pepper
1 (4-inch) piece lemongrass (white part only), bruised with the back of a knife
2 cups cubed butternut squash
2 cups chopped broccoli
1 (13½-ounce / 383-g) can unsweetened coconut milk
1 cup vegetable broth, or chicken broth
1 pound (454 g) firm whitefish fillets
¼ cup chopped fresh cilantro
1 scallion, sliced thin
Lemon wedges, for garnish

1. In a large pot over medium-high heat, melt the coconut oil. Add the onion, garlic, ginger, curry powder, salt, and pepper. Sauté for 5 minutes.
2. Add the lemongrass, butternut squash, and broccoli. Sauté for 2 minutes more.
3. Stir in the coconut milk and vegetable broth and bring to a boil. Reduce the heat to simmer and add the fish. Cover the pot and simmer for 5 minutes, or until the fish is cooked through. Remove and discard the lemongrass.
4. Ladle the curry into a serving bowl. Garnish with the cilantro and scallion and serve with the lemon wedges.

Per Serving

calories: 553 | fat: 39g | protein: 34g | carbs: 22g | fiber: 6g | sugar: 7g | sodium: 881mg

Poached Halibut and Mushrooms

Prep time: 10 minutes | Cook time: 25 minutes | Serves 8

2 pounds (907 g) halibut, cut into bite-sized pieces
1 teaspoon fresh lemon juice
½ teaspoon soy sauce
⅛ teaspoon sesame oil
4 cups mushrooms, sliced
¼ cup water
Salt and pepper, to taste
¾ cup green onions

1. Place a heavy bottomed pot on medium high fire.
2. Add all ingredients and mix well.
3. Cover and bring to a boil. Once boiling, lower fire to a simmer. Cook for 25 minutes.
4. Adjust seasoning to taste.
5. Serve and enjoy.

Per Serving

calories: 217 | fat: 15.8g | protein: 16.5g | carbs: 1.1g | fiber: 0.4g | sugar: 0g | sodium: 97mg

Halibut Stir Fry

Prep time: 10 minutes | Cook time: 19 minutes | Serves 6

2 pounds (907 g) halibut fillets
2 tablespoon olive oil
½ cup fresh parsley
1 onion, sliced
2 stalks celery, chopped
2 tablespoons capers
4 garlic cloves, minced
Salt and pepper, to taste

1. Place a heavy bottomed pot on high fire and heat for 2 minutes. Add oil and heat for 2 more minutes.
2. Stir in garlic and onions. Sauté for 5 minutes.
3. Add remaining ingredients, except for parsley and stir fry for 10 minutes or until fish is cooked.
4. Adjust seasoning to taste and serve with a sprinkle of parsley.

Per Serving
calories: 331 | fat: 26g | protein: 22g | carbs: 2g | fiber: 0.5g | sugar: 0.6g | sodium: 197mg

Molasses Glazed Salmon

Prep time: 5 minutes | Cook time: 15 minutes | Serves 4

1 tablespoon coconut oil
2 tablespoons pomegranate molasses
¼ cup fresh orange juice
4 garlic cloves, crushed
1 tablespoon fresh ginger, grated
4 (8 ounces / 227 g) salmon fillets

1. Mix the garlic, ginger, pomegranate molasses and orange juice in a small bowl.
2. Pour the mixture over the salmon and marinate at room temperature for 15 minutes.
3. Preheat the oven to 425°F (220°C).
4. Line a baking sheet with foil and grease it with coconut oil.
5. Place the salmon skin-side-down on the baking sheet.
6. Drizzle more pomegranate molasses on top of the salmon.
7. Bake the fillets for 15 minutes or until the salmon becomes flaky.

Per Serving
calories: 203 | fat: 7g | protein: 9g | carbs: 29g | fiber: 6g | sugar: 21g | sodium: 128mg

Steamed Garlic-Dill Halibut

Prep time: 5 minutes | Cook time: 15 minutes | Serves 4

1-pound (454-g) halibut fillet
1 lemon, freshly squeezed
Salt and pepper, to taste
1 teaspoon garlic powder
1 tablespoon dill weed, chopped

1. Place a large pot on medium fire and fill up to 1½-inch of water. Place a trivet inside pot.
2. In a baking dish that fits inside your large pot, add all ingredients and mix well. Cover dish with foil. Place the dish on top of the trivet inside the pot.
3. Cover pot and steam fish for 15 minutes.
4. Let fish rest for at least 10 minutes before removing from pot.
5. Serve and enjoy.

Per Serving
calories: 270 | fat: 6.5g | protein: 47.8g | carbs: 3.9g | fiber: 2.1g | sugar: 0g | sodium: 565mg

Italian Halibut Chowder

Prep time: 5 minutes | Cook time: 16 minutes | Serves 8

2 tablespoons olive oil
1 onion, chopped
3 stalks of celery, chopped
3 garlic cloves, minced
2½ pounds (1134 g) halibut steaks, cubed
1 red bell pepper, seeded and chopped
1 cup tomato juice
½ cup apple juice, organic and unsweetened
½ teaspoon dried basil
⅛ teaspoon dried thyme
Salt and pepper, to taste

1. Place a heavy bottomed pot on medium high fire and heat pot for 2 minutes. Add oil and heat for 1 minute.
2. Sauté the onion, celery and garlic until fragrant.
3. Stir in the halibut steaks and bell pepper. Sauté for 3 minutes.
4. Pour in the rest of the ingredients and mix well.
5. Cover and bring to a boil. Once boiling, lower fire to a simmer and simmer for 10 minutes.
6. Adjust seasoning to taste.
7. Serve and enjoy.

Per Serving
calories: 318 | fat: 23g | protein: 21g | carbs: 6g | fiber: 1g | sugar: 4g | sodium: 155mg

Thai Cod Curry

Prep time: 10 minutes | Cook time: 16 minutes | Serves 1

1 teaspoon coconut oil
1 tablespoon organic Thai red curry paste
1 garlic cloves, minced
1 shallot, minced
¼ cup coconut cream
3 tablespoons water
1 cod fillet

1. Place a heavy bottomed pot on medium high fire and heat pot for 2 minutes. Add oil and heat for 1 minute.
2. Sauté the curry paste, garlic, and shallots until fragrant.
3. Stir in coconut cream and fillet. Sauté for 3 minutes. Season with pepper and salt, to taste.
4. Cover and bring to a boil. Once boiling, lower fire to a simmer and simmer for 10 minutes.
5. Adjust seasoning to taste.
6. Serve and enjoy.

Per Serving

calories: 458 | fat: 28g | protein: 45g | carbs: 10g | fiber: 5g | sugar: 1g | sodium: 132mg

Salmon with Dried Tomatoes

Prep time: 10 minutes | Cook time: 15 minutes | Serves 2

1 salmon fillet
½ lemon, freshly squeezed
Salt and pepper, to taste
¼ teaspoon cayenne pepper
½ teaspoon dried oregano
½ teaspoon dried thyme
2 garlic cloves, minced
2 tablespoons chopped sun-dried tomatoes
1 tablespoon capers
¼ cup water

1. Place a heavy bottomed pot on medium high fire and add all ingredients.
2. Mix well, cover and bring to a boil. Once boiling, lower fire to a simmer and simmer for 10 minutes.
3. Adjust seasoning to taste and continue cooking for another 5 minutes.
4. Serve and enjoy.

Per Serving

calories: 265 | fat: 8g | protein: 41g | carbs: 6g | fiber: 1g | sugar: 3g | sodium: 221mg

Island Style Sardines

Prep time: 10 minutes | Cook time: 8 hours | Serves 4

2 tablespoons olive oil
1 roma tomato, diced
¼ cup sliced onion
1 garlic clove, minced
1 teaspoon cayenne pepper flakes
½ pound (226 g) sardines, gutted and scales removed
1 tablespoon lemon juice, freshly squeezed
A dash of rosemary
A dash of sage
Salt and pepper, to taste

1. In a slow cooker, add all ingredients and mix well.
2. Cover and cook on low settings for 8 hours.
3. Adjust seasoning if needed.
4. Serve and enjoy.

Per Serving

calories: 195 | fat: 13.5g | protein: 15g | carbs: 4g | fiber: 1g | sugar: 2g | sodium: 177mg

Multi-Spice Cod Curry

Prep time: 15 minutes | Cook time: 19 minutes | Serves 6

Ingredients:
2 tablespoons olive oil
1 onion, chopped
1 teaspoon garlic paste
1 teaspoon grated ginger
2 teaspoons cumin
2 teaspoons coriander
1 teaspoon cardamom
½ teaspoon turmeric
Salt and pepper, to taste
2 fresh jalapeno peppers, chopped
1 tablespoon lemon juice, freshly squeezed
1 cup tomatoes, diced
1-pound (454-g) cod fillets, cut into chunks
1 cup water
¼ cup cilantro, chopped

Instructions:
1. Place a heavy bottomed pot on medium high fire and heat pot for 2 minutes. Add oil and heat for 1 minute.
2. Sauté the onion, garlic, and ginger until fragrant.
3. Stir in the cumin, coriander, cardamom, turmeric, salt, and pepper. Sauté for 1 minute.
4. Pour in the rest of the ingredients and mix well.
5. Cover and bring to a boil. Once boiling, lower fire to a simmer and simmer for 10 minutes.
6. Adjust seasoning to taste and continue cooking for another 5 minutes.
7. Serve and enjoy.

Per Serving

calories: 114 | fat: 5g | protein: 12g | carbs: 5g | fiber: 1g | sugar: 2g | sodium: 234mg

Asian Poached Cod

Prep time: 10 minutes | Cook time: 6 minutes | Serves 4

1-pound (454-g) cod, cut into chunks
6 tablespoons water
5 tablespoons soy sauce
1 thumb-size ginger, cut into thin strips
4 garlic cloves, minced
1 tablespoon sesame oil
¾ teaspoon red pepper flakes
¼ teaspoon Chinese five spice powder

1. Place a heavy bottomed pot on medium high fire and heat pot for 2 minutes. Add oil and heat for 1 minute.
2. Sauté the garlic and ginger until fragrant.
3. Stir in red pepper flakes and Chinese five spice. Sauté for 1 minute.
4. Pour in the rest of the ingredients and toss well.
5. Cover and bring to a boil. Boil for 2 minutes and then turn off fire and let it sit untouched for 5 minutes.
6. Serve and enjoy.

Per Serving

calories: 175 | fat: 8g | protein: 19g | carbs: 7g | fiber: 1g | sugar: 4g | sodium: 646mg

Lemon Sardines with Olives

Prep time: 10 minutes | Cook time: 14 minutes | Serves 2

10 sardines, scaled and cleaned (8 if large)
Zest of 2 whole lemons
Handful of flat-leaf parsley, chopped
2 garlic cloves, finely chopped
½ cup black olives (pitted and halved)
3 tablespoons olive oil
1 can chopped tomatoes (optional)
½ can chickpeas or butter beans, drained and rinsed
8 cherry tomatoes, halved (optional)
Pinch of black pepper

1. In a bowl, add the lemon zest to the chopped parsley (save 1 pinch for garnishing) and half of the chopped garlic, ready for later.
2. Put a very large skillet on the hob over high heat.
3. Now add the oil and once very hot, lay the sardines flat on the pan.
4. Saute for 3 minutes until golden underneath and turn over to fry for another 3 minutes. Place onto a plate to rest.
5. Sauté the remaining garlic (add another splash of oil if you need to) for 1 minute until softened. Pour in the tin of chopped tomatoes, mix and let simmer for 4 to 5 minutes.
6. If you're avoiding tomatoes, just avoid this step and go straight to chickpeas.
7. Tip in the chickpeas or butter beans and fresh tomatoes and stir until heated through.
8. Here's when you add the sardines into the lemon and parsley dressing prepared earlier and add to the pan, cooking for a further 3 to 4 minutes.
9. Once heated through, serve with 1 pinch of parsley and remaining lemon zest to garnish.

Per Serving

calories: 454 | fat: 32g | protein: 21g | carbs: 23g | fiber: 8g | sugar: 6g | sodium: 580mg

Baked Spicy Cod

Prep time: 10 minutes | Cook time: 15 minutes | Serves 5

2 tablespoons plain non-fat yogurt
1 teaspoon ginger, grated
2 tablespoons curry powder
1 teaspoon soy sauce
1 teaspoon rice wine vinegar
2½ teaspoons cayenne pepper
5 cod fillets
2 tablespoons olive oil

1. In a shallow dish mix all ingredients except for oil. Let fish sit in marinade for at least 1 hour.
2. When ready, lightly grease cookie sheet with oil and preheat oven to 400°F (205°C).
3. Once preheated, place cod filets on prepped cookie sheet and bake to desired doneness, around 15 minutes baking time.
4. Serve and enjoy.

Per Serving

calories: 254 | fat: 8g | protein: 42g | carbs: 2g | fiber: 1.6g | sugar: 0.5g | sodium: 144mg

Salmon in Parchment

Prep time: 5 minutes | Cook time: 15 minutes | Serves 2

2 potatoes, peeled and sliced
10 spears asparagus
2 (6 ounces / 170 g) skinless salmon fillets
Salt and pepper, to taste
1 tablespoon lemon juice, freshly squeezed
1 teaspoon olive oil

1. Place a steamer basket inside your pot and pour water up to an inch high. Bring to a boil.
2. In a large parchment paper, layer the potatoes and asparagus.
3. Place the salmon on top and season with salt and pepper.
4. Drizzle with lemon juice and olive oil.
5. Fold over the parchment paper to create a pocket and seal off the edges by crimping.
6. Place the parchment paper inside the steamer basket.
7. Close the lid and steam fish for 15 minutes. Turn off fire and let fish sit for another 5 minutes.
8. Serve and enjoy.

Per Serving

calories: 369 | fat: 9g | protein: 39g | carbs: 33g | fiber: 5g | sugar: 3g | sodium: 97mg

Portuguese Cod Casserole

Prep time: 10 minutes | Cook time: 10 minutes | Serves 5

2 tablespoons olive oil
2 garlic cloves, minced
3 large onions, sliced
2 pounds (907 g) cod fish, sliced into strips
4 potatoes, peeled and sliced
1 teaspoon paprika
¼ cup tablespoons tomato sauce
¼ cup water
1½ teaspoons crushed pepper flakes
1 tablespoon chopped parsley

1. Place a heavy bottomed pot on medium high fire and heat pot for 2 minutes. Add oil and heat for 1 minute.
2. Sauté the garlic and onions until fragrant.
3. Stir in the cod slices and add the rest of the ingredients.
4. Season with salt and pepper, to taste.
5. Cover and bring to a boil. Boil for 2 minutes and then lower fire to a simmer. Simmer for 5 minutes. Turn off fire and let it sit untouched for 5 minutes.
6. Serve and enjoy.

Per Serving

calories: 337 | fat: 6g | protein: 32g | carbs: 37g | fiber: 6g | sugar: 7g | sodium: 747mg

Salmon with Lemon

Prep time: 5 minutes | Cook time: 20 minutes | Serves 4

1-pound (454-g) salmon fillets
2 tablespoons olive oil
5 tablespoons lemon juice, freshly squeezed
1 tablespoon fresh dill, chopped
¼ teaspoon garlic powder
Salt and pepper, to taste

7. Place a trivet or steamer basket inside your pot and pour water up to an inch high. Bring to a boil.
8. Place the salmon fillets in a baking dish that will fit in the Pot.
9. Pour over the rest of the ingredients. Mix well and cover dish securely with foil.
10. Place the baking dish on the steam rack.
11. Close the lid and steam fish for 15 minutes. Turn off fire and let fish sit for another 5 minutes.
12. Serve and enjoy.

Per Serving

calories: 320 | fat: 22.1g | protein: 25.7g | carbs: 2.4g | fiber: 1.7g | sugar: 0g | sodium: 197mg

Steamed Lemon Pepper Salmon

Prep time: 5 minutes | Cook time: 20 minutes | Serves 4

4 salmon fillets
2 tablespoons olive oil
2 tablespoons soy sauce
1 teaspoon lemon juice
Salt and pepper, to taste

1. Place a trivet or steamer basket inside your pot and pour water up to an inch high. Bring to a boil.
2. Place the salmon fillets in a baking dish that will fit in the Pot.
3. Pour over the rest of the ingredients. Mix well and cover dish securely with foil.
4. Place the baking dish on the steam rack.
5. Close the lid and steam fish for 15 minutes. Turn off fire and let fish sit for another 5 minutes.
6. Serve and enjoy.

Per Serving

calories: 239 | fat:16.7g | protein: 20.2g | carbs: 0.9g | fiber: 0.3g | sugar: 0g | sodium: 892mg

Minted Salmon

Prep time: 10 minutes | Cook time: 9 minutes | Serves 4

2 tablespoons olive oil
4 garlic cloves, minced
1 bunch fresh mint, stems removed
1 bunch flat-leaf parsley
½ cup lemon juice, freshly squeezed
2 tablespoons honey
1 teaspoon salt
1 teaspoon ground black pepper
4 (6 ounces / 170 g) salmon fillets

1. In a food processor, pulse the olive oil, garlic, mint, parsley, lemon juice, honey, salt, and pepper until smooth.
2. Place a heavy bottomed pan on medium high fire and heat pot for 2 minutes.
3. Add sauce and fish. Sauté for 2 to 3 minutes.
4. Add a splash of water and turn fish over. Continue cooking for another 2 minutes or until fish is pink.
5. Turn off fire and leave fish untouched and covered for 3 minutes to continue cooking.
6. Serve and enjoy.
7. Sauté the until fragrant.

Per Serving

calories: 309 | fat: 13g | protein: 35g | carbs: 12g | fiber: 0.4g | sugar: 9.4g | sodium: 668mg

Miso Salmon and Asian Sesame

Prep time: 10 minutes | Cook time: 14 minutes | Serves 6

2½ pounds (1134 g) salmon fillets, skin removed
1 cup miso paste
2 tablespoons sesame seeds
1 teaspoon sesame oil
¼ cup water
1 thumb-size ginger, grated
3 tablespoons rice wine vinegar

1. Place a heavy bottomed pot on medium high fire and heat pot for 2 minutes.
2. Add all ingredients and mix well.
3. Cover and bring to a boil. Boil for 2 minutes and then lower fire to a simmer. Simmer for 10 minutes.
4. Serve and enjoy.

Per Serving

calories: 343 | fat: 12g | protein: 44g | carbs: 12g | fiber: 3g | sugar: 3g | sodium: 1805mg

Orange Herbed Sauced White Bass

Prep time: 10 minutes | Cook time: 33 minutes | Serves 6

1½ tablespoons fresh lemon juice
¼ cup thinly sliced green onions
½ cup orange juice
3 tablespoons chopped fresh dill
6 (3 ounces / 85 g) skinless white bass fillets
1½ tablespoons olive oil
1 large onion, halved, thinly sliced
1 large orange, unpeeled, sliced
Additional unpeeled orange slices

1. Grease a 13-inch by 9-inch glass baking dish and preheat oven to 400°F (205°C).
2. Arrange orange slices in single layer on baking dish, top with onion slices, seasoned with pepper and salt plus drizzled with oil.
3. Pop in the oven and roast for 25 minutes or until onions are tender and browned.
4. Remove from oven and increased oven temperature to 450°F (235°C).
5. Push onion and orange slices on sides of dish and place bass fillets in middle of dish. Season with 1½ tablespoons dill, pepper and salt. Arrange onions and orange slices on top of fish and pop into the oven.
6. Roast for 8 minutes or until salmon is opaque and flaky.
7. In a small bowl, mix 1½ tablespoons dill, lemon juice, green onions and orange juice.
8. Transfer salmon to a serving plate, discard roasted onions, drizzle with the newly made orange sauce and garnish with fresh orange slices.
9. Serve and enjoy.

Per Serving

calories: 159 | fat: 6g | protein: 17g | carbs: 10g | fiber: 2g | sugar: 5g | sodium: 62mg

Pecan Crusted Trout

Prep time: 10 minutes | Cook time: 10 minutes | Serves 4

1 egg, beaten
4 (4 ounces / 113 g) trout fillets
Whole wheat flour, as needed
Black pepper, to taste
1 teaspoon salt
1 teaspoon crush dried rosemary
½ teaspoon grated fresh ginger
½ cup crushed pecans
cooking spray

1. Grease baking sheet lightly with cooking spray and preheat oven to 400°F (205°C).
2. In a shallow bowl, combine black pepper, salt, rosemary and pecans. In another shallow bowl, add whole wheat flour. In a third bowl, add beaten egg.
3. To prepare fish, dip in flour until covered well. Shake off excess flour. Then dip into beaten egg until coated well. Let excess egg drip off before dipping trout fillet into pecan crumbs. Press the trout lightly onto pecan crumbs to make it stick to the fish.
4. Place breaded fish onto prepared pan. Repeat process for remaining fillets.
5. Pop into the oven and bake for 10 to 12 minutes or until fish is flaky.

Per Serving
calories: 247 | fat: 14g | protein: 26g | carbs: 4g | fiber: 2g | sugar: 1g | sodium: 633mg

Seared Scallops with Honey

Prep time: 10 minutes | Cook time: 11 minutes | Serves 4

1 pound (454 g) large scallops, rinsed and patted dry
Dash sea salt
Dash freshly ground black pepper
2 tablespoons avocado oil
¼ cup raw honey
3 tablespoons coconut aminos
1 tablespoon apple cider vinegar
2 garlic cloves, minced

1. In a bowl, add the scallops, sea salt, and pepper and toss until coated well.
2. In a large skillet, heat the avocado oil over medium-high heat.
3. Sear the scallops for 2 to 3 minutes on each side, or until the scallops turn milky white or opaque and firm.
4. Remove the scallops from the heat to a plate and loosely tent with foil to keep warm. Set aside.
5. Add the honey, coconut aminos, vinegar, and garlic to the skillet and stir well.
6. Bring to a simmer and cook for about 7 minutes until the liquid is reduced, stirring occasionally.
7. Return the seared scallops to the skillet, stirring to coat them with the glaze.
8. Divide the scallops among four plates and serve warm.

Per Serving
calories: 382 | fat: 19g | protein: 21g | carbs: 26g | fiber: 1g | sugar: 18g | sodium: 496mg

THE ULTIMATE ANTI-INFLAMMATORY DIET COOKBOOK

Oysters on the Shell

Prep time: 5 minutes | Cook time: 3 minutes | Serves 4

24 medium oysters
2 lemons
Tabasco sauce

1. If you are a newbie when it comes to eating oysters, then I suggest that you blanch the oysters before eating.
2. For some, eating oysters raw is a great way to enjoy this dish because of the consistency and juiciness of raw oysters. Plus, adding lemon juice prior to eating the raw oysters cooks it a bit.
3. So, to blanch oysters, bring a big pot of water to a rolling boil. Add oysters in batches of 6-10 pieces. Leave on boiling pot of water between 3 to 5 minutes and remove oysters right away.
4. To eat oysters, squeeze lemon juice on oyster on shell, add tabasco as desired and enjoy.

Per Serving

calories: 250 | fat: 7g | protein: 29g | carbs: 17g | fiber: 0.6g | sugar: 0.2g | sodium: 409mg

Breaded and Spiced Halibut

Prep time: 10 minutes | Cook time: 10 minutes | Serves 4

4 (6 ounces / 170 g) halibut fillets
¼ teaspoon ground black pepper
1 teaspoon sea salt
1 teaspoon finely grated lemon zest
1 tablespoon extra-virgin olive oil
¼ cup chopped fresh chives
¼ cup chopped fresh dill
1/3 cup chopped fresh parsley
¾ cup panko breadcrumbs

1. Line a baking sheet with foil, grease with cooking spray and preheat oven to 400°F (205°C).
2. In a small bowl, mix black pepper, sea salt, lemon zest, olive oil, chives, dill, parsley and breadcrumbs. If needed add more salt to taste. Set aside.
3. Meanwhile, wash halibut fillets on cold tap water. Dry with paper towels and place on prepared baking sheet.
4. Generously spoon crumb mixture onto halibut fillets. Ensure that fillets are covered with crumb mixture. Press down on crumb mixture onto each fillet.
5. Pop into the oven and bake for 10 to 15 minutes or until fish is flaky and crumb topping are already lightly browned.

Per Serving

calories: 334 | fat: 25g | protein: 25g | carbs: 1g | fiber: 0.3g | sugar: 0.2g | sodium: 751mg

Baked Salmon with Greens

Prep time: 10 minutes | Cook time: 10 minutes | Serves 2

1 tablespoon red-wine vinegar
1 tablespoon extra-virgin olive oil
Pepper and salt, to taste
¼ cup red onion, sliced thinly
⅔ cup cherry tomatoes, halved
3 cups baby arugula leaves
1½ tablespoons olive oil
1½ tablespoons fresh lemon juice
2 (6 ounces / 170 g) center cut salmon fillets

1. In a shallow bowl, mix pepper, salt, 1½ tablespoons olive oil and lemon juice. Toss in salmon fillets and rub with the marinade. Allow to marinate for at least 15 minutes.
2. Grease a baking sheet and preheat oven to 350°F (180°C).
3. Bake marinated salmon fillet for 10 to 12 minutes or until flaky with skin side touching the baking sheet.
4. Meanwhile, in a salad bowl mix onion, tomatoes and arugula.
5. Season with pepper and salt. Drizzle with vinegar and oil. Toss to combine and serve right away with baked salmon on the side.

Per Serving

calories: 565 | fat: 36g | protein: 46g | carbs: 13g | fiber: 2g | sugar: 9g | sodium: 179mg

Oysters Rockefeller

Prep time: 15 minutes | Cook time: 5 minutes | Serves 8

36 oysters on the half shell
Pepper and salt, to taste
1 pinch cayenne pepper
2 tablespoons anise-flavored liqueur, like Pernod
2 tablespoons chopped fresh parsley
2 tablespoons chopped fresh tarragon
2 tablespoons chopped celery
2 tablespoons minced green onion
¼ cup breadcrumbs
½ cup olive oil, room temperature
1 cup chopped watercress
2 teaspoons salt

1. In a large casserole dish, pour salt rock. Preheat oven to 500°F (260°C).
2. In food processor mix anise-flavored liqueur, Italian parsley, tarragon, celery, green onions, breadcrumbs, olive oil, cayenne pepper and watercress. Blend well until smooth and creamy. Season with pepper and salt, to taste.
3. On top of casserole dish with rock salt, place 8 to 12 oysters on a half shell. Evenly place a teaspoonful of the processed mixture on top of each oyster. Pop in the oven and bake for 5 minutes or until oysters are firm.
4. Repeat process to the next batch of oysters until all are cooked. Serve oysters right away while still hot.

Per Serving

calories: 312 | fat: 19g | protein: 22g | carbs: 13g | fiber: 0.5g | sugar: 0.4g | sodium: 825mg

Smoked Herring Sandwich

Prep time: 10 minutes | Cook time: 0 minutes | Serves 4

6 ounces (170 g) can kipper, drained
⅛ teaspoon pepper
⅛ teaspoon salt
1 garlic clove, minced
1 teaspoon lemon juice
1 tablespoon chopped fresh parsley
1 celery stalk, finely chopped
1 small onion, finely chopped
½ cup reduced fat mayonnaise
8 lettuce leaves
4 slices of multi-grain bread

1. Mix pepper, salt, garlic, lemon juice, parsley, celery, onion and mayonnaise in a medium bowl. Combine well.
2. Add drained kippers and mix well.
3. To assemble sandwich, cut each slice of bread diagonally to form a triangle. On one slice, add 1 lettuce leaf, slather with 2 tablespoons of kipper mixture, top with another lettuce and cover with another triangular slice of bread.
4. Repeat process to remaining bread slices.
5. Serve and enjoy.

Per Serving

calories: 278 | fat: 18g | protein: 15g | carbs: 14g | fiber: 2.5g | sugar: 2.7g | sodium: 346mg

Roasted Salmon Garden Salad

Prep time: 10 minutes | Cook time: 8 minutes | Serves 3

7 teaspoons olive oil, divided
3 tablespoons apple cider vinegar
1 cup diced fennel bulb
1 cup diced red onions
1 cup cucumber, peeled and diced
½ pound (227 g) salmon
Pepper and salt, to taste

1. Preheat oven to 400°F (205°C).
2. Grease a small baking dish with 1 teaspoon olive oil. Place salmon with skin side down and season with pepper and salt. Pop in preheated oven and bake for 8 minutes or until salmon is flaky.
3. Remove salmon from oven. Coarsely flake salmon with two forks and discard skin of salmon. Let it cool.
4. Meanwhile, in a large salad bowl whisk well remaining olive oil and vinegar. Toss in fennel, onions, cooled salmon and cucumber. Toss to coat well and serve.

Per Serving

calories: 196 | fat: 9g | protein: 18g | carbs: 12g | fiber: 4g | sugar: 6g | sodium: 372mg

Tuna Caprese Open-Faced Flatbread

Prep time: 10 minutes | Cook time: 0 minutes | Serves 1

1 whole flatbread, whole wheat or gluten-free
½ cup spinach leaves
4 medium basil leaves
1 packet StarKist Selects Wild-Caught Yellowfin Tuna in E.V.O.O
½ whole avocado, sliced
4 small cherry tomatoes, diced
1 ounce (28 g) mozzarella cheese, diced
1 tablespoon balsamic glaze
Salt and pepper, to taste

1. Lay flatbread on a plate.
2. Evenly spread basil and spinach leaves on top of bread.
3. Spread avocado and tomato slices on top of the greens.
4. Add the packet of tuna on top and spread evenly.
5. Drizzle balsamic. Sprinkle cheese. Season with pepper and salt.
6. Serve and enjoy.

Per Serving

calories: 442 | fat: 18g | protein: 29g | carbs: 48g | fiber: 15g | sugar: 10g | sodium: 709mg

Tuna-Avo Boat Salad

Prep time: 15 minutes | Cook time: 0 minutes | Serves 2

2 tablespoons 0% plain Greek yogurt
4 teaspoons apple cider vinegar
1 teaspoon curry powder
¼ teaspoon salt
1 medium pinch ground cinnamon
5-ounce can solid white albacore, drained and flaked
¼ cup finely diced carrot
4 teaspoons chopped toasted cashews
2 tablespoons roughly chopped raisins
1 tablespoon chopped red onion
1 medium avocado, sliced in half and seed removed
2 teaspoons chopped parsley

1. Mix well cinnamon, salt, curry, vinegar, and yogurt in a medium bowl. Whisk in tuna and mix well.
2. Add remaining ingredients in bowl except for parsley and avocado. Mix thoroughly and adjust seasoning, to taste.
3. Evenly divide the tuna mixture inside the avocado hole left by the seed.
4. To enjoy, scoop out avocado flesh along with the tuna mixture with each bite.

Per Serving

calories: 241 | fat: 13g | protein: 18g | carbs: 18g | fiber: 6g | sugar: 8g | sodium: 491mg

Tuna & Sun-Dried Tomato-Wich

Prep time: 10 minutes | Cook time: 0 minutes | Serves 1

1 whole flat bread
½ whole avocado
1 packet StarKist Selects Wild Caught Yellowfin Tuna Sun Dried Tomato in E.V.O.O
¼ cup sprouts or microgreens
1 tablespoon hemp seeds
½ whole lemon, juiced
Salt and pepper, to taste

1. In a small bowl, mash avocado, hemp seeds and lemon juice. Lightly season with pepper and salt.
2. Lay flatbread on a plate.
3. Evenly spread avocado mixture on top of bread.
4. Add the packet of tuna on top and spread evenly.
5. Spread sprouts on top.
6. Serve and enjoy.

Per Serving

calories: 490 | fat: 31g | protein: 34g | carbs: 23g | fiber: 7g | sugar: 3g | sodium: 201mg

Grilled Salmon-Lettuce Wraps

Prep time: 15 minutes | Cook time: 6 minutes | Serves 6

¼ cup Avocado Sauce recipe link here
2 (6 ounces / 170 g) fresh salmon fish fillets
1 head of butter lettuce
2 cup coleslaw mix or shredded cabbage
¼ cup fresh cilantro leaves, chopped
1 lime, juiced
Salt and pepper, to taste
Avocado Sauce Ingredients:
½ avocado, pitted
½ cup cilantro, fresh
½ Jalapeño, seeded, to taste
½ cup low fat mayo
¼ cup water
2 tablespoons lime juice, fresh, to taste
1 garlic clove
½ teaspoon Salt

1. In a blender, puree all avocado sauce ingredients. Adjust seasoning to taste and puree again. Transfer to a bowl and refrigerate until ready to use.
2. Preheat grill to medium high and lightly grease grate.
3. Season fish with pepper and salt to taste. Grill fish for 3 to 4 minutes per side. Transfer to a bowl and shred.
4. In bowl of fish, add shredded cabbage, juice of lime and mix well. If needed, adjust seasoning to taste.
5. To serve, slowly separate butter lettuce into one huge leaf. In one leaf, place a good amount of the salmon filling and a dollop of the avocado sauce. Roll leaf and enjoy.

Per Serving

calories: 247 | fat: 10g | protein: 31g | carbs: 9g | fiber: 3g | sugar: 5g | sodium: 488mg

Black Bean and Salmon Salad

Prep time: 15 minutes | Cook time: 0 minutes | Serves 4

2 (5 ounces / 142 g) cans wild salmon (skinless/boneless), drained and flaked
1 (15-ounce / 425-g) can black beans or lentils, drained and rinsed
1 garlic clove, minced
¼ cup scallions, minced
¼ cup celery, finely minced
1 tomato or 1cup cherry tomatoes, diced
½ lime, juiced
¼ teaspoon. sea salt
1 jalapeño, finely minced, ribs and seeds removed
¼ cup fresh cilantro, roughly chopped
1½ tablespoons ground flaxseed
Salad Ingredients:
4 cup Spinach leaves
4 teaspoons extra virgin olive oil
1 avocado, diced

1. In a large bowl, add all ingredients and mix well. Let it rest for 10 minutes to let the flavors meld. Mix once again.
2. Evenly divide spinach leaves on to 4 salad bowls.
3. Evenly divide salmon mixture on to each bowl.
4. Top with diced avocado and drizzle with olive oil.
5. Serve and enjoy.

Per Serving

calories: 433 | fat: 21g | protein: 41g | carbs: 23g | fiber: 11g | sugar: 2g | sodium: 727mg

Easy and Healthy Tuna Salad

Prep time: 10 minutes | Cook time: 0 minutes | Serves 2

5 ounces (142 g) olive oil packed tuna, drained
1 tablespoon fresh chopped basil
½ stalk celery, minced
1 finely chopped scallion - green part only
2 tablespoons lemon juice, or more to taste
Extra virgin olive oil, to taste
Salt and pepper, to taste
6 large leaves of Boston Bibb Lettuce

1. Mix all ingredients in a bowl except for the lettuce.
2. Adjust seasoning if needed and mix well once more.
3. Evenly divide lettuce leaves on two plates.
4. Evenly divide tuna salad on top of the leaves.
5. Serve and enjoy.

Per Serving

calories: 209 | fat: 11g | protein: 20g | carbs: 3g | fiber: 2g | sugar: 0g | sodium: 260mg

Fresh Tomato 'n Tuna Salad Sandwich

Prep time: 10 minutes | Cook time: 0 minutes | Serves 3

½ cup celery (finely chopped)
2 (5 ounces / 142 g) can tuna in water (drained)
2 teaspoons whole grain mustard
¼ cup light mayonnaise
½ teaspoon turmeric
Salt and pepper, to taste
3 Whole pita bread
1 avocado, peeled, pitted and sliced
2 roma tomatoes sliced

1. Mix all ingredients in a bowl except for the pita bread, avocado and tomatoes.
2. Adjust seasoning if needed and mix well once more.
3. Evenly divide tuna salad on top of each pita bread.
4. Top evenly by avocado and tomato slices. Fold pita bread in half to form half-moons.
5. Serve and enjoy.

Per Serving

calories: 323 | fat: 10.1g | protein: 30.1g | carbs: 26.8g | fiber: 4.9g | sugar: 4.9g | sodium: 433mg

Whitefish and Tomato Stew

Prep time: 15 minutes | Cook time: 15 minutes | Serves 4

1 tablespoon extra-virgin olive oil, plus additional as needed
1 white onion, sliced thin
1 fennel bulb, sliced thin
2 garlic cloves, minced
1 (28-ounce / 794-g) can crushed tomatoes
Pinch saffron threads
1 teaspoon ground cumin
1 teaspoon ground oregano
1 teaspoon salt
½ teaspoon freshly ground black pepper
2 pounds (907 g) firm whitefish fillets, cut into 2-inch pieces
2 tablespoons chopped fresh parsley
½ lemon, for garnish

1. In a large pot or pan over medium-high heat, heat 1 tablespoon of olive oil. Add the onion, fennel, and garlic. Sauté for 5 minutes.
2. Stir in the crushed tomatoes, saffron threads, cumin, oregano, salt, and pepper. Bring the mixture to a simmer.
3. Lay the fish fillets in a single layer over the vegetables, cover the pan, and simmer for 10 minutes.
4. Transfer the fish and vegetables to a serving platter. Garnish with the parsley, a drizzle of olive oil, and a generous squeeze of lemon juice.

Per Serving

calories: 535 | fat: 21g | protein: 62g | carbs: 24g | fiber: 9g | sugar: 12g | sodium: 944mg

Salmon Quinoa with Cherry Tomatoes

Prep time: 10 minutes | Cook time: 24 minutes | Serves 4

1 tablespoon extra-virgin olive oil, plus additional for brushing
1 pound (454 g) salmon fillets
Salt
Freshly ground black pepper
1 red onion, diced
2 cups cooked quinoa
1 pint cherry tomatoes, halved
½ cup chopped fresh basil
¼ cup chopped green olives
1 tablespoon apple cider vinegar

1. Preheat the oven to 375°F (190°C).
2. Brush a rimmed baking sheet with olive oil. Place the salmon fillets on the prepared sheet and brush the top of each with olive oil. Season with salt and pepper.
3. Place the sheet in the preheated oven and bake for 20 minutes.
4. In a large pan over medium-high heat, heat 1 tablespoon of olive oil. Add the onion and sauté for 3 minutes.
5. Stir in the quinoa, cherry tomatoes, basil, olives, and cider vinegar. Cook for 1 to 2 minutes, or until the tomatoes and quinoa are warmed through.
6. Transfer the tomatoes, quinoa, and salmon to a serving platter and serve.

Per Serving

calories: 396 | fat: 16g | protein: 30g | carbs: 36g | fiber: 6g | sugar: 4g | sodium: 395mg

Trout Fillets with Chard and Raisins

Prep time: 10 minutes | Cook time: 15 minutes | Serves 4

4 boneless trout fillets
Salt
Freshly ground black pepper
1 tablespoon extra-virgin olive oil
1 onion, chopped
2 garlic cloves, minced
2 bunches chard, sliced
¼ cup golden raisins
1 tablespoon apple cider vinegar
½ cup vegetable broth

1. Preheat the oven to 375°F (190°C).
2. Season the trout with salt and pepper.
3. In a large oven-proof pan over medium-high heat, heat the olive oil. Add the onion and garlic. Sauté for 3 minutes; add the chard and sauté for 2 minutes more.
4. Add the raisins, cider vinegar, and broth to the pan. Layer the trout fillets on top. Cover the pan and place it in the preheated oven for about 10 minutes, or until the trout is cooked through.

Per Serving

calories: 231 | fat: 10g | protein: 24g | carbs: 13g | fiber: 2g | sugar: 7g | sodium: 235mg

Pecan-Crusted Trout with Thyme

Prep time: 10 minutes | Cook time: 15 minutes | Serves 4

Extra virgin olive oil, for brushing
4 large boneless trout fillets
Salt
Freshly ground black pepper
1 cup pecans, finely ground, divided
1 tablespoon coconut oil, melted, divided
2 tablespoons chopped fresh thyme leaves
Lemon wedges, for garnish

1. Preheat the oven to 375°F (190°C).
2. Brush a rimmed baking sheet with olive oil.
3. Place the trout fillets on the baking sheet skin-side down. Season with salt and pepper.
4. Gently press ¼ cup of ground pecans into the flesh of each fillet.
5. Drizzle the melted coconut oil over the nuts and then sprinkle the thyme over the fillets.
6. Give each fillet another sprinkle of salt and pepper.
7. Place the sheet in the preheated oven and bake for 15 minutes, or until the fish is cooked through.

Per Serving

calories: 672 | fat: 59g | protein: 30g | carbs: 13g | fiber: 9g | sugar: 3g | sodium: 110mg

Sea Bass with Spinach and Olives

Prep time: 10 minutes | Cook time: 15 minutes | Serves 4

2 tablespoons extra virgin olive oil
4 (5-ounce / 142-g) sea bass fillets
1 small onion, diced
½ cup vegetable or chicken broth
1 cup canned diced tomatoes
½ cup pitted and chopped Kalamata olives
2 tablespoons capers, drained
2 cups packed spinach
1 teaspoon salt
¼ teaspoon freshly ground black pepper

1. Preheat the oven to 375°F (190°C).
2. In a baking dish, add the olive oil. Place the fish fillets in the dish, turning to coat both sides with the oil.
3. Top the fish with the onion, vegetable broth, tomatoes, olives, capers, spinach, salt, and pepper.
4. Cover the baking dish with aluminum foil and place it in the preheated oven.
5. Bake for 15 minutes, or until the fish is cooked through.

Per Serving

calories: 273 | fat: 12g | protein: 35g | carbs: 5g | fiber: 2g | sugar: 2g | sodium: 938mg

Sole and Veggie Bake

Prep time: 10 minutes | Cook time: 15 minutes | Serves 4

4 (5-ounce / 142-g) sole fillets
Salt
Freshly ground black pepper
1 zucchini, sliced thin, divided
1 carrot, sliced thin, divided
2 shallots, sliced thin, divided
2 tablespoons snipped fresh chives, divided
4 teaspoons extra-virgin olive oil, divided
½ cup vegetable broth, or water, divided
Lemon wedges, for garnish

1. Preheat the oven to 425°F (220°C).
2. Tear off 4 pieces of aluminum foil.
3. Place 1 fillet on one half of a foil piece. Season with salt and pepper.
4. Top the fillet with one-quarter each of the zucchini, carrot, and shallots. Sprinkle with 1½ teaspoons of chives.
5. Drizzle 1 teaspoon of olive oil and 2 tablespoons of vegetable broth over the vegetables and fish.
6. Fold the other half of the foil over the fish and vegetables, sealing the edges so the ingredients are completely encased in the packet and the contents won't leak. Place the packet on a large baking sheet.
7. Repeat steps 3 through 6 with the remaining ingredients.
8. Place the sheet in the preheated oven and bake the packets for 15 minutes, or until the fish is cooked through and the vegetables are tender.
9. Carefully peel back the foil (the escaping steam will be hot) and transfer the contents with the liquid to a plate. Serve garnished with the lemon wedges.

Per Serving

calories: 224 | fat: 7g | protein: 35g | carbs: 4g | fiber: 1g | sugar: 2g | sodium: 205mg

Cilantro Swordfish with Pineapple

Prep time: 10 minutes | Cook time: 15 minutes | Serves 4

1 tablespoon coconut oil
2 pounds (907 g) swordfish, or other firm whitefish, cut into 2-inch pieces
1 cup fresh pineapple chunks
¼ cup chopped fresh cilantro
2 tablespoons chopped fresh parsley
2 garlic cloves, minced
1 tablespoon coconut aminos
1 teaspoon salt
¼ teaspoon freshly ground black pepper

1. Preheat the oven to 400°F (205°C).
2. Grease a baking dish with the coconut oil.
3. Add the swordfish, pineapple, cilantro, parsley, garlic, coconut aminos, salt, and pepper to the dish. Gently mix the ingredients together.
4. Place the dish in the preheated oven and bake for 15 to 20 minutes, or until the fish feels firm to the touch. Serve warm.

Per Serving

calories: 408 | fat: 16g | protein: 60g | carbs: 7g | fiber: 1g | sugar: 4g | sodium: 858mg

Cod Fillets with Shiitake Mushrooms

Prep time: 10 minutes | Cook time: 20 minutes | Serves 4 to 6

1½ pounds (680 g) cod fillets
½ teaspoon salt, plus additional for seasoning
Freshly ground black pepper
1 tablespoon extra-virgin olive oil
1 leek, white part only, sliced thin
8 ounces (227 g) shiitake mushrooms, stemmed, sliced
1 tablespoon coconut aminos
1 teaspoon sweet paprika
½ cup vegetable broth, or chicken broth

1. Preheat the oven to 375°F (190°C).
2. Season the cod with salt and pepper. Set aside.
3. In a shallow baking dish, combine the olive oil, leek, mushrooms, coconut aminos, paprika, and ½ teaspoon of salt. Season with pepper and give everything a gentle toss to coat with the oil and spices.
4. Place the dish in the preheated oven and bake the vegetables for 10 minutes.
5. Stir the vegetables and place the cod fillets on top in a single layer.
6. Pour in the vegetable broth. Return the dish to the oven and bake for an additional 10 to 15 minutes, or until the cod is firm but cooked through.

Per Serving
calories: 221 | fat: 6g | protein: 32g | carbs: 12g | fiber: 2g | sugar: 3g | sodium: 637mg

Tuna Skewers with Sesame Seeds

Prep time: 5 minutes | Cook time: 10 minutes | Serves 4 to 6

Cooking spray
¾ cup sesame seeds (mixture of black and white)
1 teaspoon salt
½ teaspoon ground ginger
¼ teaspoon freshly ground black pepper
2 tablespoons toasted sesame oil, or extra-virgin olive oil
4 (6-ounce / 170-g) thick tuna steaks, cut into 1-inch cubes

1. Preheat the oven to 400°F (205°C).
2. Lightly coat a rimmed baking sheet with cooking spray.
3. Soak 12 (6-inch) wooden skewers in water so they won't burn while the tuna bakes.
4. In a shallow dish, combine the sesame seeds, salt, ground ginger, and pepper.
5. In a medium bowl, toss the tuna with the sesame oil to coat. Press the oiled cubes into the sesame seed mixture. Put three cubes on each skewer.
6. Place the skewers on the prepared baking sheet and place the sheet into the preheated oven. Bake for 10 to 12 minutes, turning once halfway through.

Per Serving
calories: 395 | fat: 22g | protein: 45g | carbs: 7g | fiber: 3g | sugar: 0g | sodium: 649mg

Lemon Salmon with Basil Gremolata

Prep time: 15 minutes | Cook time: 20 minutes | Serves 4

4 (5-ounce / 142-g) skin-on salmon fillets
1 tablespoon plus 2 teaspoons extra-virgin olive oil, divided
¼ cup freshly squeezed lemon juice
1 teaspoon salt, plus additional for seasoning
¼ teaspoon freshly ground black pepper, plus additional for seasoning
1 bunch basil
1 garlic clove
1 tablespoon lemon zest
1 (8-ounce / 227-g) bag mixed greens
1 small cucumber, halved lengthwise and sliced thin
1 cup sprouts (radish, onion, or sunflower)

1. Preheat the oven to 375°F (190°C).
2. In a shallow baking dish, place the salmon fillets and brush them with 2 teaspoons of olive oil.
3. Add the lemon juice. Season with 1 teaspoon of salt and ¼ teaspoon of pepper.
4. Place the dish in the preheated oven and bake the fillets for about 20 minutes, or until firm and cooked through.
5. In a food processor, combine the basil, garlic, and lemon zest. Process until coarsely chopped.
6. Arrange the greens, cucumber, and sprouts on a serving platter. Drizzle the greens with the remaining 2 tablespoons of olive oil and season with salt and pepper. Place the salmon fillets on top of the greens and spoon the gremolata over the salmon.

Per Serving
calories: 274 | fat: 12g | protein: 32g | carbs: 11g | fiber: 5g | sugar: 5g | sodium: 908mg

Baked Salmon with Fennel and Leek

Prep time: 10 minutes | Cook time: 20 minutes | Serves 4

1 tablespoon extra-virgin olive oil, plus additional for brushing
1 leek, white part only, sliced thin
1 fennel bulb, sliced thin
4 (5- to 6-ounce / 142- to 170-g) salmon fillets
1 teaspoon salt
¼ teaspoon freshly ground black pepper
½ cup vegetable broth, or water
1 fresh rosemary sprig

1. Preheat the oven to 375°F (190°C).
2. In a shallow roasting pan, add 1 tablespoon of olive oil. Add the leek and fennel. Stir to coat with the oil.
3. Place the salmon fillets over the vegetables and sprinkle with salt and pepper.
4. Pour in the vegetable broth and add the rosemary sprig to the pan. Cover tightly with aluminum foil.
5. Place the pan in the preheated oven and bake for 20 minutes, or until the salmon is cooked through.
6. Remove and discard the rosemary sprig. Transfer the salmon and vegetables to a platter and serve.

Per Serving
calories: 288 | fat: 14g | protein: 34g | carbs: 8g | fiber: 2g | sugar: 1g | sodium: 692mg

Baked Salmon Burger Patty

Prep time: 10 minutes | Cook time: 20 minutes | Serves 3

1-pound (454-g) salmon skin removed and chopped into cubes
1 tablespoon stone ground mustard
1 tablespoon avocado oil
1 teaspoon ground paprika
½ teaspoon sea salt
3 whole wheat flat bread
3 lettuce leaves
1 roma tomato sliced into 3 circles
3 onion rings

1. Preheat oven to 450°F (235°C).
2. Lightly grease a cookie sheet with cooking spray.
3. In a food processor, add salmon, mustard, oil, paprika, and salt. Process until you form a thick paste. Scraping sides and bottom.
4. Evenly divide mixture into three and form into equal patties.
5. Place on prepared sheet and bake for 20 minutes. Flip burger halfway through cooking time.
6. Assemble burger, serve and enjoy.

Per Serving

calories: 372 | fat: 15g | protein: 43g | carbs: 17g | fiber: 3g | sugar: 1g | sodium: 1097mg

Salmon with Oregano-Almond Pistou

Prep time: 10 minutes | Cook time: 18 minutes | Serves 3

Pistou:
1 cup fresh oregano leaves
¼ cup almonds
2 garlic cloves
Juice of 1 lime (1 or 2 tablespoons)
Zest of 1 lime (optional)
1 tablespoon olive oil
Pinch sea salt
Fish:
4 (6-ounce / 170-g) salmon fillets
Sea salt
Freshly ground black pepper
1 tablespoon olive oil

Make the Pistou
1. In a blender, combine the oregano, almonds, garlic, lime juice, lime zest (if using), olive oil, and sea salt. Pulse until very finely chopped. Transfer the pistou to a bowl and set it aside.
Make the Fish
2. Preheat the oven to 400°F (205°C).
3. Lightly season the salmon with sea salt and pepper.
4. Place a large oven-proof skillet over medium-high heat and add the olive oil.
5. Add the salmon and pan-sear for 4 minutes per side.
6. Place the skillet in the oven and bake the fish for about 10 minutes, or until it is just cooked through.
7. Serve the salmon topped with a spoonful of pistou.

Per Serving

calories: 458 | fat: 25g | protein: 49g | carbs: 8g | fiber: 4g | sugar: 1g | sodium: 276mg

Roasted Sole with Coconut-Saffron Sauce

Prep time: 10 minutes | Cook time: 18 minutes | Serves 4

2 tablespoons warm water
Pinch saffron threads
2 pounds (907 g) sole fillets
Sea salt
2 tablespoons freshly squeezed lemon juice
1 tablespoon coconut oil
1 sweet onion, chopped, or about 1 cup pre-cut packaged onion
2 teaspoons bottled minced garlic
1 teaspoon grated fresh ginger
1 cup canned full-fat coconut milk
2 tablespoons chopped fresh cilantro

1. Place the water in a small bowl and sprinkle the saffron threads on top. Let it stand for 10 minutes.
2. Preheat the oven to 350°F (180°C).
3. Rub the fish with sea salt and the lemon juice, and place the fillets in a baking dish. Roast the fish for 10 minutes.
4. While the fish is roasting, place a large skillet over medium-high heat and add the coconut oil.
5. Add the onion, garlic, and ginger. Sauté for about 3 minutes, or until softened.
6. Stir in the coconut milk and the saffron water. Bring to a boil. Reduce the heat to low and simmer the sauce for 5 minutes. Remove the skillet from the heat.
7. Pour the sauce over the fish. Cover and bake for about 10 minutes, or until the fish flakes easily with a fork.
8. Serve the fish topped with the cilantro.

Per Serving

calories: 349 | fat: 21g | protein: 30g | carbs: 7g | fiber: 2g | sugar: 4g | sodium: 725mg

Halibut Fillets with Avocado Salsa

Prep time: 10 minutes | Cook time: 14 minutes | Serves 4

Salsa:
1 avocado, peeled, pitted, and diced
½ mango, diced, or about 1 cup frozen chunks, thawed
½ cup chopped fresh strawberries
1 teaspoon chopped fresh mint
Juice of 1 lemon (3 tablespoons)
Zest of 1 lemon (optional)
Fish:
4 (6-ounce / 170-g) boneless, skinless halibut fillets, patted dry
Sea salt
Freshly ground black pepper
1 tablespoon olive oil

Make the Salsa
1. In a medium bowl, stir together the avocado, mango, strawberries, mint, lemon juice, and lemon zest (if using). Set it aside.
Make the Fish
2. Lightly season the halibut with sea salt and pepper.
3. Place a large skillet over medium heat and add the olive oil.
4. Add the fish and pan-fry for about 7 minutes per side, turning once, or until it is just cooked through.
5. Top with the avocado salsa and serve.

Per Serving
calories: 354 | fat: 15g | protein: 43g | carbs: 12g | fiber: 7g | sugar: 8g | sodium: 160mg

Salmon Patties with Lime and Scallion

Prep time: 10 minutes | Cook time: 10 minutes | Serves 4

½ pound (227 g) cooked boneless salmon fillet, flaked
2 eggs
¾ cup almond flour, plus more as needed
1 scallion, white and green parts, chopped
Juice of 2 limes (2 to 4 tablespoons), plus more as needed
Zest of 2 limes (optional)
1 tablespoon chopped fresh dill
Pinch sea salt
1 tablespoon olive oil
1 lime, cut into wedges

1. In a large bowl, mix together the salmon, eggs, almond flour, scallion, lime juice, lime zest (if using), dill, and sea salt until the mixture holds together when pressed. If the mixture is too dry, add more lime juice; if it is too wet, add more almond flour.
2. Divide the salmon mixture into 4 equal portions, and press them into patties about ½ inch thick. Refrigerate them for about 30 minutes to firm up.
3. Place a large skillet over medium-high heat and add the olive oil.
4. Add the salmon patties and brown for about 5 minutes per side, turning once.
5. Serve the patties with lime wedges.

Per Serving
calories: 243 | fat: 18g | protein: 18g | carbs: 5g | fiber: 2g | sugar: 1g | sodium: 123mg

Tilapia, Carrot and Parsnip Casserole

Prep time: 10 minutes | Cook time: 30 minutes | Serves 4

2 cups diced sweet potato
2 cups diced carrot
2 cups diced parsnip
1 sweet onion, cut into eighths
1 cup (2-inch) asparagus pieces
2 teaspoons chopped fresh thyme
1 teaspoon bottled minced garlic
¼ teaspoon sea salt
1 tablespoon olive oil
4 (6-ounce / 170-g) skinless tilapia fillets
Juice of 1 lemon (3 tablespoons)

1. Preheat the oven to 350°F (180°C).
2. Tear off 4 pieces of aluminum foil and fold each piece in half to make four 18-by-12-inch pieces.
3. In a large bowl, toss together the sweet potato, carrot, parsnip, onion, asparagus, thyme, garlic, sea salt, and olive oil. Place one-fourth of the vegetables in the center of each foil piece.
4. Top each vegetable mound with one tilapia fillet.
5. Sprinkle the fish with lemon juice.
6. Fold the foil to create sealed packages that have a bit of space at the top, and arrange the packets on a baking sheet.
7. Bake for about 30 minutes, or until the fish begins to flake and the vegetables are tender.
8. Carefully open the packets, plate, and serve.

Per Serving
calories: 353 | fat: 6g | protein: 36g | carbs: 43g | fiber: 9g | sugar: 13g | sodium: 323mg

Chipotle Trout with Spinach

Prep time: 10 minutes | Cook time: 15 minutes | Serves 4

Extra virgin olive oil, for brushing
½ red onion, thinly sliced
1 (10-ounce / 284-g) package frozen spinach, thawed
4 boneless trout fillets
1 teaspoon salt
¼ teaspoon chipotle powder
¼ teaspoon garlic powder
2 tablespoons fresh lemon juice

1. Preheat the oven to 375°F (190°C). Brush a baking pan with olive oil.
2. Scatter the red onion and spinach in the pan.
3. Lay the trout fillets over the spinach.
4. Sprinkle the salt, chipotle powder, and garlic powder over the fish.
5. Cover with aluminum foil and bake until the trout is firm, about 15 minutes.
6. Drizzle with the lemon juice and serve.

Per Serving
calories: 160 | fat: 7g | protein: 19g | carbs: 5g | fiber: 2g | sugar: 1g | sodium: 670mg

Sea Bass with Ginger and Chili
Prep time: 10 minutes | Cook time: 9 minutes | Serves 2

2 sea bass fillets
1 teaspoon black pepper
1 tablespoon extra-virgin olive oil
1 teaspoon ginger, peeled and chopped
1 garlic clove, thinly sliced
1 red chili, deseeded and thinly sliced
2 green onion stems, sliced

1. Get a skillet and heat the oil over medium-high heat.
2. Sprinkle black pepper over the Sea Bass and score the skin of the fish a few times with a sharp knife.
3. Add the sea bass fillet to the very hot pan with the skin side down.
4. Cook for 5 minutes and turn over.
5. Cook for a further 2 minutes.
6. Remove sea bass from the pan and rest.
7. Add the chili, garlic and ginger and cook for approximately 2 minutes or until golden.
8. Remove from the heat and add the green onions.
9. Scatter the vegetables over your sea bass to serve.
10. Try with a steamed sweet potato or side salad.

Per Serving
calories: 204 | fat: 10g | protein: 25g | carbs: 4g | fiber: 1g | sugar: 2g | sodium: 92mg

Caper-Lemon Trout with Shallots
Prep time: 10 minutes | Cook time: 26 minutes | Serves 2

Shallots:
2 shallots, thinly sliced
1 teaspoon ghee
Dash salt
Trout:
1 tablespoon plus 1 teaspoon ghee, divided
2 (4-ounce / 113-g) trout fillets
¼ cup freshly squeezed lemon juice
3 tablespoons capers
¼ teaspoon salt
Dash freshly ground black pepper
1 lemon, thinly sliced

Make the Shallots
1. In a large skillet over medium heat, cook the shallots, ghee, and salt for 20 minutes, stirring every 5 minutes, until the shallots have fully wilted and caramelized.
Make the Trout
2. While the shallots cook, in another large skillet over medium heat, heat 1 teaspoon of ghee.
3. Add the trout fillets. Cook for 3 minutes per side, or until the center is flaky. Transfer to a plate and set aside.
4. In the skillet used for the trout, add the lemon juice, capers, salt, and pepper. Bring to a simmer. Whisk in the remaining 1 tablespoon of ghee. Spoon the sauce over the fish.
5. Garnish the fish with the lemon slices and caramelized shallots before serving.

Per Serving
calories: 299 | fat: 22g | protein: 21g | carbs: 9g | fiber: 2g | sugar: 3g | sodium: 735mg

Almond-Crusted Trout
Prep time: 5 minutes | Cook time: 12 minutes | Serves 1

2 trout fillets
½ cup whole wheat breadcrumbs
1 tablespoon extra-virgin olive oil
½ cup fresh parsley, finely chopped
Zest and juice of 1 lemon
½ cup chopped almonds

1. Preheat the broiler to high heat.
2. Lightly oil a baking tray.
3. Mix the breadcrumbs, parsley, lemon zest and juice and half of the nuts together in a shallow dish.
4. Lay the fillets skin side down onto the oiled baking tray and then flip over so that both sides of your fish are coated in the oil.
5. Now, dip the fillets into the nut mixture on both sides to coat.
6. Return to the baking tray.
7. Broil for 6 to 7 minutes on each side and serve with a side salad or vegetables of your choice.

Per Serving
calories: 869 | fat: 51g | protein: 51g | carbs: 56g | fiber: 11g | sugar: 7g | sodium: 496mg

Lemon-Garlic Shrimp Paella
Prep time: 10 minutes | Cook time: 23 minutes | Serves 2

2 cups wild or basmati rice
4 cups water
12 whole shrimp, peeled, deveined and the tails still intact
2 garlic cloves, crushed
1 white onion, diced
2 tablespoons extra-virgin olive oil
½ teaspoon red pepper flakes
1 tablespoon parsley, crushed
1 lemon, juice and zest
1 lemon, cut into quarters

1. Add the rice and 4 cups of water to a saucepan and boil over high heat.
2. Once boiling, lower the heat, cover and simmer for 15 minutes.
3. Meanwhile, heat the oil in a skillet over medium heat and then sauté the onion, garlic and red pepper flakes for 5 minutes until softened and then add the shrimp.
4. Sauté for 5 to 8 minutes or until shrimp is opaque
5. Drain the rice and return to the heat for a further 3 minutes with the lid on.
6. Add the rice to the shrimps.
7. Add in the parsley, zest and juice of 1 lemon and mix well.
8. Serve in a wide paella dish if possible or a large serving dish—scatter the lemon wedges around the edge and sprinkle with a little more fresh parsley.
9. Season with black pepper to taste.

Per Serving
calories: 761 | fat: 16g | protein: 30g | carbs: 132g | fiber: 13g | sugar: 8g | sodium: 230mg

Tilapia and Kale with Nuts

Prep time: 10 minutes | Cook time: 5½ minutes | Serves 2

2 teaspoons extra-virgin olive oil
2 tablespoons low fat hard cheese, grated
½ cup roasted and ground Brazil nuts, hazelnuts or any other hard nuts
½ cup 100% whole-grain bread crumbs
2 tilapia fillets, skinless
2 teaspoons whole-grain mustard
1 head kale, chopped
1 tablespoon sesame seeds, lightly toasted
1 garlic clove, mashed

1. Preheat the oven to 350°F (180°C).
2. Lightly oil a baking sheet with 1 teaspoon extra-virgin olive oil.
3. Mix in the nuts, breadcrumbs, and cheese in a separate bowl.
4. Spread a thin layer of the mustard over the fish and then dip into the breadcrumb mixture.
5. Transfer to baking dish.
6. Bake for 12 minutes or until cooked through.
7. Meanwhile, heat 1 teaspoon oil in a skillet over medium heat and sauté the garlic for 30 seconds, adding in the kale for a further 5 minutes.
8. Mix in the sesame seeds.
9. Serve the fish at once with the kale on the side.

Per Serving
calories: 538 | fat: 33g | protein: 35g | carbs: 29g | fiber: 6g | sugar: 4g | sodium: 375mg

Lime Salmon with Arugula Salad

Prep time: 10 minutes | Cook time: 8 minutes | Serves 2

Fish:
2 skinless salmon fillets
1 tablespoon extra-virgin olive oil
½ fresh lime, juiced
Pinch of black pepper
Salad:
4 cups baby arugula leaves
1 cup grapes or cherry tomatoes, cut into halves
½ cup slivered red onion
1 tablespoon olive oil
1 tablespoon balsamic vinegar

1. In a bowl, coat the salmon with the olive oil, lime juice and pepper (if you can, leave for at least 15 minutes up to an hour but don't worry if not).
2. Heat the oil in a skillet over medium heat and cook the salmon skin-side for about 4 to 5 minutes each side or until completely cooked through.
3. Add the arugula, onion and tomatoes with oil and vinegar to a separate bowl and toss.
4. Serve the fish on the bed of salad.

Per Serving
calories: 568 | fat: 28g | protein: 67g | carbs: 9g | fiber: 2g | sugar: 5g | sodium: 257mg

Black Cod and Veggie Udon Broth

Prep time: 15 minutes | Cook time: 12 minutes | Serves 2

2 black cod fillets
Pinch of black pepper
1 teaspoon reduced sodium soy sauce
2 cups homemade chicken broth (use vegetable if you've given up meat)
1 teaspoon coconut oil
1 teaspoon five-spice powder
1 tablespoon olive oil
3 heads bok choy
1 carrot, sliced
1 tablespoon ginger, minced
2 cups udon noodles
1 green onion, thinly sliced
2 teaspoons cilantro, finely chopped
1 teaspoon sesame seeds

1. Rub the fish with pepper.
2. In a bowl, combine pepper, soy sauce, 1 cup chicken broth, coconut oil and spice blend. Mix together and place to one side.
3. In a large saucepan, heat the oil over medium heat and cook the boy choy, ginger and carrot for about 2 minutes until the bok choy is green.
4. Add the rest of the reserved chicken stock and heat through.
5. Add the udon noodles and stir, bringing to a simmer.
6. Add the green onion and the fish and cook for 10 to 15 minutes until fish is tender.
7. Add the fish, noodles and vegetables into serving bowls and pour the broth over the top.
8. Garnish with the cilantro and sesame seeds and serve with chopsticks for real authenticity!

Per Serving
calories: 484 | fat: 14g | protein: 37g | carbs: 43g | fiber: 8g | sugar: 5g | sodium: 998mg

Thyme Shark Steaks with Worcestershire

Prep time: 10 minutes | Cook time: 30 minutes | Serves 2

2 shark steaks, skinless
2 tablespoons onion powder
2 teaspoons chili powder
1 garlic clove, minced
¼ cup Worcestershire sauce
1 tablespoon ground black pepper
2 tablespoons thyme, chopped

1. In a bowl, mix all the seasonings and spices to form a paste before setting aside.
2. Spread a thin layer of paste on both sides of the fish, cover and chill for 30 minutes (If possible).
3. Preheat the oven to 325°F (163°C).
4. Bake the fish in parchment paper for 30 to 40 minutes, until well cooked.
5. Serve on a bed of quinoa or wholegrain couscous and your favorite salad.

Per Serving
calories: 292 | fat: 8g | protein: 37g | carbs: 17g | fiber: 3g | sugar: 4g | sodium: 555mg

Garlic Halibut with Lemon

Prep time: 5 minutes | Cook time: 15 minutes | Serves 2

2 halibut fillets
Pinch of black pepper
2 garlic cloves, pressed
2 tablespoons olive oil
2 tablespoons low fat Greek yogurt
4 lemon wedges for garnish

1. Preheat the oven to 400°F (205°C).
2. Season the fish with the pepper and add to a parchment paper-lined baking dish.
3. Scatter the garlic cloves (no need to peel) around the fish and drizzle with the oil.
4. Squeeze the lemon juice over the fish.
5. Bake for approximately 15 minutes until the fish is firm and well cooked.
6. Serve and pour over the juices for a delicious garlic feast.

Per Serving

calories: 489 | fat: 19g | protein: 56g | carbs: 3g | fiber: 1g | sugar: 1g | sodium: 289mg

Tuna Steaks with Fennel Salad

Prep time: 10 minutes | Cook time: 20 minutes | Serves 2

2 tuna steaks, each 1 inch thick
2 tablespoons olive oil
1 tablespoon olive oil for brushing
1 teaspoon crushed black peppercorns
1 teaspoon crushed fennel seeds
1 fennel bulb, trimmed and sliced
½ cup water
1 lemon, juiced
1 teaspoon fresh parsley, chopped

1. Coat the fish with oil and then season with peppercorns and fennel seeds.
2. Heat the oil over medium heat and sauté the fennel bulb slices for 5 minutes or until light brown, stir in the garlic and cook for 1 minute.
3. Add the water to the pan and cook for 10 minutes until fennel is tender.
4. Stir in the lemon juice and lower heat to a simmer.
5. Meanwhile, heat another skillet and sauté the tuna steaks for about 2 to 3 minutes each side for medium-rare. (Add 1 minute each side for medium and 2 minutes each side for medium well).
6. Serve the fennel mix with the tuna steaks on top and garnish with the fresh parsley.

Per Serving

calories: 635 | fat: 25g | protein: 88g | carbs: 12g | fiber: 4g | sugar: 5g | sodium: 211mg

Sesame Mahi-Mahi with Pineapple Salsa

Prep time: 10 minutes | Cook time: 16 minutes | Serves 1

Salsa:
1 cup fresh pineapple, peeled and cubed
½ red chili, finely chopped
1 lime, juiced
2 teaspoons cilantro, chopped
1 onion, finely chopped
Fish:
2 mahi mahi fillets
2 teaspoons coconut oil
2 tablespoons sesame seeds

1. Get a bowl and mix all the ingredients for the salsa.
2. Drizzle 1 teaspoon coconut oil on the fillets and coat each side with the sesame seeds.
3. Heat 1 tablespoon oil over medium heat and then sauté the fillets for about 8 minutes each side or until the flesh flakes away.
4. Serve with the salsa on the side.

Per Serving

calories: 734 | fat: 22g | protein: 83g | carbs: 54g | fiber: 8g | sugar: 35g | sodium: 398mg

Avocado Baked Salmon

Prep time: 10 minutes | Cook time: 15 minutes | Serves 4

1 tablespoon coconut oil
4 (8 ounces / 227 g) salmon fillets
1 tablespoon lemon zest
1 teaspoon capers
1 ripe avocado
3 garlic cloves, crushed
½ cup chopped fresh basil

1. Grease a baking sheet with coconut oil.
2. On a bowl, mash avocado until it becomes creamy. Add in the chopped garlic, capers, lemon zest and basil. Set aside.
3. Lay the salmon fillets on the baking sheet and spread the avocado topping on top of the salmon.
4. Bake in a preheated 350°F (180°C) oven for 15 minutes.

Per Serving

calories: 387 | fat: 19g | protein: 47g | carbs: 5g | fiber: 3.5g | sugar: 0.5g | sodium: 133mg

Salmon with Honey-Mustard Glaze

Prep time: 5 minutes | Cook time: 11 minutes | Serves 4

4 tablespoons honey
2 tablespoons Dijon mustard
4 (4-ounce / 113-g) skin-on salmon fillets, about 1 inch thick, pin bones removed
Olive oil for brushing
Kosher salt
Freshly ground black pepper

1. In a small bowl, whisk together the honey and mustard. Set aside.
2. Rinse the salmon and pat dry with a paper towel. Brush all sides of each fillet with olive oil and season with 1 pinch each of salt and pepper.
3. To grill the salmon, prepare a grill for direct cooking over medium-high heat. Fold a piece of aluminum foil to create a square. Crimp the edges upward to form a rim. Prick the foil several times with a fork, then brush with olive oil.
4. Place the foil directly on the grill grate, then set the salmon, skin-side down, on the foil, leaving 1 inch between each piece. Close the lid and grill for 4 minutes. Lift the lid and generously brush the fish with the honey mustard. Close the lid and grill for 2 to 3 minutes more for medium, or until the salmon is cooked to the desired doneness. Remove the salmon from the grill.
5. To cook the salmon in the oven, place a rack in the top third of the oven, and preheat the oven to broil. Line a baking sheet with aluminum foil and brush with olive oil. Place the salmon, skin-side down, on the foil, leaving 1 inch between each piece. Broil for 2 minutes, then liberally brush each fillet with the honey mustard. Continue broiling for 3 to 4 minutes more, or until the salmon is cooked to the desired doneness. Remove the salmon from the oven.
6. Brush the salmon with more honey mustard and let rest for 3 to 5 minutes before serving.

Per Serving
calories: 223 | fat: 6g | protein: 24g | carbs: 18g | fiber: 1g | sugar: 17g | sodium: 211mg

Fish en Papillote with Asparagus

Prep time: 10 minutes | Cook time: 15 minutes | Serves 4

4 (4-ounce / 113-g) fish fillets, such as halibut, salmon, or snapper, pin bones removed
Kosher salt
Freshly ground black pepper
Extra virgin olive oil for drizzling
2 lemons, preferably Meyer, ends trimmed, cut into 12 slices about ⅛ inch thick
Kernels from 2 ears of corn
16 asparagus spears, bottoms trimmed, sliced on the bias into ½-inch pieces
1 cup cherry tomatoes (optional if nightshade-sensitive)
2 tablespoons finely chopped assorted herbs, such as basil, chives, parsley, tarragon, and dill

1. Preheat the oven to 400°F (205°C). Cut four pieces of parchment paper each 18 inch long.
2. Place a fish fillet on the center of a piece of parchment. Season with a small pinch each of salt and pepper, then drizzle with olive oil. Place three lemon slices on the fillet, overlapping them slightly to cover the fish. Sprinkle one-fourth each of the corn, asparagus, and tomatoes (if using) evenly around the fish, then drizzle with a little olive oil and season again with a small pinch each of salt and pepper.
3. Bring the long sides of the paper together, and fold the top edges down together to create a 1-inch seal, then continue to fold down tightly over the fish and vegetables. Twist the open ends of the parchment in opposite directions to prevent steam from escaping.
4. Repeat the process with the remaining ingredients and parchment. Place the packets on a baking sheet. (If not baking immediately, refrigerate for up to 4 hours.)
5. Bake until the packets are lightly browned and have puffed up, about 15 minutes. Transfer each packet to a plate and let stand for 5 minutes. Using sharp scissors, cut an X into the center of each packet and carefully pull back the parchment and sprinkle with the herbs. Serve immediately.

Per Serving
calories: 166 | fat: 4g | protein: 24g | carbs: 12g | fiber: 2g | sugar: 4g | sodium: 132mg

Chipotle-Lime Shrimp Skewers

Prep time: 15 minutes | Cook time: 4 minutes | Serves 4

½ cup olive oil
¼ cup lime juice
2 to 3 tablespoons chipotles in adobo (optional if nightshade-sensitive)
1 tablespoon honey
¼ red onion, coarsely chopped
2 garlic cloves, coarsely chopped
2 to 3 teaspoons hot sauce
2 teaspoons ancho chile powder
1 teaspoon ground cumin
1 teaspoon dried oregano
1 teaspoon kosher salt
½ teaspoon freshly ground black pepper
1½ pounds (680 g) shrimp, peeled and deveined, tails on

1. Place the olive oil, lime juice, 2 tablespoons of the chipotles in adobo, honey, onion, garlic, 2 teaspoons of the hot sauce, chile powder, cumin, oregano, salt, and pepper in a blender or food processor. Puree until smooth to make a marinade. Taste and adjust with more chipotle or hot sauce as desired.
2. Place the shrimp in a nonreactive dish, such as ceramic or glass, or in a sealable plastic bag. Pour half of the marinade over the shrimp. Toss the shrimp to evenly coat. Cover and refrigerate for 2 hours, or up to 12 hours.
3. Prepare a grill for cooking over medium-high heat. Alternatively, preheat a grill pan over medium-high heat. When the grill or pan is hot, use a folded paper towel to lightly oil the grill rack or pan. Soak eight 9-inch bamboo skewers in water for at least 30 minutes before cooking.
4. Thread the shrimp onto the skewers, allowing the marinade to drip off over the bowl, and set on a baking sheet (to transport the skewers to the grill).
5. Place the shrimp skewers on the grill or grill pan and cook until they are just pink and opaque, about 2 minutes per side. Serve warm or at room temperature.

Per Serving

calories: 441 | fat: 30g | protein: 35g | carbs: 8g | fiber: 1g | sugar: 6g | sodium: 1122mg

Garlic Scallops with Cilantro

Prep time: 10 minutes | Cook time: 4 minutes | Serves 1

8 queen or king scallops (row on)
1 tablespoon extra sesame oil
2 large garlic cloves, finely chopped
1 red chili, finely chopped
Juice of ½ lime
2 tablespoons of chopped cilantro
Pinch of black pepper

1. Heat oil in a skillet over medium-high heat and fry scallops for about 1 minute each side until lightly golden.
2. Add the chopped chili and garlic cloves to the pan and squeeze the lime juice over the scallops. Saute for 2 to 3 minutes.
3. Remove the scallops and sprinkle the cilantro over the top to serve.

Per Serving

calories: 236 | fat: 15g | protein: 16g | carbs: 12g | fiber: 1g | sugar: 3g | sodium: 477mg

Seared Scallops with Kale and Spinach

Prep time: 10 minutes | Cook time: 14 minutes | Serves 4

1½ pounds (680 g) sea scallops, cleaned and patted dry
Sea salt
Freshly ground black pepper
2 tablespoons olive oil, divided
2 garlic cloves, thinly sliced
2 cups chopped kale leaves
2 cups fresh spinach

1. Lightly season the scallops all over with sea salt and pepper.
2. Place a large skillet over medium-high heat and add 1 tablespoon of olive oil.
3. Pan-sear the scallops for about 2 minutes per side, or until opaque and just cooked through. Transfer to a plate and cover loosely with aluminum foil to keep them warm. Wipe the skillet with a paper towel and place it back on the heat.
4. Add the remaining 1 tablespoon of olive oil to the skillet and sauté the garlic for about 4 minutes, or until caramelized.
5. Stir in the kale and spinach. Cook, tossing with tongs, for about 6 minutes, or until the greens are tender and wilted.
6. Divide the greens with any juices equally among four plates and top each with the scallops.

Per Serving

calories: 232 | fat: 8g | protein: 30g | carbs: 9g | fiber: 1g | sugar: 0g | sodium: 721mg

Coconut Crab Cakes with Carrots

Prep time: 10 minutes | Cook time: 12 minutes | Serves 4

2 pounds (907 g) cooked lump crabmeat, drained and picked over
½ cup shredded unsweetened coconut
½ cup coconut flour, plus more as needed
½ cup shredded carrot
2 scallions, white and green parts, finely chopped
2 eggs
1 teaspoon freshly grated lemon zest (optional)
2 tablespoons olive oil

1. In a large bowl, stir together the crab, coconut, coconut flour, carrot, scallions, eggs, and lemon zest (if using) until the mixture holds together when pressed. Add more coconut flour if the mixture is too wet.
2. Divide the mixture into 8 portions and flatten them until they are about 1 inch thick. Cover the crab cakes and refrigerate for about 1 hour to firm up.
3. Place a large skillet over medium-high heat and add the olive oil.
4. Add the crab cakes and sear for about 6 minutes per side until cooked through and golden on both sides, turning just once.
5. Serve 2 crab cakes per person.

Per Serving (2 crab cakes)

calories: 406 | fat: 20g | protein: 50g | carbs: 5g | fiber: 2g | sugar: 2g | sodium: 901mg

Cod Fillets with Shiitake Mushrooms

Prep time: 10 minutes | Cook time: 15 minutes | Serves 4

1 garlic clove, minced
1 leek, thinly sliced
1 teaspoon minced fresh ginger root
1 tablespoon olive oil
½ cup dry white wine
½ cup sliced shiitake mushrooms
4 (6-ounce / 170-g) cod fillets
1 teaspoon sea salt
⅛ teaspoon freshly ground black pepper

1. Preheat the oven to 375°F (190°C).
2. Mix together the garlic, leek, ginger root, wine, olive oil, and mushrooms in a baking pan, and toss until the mushrooms are evenly coated.
3. Bake in the preheated oven for 10 minutes until lightly browned.
4. Remove the baking pan from the oven. Spread the cod fillets on top and season with sea salt and pepper.
5. Cover with aluminum foil and return to the oven. Bake for 5 to 8 minutes more, or until the fish is flaky.
6. Remove the aluminum foil and cool for 5 minutes before serving.

Per Serving
calories: 166 | fat: 7g | protein: 21g | carbs: 5g | fiber: 1g | sugar: 1g | sodium: 857mg

Simple Salmon Patties

Prep time: 10 minutes | Cook time: 8 minutes | Serves 4

1 pound (454 g) skinless boned salmon fillets, minced
¼ cup minced sweet onion
½ cup almond flour
2 garlic cloves, minced
2 eggs, whisked
1 teaspoon Dijon mustard
1 tablespoon freshly squeezed lemon juice
Dash red pepper flakes
½ teaspoon sea salt
¼ teaspoon freshly ground black pepper
1 tablespoon avocado oil

1. Mix together the minced salmon, sweet onion, almond flour, garlic, whisked eggs, mustard, lemon juice, red pepper flakes, sea salt, and pepper in a large bowl, and stir until well incorporated.
2. Allow the salmon mixture to rest for 5 minutes.
3. Scoop out the salmon mixture and shape into four ½-inch-thick patties with your hands.
4. Heat the avocado oil in a large skillet over medium heat. Add the patties to the hot skillet and cook each side for 4 to 5 minutes until lightly browned and cooked through.
5. Remove from the heat and serve on a plate.

Per Serving
calories: 248 | fat: 13g | protein: 28g | carbs: 4g | fiber: 2g | sugar: 2g | sodium: 443mg

Baked Salmon with Miso Sauce

Prep time: 10 minutes | Cook time: 15 minutes | Serves 4

4 (3- to 4-ounce / 85- to 113-g) boneless salmon fillets
1 sliced scallion, for garnish
⅛ teaspoon red pepper flakes, for garnish
Sauce:
¼ cup apple cider
¼ cup white miso
1 tablespoon olive oil
1 tablespoon white rice vinegar
⅛ teaspoon ground ginger

1. Preheat the oven to 375°F (190°C).
2. Make the sauce: Whisk together the apple cider, white miso, olive oil, rice vinegar, ginger in a small bowl. Add a little water if a thinner consistency is desired.
3. Arrange the salmon fillets in a baking pan, skin-side down. Spoon the prepared sauce over the fillets to coat evenly.
4. Bake in the preheated oven for 15 to 20 minutes, or until the fish flakes easily with a fork.
5. Garnish with the sliced scallion and red pepper flakes and serve.

Per Serving
calories: 466 | fat: 18g | protein: 68g | carbs: 9g | fiber: 1g | sugar: 3g | sodium: 819mg

Quinoa Salmon Bowl with Vegetables

Prep time: 10 minutes | Cook time: 0 minutes | Serves 4

1 pound (454 g) cooked salmon, flaked
4 cups cooked quinoa
6 radishes, thinly sliced
1 zucchini, sliced into half moons
3 cups arugula
3 scallions, minced
½ cup almond oil
1 teaspoon sugar-free hot sauce
1 tablespoon apple cider vinegar
1 teaspoon sea salt
½ cup toasted slivered almonds, for garnish (optional)

1. In a large bowl, mix together the flaked salmon, cooked quinoa, radishes, zucchini, arugula, and scallions, and stir well.
2. Fold in the almond oil, hot sauce, apple cider vinegar, and sea salt and toss to combine.
3. Divide the mixture into four bowls. Scatter each bowl evenly with the slivered almonds for garnish, if desired. Serve immediately.

Per Serving
calories: 769 | fat: 52g | protein: 37g | carbs: 45g | fiber: 8g | sugar: 4g | sodium: 681mg

THE ULTIMATE ANTI-INFLAMMATORY DIET COOKBOOK

Trout With Cucumber Salsa

Prep time: 10 minutes | Cook time: 10 minutes | Serves 4

Salsa:
1 English cucumber, diced
¼ cup unsweetened coconut yogurt
2 tablespoons chopped fresh mint
1 scallion, white and green parts, chopped
1 teaspoon raw honey
Sea salt
Fish:
4 (5-ounce) trout fillets, patted dry
1 tablespoon olive oil
Sea salt and freshly ground black pepper, to taste

1. Make the salsa: Stir together the yogurt, cucumber, mint, scallion, honey, and sea salt in a small bowl until completely mixed. Set aside.
2. On a clean work surface, rub the trout fillets lightly with sea salt and pepper.
3. Heat the olive oil in a large skillet over medium heat. Add the trout fillets to the hot skillet and panfry for about 10 minutes, flipping the fish halfway through, or until the fish is cooked to your liking.
4. Spread the salsa on top of the fish and serve.

Per Serving

calories: 328 | fat: 16g | protein: 39g | carbs: 6g | fiber: 1g | sugar: 3g | sodium: 477mg

Cucumber Ahi Poke

Prep time: 10 minutes | Cook time: 0 minutes | Serves 4

1 cucumber, sliced into ½-inch-thick rounds
Ahi Poke:
1 pound (454 g) sushi-grade ahi tuna, cut into 1-inch cubes
3 tablespoons coconut aminos
3 scallions, thinly sliced
1 serrano chile, deseeded and minced (optional)
1 teaspoon olive oil
1 teaspoon rice vinegar
1 teaspoon toasted sesame seeds
Dash ground ginger
1 large avocado, diced

1. Make the ahi poke: Toss the ahi tuna cubes with the coconut aminos, scallions, serrano chile (if desired), olive oil, vinegar, sesame seeds, and ginger in a large bowl.
2. Cover the bowl with plastic wrap and marinate in the fridge for 15 minutes.
3. Add the diced avocado to the bowl of ahi poke and stir to incorporate.
4. Arrange the cucumber rounds on a serving plate. Spoon the ahi poke over the cucumber and serve.

Per Serving

calories: 213 | fat: 15g | protein: 10g | carbs: 11g | fiber: 4g | sugar: 1g | sodium: 70mg

Seared Haddock with Beets

Prep time: 10 minutes | Cook time: 38 minutes | Serves 4

8 beets, peeled and cut into eighths
2 shallots, thinly sliced
2 tablespoons apple cider vinegar
2 tablespoons olive oil, divided
1 teaspoon bottled minced garlic
1 teaspoon chopped fresh thyme
Pinch sea salt
4 (5-ounce / 142-g) haddock fillets, patted dry

1. Preheat the oven to 400°F (205°C).
2. Combine the beets, shallots, vinegar, 1 tablespoon of olive oil, garlic, thyme, and sea salt in a medium bowl, and toss to coat well. Spread out the beet mixture in a baking dish.
3. Roast in the preheated oven for about 30 minutes, turning once or twice with a spatula, or until the beets are tender.
4. Meanwhile, heat the remaining 1 tablespoon of olive oil in a large skillet over medium-high heat.
5. Add the haddock and sear each side for 4 to 5 minutes, or until the flesh is opaque and it flakes apart easily.
6. Transfer the fish to a plate and serve topped with the roasted beets.

Per Serving

calories: 343 | fat: 9g | protein: 38g | carbs: 21g | fiber: 4g | sugar: 12g | sodium: 540mg

White Fish Chowder with Vegetables

Prep time: 10 minutes | Cook time: 32 minutes | Serves 6 to 8

3 sweet potatoes, peeled and cut into ½-inch pieces
4 carrots, peeled and cut into ½-inch pieces
3 cups full-fat coconut milk
2 cups water
1 teaspoon dried thyme
½ teaspoon sea salt
10½ ounces (298 g) white fish, skinless and firm, such as cod or halibut, cut into chunks

1. Add the sweet potatoes, carrots, coconut milk, water, thyme, and sea salt to a large saucepan over high heat, and bring to a boil.
2. Reduce the heat to low, cover, and simmer for 20 minutes until the vegetables are tender, stirring occasionally.
3. Pour half of the soup to a blender and purée until thoroughly mixed and smooth, then return it to the pot.
4. Stir in the fish chunks and continue cooking for an additional 12 to 15 minutes, or until the fish is cooked through.
5. Remove from the heat and serve in bowls.

Per Serving

calories: 450 | fat: 29g | protein: 14g | carbs: 39g | fiber: 8g | sugar: 7g | sodium: 250mg

Coconut Shrimp with Arugula Salad

Prep time: 10 minutes | Cook time: 10 minutes | Serves 2

2 cups shrimp, peeled and deveined
¼ cup coconut flour
½ teaspoon cayenne pepper
1 teaspoon garlic powder
2 beaten free-range eggs
½ cup shredded coconut
¼ cup almond flour
Pinch of black pepper, to taste
1 cup arugula or watercress

1. Preheat the oven to 400°F (205°C).
2. Line a baking sheet with parchment paper.
3. Mix the coconut flour, cayenne pepper, and garlic powder in a bowl.
4. In a separate bowl, whisk the eggs.
5. In a third bowl, add the shredded coconut, almond flour and pepper.
6. Dip the shrimp into each dish in consecutive order, and then place on the baking sheet and bake for 10 to 15 minutes or until cooked through.
7. Serve piping hot and straight from the oven with a side salad of arugula or watercress.

Per Serving

calories: 476 | fat: 15g | protein: 55g | carbs: 30g | fiber: 5g | sugar: 2g | sodium: 910mg

---

Wasabi-Ginger Salmon Burgers

Prep time: 10 minutes | Cook time: 8¼ minutes | Serves 2

½ teaspoon honey
2 tablespoons reduced-salt soy sauce
1 teaspoon wasabi powder
1 beaten free range egg
2 cans wild salmon, drained
2 scallions, chopped
2 tablespoons coconut oil
1 tablespoon fresh ginger, minced

1. Combine the salmon, egg, ginger, scallions and 1 tablespoon oil in a bowl, mixing well with your hands to form 4 patties.
2. In a separate bowl, add the wasabi powder and soy sauce with the honey and whisk until blended.
3. Heat 1 tablespoon oil over medium heat in a skillet and cook the patties for 4 minutes on each side until firm and browned.
4. Glaze the top of each patty with the wasabi mixture and cook for another 15 seconds before you serve.
5. Serve with your favorite side salad or vegetables for a healthy treat.

Per Serving

calories: 553 | fat: 30g | protein: 68g | carbs: 4g | fiber: 1g | sugar: 2g | sodium: 988mg

---

Lemon Zoodles With Shrimp

Prep time: 10 minutes | Cook time: 0 minutes | Serves 4

1 large yellow squash, julienned or spiralized
1 large zucchini, julienned or spiralized
1 pound (454 g) shrimp, deveined, boiled, peeled, and chilled
Zest of 1 lemon (optional)
Sauce:
½ cup packed fresh basil leaves
Juice of 1 lemon (or 3 tablespoons)
1 teaspoon bottled minced garlic
Pinch sea salt
Pinch freshly ground black pepper
¼ cup canned full-fat coconut milk

1. Make the sauce: Process the basil leaves, lemon juice, garlic, sea salt, and pepper in a food processor until chopped thoroughly.
2. Slowly pour in the coconut milk while the processor is still running. Pulse until smooth.
3. Transfer the sauce to a large bowl, along with the yellow squash and zucchini. Toss well.
4. Scatter the shrimp and lemon zest (if desired) on top of the noodles. Serve immediately.

Per Serving

calories: 246 | fat: 13g | protein: 28g | carbs: 5g | fiber: 2g | sugar: 3g | sodium: 139mg

---

Coconut Shrimp

Prep time: 10 minutes | Cook time: 6 minutes | Serves 4

2 eggs
1 cup unsweetened dried coconut
¼ cup coconut flour
¼ teaspoon paprika
Dash cayenne pepper
½ teaspoon sea salt
Dash freshly ground black pepper
¼ cup coconut oil
1 pound (454 g) raw shrimp, peeled, deveined, and patted dry

1. Beat the eggs in a small shallow bowl until frothy. Set aside.
2. In a separate bowl, mix together the coconut, coconut flour, paprika, cayenne pepper, sea salt, and black pepper, and stir until well incorporated.
3. Dredge the shrimp in the beaten eggs, then coat the shrimp in the coconut mixture. Shake off any excess.
4. Heat the coconut oil in a large skillet over medium-high heat.
5. Add the shrimp and cook for 3 to 6 minutes, stirring occasionally, or until the flesh is totally pink and opaque.
6. Transfer the cooked shrimp to a plate lined with paper towels to drain. Serve warm.

Per Serving

calories: 278 | fat: 2g | protein: 19g | carbs: 6g | fiber: 3g | sugar: 2g | sodium: 556mg

CHAPTER 7:
POULTRY AND MEAT

Curried Chicken, Chickpeas

Prep time: 20 minutes | Cook time: 18 minutes | Serves 5

1 cup red grapes, halved
3 to 4 cups rotisserie chicken, meat coarsely shredded
2 tablespoons cilantro
1 cup plain yogurt
2 medium tomatoes, chopped
1 teaspoon ground cumin
1 tablespoon curry powder
2 tablespoons vegetable oil
1 tablespoon minced peeled ginger
1 tablespoon minced garlic
1 medium onion, chopped
For Chickpeas:
¼ teaspoon cayenne
½ teaspoon turmeric
1 teaspoon ground cumin
1 (19-ounce / 539-g) can chickpeas, rinsed, drained and patted dry
1 tablespoon vegetable oil
For Topping and Raita:
½ cup sliced and toasted almonds
2 tablespoons chopped mint
2 cups cucumber, peeled, cored and chopped
1 cup plain yogurt

1. To make the chicken salad, on medium low fire, place a medium nonstick saucepan and heat oil.
2. Sauté ginger, garlic and onion for 5 minutes or until softened while stirring occasionally.
3. Add 1½ teaspoons salt, cumin and curry. Sauté for 2 minutes.
4. Increase fire to medium high and add tomatoes. Stirring frequently, cook for 5 minutes.
5. Pour sauce into a bowl, mix in chicken, cilantro and yogurt. Stir to combine and let it stand to cool to room temperature.
6. To make the chickpeas, on a nonstick fry pan, heat oil for 3 minutes.
7. Add chickpeas and cook for 1 minute while stirring frequently.
8. Add ¼ teaspoon salt, cayenne, turmeric and cumin. Stir to mix well and cook for 2 minutes or until sauce is dried.
9. Transfer to a bowl and let it cool to room temperature.
10. To make the raita, mix ½ teaspoon salt, mint, cucumber and yogurt. Stir thoroughly to combine and dissolve salt.
11. To assemble, in 4 (16-ounce / 454-g) lidded jars or bowls layer the following: curried chicken, raita, chickpeas and garnish with almonds.
12. You can make this recipe one day ahead and refrigerate for 6 hours before serving.

Per Serving
calories: 403 | fat: 16g | protein: 26g | carbs: 42g | fiber: 9g | sugar: 17g | sodium: 312mg

Balsamic Vinaigrette on Chicken

Prep time: 10 minutes | Cook time: 1 hour | Serves 8

1 tablespoon chopped fresh parsley
1 teaspoon lemon zest
½ cup low-salt chicken broth
1 (4 pounds / 1.8 kg) whole chicken, cut into pieces
Freshly ground black pepper
Salt
2 tablespoons olive oil
2 garlic cloves, chopped
2 tablespoons fresh lemon juice
2 tablespoons Dijon mustard
¼ cup balsamic vinegar

1. In a small bowl, whisk to blend pepper, salt, olive oil, garlic, lemon juice, mustard and vinegar.
2. In a re-sealable bag, combine above mixture and chicken pieces. Refrigerate and marinate for at least 2 hours to a whole day. Ensure to turn bag upside down occasionally.
3. Grease a baking dish and preheat oven to 400°F (205°C).
4. Arrange marinated chicken pieces onto baking dish and pop into the oven.
5. Roast chicken for 1 hour or until cooked through. If chicken is browned and not yet fully cooked, cover with foil and continue cooking.
6. Remove from oven, and transfer chicken to a serving plate.
7. Garnish with parsley and drizzle with lemon juice before serving.

Per Serving
calories: 296 | fat: 10g | protein: 47g | carbs: 2g | fiber: 0.2g | sugar: 1.4g | sodium: 278mg

Chicken Pasta Parmesan

Prep time: 5 minutes | Cook time: 16 minutes | Serves 1

½ cup cooked whole wheat spaghetti
1 ounce (28 g) reduced fat mozzarella cheese, grated
¼ cup prepared marinara sauce
2 tablespoons seasoned dry breadcrumbs
4 ounces (113 g) skinless chicken breast
1 tablespoon olive oil

1. On medium high fire, place an ovenproof skillet and heat oil.
2. Pan fry chicken for 3 to 5 minutes per side or until cooked through.
3. Pour marinara sauce, stir and continue cooking for 3 minutes.
4. Turn off fire, add mozzarella and breadcrumbs on top.
5. Pop into a preheated broiler on high and broil for 10 minutes or until breadcrumbs are browned and mozzarella is melted.
6. Remove from broiler, serve and enjoy.

Per Serving
calories: 492 | fat: 19g | protein: 49g | carbs: 32g | fiber: 6g | sugar: 11g | sodium: 488mg

Chicken and White Bean

Prep time: 15 minutes | Cook time: 1²⁄₁₅ hours | Serves 6

2 tablespoons fresh cilantro, chopped
2 cups grated low-fat Monterey Jack cheese
3 cups water
⅛ teaspoon cayenne pepper
2 teaspoons pure chile powder
2 teaspoons ground cumin
1 (4 ounces / 113 g) can chopped green chiles
1 cup corn kernels
2 (15 ounces / 425 g) cans shite beans, drained and rinsed
2 garlic cloves
1 medium onion, diced
2 tablespoons extra-virgin olive oil
1 pound (454 g) chicken breasts, boneless and skinless

1. Slice chicken breasts into ½-inch cubes and with pepper and salt, season it.
2. On high fire, place a large nonstick fry pan and heat oil.
3. Sauté chicken pieces for 3 to 4 minutes or until lightly browned.
4. Reduce fire to medium and add garlic and onion.
5. Cook for 5 to 6 minutes or until onions are translucent.
6. Add water, spices, chilies, corn and beans. Bring to a boil.
7. Once boiling, slow fire to a simmer and continue simmering for 1 hour, uncovered.
8. To serve, garnish with a sprinkling of cilantro and a tablespoon of cheese.

Per Serving

calories: 550 | fat: 18g | protein: 48g | carbs: 51g | fiber: 14g | sugar: 2g | sodium: 817mg

Chicken Pad Thai

Prep time: 10 minutes | Cook time: 6 minutes | Serves 6

2 medium sized carrots, julienned
1 (12 ounces / 340 g) package broccoli slaw
5 green onions, chopped
5 tablespoons fresh cilantro, chopped
½ tablespoon coconut vinegar
4 tablespoons fresh lime juice
1 tablespoon coconut aminos
3 tablespoon fish sauce
5 garlic cloves, crushed
2 tablespoons extra-virgin coconut oil
1½ pounds (680 g) organic chicken meat, cut into chunks

1. Heat the skillet over medium high heat and add the coconut oil.
2. Sauté the garlic and onion for 1 minute.
3. Add the chicken and cook for 5 minutes.
4. Add the coconut aminos, fish sauce, vinegar and lime juice. Increase the heat to high and simmer until the chicken is thoroughly cooked.
5. Add the broccoli slaw and carrots. Stir constantly until the vegetables become soft.
6. Garnish with cilantro and green onions.

Per Serving

calories: 287 | fat: 10g | protein: 38g | carbs: 10g | fiber: 2g | sugar: 4g | sodium: 836mg

Chicken Thighs with Butternut Squash

Prep time: 5 minutes | Cook time: 35 minutes | Serves 6

3 cups butternut squash, cubed
6 boneless chicken thighs
A sprig of fresh sage, chopped
1 tablespoon olive oil
Salt and pepper, to taste

1. Preheat the oven to 425°F (220°C).
2. In a skillet, sauté the butternut squash and season with salt and pepper to taste. Once the squash is cooked, remove from the skillet and set aside.
3. Using the same skillet, add oil and cook the chicken thighs for 10 minutes on each side.
4. Season with salt and pepper and add the squash back.
5. Remove the skillet from the stove and bake in the oven for 15 minutes.
6. Serve and enjoy.

Per Serving

calories: 300 | fat: 13g | protein: 35g | carbs: 9g | fiber: 1.5g | sugar: 2g | sodium: 419mg

Cajun Rice & Chicken

Prep time: 10 minutes | Cook time: 20 minutes | Serves 6

1 tablespoon oil
1 onion, diced
3 garlic cloves, minced
1-pound (454-g) chicken breasts, sliced
1 tablespoon Cajun seasoning
1 tablespoon tomato paste
3 cups chicken broth
1½ cups brown rice, rinsed
1 bell pepper, chopped

1. Place a heavy bottomed pot on medium high fire and heat for 2 minutes.
2. Add oil and heat for a minute.
3. Sauté the onion and garlic until fragrant.
4. Stir in the chicken breasts and season with Cajun seasoning.
5. Continue cooking for 3 minutes.
6. Add the tomato paste, rice, and chicken broth. Bring to a boil while stirring to dissolve the tomato paste.
7. Once boiling, lower fire to a simmer, cover and cook until liquid is fully absorbed, around 15 minutes.
8. Turn off fire and let it stand for another 5 minutes before serving.

Per Serving

calories: 224 | fat: 6g | protein: 26g | carbs: 16g | fiber: 2g | sugar: 2g | sodium: 646mg

Vegetable Lover's Chicken Soup

Prep time: 10 minutes | Cook time: 12 minutes | Serves 4

1½ cups baby spinach
2 tablespoons orzo (tiny pasta)
¼ cup dry white wine
1 (14 ounces / 397 g) low sodium chicken broth
2 plum tomatoes, chopped
⅛ teaspoon salt
½ teaspoon Italian seasoning
1 large shallot, chopped
1 small zucchini, diced
8 ounces (227 g) chicken tenders
1 tablespoon extra-virgin olive oil

1. In a large saucepan, heat oil over medium heat and add the chicken. Stir occasionally for 8 minutes until browned. Transfer in a plate. Set aside.
2. In the same saucepan, add the zucchini, Italian seasoning, shallot and salt and stir often until the vegetables are softened, around 4 minutes.
3. Add the tomatoes, wine, broth and orzo and increase the heat to high to bring the mixture to boil. Reduce the heat and simmer.
4. Add the cooked chicken and stir in the spinach last.
5. Serve hot.

Per Serving

calories: 171 | fat: 7g | protein: 19g | carbs: 7g | fiber: 1g | sugar: 4g | sodium: 582mg

Herbed Chicken Salad

Prep time: 15 minutes | Cook time: 0 minutes | Serves 4

6 pitted kalamata olives, halved
1 cup grape tomatoes, halved
1 cup peeled and chopped English cucumbers
8 cups chopped romaine lettuce
1 teaspoon bottled minced garlic
2 teaspoons sesame seed paste or tahini
1 cup plain fat-free yogurt
5 teaspoons fresh lemon juice, divided
1-pound (454-g) skinless, boneless chicken breast, cut into 1-inch cubes
Cooking spray
½ teaspoon salt
¾ teaspoon black pepper, divided
½ teaspoon garlic powder
1 teaspoon ground oregano

1. In a bowl, mix together ¼ teaspoon salt, ½ teaspoon pepper, garlic powder and oregano.
2. Then on medium high heat place a skillet and coat with cooking spray and sauté together the spice mixture and chicken until chicken is cooked. Before transferring to bowl, drizzle with juice.
3. In a small bowl, mix thoroughly the following: garlic, tahini, yogurt, ¼ teaspoon pepper, ¼ teaspoon salt, and 2 teaspoons juice.
4. In another bowl, mix together olives, tomatoes, cucumber and lettuce.
5. To Serve salad, place 2½ cups of lettuce mixture on plate, topped with ½ cup chicken mixture, 3 tablespoons yogurt mixture and 1 tablespoon of cheese.

Per Serving

calories: 291 | fat: 8g | protein: 40g | carbs: 17g | fiber: 3g | sugar: 12g | sodium: 965mg

Chicken in Pita Bread

Prep time: 15 minutes | Cook time: 8 minutes | Serves 4

½ cup diced tomato
2 cups shredded lettuce
4 (6-inch) pieces pice pitas, cut in half
1½ teaspoons chopped fresh oregano
½ cup plain low-fat yogurt
1 tablespoon olive oil
2 teaspoons grated lemon rind, divided
1 pound (454 g) ground chicken
2 large egg whites, lightly beaten
½ teaspoon coarsely ground black pepper
1 tablespoon Greek or Moroccan seasoning blend
½ cup chopped green onions

1. Mix thoroughly the ground chicken, 1 teaspoon lemon rind, egg whites, black pepper, Greek or Moroccan seasoning and green onions. Equally separate into eight parts and shaping each part into ¼ inch thick patty.
2. Turn fire on medium high and place a large nonstick skillet. Fry the patties until browned or for 2 minutes each side. Then slow the fire to medium, cover the skillet and continue cooking for another 4 minutes.
3. In a small bowl, mix thoroughly the oregano, yogurt and 1 teaspoon lemon rind.
4. To serve, spread the mixture on the pita, add cooked patty, 1 tablespoon tomato and ¼ cup lettuce.

Per Serving

calories: 408 | fat: 15g | protein: 30g | carbs: 41g | fiber: 6g | sugar: 4g | sodium: 560mg

Greek Chicken Stew

Prep time: 10 minutes | Cook time: 40 minutes | Serves 8

1½ cups chicken stock or more if needed
2 bay leaves
1 pinch dried oregano, to taste
Salt and ground black pepper, to taste
2 tablespoons chopped fresh parsley
1 cup tomato sauce
½ cup water
2 garlic cloves, finely chopped
1 (2-pound / 907-g) whole chicken cut into pieces
1 tablespoon olive oil
10 small shallots, peeled

1. Bring to a boil a small pot of lightly salted water. Mix in the shallots and let boil uncovered until tender for around 3 minutes. Then drain the shallots and dip in cold water until no longer warm.
2. In another large pot over medium fire, heat olive oil for 1 minute. Then sauté in the chicken and shallots for 15 minutes or until chicken is cooked and shallots are soft and translucent. Then add the chopped garlic and cook for three mins more.
3. Then add bay leaves, oregano, salt and pepper, parsley, tomato sauce and the water. Let simmer for 1 minute before adding the chicken stock. Stir before covering and let cook for 20 minutes on medium-low fire or until chicken is tender.

Per Serving

calories: 129 | fat: 3g | protein: 13g | carbs: 10g | fiber: 3g | sugar: 5g | sodium: 651mg

Easy Stir-Fried Chicken

Prep time: 5 minutes | Cook time: 8 minutes | Serves 3

1 tablespoon soy sauce
1 tablespoon virgin coconut oil
¼ medium onion, sliced thinly
¼ pound (113 g) brown mushrooms
1 large orange bell pepper
2 (7 ounces / 198 g) skinless and boneless chicken breast

1. On medium high fire, place a nonstick saucepan and heat coconut oil.
2. Add soy sauce, onion powder, mushrooms, bell pepper and chicken.
3. Stir fry for 8 to 10 minutes.
4. Remove from pan and serve.

Per Serving

calories: 277 | fat: 10g | protein: 44g | carbs: 4g | fiber: 1g | sugar: 2g | sodium: 146mg

---

African Chicken Stew

Prep time: 15 minutes | Cook time: 1⅓ hours | Serves 8

1 lime cut into wedges
2-pound (907-g) bone in, skin on drumsticks and chicken thighs
¼ teaspoon ground allspice
½ teaspoon salt
½ teaspoon pepper
2 bay leaves
1 jalapeno pepper, seeds removed, diced
6 garlic cloves, minced
4 onions, sliced
1 tablespoon zest of lemon
¼ cup lemon juice
¼ cup apple cider vinegar
2 tablespoons olive oil
¼ cup water

1. In wide and shallow bowl with lid, combine allspice, salt, pepper, bay leaves, jalapeno, garlic, lemon zest, lemon juice, vinegar and oil. Mix well.
2. Add chicken, cover and marinate in the ref. Ensuring to turn chicken in two hours. Chicken is best left overnight or for at least 4 hours.
3. Once you are done marinating, grease a roasting pan and preheat oven to 400°F (205°C).
4. Remove chicken from marinade and arrange on prepared pan. Pop in the oven and bake until juices run clear around 35 to 40 minutes.
5. Meanwhile, discard ¾ of the marinade while reserving onions. Then place a nonstick pan on low fire and add remaining marinade with bay leaves and onions.
6. Sauté for 45 minutes until caramelized while stirring every once in a while.
7. To serve, place baked chicken on a serving plate drizzled with caramelized onion sauce and lime wedges on the side.

Per Serving

calories: 543 | fat: 54g | protein: 11g | carbs: 4g | fiber: 0.3g | sugar: 1.5g | sodium: 205mg

Roasted Chicken

Prep time: 10 minutes | Cook time: 50 minutes | Serves 8

1 bay leaf
4 tablespoons orange peel, chopped coarsely
3 garlic cloves
½ teaspoon thyme
½ teaspoon black pepper
½ tablespoon. salt
1 whole chicken (3-pound / 1.4-kg)

1. Prepare chicken by placing in room temperature for at least 1 hour.
2. With paper towels, pat dry chicken inside and out.
3. As you begin preparing chicken seasoning, preheat oven to 450°F (235°C).
4. In a small bowl, mix thyme, pepper and salt.
5. Get ⅓ of the seasoning and wipe inside the chicken. Also place inside of the chicken the bay leaf, citrus peel and garlic.
6. Tuck the wing tips and tie chicken legs together. Spread remaining seasoning all over and around the chicken. Then place on a roasting pan.
7. Pop in the oven and bake for 50 to 60 minutes or until chicken is a golden brown, juices run clear or chicken things or breasts register a 160°F (71°C) temperature.
8. Remove from oven and let it sit for 15 minutes more before cutting up and serving the roasted chicken.

Per Serving

calories: 270 | fat: 6g | protein: 49g | carbs: 1g | fiber: 0.4g | sugar: 0g | sodium: 615mg

---

Chicken Breasts with Stuffing

Prep time: 5 minutes | Cook time: 27 minutes | Serves 8

8 (6 ounces / 170 g) boneless and skinless chicken breasts
1 tablespoon minced fresh basil
2 tablespoons finely chopped, pitted Kalamata olives
¼ cup crumbled feta cheese
1 large bell pepper, halved and seeded

1. In a greased baking sheet place bell pepper with skin facing up and pop into a preheated broiler on high. Broil until blackened around 15 minutes. Remove from broiler and place right away into a re-sealable bag, seal and leave for 15 minutes.
2. After, peel bell pepper and mince. Preheat grill to medium high fire.
3. In a medium bowl, mix well basil, olives, cheese and bell pepper.
4. Form a pocket on each chicken breast by creating a slit through the thickest portion; add 2 tablespoons bell pepper mixture and seal with a wooden pick. (At this point, you can stop and freeze chicken and just thaw when needed for grilling already)
5. Season chicken breasts with pepper and salt.
6. Grill for 6 minutes per side, remove from grill and cover loosely with foil and let stand for 10 minutes before serving.

Per Serving

calories: 221 | fat: 6g | protein: 39g | carbs: 1g | fiber: 0.2g | sugar: 0.5g | sodium: 135mg

Easy Stir-Fried Chicken

Prep time: 5 minutes | Cook time: 8 minutes | Serves 3

1 tablespoon soy sauce
1 tablespoon virgin coconut oil
¼ medium onion, sliced thinly
¼ pound (113 g) brown mushrooms
1 large orange bell pepper
2 (7 ounces / 198 g) skinless and boneless chicken breast

1. On medium high fire, place a nonstick saucepan and heat coconut oil.
2. Add soy sauce, onion powder, mushrooms, bell pepper and chicken.
3. Stir fry for 8 to 10 minutes.
4. Remove from pan and serve.

Per Serving

calories: 277 | fat: 10g | protein: 44g | carbs: 4g | fiber: 1g | sugar: 2g | sodium: 146mg

---

African Chicken Stew

Prep time: 15 minutes | Cook time: 1⅓ hours | Serves 8

1 lime cut into wedges
2-pound (907-g) bone in, skin on drumsticks and chicken thighs
¼ teaspoon ground allspice
½ teaspoon salt
½ teaspoon pepper
2 bay leaves
1 jalapeno pepper, seeds removed, diced
6 garlic cloves, minced
4 onions, sliced
1 tablespoon zest of lemon
¼ cup lemon juice
¼ cup apple cider vinegar
2 tablespoons olive oil
¼ cup water

1. In wide and shallow bowl with lid, combine allspice, salt, pepper, bay leaves, jalapeno, garlic, lemon zest, lemon juice, vinegar and oil. Mix well.
2. Add chicken, cover and marinate in the ref. Ensuring to turn chicken in two hours. Chicken is best left overnight or for at least 4 hours.
3. Once you are done marinating, grease a roasting pan and preheat oven to 400°F (205°C).
4. Remove chicken from marinade and arrange on prepared pan. Pop in the oven and bake until juices run clear around 35 to 40 minutes.
5. Meanwhile, discard ¾ of the marinade while reserving onions. Then place a nonstick pan on low fire and add remaining marinade with bay leaves and onions.
6. Sauté for 45 minutes until caramelized while stirring every once in a while.
7. To serve, place baked chicken on a serving plate drizzled with caramelized onion sauce and lime wedges on the side.

Per Serving

calories: 543 | fat: 54g | protein: 11g | carbs: 4g | fiber: 0.3g | sugar: 1.5g | sodium: 205mg

---

Roasted Chicken

Prep time: 10 minutes | Cook time: 50 minutes | Serves 8

1 bay leaf
4 tablespoons orange peel, chopped coarsely
3 garlic cloves
½ teaspoon thyme
½ teaspoon black pepper
½ tablespoon. salt
1 whole chicken (3-pound / 1.4-kg)

1. Prepare chicken by placing in room temperature for at least 1 hour.
2. With paper towels, pat dry chicken inside and out.
3. As you begin preparing chicken seasoning, preheat oven to 450°F (235°C).
4. In a small bowl, mix thyme, pepper and salt.
5. Get ⅓ of the seasoning and wipe inside the chicken. Also place inside of the chicken the bay leaf, citrus peel and garlic.
6. Tuck the wing tips and tie chicken legs together. Spread remaining seasoning all over and around the chicken. Then place on a roasting pan.
7. Pop in the oven and bake for 50 to 60 minutes or until chicken is a golden brown, juices run clear or chicken things or breasts register a 160°F (71°C) temperature.
8. Remove from oven and let it sit for 15 minutes more before cutting up and serving the roasted chicken.

Per Serving

calories: 270 | fat: 6g | protein: 49g | carbs: 1g | fiber: 0.4g | sugar: 0g | sodium: 615mg

---

Chicken Breasts with Stuffing

Prep time: 5 minutes | Cook time: 27 minutes | Serves 8

8 (6 ounces / 170 g) boneless and skinless chicken breasts
1 tablespoon minced fresh basil
2 tablespoons finely chopped, pitted Kalamata olives
¼ cup crumbled feta cheese
1 large bell pepper, halved and seeded

1. In a greased baking sheet place bell pepper with skin facing up and pop into a preheated broiler on high. Broil until blackened around 15 minutes. Remove from broiler and place right away into a re-sealable bag, seal and leave for 15 minutes.
2. After, peel bell pepper and mince. Preheat grill to medium high fire.
3. In a medium bowl, mix well basil, olives, cheese and bell pepper.
4. Form a pocket on each chicken breast by creating a slit through the thickest portion; add 2 tablespoons bell pepper mixture and seal with a wooden pick. (At this point, you can stop and freeze chicken and just thaw when needed for grilling already)
5. Season chicken breasts with pepper and salt.
6. Grill for 6 minutes per side, remove from grill and cover loosely with foil and let stand for 10 minutes before serving.

Per Serving

calories: 221 | fat: 6g | protein: 39g | carbs: 1g | fiber: 0.2g | sugar: 0.5g | sodium: 135mg

Chicken-Bell Pepper Sauté

Prep time: 10 minutes | Cook time: 31 minutes | Serves 6

6 (4 ounces / 113 g) skinless, boneless chicken breast halves, cut in half horizontally
Cooking spray
20 Kalamata olives
1 teaspoon chopped fresh oregano
2 tablespoons finely chopped fresh flat-leaf parsley
¼ teaspoon freshly ground black pepper
½ teaspoon salt
2⅓ cups coarsely chopped tomato
1 large red bell pepper, cut into ¼-inch strips
1 large yellow bell pepper, cut into ¼-inch strips
3 cups onion sliced crosswise
1 tablespoon olive oil

1. On medium high fire, place a large nonstick fry pan and heat oil. Once oil is hot, sauté onions until soft and translucent, around 6 to 8 minutes.
2. Add bell peppers and sauté for another 10 minutes or until tender.
3. Add black pepper, salt and tomato. Cook until tomato juice has evaporated, around 7 minutes.
4. Add olives, oregano and parsley, cook until heated through around 1 to 2 minutes. Transfer to a bowl and keep warm.
5. Wipe pan with paper towel and grease with cooking spray. Return to fire and place chicken breasts. Cook for 3 minutes per side or until desired doneness is reached. If needed, cook chicken in batches.
6. When cooking the last batch of chicken is done, add back the previous batch of chicken and the onion-bell pepper mixture and cook for 1 to 2 minutes while tossing chicken to coat well in the onion-bell pepper mixture.
7. Serve and enjoy.

Per Serving

calories: 81 | fat: 3g | protein: 10g | carbs: 4g | fiber: 1g | sugar: 1.7g | sodium: 148mg

Avocado-Orange Grilled Chicken

Prep time: 10 minutes | Cook time: 6 minutes | Serves 4

1 small red onion, sliced thinly
2 oranges, peeled and sectioned
¼ cup fresh lime juice
1 avocado
4 (4- to 6-pound / 1.8- to 2.7-kg) boneless, skinless chicken breasts
Pepper and salt, to taste
1 tablespoon honey
2 tablespoons chopped cilantro
¼ cup minced red onion
1 cup low fat yogurt

1. In a large bowl mix honey, cilantro, minced red onion and yogurt.
2. Submerge chicken into mixture and marinate for at least 30 minutes.
3. Grease grate and preheat grill to medium high fire.
4. Remove chicken from marinade and season with pepper and salt.
5. Grill for 6 minutes per side or until chicken is cooked and juices run clear.
6. Meanwhile, peel avocado and discard seed. Chop avocados and place in bowl. Quickly add lime juice and toss avocado to coat well with juice.
7. Add cilantro, thinly sliced onions and oranges into bowl of avocado, mix well.
8. Serve grilled chicken and avocado dressing on the side.

Per Serving

calories: 443 | fat: 14g | protein: 53g | carbs: 26g | fiber: 6g | sugar: 17g | sodium: 815mg

Honey Chicken Tagine

Prep time: 15 minutes | Cook time: 1¹³⁄₆₀ minutes | Serves 8

1½ tablespoons honey
1 (15 ounces / 425 g) can chickpeas, rinsed
12 ounces (340 g) kumquats, seeded and roughly chopped
1 (14 ounces / 397 g) can vegetable broth
⅛ teaspoon ground cloves
½ teaspoon ground pepper
½ teaspoon salt
¾ teaspoon ground cinnamon
1 teaspoon ground cumin
1 teaspoon ground coriander
2-pound (907-g) boneless, skinless chicken thighs, trimmed of fat and cut into 2-inch pieces
1 tablespoon minced fresh ginger
4 garlic cloves, slivered
2 onions, thinly sliced
1 tablespoon extra-virgin olive oil

1. Preheat oven to 375°F (190°C).
2. On medium fire, place a heatproof casserole and heat oil.
3. Add onions and sauté for 4 minutes or until soft.
4. Add ginger and garlic, sauté for 1 minute.
5. Add chicken and sauté for 8 minutes.
6. Season with cloves, pepper, salt, cinnamon, cumin, and coriander. Sauté for a minute or until aromatic.
7. Add honey, chickpeas, kumquats, and broth. Bring to a boil and turn off fire.
8. Cover casserole and pop in the oven. Bake for 1 hour while stirring every after 15-minute intervals.

Per Serving

calories: 541 | fat: 46g | protein: 20g | carbs: 16g | fiber: 4g | sugar: 6g | sodium: 521mg

Brussels Sprouts and Chicken Thighs

Prep time: 10 minutes | Cook time: 20 minutes | Serves 4

4 large bone-in chicken thighs, skin removed
1 teaspoon dried thyme
1 tablespoon smoked paprika
2 garlic cloves, minced
½ teaspoon ground pepper, divided
¾ teaspoon salt, divided
3 tablespoons extra-virgin olive oil, divided
1 lemon, sliced
4 small shallots, quartered
1 pound (454 g) Brussels sprouts, trimmed and halved

1. Preheat oven to 450°F (235°C) and position rack to lower third in oven.
2. On a large and rimmed baking sheet, mix ¼ teaspoon pepper, ¼ teaspoon salt, 2 tablespoons oil, lemon, shallots, and Brussels sprouts.
3. With a chef's knife, mash ½ teaspoon salt and garlic to form a paste.
4. In small bowl, mix ¼ teaspoon pepper, 1 tablespoon oil, thyme, paprika, and garlic paste. Rub all over chicken and place around Brussels sprouts in pan.
5. Pop in the oven and roast for 20 to 25 minutes or until chicken is cooked and juices run clear.
6. Serve and enjoy.

Per Serving

calories: 293 | fat: 14g | protein: 29g | carbs: 10g | fiber: 5g | sugar: 4g | sodium: 992mg

Sweet Potato, Kale and Chicken Patties

Prep time: 10 minutes | Cook time: 20 minutes | Serves 7

2 tablespoons coconut flour
1 egg
1 tablespoon fresh rosemary, chopped
1 teaspoon Dijon mustard
1 teaspoon paprika powder
1 garlic clove, minced
½ teaspoon sea salt
1 pound (454 g) skinless and boneless chicken, chopped finely
2 ½ cups kale, chopped
½ medium sweet potato, chopped
2 green onions, chopped

1. Heat oil in a large skillet and sauté the green onions for 5 minutes.
2. Add the sweet potatoes and cook for 5 minutes until almost tender.
3. Mix in the kale and cook until the kale has wilted. Set aside.
4. In a mixing bowl, mix together the chicken and season with salt, paprika, mustard, garlic and rosemary. Add the egg, coconut flour and sweet potato mix.
5. Cover with plastic wrap and refrigerate for 4 hours.
6. Make patties out of the chicken mixture.
7. Cook the patties in a hot skillet for 5 minutes each side.

Per Serving
calories: 106 | fat: 3g | protein: 16g | carbs: 4g | fiber: 1g | sugar: 1.7g | sodium: 225mg

Chicken Burger with Brussel Sprouts Slaw

Prep time: 10 minutes | Cook time: 10 minutes | Serves 4

Salt and pepper, to taste
½ avocado, cubed
⅓ cup apple, sliced into strips
½ pound (227 g) Brussels sprouts, shredded
⅛ teaspoon red pepper flakes, optional
1 garlic clove, minced
¼ cup apple, diced
¼ cup green onion, diced
1 tablespoon Dijon mustard
1-pound (454-g) cooked ground chicken

1. In a mixing bowl, combine together chicken, green onion, Dijon mustard, garlic, apple, and pepper flakes.
2. Season with salt and pepper to taste. Mix the ingredients then form 4 burger patties.
3. Heat a grill pan over medium-high flame and grill the burgers. Cook for 5 minutes on side. Set aside.
4. In another bowl, toss the Brussels sprouts and apples.
5. In a small pan, heat coconut oil and add the Brussels sprouts mixture until everything is slightly wilted. Season with salt and pepper, to taste.
6. Serve burger patties with the Brussels sprouts slaw.

Per Serving
calories: 324 | fat: 21g | protein: 25g | carbs: 11g | fiber: 5g | sugar: 4g | sodium: 220mg

Chicken and Avocado Lettuce Wraps

Prep time: 10 minutes | Cook time: 0 minutes | Serves 3

⅛ teaspoon black pepper
⅛ teaspoon salt
2 tablespoons cilantro chopped
2 tablespoons lime juice
1 tablespoon lemon juice
½ cups avocado, pitted and mashed
1 cup cooked chicken, shredded
6 leaves of Romaine lettuce
1 cup grape tomatoes, halved

1. In a mixing bowl, mix together the avocado, lime juice, lemon juice and stir to combine.
2. Add the chicken and cilantro. Season with salt and pepper, to taste.
3. Spoon into the lettuce leaves and add chopped tomatoes.

Per Serving
calories: 134 | fat: 6g | protein: 14g | carbs: 7g | fiber: 4g | sugar: 2.4g | sodium: 136mg

Grilled Veggies 'n Chicken

Prep time: 15 minutes | Cook time: 19 minutes | Serves 3

Salt, to taste
1 teaspoon Italian seasoning
1 teaspoon rosemary
4 tablespoons extra-virgin olive oil
1-pound (454-g) organic chicken breast
1 red onion
2 cups fresh cherry tomatoes, halved
1 red pepper, chopped
1 yellow squash, chopped
1 zucchini, chopped
¼ teaspoon cayenne pepper
½ teaspoon onion powder
½ teaspoon garlic granules
Pepper, to taste
1 tablespoon vinegar
1 cup organic tomatoes, blended

1. Marinade the chicken by mixing together 1 tablespoon of extra-virgin olive oil, Italian seasoning, and rosemary. Season with salt the set aside for at least 2 hours.
2. In another bowl, make the salad by combining the red onion, fresh cherry tomatoes, red pepper, squash and zucchini. Add 1 tablespoon of extra-virgin olive oil and season with salt and pepper to taste. Place inside a greased tinfoil then set aside.
3. Prepare the grill and heat it to 350ºF (180ºC). Cook the chicken breast and let it cook for 7 minutes on each side. Place the tinfoil with the veggies on the grill and cook it for 5 to 7 minutes.
4. Meanwhile, make the vinaigrette my combining the cayenne pepper, onion powder, garlic granules, vinegar and blended organic tomatoes in a food processor.
5. Add 2 tablespoons of extra-virgin olive oil and season with salt and pepper to taste.

Per Serving
calories: 448 | fat: 14g | protein: 51g | carbs: 28g | fiber: 6g | sugar: 19g | sodium: 523mg

Lettuce Tacos with Chipotle Chicken

Prep time: 15 minutes | Cook time: 20 minutes | Serves 4

Lime wedges for garnish
Fresh tomatoes, sliced for garnish
½ avocado, sliced
2 pickled jalapenos, chopped
A handful coriander leaves
1 head lettuce, leaves separated and washed
1 pinch of coconut sugar
Salt and pepper, to taste
½ teaspoon cumin
1 tablespoon chopped chipotle in adobo sauce
1 can tomatoes
1 red onion, sliced
1 tablespoon olive oil
1 cup skinless chicken, cut into strips

1. Heat the olive oil in a skillet and fry the chicken until they are golden brown. Set aside.
2. In the same pan, fry the onions until they become soft. Add the canned tomatoes, chipotle, cumin and sugar.
3. Let it simmer for 15 minutes until the tomatoes become soft and thickened.
4. Add the chicken to the sauce and cook for 5 minutes.
5. Assemble the tacos by putting the chicken inside the lettuce wraps. Garnish with lime wedges, fresh tomatoes, avocado, jalapeno and coriander leaves.

Per Serving

calories: 187 | fat: 10g | protein: 12g | carbs: 8g | fiber: 3g | sugar: 3g | sodium: 72mg

Chicken in A Bowl

Prep time: 10 minutes | Cook time: 5 minutes | Serves 2

½ cup cooked chicken, cut into strips
4 green onions, diced
2 garlic cloves, minced
1 tablespoon sesame oil
⅓ cup coconut aminos
1 tablespoon coconut oil
2 large carrots, cut into strips
1 head of cabbage, chopped

1. Melt coconut oil in a skillet over medium high heat.
2. Sauté the cabbage then add the carrots. Continue sautéing until soft. If it gets too dry, add a little bit of water.
3. Season with sesame oil and coconut aminos.
4. Add the garlic and cook for 5 minutes.
5. Throw in the chicken strips and toss the green onions.

Per Serving

calories: 280 | fat: 15.7g | protein: 14g | carbs: 25g | fiber: 7g | sugar: 13g | sodium: 143mg

Chicken with Balsamic Cherry Sauce

Prep time: 10 minutes | Cook time: 26 minutes | Serves 4

1 tablespoon coconut oil
4 boneless, skinless chicken breasts
Salt
Freshly ground black pepper
2 scallions, sliced
¾ cup chicken broth
1 tablespoon balsamic vinegar
½ cup dried cherries

1. Preheat the oven to 375°F (190°C).
2. In a large oven-proof skillet over medium-high heat, melt the coconut oil.
3. Season the chicken with salt and pepper. Place the chicken in the pan and brown it on both sides, about 3 minutes per side.
4. Add the scallions, chicken broth, balsamic vinegar, and dried cherries. Cover with an oven-proof lid or aluminum foil and place the pan in the preheated oven.
5. Bake for 20 minutes, or until the chicken is cooked through.

Per Serving

calories: 379 | fat: 14g | protein: 43g | carbs: 17g | fiber: 5g | sugar: 9g | sodium: 308mg

Chicken, Butternut Squash and Hazelnut

Prep time: 10 minutes | Cook time: 48 minutes | Serves 4

¼ cup unsweetened coconut milk
½ cup hazelnut, crushed
6 cups baby spinach leaves, chopped
1 orange, juiced
Salt and pepper, to taste
1 medium-sized boneless chicken breast, sliced in half
1 medium-sized butternut squash, halved and deseeded

1. Preheat the oven to 350°F (180°C).
2. Sprinkle the butternut squash with salt and paper and place them face down in a baking pan. Put the chicken breasts in the same baking pan. Squeeze orange juice over the chicken. Bake for 35 minutes until both squash and chicken are cooked through.
3. Meanwhile, sauté spinach in a skillet and cook for 3 minutes or until wilted.
4. In another pan, toast the crushed hazelnuts over medium heat.
5. Once the chicken and squash are cooked, it is time to assemble everything.
6. Scoop the squash and shred the chicken and put them in a mixing bowl. Add the hazelnut, spinach and coconut cream. Mix until well combined.
7. Place in a baking dish and cook in the broiler for 1o minutes or until the top takes on a golden brown.

Per Serving

calories: 301 | fat: 17g | protein: 26g | carbs: 18g | fiber: 9.5g | sugar: 6g | sodium: 209mg

Chicken, Carrot and Broccoli Stir-Fry

Prep time: 10 minutes | Cook time: 10 minutes | Serves 4 to 6

1 pound (454 g) boneless, skinless chicken thighs, cut into thin strips
1 tablespoon coconut oil
2 cups broccoli florets
2 carrots, cut into matchsticks
1 garlic clove, minced
1 teaspoon minced fresh ginger
1 teaspoon salt
¼ teaspoon red pepper flakes
½ cup chicken broth
1 teaspoon toasted sesame oil
1 teaspoon coconut aminos
1 tablespoon sesame seeds

1. In a large pan or Dutch oven over high heat, melt the coconut oil. Add the chicken and sauté for 5 to 8 minutes, or until the chicken browns.
2. Stir in the broccoli, carrots, garlic, ginger, salt, red pepper flakes, and chicken broth. Cover the pan and cook for 5 minutes, or until the broccoli turns bright green.
3. Remove the pan from the heat and stir in the sesame oil, coconut aminos, and sesame seeds.

Per Serving

calories: 305 | fat: 14g | protein: 35g | carbs: 8g | fiber: 2g | sugar: 2g | sodium: 812mg

Chicken with Snow Peas and Brown Rice

Prep time: 10 minutes | Cook time: 5 minutes | Serves 4

1 tablespoon coconut oil
2 cups cooked brown rice
1 cup cooked chicken, cut into ½-inch cubes
4 ounces (113 g) snow peas, strings removed
½ cup chicken broth
1 teaspoon salt
½ teaspoon ground ginger
1 teaspoon toasted sesame oil
1 teaspoon coconut aminos
2 scallions, sliced

1. In a large pan over high heat, melt the coconut oil. Add the rice and chicken. Sauté for about 2 minutes.
2. Add the snow peas, chicken broth, salt, and ginger. Cover the pan, reduce the heat to low, and cook for 3 minutes, or until the snow peas turn bright green.
3. Remove the pan from the heat. Stir in the sesame oil, coconut aminos, and scallions.

Per Serving

calories: 285 | fat: 7g | protein: 15g | carbs: 39g | fiber: 3g | sugar: 1g | sodium: 705mg

Chipotle Chicken with Butternut Squash

Prep time: 10 minutes | Cook time: 29 minutes | Serves 4

4 boneless, skinless chicken breasts
1 teaspoon salt
½ teaspoon chipotle powder
½ teaspoon ground cumin
2 tablespoons extra-virgin olive oil
1 onion, chopped
1 cup brown basmati rice
2 cups butternut squash, cut into ½-inch pieces
2 cups chicken broth
1 cup cooked black beans
1 lime, cut into 8 wedges

1. Place the chicken on a large plate.
2. In a small bowl, mix together the salt, chipotle powder, and cumin. Rub the mixture onto the chicken breasts.
3. Place a large pan or Dutch oven over high heat and add the olive oil. When the oil is hot, add the chicken and brown it, about 3 minutes per side. Remove the chicken from the pan and transfer it to a plate.
4. Add the onions to the pan. Sauté for about 3 minutes, or until just softened.
5. Stir in the rice, butternut squash, and chicken broth.
6. Return the chicken to the pan and cover it. Bring to a boil, reduce the heat to simmer, and cook for 20 minutes.
7. Remove the pan from the heat and stir in the black beans. Serve with the lime wedges.

Per Serving

calories: 623 | fat: 19g | protein: 52g | carbs: 60g | fiber: 7g | sugar: 3g | sodium: 992mg

Whole Chicken with Apple Juice

Prep time: 10 minutes | Cook time: 35 minutes | Serves 4 to 6

1 whole chicken, cut into 8 pieces
1 tablespoon brown rice flour, or coconut flour
1 teaspoon salt
1 teaspoon ground cumin
2 teaspoons sweet paprika
½ teaspoon garlic powder
½ teaspoon freshly ground black pepper
1 cup no-added-sugar apple juice

1. Preheat the oven to 375°F (190°C).
2. Place the chicken pieces in a baking pan.
3. In a small bowl, combine the brown rice flour, salt, cumin, paprika, garlic powder, and pepper. Rub the spice mix onto the chicken pieces.
4. Carefully pour the apple juice into the pan; avoid washing the spice mixture off the chicken.
5. Place the pan in the preheated oven and bake for 35 to 45 minutes, or until the chicken is golden brown and cooked through.

Per Serving

calories: 375 | fat: 21g | protein: 39g | carbs: 10g | fiber: 1g | sugar: 7g | sodium: 930mg

Cumin Chicken Thighs with Sweet Potatoes

Prep time: 10 minutes | Cook time: 35 minutes | Serves 4 to 6

2 tablespoons extra-virgin olive oil or coconut oil
2 shallots, sliced thin
1 teaspoon salt
½ teaspoon ground cumin
½ teaspoon ground cinnamon
¼ teaspoon freshly ground black pepper
1 cup chicken broth
6 bone-in chicken thighs
2 small sweet potatoes, peeled and cut into ½-inch cubes

1. Preheat the oven to 425°F (220°C).
2. In a large baking dish, stir together the oil, shallots, salt, cumin, cinnamon, pepper, and chicken broth.
3. Add the chicken and sweet potatoes. Stir to coat with the spices.
4. Place the dish in the preheated oven and bake for 35 to 45 minutes, or until the chicken is cooked through and the sweet potatoes are tender.

Per Serving

calories: 524 | fat: 33g | protein: 33g | carbs: 22g | fiber: 3g | sugar: 1g | sodium: 908mg

Honey-Lime Chicken Drumsticks

Prep time: 10 minutes | Cook time: 25 minutes | Serves 4 to 6

6 chicken drumsticks
1 cup unsweetened coconut yogurt
½ cup extra-virgin olive oil
Juice of 2 limes
2 garlic cloves, smashed
1 tablespoon raw honey
1 teaspoon salt
1 teaspoon ground cumin
½ teaspoon paprika
½ teaspoon ground turmeric
¼ teaspoon freshly ground black pepper
Olive oil cooking spray

1. Place the chicken in a shallow baking dish.
2. In a small bowl, whisk together the yogurt, olive oil, lime juice, garlic, honey, salt, cumin, paprika, turmeric, and pepper until smooth.
3. Pour the yogurt mixture over the chicken. Cover with plastic wrap and chill for 30 minutes or overnight.
4. Preheat the oven to 375°F (190°C).
5. Line a rimmed baking sheet with aluminum foil and lightly grease it with cooking spray.
6. Remove the drumsticks from the marinade and place them on the prepared sheet. Discard the marinade.
7. Place the sheet in the preheated oven and bake the drumsticks for 25 to 35 minutes, or until they start to brown and are cooked through.

Per Serving

calories: 380 | fat: 31g | protein: 19g | carbs: 9g | fiber: 2g | sugar: 5g | sodium: 686mg

Chicken Satay with Ginger-Lime Sauce

Prep time: 15 minutes | Cook time: 8 minutes | Serves 4

Sauce:
½ cup almond butter
¼ cup water
2 tablespoons coconut aminos
1 tablespoon grated fresh ginger
1 tablespoon freshly squeezed lime juice
1 garlic clove
1 teaspoon raw honey
Satay:
Juice of 2 limes (2 to 4 tablespoons)
2 tablespoons olive oil
2 tablespoons raw honey
1 tablespoon finely chopped fresh cilantro
1 tablespoon bottled minced garlic
1½ pounds (680 g) boneless, skinless chicken breast, cut into strips

Make the Sauce
1. In a blender, combine the almond butter, water, coconut aminos, ginger, lime juice, garlic, and honey. Pulse until smooth. Set it aside.
Make the Satay
2. In a large bowl, whisk the lime juice, olive oil, honey, cilantro, and garlic until well mixed.
3. Add the chicken strips and toss to coat. Cover the bowl with plastic wrap and refrigerate for 1 hour to marinate.
4. Preheat the broiler.
5. Place a rack in the upper quarter of the oven.
6. Thread each chicken strip onto a wooden skewer and lay them on a rimmed baking sheet.
7. Broil the chicken for about 4 minutes per side until cooked through and golden, turning once.
8. Serve with the sauce.

Per Serving

calories: 510 | fat: 29g | protein: 46g | carbs: 15g | fiber: 4g | sugar: 12g | sodium: 584mg

Coconut Chicken Curry with Cilantro

Prep time: 10 minutes | Cook time: 6 hours | Serves 4 to 6

1 tablespoon coconut oil
6 bone-in skin-on chicken thighs
1 onion, sliced
2 garlic cloves, smashed
2 teaspoons curry powder
1 teaspoon salt
¼ teaspoon freshly ground black pepper
1 (13½-ounce / 383-g) can unsweetened coconut milk
3 cups chicken broth
¼ cup chopped fresh cilantro
2 scallions, sliced

1. Coat the slow cooker with the coconut oil.
2. Add the chicken, onion, garlic, curry powder, salt, pepper, coconut milk, and chicken broth. Cover the slow cooker and cook on high for 6 hours.
3. Garnish with the cilantro and scallions before serving.

Per Serving

calories: 652 | fat: 56g | protein: 32g | carbs: 10g | fiber: 3g | sugar: 5g | sodium: 1077mg

Rosemary-Thyme Whole Chicken

Prep time: 10 minutes | Cook time: 1½ hour | Serves 4

1 (4-pound / 1.8-kg) whole chicken, rinsed and patted dry
2 lemons, halved
1 sweet onion, quartered
4 garlic cloves, crushed
6 fresh thyme sprigs
6 fresh rosemary sprigs
3 bay leaves
2 tablespoons olive oil
Sea salt
Freshly ground black pepper

1. Preheat the oven to 400°F (205°C).
2. Place the chicken in a roasting pan. Stuff the lemons, onion, garlic, thyme, rosemary, and bay leaves into the cavity.
3. Brush the chicken with the olive oil, and season lightly with sea salt and pepper.
4. Roast the chicken for about 1½ hours until golden brown and cooked through.
5. Remove the chicken from the oven and let it sit for 10 minutes. Remove the lemons, onion, and herbs from the cavity and serve.

Per Serving

calories: 261 | fat: 9g | protein: 38g | carbs: 5g | fiber: 2g | sugar: 5g | sodium: 364mg

Coconut-Lime Chicken Thighs

Prep time: 10 minutes | Cook time: 35 minutes | Serves 4

1½ cups canned lite coconut milk
2 tablespoons grated fresh ginger
Juice of 1 lime (1 or 2 tablespoons)
Zest of 1 lime (optional)
1 tablespoon raw honey
½ teaspoon ground cardamom
1 tablespoon olive oil
1 pound (454 g) bone-in skin-on chicken thighs
1 scallion, white and green parts, chopped

1. In a medium bowl, whisk the coconut milk, ginger, lime juice, lime zest (if using), honey, and cardamom. Set it aside.
2. Place a large skillet over medium-high heat and add the olive oil.
3. Add the chicken thighs and pan-sear for about 20 minutes, or until golden, turning once.
4. Pour the coconut milk mixture over the chicken and bring the liquid to a boil. Reduce the heat to low, cover, and simmer for about 15 minutes, or until the chicken is tender and cooked through.
5. Serve garnished with the scallions.

Per Serving

calories: 480 | fat: 34g | protein: 35g | carbs: 12g | fiber: 3g | sugar: 5g | sodium: 105mg

Thyme Turkey Meatballs

Prep time: 10 minutes | Cook time: 15 minutes | Serves 4

1½ pounds (680 g) lean ground turkey
½ sweet onion, chopped, or about ½ cup pre-cut packaged onion
¼ cup almond flour
1 tablespoon chopped fresh thyme
2 teaspoons bottled minced garlic
1 egg
¼ teaspoon ground nutmeg
Pinch sea salt

1. Preheat the oven to 350°F (180°C).
2. Line a rimmed baking sheet with aluminum foil and set it aside.
3. In a large bowl, combine the turkey, onion, almond flour, thyme, garlic, egg, nutmeg, and sea salt until well mixed.
4. Roll the turkey mixture into 1½-inch meatballs. Arrange the meatballs on the prepared baking sheet.
5. Bake for about 15 minutes, or until browned and cooked through.

Per Serving

calories: 303 | fat: 16g | protein: 36g | carbs: 4g | fiber: 1g | sugar: 2g | sodium: 176mg

Braised Whole Chicken with Thyme

Prep time: 10 minutes | Cook time: 6 hours | Serves 4 to 6

1 teaspoon garlic powder
1 teaspoon chili powder
1 teaspoon paprika
1 teaspoon dried thyme leaves
1 teaspoon sea salt
Pinch cayenne pepper
Freshly ground black pepper
1 whole chicken (about 4 to 5 pounds / 1.8 to 2.3 kg), neck and giblets removed
½ medium onion, sliced

1. In a small bowl, stir together the garlic powder, chili powder, paprika, thyme, salt, and cayenne. Season with black pepper and stir again to combine. Rub the spice mix all over the exterior of the chicken.
2. Place the chicken in the slow cooker with the sliced onion sprinkled around it.
3. Cover the cooker and set to low. Cook for 6 to 8 hours, or until the internal temperature reaches 165°F (74°C) on a meat thermometer and the juices run clear and serve.

Per Serving

calories: 862 | fat: 59g | protein: 86g | carbs: 7g | fiber: 0g | sugar: 6g | sodium: 920mg

Coconut Chicken Stew with Turmeric

Prep time: 15 minutes | Cook time: 4 hours | Serves 4 to 6

1 tablespoon extra-virgin olive oil
3 pounds (1.4 kg) boneless, skinless chicken thighs
1 large onion, thinly sliced
2 garlic cloves, thinly sliced
1 teaspoon minced fresh ginger root
2 teaspoons ground turmeric
1 teaspoon whole coriander seeds, lightly crushed
1 teaspoon salt
¼ teaspoon freshly ground black pepper
2 cups chicken broth
1 cup unsweetened coconut milk
¼ cup chopped fresh cilantro (optional)

1. Drizzle the oil into a slow cooker.
2. Add the chicken, onion, garlic, ginger root, turmeric, coriander, salt, pepper, chicken broth, and coconut milk, and toss to combine.
3. Cover and cook on high for 4 hours. Garnish with the chopped cilantro (if using) and serve.

Per Serving

calories: 370 | fat: 19g | protein: 46g | carbs: 4g | fiber: 1g | sugar: 1g | sodium: 770mg

Sesame Chicken Thighs in Miso

Prep time: 10 minutes | Cook time: 4 hours | Serves 4 to 6

¼ cup white miso
2 tablespoons coconut oil, melted
2 tablespoons honey
1 tablespoon unseasoned rice wine vinegar
2 garlic cloves, thinly sliced
1 teaspoon minced fresh ginger root
1 cup chicken broth
8 boneless, skinless chicken thighs
2 scallions, sliced
1 tablespoon sesame seeds

1. In a slow cooker, combine the miso, coconut oil, honey, rice wine vinegar, garlic, and ginger root, mixing well.
2. Add the chicken and toss to combine. Cover and cook on high for 4 hours.
3. Transfer the chicken and sauce to a serving dish. Garnish with the scallions and sesame seeds and serve.

Per Serving

calories: 320 | fat: 15g | protein: 32g | carbs: 17g | fiber: 1g | sugar: 11g | sodium: 1020mg

Dijon Chicken and Fruit Salad

Prep time: 10 minutes | Cook time: 0 minutes | Serves 4

1 large avocado, diced
2 tablespoons Dijon mustard
½ teaspoon garlic powder
Dash salt
Dash freshly ground black pepper
2 (8-ounce / 227-g) grilled boneless, skinless chicken breasts, chopped
2 small green apples, diced
1 cup grapes, halved
¼ cup sliced scallions
2 tablespoons minced celery

1. In a large bowl, combine the avocado, mustard, garlic powder, salt, and pepper, stirring until creamy.
2. Add the chicken, apples, grapes, scallions, and celery. Stir well to combine.
3. Serve chilled, if desired.

Per Serving

calories: 234 | fat: 7g | protein: 24g | carbs: 19g | fiber: 5g | sugar: 14g | sodium: 640mg

Turkey-Veggie Tagine with Apricots

Prep time: 15 minutes | Cook time: 7 hours | Serves 4 to 6

4 cups boneless, skinless turkey breast chunks
1 (14-ounce / 397-g) can diced tomatoes
1 (14-ounce / 397-g) can chickpeas, rinsed and drained well
2 large carrots, finely chopped
½ cup dried apricots
½ red onion, chopped
2 tablespoons raw honey
1 tablespoon tomato paste
1 teaspoon garlic powder
1 teaspoon ground turmeric
½ teaspoon sea salt
¼ teaspoon ground ginger
¼ teaspoon ground coriander
¼ teaspoon paprika
½ cup water
2 cups broth of choice
Freshly ground black pepper

1. In your slow cooker, combine the turkey, tomatoes, chickpeas, carrots, apricots, onion, honey, tomato paste, garlic powder, turmeric, salt, ginger, coriander, paprika, water, and broth, and season with pepper. Gently stir to blend the ingredients.
2. Cover the cooker and set to low. Cook for 7 to 8 hours and serve.

Per Serving

calories: 428 | fat: 5g | protein: 49g | carbs: 46g | fiber: 8g | sugar: 25g | sodium: 983mg

Maple-Dijon Turkey with Veggies

Prep time: 15 minutes | Cook time: 4 hours | Serves 4 to 6

1 tablespoon extra-virgin olive oil
1 pound (454 g) ground turkey
1 celery stalk, minced
1 carrot, minced
½ medium sweet onion, diced
½ red bell pepper, finely chopped
6 tablespoons tomato paste
2 tablespoons apple cider vinegar
1 tablespoon pure maple syrup
1 teaspoon Dijon mustard
1 teaspoon chili powder
½ teaspoon garlic powder
½ teaspoon sea salt
½ teaspoon dried oregano

1. In your slow cooker, combine the olive oil, turkey, celery, carrot, onion, red bell pepper, tomato paste, vinegar, maple syrup, mustard, chili powder, garlic powder, salt, and oregano.
2. Using a large spoon, break up the turkey into smaller chunks as it combines with the other ingredients.
3. Cover the cooker and set to low. Cook for 4 to 6 hours, stir thoroughly, and serve.

Per Serving
calories: 251 | fat: 12g | protein: 24g | carbs: 14g | fiber: 3g | sugar: 9g | sodium: 690mg

Turkey Wings with Balsamic-Honey Glaze

Prep time: 5 minutes | Cook time: 7 hours | Serves 4 to 6

1¼ cups balsamic vinegar
2 tablespoons raw honey
1 teaspoon garlic powder
2 pounds (907 g) turkey wings

1. In a small bowl, whisk the vinegar, honey, and garlic powder.
2. Put the wings in the bottom of the slow cooker and pour the vinegar sauce on top.
3. Cover the cooker and set to low. Cook for 7 to 8 hours.
4. Baste the wings with the sauce from the bottom of the slow cooker and serve.

Per Serving
calories: 501 | fat: 25g | protein: 47g | carbs: 23g | fiber: 0g | sugar: 9g | sodium: 162mg

Ginger-Cilantro Turkey Burgers

Prep time: 10 minutes | Cook time: 6 minutes | Serves 4

1½ pounds (680 g) ground turkey
1 large egg, lightly beaten
2 tablespoons coconut flour (or almond flour)
½ cup finely chopped onion
1 garlic clove, minced
2 teaspoons minced fresh ginger root
1 tablespoon fresh cilantro
1 teaspoon salt
¼ teaspoon freshly ground black pepper
1 tablespoon extra-virgin olive oil

1. In a medium bowl, combine the ground turkey, egg, flour, onion, garlic, ginger root, cilantro, salt, and pepper and mix well.
2. Form the turkey mixture into four patties.
3. Heat the olive oil in a large skillet over medium-high heat.
4. Cook the burgers, flipping once, until firm to the touch, 3 to 4 minutes on each side. Serve.

Per Serving
calories: 320 | fat: 20g | protein: 34g | carbs: 2g | fiber: 1g | sugar: 1g | sodium: 720mg

Turkey Meatballs with Tomato Sauce

Prep time: 15 minutes | Cook time: 6 hours | Serves 4 to 6

1 spaghetti squash, halved lengthwise and seeded
Sauce:
1 (15-ounce / 425-g) can diced tomatoes
½ teaspoon garlic powder
½ teaspoon dried oregano
½ teaspoon sea salt
Meatballs:
1 pound (454 g) ground turkey
1 large egg, whisked
½ small white onion, minced
1 teaspoon garlic powder
½ teaspoon sea salt
½ teaspoon dried oregano
½ teaspoon dried basil leaves
Freshly ground black pepper

1. Place the squash halves in the bottom of your slow cooker, cut-side down.
Make the Sauce
2. Pour the diced tomatoes around the squash in the bottom of the slow cooker.
3. Sprinkle in the garlic powder, oregano, and salt.
Make the Meatballs
4. In a medium bowl, mix together the turkey, egg, onion, garlic powder, salt, oregano, and basil, and season with pepper. Form the turkey mixture into 12 balls, and place them in the slow cooker around the spaghetti squash.
5. Cover the cooker and set to low. Cook for 6 to 7 hours.
6. Transfer the squash to a work surface and use a fork to shred it into spaghetti-like strands. Combine the strands with the tomato sauce, top with the meatballs, and serve.

Per Serving
calories: 253 | fat: 8g | protein: 24g | carbs: 22g | fiber: 1g | sugar: 4g | sodium: 948mg

Mushroom Turkey Thighs in Wine

Prep time: 15 minutes | Cook time: 4 hours | Serves 4

1 tablespoon extra-virgin olive oil
2 turkey thighs
2 cups button or cremini mushrooms, sliced
1 large onion, sliced
1 garlic clove, sliced
1 rosemary sprig
1 teaspoon salt
¼ teaspoon freshly ground black pepper
2 cups chicken broth
½ cup dry red wine

1. Drizzle the olive oil into a slow cooker. Add the turkey thighs, mushrooms, onion, garlic, rosemary sprig, salt, and pepper. Pour in the chicken broth and wine. Cover and cook on high for 4 hours.
2. Remove and discard the rosemary sprig. Use a slotted spoon to transfer the thighs to a plate and allow them to cool for several minutes for easier handling.
3. Cut the meat from the bones, stir the meat into the mushrooms, and serve.

Per Serving

calories: 280 | fat: 9g | protein: 43g | carbs: 3g | fiber: 1g | sugar: 1g | sodium: 850mg

Garlic-Lemon Chicken Thighs

Prep time: 5 minutes | Cook time: 7 hours | Serves 4 to 6

2 cups chicken broth
1½ teaspoons garlic powder
1 teaspoon sea salt
Juice and zest of 1 large lemon
2 pounds (907 g) boneless, skinless chicken thighs

1. Pour the broth into the slow cooker.
2. In a small bowl, stir together the garlic powder, salt, lemon juice, and lemon zest.
3. Baste each chicken thigh with an even coating of the mixture. Place the thighs along the bottom of the slow cooker.
4. Cover the cooker and set to low. Cook for 7 to 8 hours, or until the internal temperature of the chicken reaches 165°F (74°C) on a meat thermometer and the juices run clear and serve.

Per Serving

calories: 290 | fat: 14g | protein: 43g | carbs: 3g | fiber: 0g | sugar: 0g | sodium: 917mg

Beef Sirloin and Veggie Kebabs

Prep time: 10 minutes | Cook time: 0 minutes | Serves 4

2 tablespoons olive oil, divided
1 tablespoon coconut aminos
1 tablespoon apple cider vinegar
1 tablespoon bottled minced garlic
1 tablespoon chopped fresh cilantro
1 pound (454 g) boneless top sirloin steak, trimmed of visible fat and cut into 1½-inch chunks
1 red onion, quartered and separated into layers
1 sweet potato, peeled, halved lengthwise, and each half cut into 8 pieces
8 medium button mushrooms

1. In a large bowl, stir together 1 tablespoon of olive oil, the coconut aminos, cider vinegar, garlic, and cilantro until well mixed.
2. Add the beef to the bowl and stir to coat the meat in the marinade. Cover the bowl and refrigerate for 1 hour to marinate.
3. Preheat the broiler.
4. Place an oven rack in the top quarter of the oven.
5. On 4 skewers, assemble the kebabs by alternating pieces of beef, onion, sweet potato, and mushrooms.
6. Lightly brush the vegetables with the remaining 1 tablespoon of olive oil and arrange the kebabs on a baking sheet.
7. Broil the kebabs for 10 minutes for medium, turning once or twice, or until the beef is cooked to your desired doneness. Transfer the kebabs to a plate and let them rest for 5 minutes before serving.

Per Serving (1 kebab)

calories: 319 | fat: 14g | protein: 37g | carbs: 10g | fiber: 2g | sugar: 3g | sodium: 333mg

Horseradish Beef Meatloaf with Basil

Prep time: 10 minutes | Cook time: 1 hour | Serves 4

1½ pounds (680 g) extra-lean ground beef
½ cup almond flour
½ cup chopped sweet onion
1 egg
1 tablespoon chopped fresh basil
1 tablespoon chopped fresh parsley
1 teaspoon grated fresh horseradish, or prepared horseradish
⅛ teaspoon sea salt

1. Preheat the oven to 350°F (180°C).
2. In a large bowl, combine the ground beef, almond flour, onion, egg, basil, parsley, horseradish, and sea salt until well mixed. Press the meatloaf mixture into a loaf pan.
3. Bake for about 1 hour until cooked through.
4. Remove the meatloaf from the oven and let it rest for 10 minutes.

Per Serving

calories: 407 | fat: 18g | protein: 56g | carbs: 4g | fiber: 2g | sugar: 1g | sodium: 212mg

Beef Lettuce Wraps

Prep time: 15 minutes | Cook time: 7 hours | Serves 4 to 6

2 pounds (907 g) beef chuck roast
1 small white onion, diced
1 cup broth of choice
3 tablespoons coconut aminos
2 tablespoons coconut sugar
1 tablespoon rice vinegar
1 teaspoon garlic powder
1 teaspoon sesame oil
½ teaspoon ground ginger
¼ teaspoon red pepper flakes
8 romaine lettuce leaves
1 tablespoon sesame seeds (optional)
2 scallions (both white and green parts), diced (optional)

1. In your slow cooker, combine the beef, onion, broth, coconut aminos, coconut sugar, vinegar, garlic powder, sesame oil, ginger, and red pepper flakes.
2. Cover the cooker and set to low. Cook for 7 to 8 hours.
3. Scoop spoonfuls of the beef mixture into each lettuce leaf. Garnish with sesame seeds and diced scallion (if using) and serve.

Per Serving

calories: 428 | fat: 23g | protein: 46g | carbs: 12g | fiber: 1g | sugar: 10g | sodium: 425mg

Garlic Beef Bolognese

Prep time: 15 minutes | Cook time: 7 hours | Serves 4 to 6

1 tablespoon extra-virgin olive oil
3 garlic cloves, minced
½ cup chopped onion
⅔ cup chopped celery
⅔ cup chopped carrot
1 pound (454 g) ground beef
1 (14-ounce / 397-g) can diced tomatoes
1 tablespoon white wine vinegar
⅛ teaspoon ground nutmeg
2 bay leaves
½ teaspoon red pepper flakes
Dash sea salt
Dash freshly ground black pepper

1. Coat the bottom of the slow cooker with the olive oil.
2. Add the garlic, onion, celery, carrot, ground beef, tomatoes, vinegar, nutmeg, bay leaves, red pepper flakes, salt, and black pepper. Using a fork, break up the ground beef as much as possible.
3. Cover the cooker and set to low. Cook for 7 to 8 hours.
4. Remove and discard the bay leaves. Stir, breaking up the meat completely, and serve.

Per Serving

calories: 314 | fat: 21g | protein: 22g | carbs: 10g | fiber: 2g | sugar: 5g | sodium: 376mg

Beef Meatballs with Tomatoes

Prep time: 15 minutes | Cook time: 7 hours | Makes 12 meatballs

1½ pounds (680 g) ground beef
1 large egg
1 small white onion, minced
¼ cup minced mushrooms
1 teaspoon garlic powder
½ teaspoon sea salt
½ teaspoon dried oregano
¼ teaspoon freshly ground black pepper
¼ teaspoon ground ginger
Dash red pepper flakes
1 (14-ounce / 397-g) can crushed tomatoes

1. In a large bowl, combine the ground beef, egg, onion, mushrooms, garlic powder, salt, oregano, black pepper, ginger, and red pepper flakes. Mix well. Form the beef mixture into about 12 meatballs.
2. Pour the tomatoes into the bottom of your slow cooker. Gently arrange the meatballs on top.
3. Cover the cooker and set to low. Cook for 7 to 8 hours and serve.

Per Serving (1 meatball)

calories: 131 | fat: 8g | protein: 11g | carbs: 2g | fiber: 0g | sugar: 1g | sodium: 214mg

Pot Roast with Carrots and Garlic

Prep time: 15 minutes | Cook time: 7 thours | Serves 6 to 8

1 teaspoon sea salt
1½ teaspoons dried thyme leaves
1 teaspoon dried rosemary
½ teaspoon freshly ground black pepper
1 (4-pound / 1.8-kg) beef chuck roast
1 medium onion, sliced
5 carrots, chopped
1 celery stalk, chopped
6 garlic cloves, minced
2 cups broth of choice
3 bay leaves
2 large sweet potatoes, peeled and cubed

1. In a small bowl, stir together the salt, thyme, rosemary, and pepper. Rub the spices all over the roast. Set aside.
2. In your slow cooker, layer the onion, carrots, celery, and garlic on the bottom.
3. Add the broth and bay leaves. Put the meat on top of the vegetables.
4. Put the sweet potatoes on top of the meat.
5. Cover the cooker and set to low. Cook for 7 to 8 hours.
6. Remove and discard the bay leaves before serving.

Per Serving

calories: 579 | fat: 29g | protein: 63g | carbs: 21g | fiber: 4g | sugar: 8g | sodium: 660mg

THE ULTIMATE ANTI-INFLAMMATORY DIET COOKBOOK

Chili-Garlic Pork Loin with Lime

Prep time: 10 minutes | Cook time: 6 hours | Serves 4 to 6

3 teaspoons chili powder
2 teaspoons garlic powder
1 teaspoon ground cumin
½ teaspoon sea salt
2 (1-pound / 454-g) pork tenderloins
1 cup broth of choice
¼ cup freshly squeezed lime juice

1. In a small bowl, stir together the chili powder, garlic powder, cumin, and salt. Rub the pork all over with the spice mixture and put it in the slow cooker.
2. Pour the broth and lime juice around the pork in the cooker.
3. Cover the cooker and set to low. Cook for 6 to 7 hours.
4. Remove the pork from the slow cooker and let rest for 5 minutes. Slice the pork against the grain into medallions before serving.

Per Serving

calories: 259 | fat: 5g | protein: 50g | carbs: 5g | fiber: 1g | sugar: 0g | sodium: 510mg

Sumptuous Indian Chicken Curry

Prep time: 15 minutes | Cook time: 32 minutes | Serves 6

2 tablespoons coconut oil, divided
2 (4-ounce / 113-g) boneless, skinless chicken breasts, cut into bite-size pieces
2 medium carrots, diced
1 small white onion, diced
1 tablespoon minced fresh ginger
6 garlic cloves, minced
1 cup sugar snap peas, diced
1 (5-ounce / 153-g) can unsweetened coconut cream
1 tablespoon sugar-free fish sauce
1 cup low-sodium chicken broth
½ cup diced tomatoes, with juice
1 tablespoon curry powder
¼ teaspoon sea salt
Pinch cayenne pepper, to taste
Freshly ground black pepper, to taste
¼ cup filtered water

1. Heat 1 tablespoon of coconut oil in a nonstick skillet over medium-high heat until melted.
2. Add the chicken breasts to the skillet and cook for 15 minutes or until an instant-read thermometer inserted in the thickest part of the chicken breasts registers at least 165°F (74°C). Flip the chicken breasts halfway through the cooking time.
3. Meanwhile, in a separate skillet, heat the remaining coconut oil over medium heat until melted.
4. Add the carrots, onion, ginger, and garlic to the skillet and sauté for 5 minutes or until fragrant and the onion is translucent.
5. Add the peas, coconut cream, fish sauce, chicken broth, tomatoes, curry powder, salt, cayenne pepper, black pepper, and water to the skillet. Stir to mix well.
6. Bring to a boil. Reduce the heat to medium-low then simmer for 10 minutes.
7. Add the cooked chicken to the second skillet, then cook for 2 more minutes to combine well.
8. Pour the curry on a large serving plate, then serve immediately.

Per Serving

calories: 223 | fat: 16g | protein: 13g | carbs: 9g | fiber: 3g | sugar: 2g | sodium: 673mg

Pork and Spinach Ragù

Prep time: 10 minutes | Cook time: 7 hours | Serves 4 to 6

1 pound (454 g) pork tenderloin
1 medium yellow onion, diced
1 red bell pepper, diced
1 (28-ounce / 794-g) can diced tomatoes
2 teaspoons chili powder
1 teaspoon garlic powder
½ teaspoon ground cumin
½ teaspoon smoked paprika
Dash red pepper flakes
1 cup fresh spinach leaves, minced

1. In your slow cooker, combine the pork, onion, bell pepper, tomatoes, chili powder, garlic powder, cumin, paprika, red pepper flakes, and spinach.
2. Cover the cooker and set to low. Cook for 7 to 8 hours.
3. Transfer the pork loin to a cutting board and shred with a fork. Return it to the slow cooker, stir it into the sauce, and serve.

Per Serving

calories: 292 | fat: 10g | protein: 36g | carbs: 15g | fiber: 3g | sugar: 8g | sodium: 532mg

Pork Chops with Apple-Raisin Salsa

Prep time: 10 minutes | Cook time: 14 minutes | Serves 4

Salsa:
1 teaspoon olive oil
¼ cup finely chopped sweet onion
½ teaspoon grated fresh ginger
2 apples, peeled, cored, and diced
½ cup dried raisins
Pinch sea salt
Pork Chops:
4 (4-ounce / 113-g) boneless center-cut pork chops, trimmed and patted dry
1 teaspoon garlic powder
1 teaspoon ground cinnamon
Sea salt
Freshly ground black pepper
1 tablespoon olive oil

Make the Salsa
1. Place a medium skillet over medium heat and add the olive oil.
2. Add the onion and ginger. Sauté for about 2 minutes, or until softened.
3. Stir in the apples and raisins. Sauté for about 5 minutes, or until the fruit is just tender. Season the salsa with sea salt and set it aside.
Make the Pork Chops
4. Sprinkle the pork chops on both sides with the garlic powder, cinnamon, sea salt, and pepper.
5. Place a large skillet over medium-high heat and add the olive oil.
6. Add the seasoned chops and pan-fry for 7 to 8 minutes per side until just cooked through and browned, turning once.
7. Serve the chops with the cooked apple salsa.

Per Serving

calories: 434 | fat: 32g | protein: 26g | carbs: 10g | fiber: 4g | sugar: 22g | sodium: 148mg

Pork Loin with Celeriac and Fennel

Prep time: 10 minutes | Cook time: 1¼ hours | Serves 4

1 fennel bulb, fronds cut off, cut into ¼-inch slices
1 celeriac, peeled and diced
2 tablespoons olive oil, divided
1 tablespoon pure maple syrup
1 teaspoon bottled minced garlic
Pinch sea salt
1 pound (454 g) boned pork loin, trimmed of visible fat
1 teaspoon chopped fresh thyme

1. Preheat the oven to 375°F (190°C).
2. In a large bowl, toss the fennel, celeriac, 1 tablespoon of olive oil, maple syrup, garlic, and sea salt until well mixed. Transfer the vegetables to a baking dish and set it aside.
3. Place a large skillet over medium-high heat and add the remaining 1 tablespoon of olive oil.
4. Add the pork loin. Brown it on all sides, turning, for about 15 minutes total. Place the browned pork on top on the vegetables and sprinkle with the thyme.
5. Roast the pork for about 1 hour until cooked through, but still juicy.
6. Transfer the roast and vegetables to a serving platter and pour any pan juices over the top.
7. Let the meat rest for 10 minutes before serving.

Per Serving
calories: 400 | fat: 23g | protein: 33g | carbs: 15g | fiber: 3g | sugar: 8| sodium: 306mg

Mustard Lamb Chops with Oregano

Prep time: 5 minutes | Cook time: 15 minutes | Serves 4

8 (4- to 5-ounce / 113- to 142-g) lamb loin chops
2 tablespoons chopped fresh oregano
4 garlic cloves, mashed
¼ cup extra-virgin olive oil
1 teaspoon Dijon mustard
1 teaspoon salt
¼ teaspoon freshly ground black pepper

1. Place the lamb chops in a shallow baking dish.
2. In a small bowl, whisk together the oregano, garlic, olive oil, Dijon mustard, salt, and pepper.
3. Rub the mixture over the lamb chops. Cover the dish with plastic wrap and marinate the chops at room temperature for 30 minutes.
4. Preheat the oven to 425°F (220°C).
5. Remove the plastic wrap and place the dish in the preheated oven. Bake the lamb chops for 15 to 20 minutes, or until they are sizzling and browned.
6. Let the chops sit for 5 minutes before serving.

Per Serving
calories: 648 | fat: 34g | protein: 80g | carbs: 3g | fiber: 1g | sugar: 0g | sodium: 812mg

Cider Vinegar Marinated Lamb Souvlaki

Prep time: 5 minutes | Cook time: 15 minutes | Makes 8 skewers

2 tablespoons olive oil
2 tablespoons apple cider vinegar
1 tablespoon dried oregano
2 teaspoons bottled minced garlic
½ teaspoon sea salt
1 pound (454 g) lamb shoulder, cut into 1-inch cubes

1. In a large bowl, stir together the olive oil, cider vinegar, oregano, garlic, and sea salt until well mixed.
2. Stir in the lamb. Cover the bowl and refrigerate it for 1 hour to marinate.
3. Preheat the broiler.
4. Place one of the racks in the upper third of the oven.
5. Using 8 wooden skewers, thread 4 or 5 pieces of lamb on each and arrange them on a baking sheet.
6. Broil, turning, for about 15 minutes total until the meat is browned evenly on all sides.

Per Serving (2 skewers)
calories: 278 | fat: 15g | protein: 32g | carbs: 1g | fiber: 1g | sugar: 0g | sodium: 375mg

Lamb Ragù with Tomatoes and Lentils

Prep time: 10 minutes | Cook time: 27 minutes | Serves 4

2 tablespoons extra-virgin olive oil
1 red onion, chopped
4 garlic cloves, minced
1 pound (454 g) lean ground lamb
1 (14-ounce / 397-g) can chopped tomatoes
1 cup chicken broth, plus additional as needed
½ cup green lentils
1 teaspoon salt
1 teaspoon dried oregano
1 teaspoon ground cumin
½ teaspoon freshly ground black pepper

1. In a large pan over high heat, heat the olive oil. Add the onion and sauté for 3 minutes. Add the garlic and sauté for 1 minute.
2. Add the ground lamb, breaking it up with a spoon. Cook for 3 to 4 minutes, or until the lamb is browned.
3. Stir in the tomatoes, chicken broth, lentils, salt, oregano, cumin, and pepper.
4. Simmer for 20 minutes, or until the lentils are cooked and most of the liquid has evaporated. If the lentils are not yet tender and most of the liquid has evaporated, stir in a little more broth or some water.

Per Serving
calories: 402 | fat: 16g | protein: 41g | carbs: 23g | fiber: 10g | sugar: 5g | sodium: 867mg

Dijon-Rosemary Leg of Lamb

Prep time: 10 minutes | Cook time: 5 thours | Serves 4 to 6

1½ teaspoons sea salt
½ teaspoon freshly ground black pepper
1 teaspoon garlic powder
1 teaspoon dried thyme leaves
1 teaspoon dried rosemary
1 teaspoons Dijon mustard
1 (4-pound / 1.8-kg) bone-in lamb leg
2 cups broth of choice
1 small onion, roughly chopped

1. In a small bowl, stir together the salt, pepper, garlic powder, thyme, rosemary, and mustard to make a paste. Rub the paste evenly onto the lamb and put it in the slow cooker.
2. Add the broth and onion around the lamb in the cooker.
3. Cover the cooker and set to low. Cook for 5 to 6 hours and serve.

Per Serving

calories: 780 | fat: 41g | protein: 93g | carbs: 3g | fiber: 0g | sugar: 1g | sodium: 1023mg

Orange-Oregano Pork Tacos

Prep time: 15 minutes | Cook time: 7 hours | Serves 4 to 6

1 teaspoon sea salt
1 teaspoon ground cumin
1 teaspoon garlic powder
½ teaspoon dried oregano
½ teaspoon freshly ground black pepper
3 to 4 pounds (1.4 to 1.8 kg) pork shoulder or butt
2 cups broth of choice
Juice of 1 orange
1 small onion, chopped
4 to 6 corn taco shells
Shredded cabbage, lime wedges, avocado, and hot sauce, for topping (optional)

1. In a small bowl, stir together the salt, cumin, garlic powder, oregano, and pepper. Rub the pork with the spice mixture and put it in your slow cooker.
2. Pour the broth and orange juice around the pork. Scatter the onion around the pork.
3. Cover the cooker and set on low. Cook for 7 to 8 hours.
4. Transfer the pork to a work surface and shred it with a fork. Serve in taco shells with any optional toppings you like.

Per Serving

calories: 1156 | fat: 84g | protein: 84g | carbs: 12g | fiber: 2g | sugar: 1g | sodium: 942mg

Stir-Fried Chicken and Broccoli

Prep time: 10 minutes | Cook time: 8½ minutes | Serves 4

3 tablespoons extra-virgin olive oil
1½ cups broccoli florets
1½ pounds (680 g) boneless, skinless chicken breasts, cut into bite-size pieces
½ onion, chopped
½ teaspoon sea salt
⅛ teaspoon freshly ground black pepper
3 garlic cloves, minced
2 cups cooked brown rice

1. Heat the olive oil in a large nonstick skillet over medium-high heat until shimmering.
2. Add the broccoli, chicken, and onion to the skillet and stir well. Season with sea salt and black pepper.
3. Stir-fry for about 8 minutes, or until the chicken is golden browned and cooked through.
4. Toss in the garlic and cook for 30 seconds, stirring constantly, or until the garlic is fragrant.
5. Remove from the heat to a plate and serve over the cooked brown rice.

Per Serving

calories: 344 | fat: 14g | protein: 14g | carbs: 41g | fiber: 3g | sugar: 1g | sodium: 275mg

Chicken Cacciatore

Prep time: 10 minutes | Cook time: 17 tminutes | Serves 4

2 tablespoons extra-virgin olive oil
1½ pounds (680 g) boneless, skinless chicken breasts, cut into bite-size pieces
2 (28-ounce / 794-g) cans crushed tomatoes, drained
½ cup chopped black olives
1 teaspoon onion powder
1 teaspoon garlic powder
½ teaspoon sea salt
⅛ teaspoon freshly ground black pepper

1. Heat the olive oil in a large nonstick skillet over medium-high heat until shimmering.
2. Add the chicken pieces and sauté for 7 to 10 minutes until evenly browned, stirring occasionally.
3. Add the tomatoes, olives, onion powder, garlic powder, sea salt, and black pepper to the skillet, and allow to simmer for 10 minutes, stirring occasionally, or until the chicken is cooked through.
4. Remove from the heat and serve on a plate.

Per Serving

calories: 304 | fat: 11g | protein: 19g | carbs: 34g | fiber: 13g | sugar: 23g | sodium: 1170mg

Chicken and Sweet Potato Stew

Prep time: 10 minutes | Cook time: 40 minutes | Serves 4

1 tablespoon extra virgin olive oil
2 garlic cloves, sliced
1 white onion, chopped
14 ounces (397 g) tomatoes, chopped
2 tablespoons chopped rosemary leaves
Sea salt and ground black pepper, to taste
4 free-range skinless chicken thighs
4 sweet potatoes, peeled and cubed
2 tablespoons basil leaves

1. Preheat the oven to 375°F (190°C).
2. Heat the olive oil in a nonstick skillet over medium heat until shimmering.
3. Add the garlic and onion to the skillet and sauté for 5 minutes or until fragrant and the onion is translucent.
4. Add the tomatoes, rosemary, salt, and ground black pepper and cook for 15 minutes or until lightly thickened.
5. Arrange the chicken thighs and sweet potatoes on a baking sheet, then pour the mixture in the skillet over the chicken and sweet potatoes. Stir to coat well. Pour in enough water to make sure the liquid cover the chicken and sweet potatoes.
6. Bake in the preheated oven for 20 minutes or until the internal temperature of the chicken reaches at least 165°F (74°C).
7. Remove the baking sheet from the oven and pour them in a large bowl. Sprinkle with basil and serve.

Per Serving

calories: 297 | fat: 9g | protein: 22g | carbs: 33g | fiber: 7g | sugar: 9g | sodium: 532mg

Mediterranean Chicken Bake with Vegetables

Prep time: 10 minutes | Cook time: 20 minutes | Serves 4

4 (4-ounce / 113-g) boneless, skinless chicken breasts
2 tablespoons avocado oil
1 cup sliced cremini mushrooms
1 cup packed chopped fresh spinach
1 pint cherry tomatoes, halved
½ cup chopped fresh basil
½ red onion, thinly sliced
4 garlic cloves, minced
2 teaspoons balsamic vinegar

1. Preheat the oven to 400°F (205°C).
2. Arrange the chicken breast in a large baking dish and brush them generously with the avocado oil.
3. Mix together the mushrooms, spinach, tomatoes, basil, red onion, cloves, and vinegar in a medium bowl, and toss to combine. Scatter each chicken breast with ¼ of the vegetable mixture.
4. Bake in the preheated oven for about 20 minutes, or until the internal temperature reaches at least 165°F (74°C) and juices run clear when pierced with a fork.
5. Allow the chicken to rest for 5 to 10 minutes before slicing to serve.

Per Serving

calories: 220 | fat: 9g | protein: 28g | carbs: 7g | fiber: 2g | sugar: 7g | sodium: 310mg

Tuscan Chicken with Tomatoes, Olives, and Zucchini

Prep time: 10 minutes | Cook time: 21 minutes | Serves 4

4 boneless, skinless chicken breast halves, pounded to ½- to ¾-inch thickness
1 teaspoon garlic powder
½ teaspoon sea salt
⅛ teaspoon freshly ground black pepper
2 tablespoons extra-virgin olive oil
2 cups cherry tomatoes
½ cup sliced green olives
1 zucchini, chopped
¼ cup dry white wine

1. On a clean work surface, rub the chicken breasts with garlic powder, salt, and ground black pepper.
2. Heat the olive oil in a nonstick skillet over medium-high heat until shimmering.
3. Add the chicken and cook for 16 minutes or until the internal temperature reaches at least 165°F (74°C). Flip the chicken halfway through the cooking time. Transfer to a large plate and cover with aluminum foil to keep warm.
4. Add the tomatoes, olives, and zucchini to the skillet and sauté for 4 minutes or until the vegetables are soft.
5. Add the white wine to the skillet and simmer for 1 minutes.
6. Remove the aluminum foil and top the chicken with the vegetables and their juices, then serve warm.

Per Serving

calories: 172 | fat: 11g | protein: 8g | carbs: 8g | fiber: 2g | sugar: 4g | sodium: 742mg

Turkey Gumbo

Prep time:10 minutes | Cook time: 1⅚ hours | Serves 12

1 whole turkey
1 stalk celery, chopped
1 onion, quartered
3 garlic cloves, chopped
2 cups water
1 tablespoon extra virgin olive oil
½ cup chopped okra
14 ounces (397 g) chopped tomatoes
1 to 2 bay leaves
Sea salt and ground black pepper, to taste

1. Put the turkey, celery, onion and garlic in a large pot, then pour in the water. Bring to a boil over high heat.
2. Reduce the heat to low and simmer for 45 minutes or until an instant-read thermometer inserted in the thickest part of the turkey reaches at least 165°F (74°C).
3. Meanwhile, heat the olive oil in the nonstick skillet over medium heat until shimmering.
4. Add the okra to the skillet and sauté for 5 minutes or until tender.
5. Add the okra, tomatoes, and bay leaves to the pot of broth, then stir and cook for an additional 1 hour or until the broth is slightly thickened.
6. Pour the gumbo in a large serving bowl, then sprinkle with salt and pepper. Discard the bay leaves. Stir to mix well. Serve warm.

Per Serving

calories: 489 | fat: 9g | protein: 95g | carbs: 3g | fiber: 1g | sugar: 2g | sodium: 534mg

General Tso's Chicken

Prep time: 15 minutes | Cook time: 15 minutes | Serves 4

Sauce:
¼ teaspoon ground ginger
1 tablespoon almond butter
3 tablespoons coconut aminos
1 tablespoon arrowroot powder
½ teaspoon red pepper flakes
2 garlic cloves, minced
2 tablespoons rice vinegar
3 tablespoons coconut sugar
Chicken:
1 tablespoon avocado oil
1 cup brown rice flour
¼ teaspoon garlic powder
¼ teaspoon sea salt
1 pound (454 g) boneless, skinless chicken thighs, cut into 1-inch pieces

Make the Sauce
1. Combine the ginger and almond butter in a saucepan. Cook over medium heat for 2 minutes or until fragrant.
2. Add the coconut aminos, arrowroot powder, red pepper flakes, garlic, vinegar, and coconut sugar to the saucepan. Stir to mix well.
3. Bring to a boil. Reduce the heat to medium-low and cook for 5 minutes or until the sauce is thickened.
Make the Chicken
4. Heat the avocado oil in a nonstick skillet over medium-high heat.
5. Combine the rice flour, garlic powder, and sea salt in a small bowl. Stir to mix well.
6. Dunk the chicken in the mixture, then place in the skillet and cook for 8 minutes or until golden brown and crispy. Flip the chicken halfway through the cooking time.
7. Transfer the chicken thighs on a large plate and baste with the sauce before serving.

Per Serving
calories: 483 | fat: 21g | protein: 33g | carbs: 41g | fiber: 3g | sugar: 7g | sodium: 1397mg

Lime Chicken Drumsticks with Cilantro

Prep time: 5 minutes | Cook time: 2 hours | Serves 4 to 6

¼ cup fresh cilantro, chopped
3 tablespoons freshly squeezed lime juice
½ teaspoon garlic powder
½ teaspoon sea salt
¼ teaspoon ground cumin
3 pounds (1.4 kg) chicken drumsticks

1. In a small bowl, stir together the cilantro, lime juice, garlic powder, salt, and cumin to form a paste.
2. Put the drumsticks in the slow cooker. Spread the cilantro paste evenly on each drumstick.
3. Cover the cooker and set to high. Cook for 2 to 3 hours, or until the internal temperature of the chicken reaches 165°F (74°C) on a meat thermometer and the juices run clear and serve.

Per Serving
calories: 417 | fat: 12g | protein: 71g | carbs: 1g | fiber: 1g | sugar: 1g | sodium: 591mg

Lemon Tenderloin

Prep time: 5 minutes | Cook time: 21 minutes | Serves 2

¼ teaspoon za'atar seasoning
Zest of 1 lemon
½ teaspoon dried thyme
¼ teaspoon garlic powder
¼ teaspoon salt
1 tablespoon olive oil
1 (8-ounce / 227-g) pork tenderloin, sliver skin trimmed

1. Preheat the oven to 425°F (220°C).
2. Combine the za'atar seasoning, lemon zest, thyme, garlic powder, and salt in a bowl, then rub the pork tenderloin with the mixture on both sides.
3. Warm the olive oil in an oven-safe skillet over medium-high heat until shimmering.
4. Add the pork tenderloin and sear for 6 minutes or until browned. Flip the pork halfway through the cooking time.
5. Arrange the skillet in the preheated oven and roast for 15 minutes or until an instant-read thermometer inserted in the thickest part of the tenderloin registers at least 145°F (63°C).
6. Transfer the cooked tenderloin to a large plate and allow to cool for a few minutes before serving.

Per Serving
calories: 184 | fat: 11g | carbs: 1g | fiber: 0g | protein: 20g | sodium: 358mg

Rosemary Beef Ribs

Prep time: 10 minutes | Cook time: 2¹⁄₁₂ hours | Serves 4

1½ pounds (680 g) boneless beef short ribs
½ teaspoon garlic powder
1 teaspoon salt
½ teaspoon freshly ground black pepper
2 tablespoons olive oil
2 cups low-sodium beef broth
1 cup red wine
4 sprigs rosemary

1. Preheat the oven to 350°F (180°C).
2. On a clean work surface, rub the short ribs with garlic powder, salt, and black pepper. Let stand for 10 minutes.
3. Heat the olive oil in an oven-safe skillet over medium-high heat.
4. Add the short ribs and sear for 5 minutes or until well browned. Flip the ribs halfway through. Transfer the ribs onto a plate and set aside.
5. Pour the beef broth and red wine into the skillet. Stir to combine well and bring to a boil.
6. Turn down the heat to low and simmer for 10 minutes until the mixture reduces to two thirds.
7. Put the ribs back to the skillet. Add the rosemary sprigs.
8. Put the skillet lid on, then braise in the preheated oven for 2 hours until the internal temperature of the ribs reads 165°F (74°C).
9. Transfer the ribs to a large plate. Discard the rosemary sprigs. Pour the cooking liquid over and serve warm.

Per Serving
calories: 731 | fat: 69g | carbs: 2g | fiber: 0g | protein: 25g | sodium: 781mg

CHAPTER 8:
SAUCES, CONDIMENTS, AND DRESSINGS

Garlic-Ginger Lime Sauce

Prep time: 5 minutes | Cook time: 0 minutes | Serves 4

¼ cup low-sodium soy sauce
3 garlic cloves, minced
Juice of 2 limes
1 tablespoon grated fresh ginger
1 tablespoon arrowroot powder

1. In a small bowl, whisk together the soy sauce, garlic, lime juice, ginger, and arrowroot powder.

Per Serving (2 tablespoons)

calories: 24 | fat: 0g | protein: 1g | carbs: 4g | fiber: 0g | sugar: 2g | sodium: 887mg

Coconut Peanut Sauce

Prep time: 10 minutes | Cook time: 0 minutes | Serves 8

1 cup lite coconut milk
¼ cup creamy peanut butter
¼ cup freshly squeezed lime juice
3 garlic cloves, minced
2 tablespoons low-sodium soy sauce, or gluten-free soy sauce, or tamari
1 tablespoon grated fresh ginger

1. In a blender or food processor, process the coconut milk, peanut butter, lime juice, garlic, soy sauce, and ginger until smooth.
2. Keep refrigerated in a tightly sealed container for up to 5 days.

Per Serving (about 2 tablespoons)

calories: 143 | fat: 11g | protein: 6g | carbs: 8g | fiber: 1g | sugar: 2g | sodium: 533mg

Lemon Tahini Sauce

Prep time: 5 minutes | Cook time: 0 minutes | Makes 1 cup

½ cup tahini
1 garlic clove, minced
Juice of 1 lemon
Zest of 1 lemon
½ teaspoon salt, plus additional as needed
½ cup warm water, plus additional as needed

1. In a small bowl, stir together the tahini and garlic.
2. Add the lemon juice, lemon zest, and salt. Stir well.
3. Whisk in ½ cup of warm water, until well mixed and creamy. Add more water if the sauce is too thick.
4. Taste and adjust the seasoning if necessary.
5. Refrigerate in a sealed container.

Per Serving (¼ cup)

calories: 180 | fat: 16g | protein: 5g | carbs: 7g | fiber: 3g | sugar: 0g | sodium: 325mg

Cashew and Butternut Squash Sauce

Prep time: 5 minutes | Cook time: 10minutes | Makes 3½ cups

3 cups cubed butternut squash
½ cup cashews, soaked in water for at least 4 hours, drained
½ cup water, plus additional for cooking and thinning
1 teaspoon salt, plus additional as needed

1. Fill a large pot with 2 inches of water and insert a steamer basket. Bring to a boil over high heat.
2. Add the butternut squash to the basket. Cover and steam for 10 to 12 minutes, or until tender.
3. Remove from the heat and cool slightly.
4. Transfer the squash to a blender. Add the cashews, ½ cup of water, and salt. Blend until smooth and creamy. Depending on the consistency, add more water to thin if necessary.
5. Taste and adjust the seasoning if necessary.

Per Serving (½ cup)

calories: 73 | fat: 5g | protein: 2g | carbs: 8g | fiber: 1g | sugar: 1g | sodium: 335mg

Dijon0-Honey Sesame Sauce

Prep time: 5 minutes | Cook time: 0 minutes | Makes 1 cup

½ cup Dijon mustard
½ cup raw honey or pure maple syrup
1 garlic clove, minced
1 teaspoon toasted sesame oil

1. In a small bowl, whisk together the Dijon, honey, garlic, and sesame oil.
2. Refrigerate in an airtight container.

Per Serving (2 tablespoons)

calories: 67 | fat: 1g | protein: 1g | carbs: 14g | fiber: 1g | sugar: 12g | sodium: 179mg

Buttery Tofu Sauce with Basil

Prep time: 10 minutes | Cook time: 0 minutes | Makes 2 cups

1 (12-ounce / 340-g) package silken tofu
½ cup chopped fresh basil
2 garlic cloves, lightly crushed
½ cup almond butter
1 tablespoon fresh lemon juice
1 teaspoon salt
¼ teaspoon freshly ground black pepper

1. In a blender or food processor, combine the tofu, basil, garlic, almond butter, lemon juice, salt, and pepper.
2. Process until smooth. If too thick, thin with a bit of water.
3. Refrigerate in an airtight container for up to 5 days.

Per Serving

calories: 120 | fat: 10g | protein: 6g | carbs: 5g | fiber: 2g | sugar: 1g | sodium: 290mg

Dijon Mustard Dressing with Lemon

Prep time: 5 minutes | Cook time: 0 minutes | Makes 6 tablespoons

¼ cup extra-virgin olive oil
2 tablespoons freshly squeezed lemon juice
1 teaspoon Dijon mustard
½ teaspoon raw honey
1 garlic clove, minced
¼ teaspoon dried basil
¼ teaspoon salt

1. In a glass jar with a lid, combine the olive oil, lemon juice, mustard, honey, garlic, basil, and salt.
2. Cover and shake vigorously until the ingredients are well combined and emulsified. Refrigerate for up to 1 week.

Per Serving (1½ tablespoons)
calories: 128 | fat: 13g | protein: 0g | carbs: 1g | fiber: 0g | sugar: 1g | sodium: 160mg

Garlic Fennel Pesto with Sunflower Seeds

Prep time: 5 minutes | Cook time: 30 minutes | Makes 2 cups

2 fennel bu-pound
8 garlic cloves, peeled
2 tablespoons extra-virgin olive oil, plus additional as needed
¾ cup sunflower seeds
¼ cup freshly squeezed lemon juice
½ teaspoon sea salt, plus additional as needed

1. Preheat the oven to 350°F (180°C).
2. Trim the fronds from the fennel bu-pound and set aside. Cut off the stalks and save them for another use. Halve the fennel bu-pound, removing and discarding the core. Chop the fennel roughly.
3. In a large roasting pan, combine the chopped fennel and garlic.
4. Drizzle with the olive oil and toss to coat.
5. Place the pan in the preheated oven and roast for 30 minutes, stirring halfway through. Remove the pan from the oven and cool.
6. In a food processor, grind the sunflower seeds into a rough meal.
7. Add the roasted fennel and garlic, along with the lemon juice and sea salt. Process until everything comes together. If the pesto is dry, add an additional 1 or 2 tablespoons of olive oil or water.
8. Roughly chop a handful of the reserved fennel fronds. Add them to the pesto. Pulse until combined. Taste and adjust the seasoning if necessary.

Per Serving (¼ cup)
calories: 80 | fat: 6g | protein: 2g | carbs: 6g | fiber: 2g | sugar: 0g | sodium: 150mg

Creamy Anti-Inflammatory Mayonnaise

Prep time: 5 minutes | Cook time: 0 minutes | Makes 1 cup

1 egg yolk
1 tablespoon apple cider vinegar
½ teaspoon Dijon mustard
Pinch sea salt
¾ cup extra-virgin olive oil

1. In a blender or food processor, combine the egg yolk, cider vinegar, mustard, and salt.
2. Turn on the blender or food processor, and while it's running, remove the top spout. Carefully, working one drip at a time to start, drip in the olive oil.
3. After about 15 drops, continue to run the processor and add the oil in a thin stream until emulsified. You may adjust the amount of oil to adjust the thickness. The more oil you add, the thicker the mayonnaise will be.
4. Keep this refrigerated for up to 4 days in a tightly sealed container.

Per Serving (2 tablespoons)
calories: 169 | fat: 20g | protein: 1g | carbs: 1g | fiber: 0g | sugar: 0g | sodium: 36mg

Raspberry-Garlic Vinaigrette

Prep time: 5 minutes | Cook time: 0 minutes | Serves 8

¾ cup extra-virgin olive oil
¼ cup apple cider vinegar
¼ cup fresh raspberries, crushed with the back of a spoon
3 garlic cloves, finely minced
½ teaspoon sea salt
⅛ teaspoon freshly ground black pepper

1. In a small bowl, whisk the olive oil, cider vinegar, raspberries, garlic, salt, and pepper.
2. Keep refrigerated in a tightly sealed container for up to 5 days.

Per Serving (about 2 tablespoons)
calories: 167 | fat: 19g | protein: 1g | carbs: 1g | fiber: 0g | sugar: 0g | sodium: 118mg

Walnut-Spinach Basil Pesto

Prep time: 5 minutes | Cook time: 0 minutes | Serves 8

½ cup walnuts
¼ cup extra-virgin olive oil
4 garlic cloves, minced
1 cup baby spinach
¼ cup basil leaves
½ teaspoon sea salt

1. In a blender or food processor, combine the walnuts, olive oil, garlic, spinach, basil, and salt.
2. Pulse for 15 to 20 (1-second) bursts, or until everything is finely chopped.

Per Serving
calories: 106 | fat: 11g | protein: 2g | carbs: 1g | fiber: 0g | sugar: 0g | sodium: 120mg

Coconut Butter with Sunflower Seeds

Prep time: 5 minutes | Cook time: 6 minutes | Makes 1½ cups

1½ cups sunflower seeds
1½ cups large-flake unsweetened coconut
⅛ teaspoon salt

1. Preheat the oven to 350°F (180°C).
2. On a baking sheet, spread the sunflower seeds and coconut.
3. Place the sheet in the preheated oven and bake for 6 to 8 minutes. Keep a close watch, as the seeds and coconut can burn quickly.
4. Remove from the oven and cool.
5. In a food processor, combine the seeds, coconut, and salt. Blend until smooth and creamy, scraping down the sides as needed.
6. Pour into a sealable jar.

Per Serving (1 tablespoon)

calories: 66 | fat: 7g | protein: 1g | carbs: 3g | fiber: 2g | sugar: 1g | sodium: 31mg

Maple Strawberry-Chia Jam

Prep time: 5 minutes | Cook time: 8 minutes | Makes 1 cup

3 cups fresh strawberries, hulled and halved
¼ cup pure maple syrup or raw honey
3 tablespoons chia seeds

1. In a large pot set over medium-low heat, cook the strawberries for 8 to 10 minutes, mashing them lightly with a fork. If the pan gets dry, add 1 or 2 tablespoons of water. Transfer to a blender.
2. Add the maple syrup. Blend until smooth. Pour the mixture into a medium bowl.
3. Stir in the chia seeds.
4. Transfer the jam to a jar. Cover and refrigerate. The jam will thicken as it cools.

Per Serving (1 tablespoon)

calories: 30 | fat: 1g | protein: 1g | carbs: 7g | fiber: 1g | sugar: 6g | sodium: 0mg

Dill-Chive Ranch Dressing

Prep time: 10 minutes | Cook time: 0 minutes | Serves 8

1 cup nonfat plain Greek yogurt
1 garlic clove, minced
2 tablespoons chopped fresh chives
¼ cup chopped fresh dill
Zest of 1 lemon
½ teaspoon sea salt
⅛ teaspoon freshly cracked black pepper

1. In a small bowl, whisk together the yogurt, garlic, chives, dill, lemon zest, salt, and pepper.
2. Keep refrigerated in a tightly sealed container for up to 5 days.

Per Serving

calories: 17 | fat: 0g | protein: 2g | carbs: 3g | fiber: 0g | sugar: 2g | sodium: 140mg

Ginger-Lemon Honey

Prep time: 5 minutes | Cook time: 0 minutes | Makes 1 cup

1 cup water
¼ cup fresh lemon juice
2 tablespoons honey
2 teaspoons grated fresh ginger root

1. Combine all the ingredients in an airtight jar and shake until the honey is dissolved.
2. Refrigerate for 24 hours before using so the ginger can permeate the mixture.
3. Store in the refrigerator up to a week.

Per Serving (2 tablespoons)

calories: 20 | fat: 0g | protein: 0g | carbs: 5g | fiber: 0g | sugar: 4g | sodium: 0mg

Parmesan Spinach-Basil Pesto

Prep time: 10 minutes | Cook time: 0 minutes | Serves 4

1 cup fresh baby spinach
½ cup fresh basil leaves
¼ cup pine nuts
¼ cup extra-virgin olive oil
4 garlic cloves, minced
2 ounces (57 g) Parmesan Cheese, grated
½ teaspoon sea salt

1. In a blender or food processor, combine the spinach, basil, pine nuts, olive oil, garlic, Parmesan Cheese, and salt.
2. Pulse for 15 to 20 (1-second) bursts, or until everything is finely chopped. This keeps refrigerated in a tightly sealed container for 5 days.

Per Serving

calories: 218 | fat: 22g | protein: 6g | carbs: 3g | fiber: 0g | sugar: 0g | sodium: 372mg

Apple-Raisin Chutney

Prep time: 10 minutes | Cook time: 5 minutes | Makes 2 cups

1 tablespoon almond oil
4 apples, peeled, cored, and diced
1 small onion, diced
½ cup white raisins (optional)
1 tablespoon apple cider vinegar
1 tablespoon honey
1 teaspoon ground cinnamon
½ teaspoon ground cardamom
½ teaspoon ground ginger
½ teaspoon salt

1. In a medium saucepan, heat the oil over low heat.
2. Add the apples, onion, raisins (if using), vinegar, honey, cinnamon, cardamom, ginger, and salt.
3. Cook briefly, just until the apples begin to release their juices. Bring to a simmer, cover, and cook until the apples are tender, 5 to 10 minutes.
4. Allow to cool completely before serving.

Per Serving

calories: 120 | fat: 2g | protein: 1g | carbs: 24g | fiber: 3g | sugar: 18g | sodium: 150mg

Tahini Dressing with Lime

Prep time: 10 minutes | Cook time: 0 minutes | Makes ¾ cup

⅓ cup tahini (sesame paste)
3 tablespoons filtered water
2 tablespoons freshly squeezed lime juice
1 tablespoon apple cider vinegar
1 teaspoon lime zest
1½ teaspoons raw honey
¼ teaspoon garlic powder
¼ teaspoon salt

1. In a glass jar with a lid, combine the tahini, water, lime juice, vinegar, lime zest, honey, garlic powder, and salt.
2. Cover and shake vigorously until the ingredients are well combined and emulsified. Refrigerate for up to 1 week.

Per Serving (1½ tablespoons)
calories: 157 | fat: 12g | protein: 6g | carbs: 5g | fiber: 0g | sugar: 1g | sodium: 146mg

Avocado-Lemon Dressing

Prep time: 5 minutes | Cook time: 0 minutes | Makes 2 cups

1 ripe avocado
1 cup plain coconut yogurt
¼ cup freshly squeezed lemon juice
1 scallion, chopped
1 tablespoon chopped fresh cilantro

1. In a food processor, blend the avocado, yogurt, lemon juice, scallion, and cilantro until smooth.
2. Refrigerate in an airtight container.

Per Serving (2 tablespoons)
calories: 33 | fat: 3g | protein: 0g | carbs: 2g | fiber: 1g | sugar: 0g | sodium: 14mg

Caesar Salad Dressing with Anchovy

Prep time: 5 minutes | Cook time: 0 minutes | Makes 1 cup

¾ cup extra-virgin olive oil
3 tablespoons apple cider vinegar
2 anchovy fillets
2 garlic cloves, minced
½ teaspoon salt
Freshly ground black pepper, to taste

1. In a blender or food processor, purée the olive oil, cider vinegar, anchovies, garlic, salt, and pepper until smooth.
2. Refrigerate in an airtight container and use within one week.

Per Serving (2 tablespoons)
calories: 166 | fat: 19g | protein: 0g | carbs: 0g | fiber: 0g | sugar: 0g | sodium: 184mg

Ginger-Mustard Vinaigrette

Prep time: 10 minutes | Cook time: 0 minutes | Makes 1½ cups

1 cup extra-virgin olive oil
¼ cup apple cider vinegar
½ teaspoon Dijon mustard
1 garlic clove, sliced
½ teaspoon minced fresh ginger root
1 teaspoon salt
½ teaspoon ground turmeric
¼ teaspoon ground coriander
¼ teaspoon freshly ground black pepper

1. In a blender or food processor, combine all the ingredients and process until smooth.
2. Refrigerate in an airtight container for up to a week.

Per Serving (2 tablespoons)
calories: 160 | fat: 18g | protein: 0g | carbs: 0g | fiber: 0g | sugar: 0g | sodium: 200mg

Homemade Mild Curry Powder

Prep time: 10 minutes | Cook time: 0 minutes | Makes ¼ cup

1 tablespoon ground turmeric
1 tablespoon ground cumin
2 teaspoons ground coriander
1 teaspoon ground cardamom
1 teaspoon ground cinnamon
1 teaspoon ground ginger
½ teaspoon fenugreek powder
½ teaspoon ground cloves

1. In a small bowl, stir together the turmeric, cumin, coriander, cardamom, cinnamon, ginger, fenugreek, and cloves until well blended.
2. Store the curry powder in an airtight container for up to 1 month.

Per Serving (1 teaspoon)
calories: 5 | fat: 0g | protein: 0g | carbs: 1g | fiber: 0g | sugar: 0g | sodium: 8mg

Mediterranean Spice Rub

Prep time: 10 minutes | Cook time: 0 minutes | Makes ¾ cup

¼ cup packed coconut sugar
3 tablespoons dried oregano leaves
2 tablespoons dried thyme leaves
1 tablespoon dried tarragon
1 teaspoon dried marjoram
1 teaspoon dried dill
1 teaspoon dried basil

1. In a small bowl, stir together the coconut sugar, oregano, thyme, tarragon, marjoram, dill, and basil until well blended.
2. Store the seasoning in a sealed container for up to 1 month.

Per Serving (1 teaspoon)
calories: 6 | fat: 0g | protein: 0g | carbs: 1g | fiber: 0g | sugar: 1g | sodium: 33mg

Spicy Vinaigrette with Parsley

Prep time: 10 minutes | Cook time: 0 minutes | Makes 1¼ cups

¾ cup olive oil
¼ cup apple cider vinegar
1 tablespoon freshly squeezed lemon juice
¼ cup chopped fresh parsley
1 teaspoon bottled minced garlic
1 teaspoon ground cumin
¼ teaspoon ground coriander
Pinch sea salt

1. In a medium bowl, whisk the olive oil, cider vinegar, and lemon juice until emulsified.
2. Whisk in the parsley, garlic, cumin, and coriander.
3. Season with sea salt.
4. Refrigerate the vinaigrette in a sealed container for up to 2 weeks.

Per Serving (2 teaspoons)
calories: 134 | fat: 15g | protein: 0g | carbs: 0g | fiber: 0g | sugar: 2g | sodium: 5mg

Creamy Tahini Dressing

Prep time: 5 minutes | Cook time: 0 minutes | Makes ¾ cup

½ cup canned full-fat coconut milk
2 tablespoons tahini
2 tablespoons freshly squeezed lime juice
1 teaspoon bottled minced garlic
1 teaspoon minced fresh chives
Pinch sea salt

1. In a small bowl, whisk the coconut milk, tahini, lime juice, garlic, and chives until well blended. You can also prepare this in a blender.
2. Season with sea salt and transfer the dressing to a container with a lid. Refrigerate for up to 1 week.

Per Serving (1 teaspoon)
calories: 42 | fat: 4g | protein: 1g | carbs: 2g | fiber: 0g | sugar: 1g | sodium: 13mg

Maple-Mustard Dressing

Prep time: 5 minutes | Cook time: 0 minutes | Makes 1¼ cups

1 cup canned full-fat coconut milk
2 tablespoons pure maple syrup
1 tablespoon Dijon mustard
1 tablespoon apple cider vinegar
Sea salt, to taste

1. In a medium bowl, whisk the coconut milk, maple syrup, mustard, and cider vinegar until smoothly blended.
2. Season with sea salt. You can also prepare this in a blender.
3. Refrigerate the dressing in a sealed container for up to 1 week.

Per Serving (2 teaspoons)
calories: 66 | fat: 6g | protein: 1g | carbs: 4g | fiber: 1g | sugar: 8g | sodium: 53mg

Avocado and Herb Spread

Prep time: 10 minutes | Cook time: 0 minutes | Makes 1 cup

1 ripe avocado, peeled and pitted
2 tablespoons freshly squeezed lemon juice
2 tablespoons chopped fresh parsley
1 teaspoon chopped fresh dill
½ teaspoon ground coriander
Sea salt, to taste
Freshly ground black pepper, to taste

1. In a blender, pulse the avocado until smoothly puréed.
2. Add the lemon juice, parsley, dill, and coriander. Pulse until well blended.
3. Season with sea salt and pepper.
4. Refrigerate the spread in a sealed container for up to 4 days.

Per Serving (2 teaspoons)
calories: 54 | fat: 5g | protein: 1g | carbs: 2g | fiber: 2g | sugar: 1g | sodium: 10mg

Chimichurri

Prep time: 5 minutes | Cook time: 0 minutes | Makes 1 cup

1 cup coarsely chopped fresh parsley
½ cup fresh mint leaves
¼ cup olive oil
2 tablespoons freshly squeezed lemon juice
2 teaspoons bottled minced garlic
Pinch sea salt

1. In a blender or food processor, combine the parsley, mint, olive oil, lemon juice, garlic, and sea salt. Pulse until the herbs are very finely chopped and the ingredients are well mixed.
2. Refrigerate the mixture in a sealed container for up to 1 week.

Per Serving (2 teaspoons)
calories: 60 | fat: 6g | protein: 1g | carbs: 1g | fiber: 1g | sugar: 0g | sodium: 9mg

Gremolata Sauce

Prep time: 5 minutes | Cook time: 0 minutes | Makes 1 cup

¾ cup finely chopped fresh parsley
Juice of 2 lemons (or 6 tablespoons)
Zest of 2 lemons (optional)
2 tablespoons olive oil
2 teaspoons bottled minced garlic
¼ teaspoon sea salt

1. In a small bowl, stir together the parsley, lemon juice, lemon zest (if using), olive oil, garlic, and sea salt until well blended.
2. Refrigerate in a sealed container for up to 4 days.

Per Serving (2 teaspoons)
calories: 34 | fat: 4g | protein: 0g | carbs: 1g | fiber: 0g | sugar: 1g | sodium: 152mg

CHAPTER 9:
SMOOTHIES AND DRINKS

**THE ULTIMATE ANTI-INFLAMMATORY
DIET COOKBOOK**

Butternut Squash Smoothie with Tahini

Prep time: 5 minutes | Cook time: 0 minutes | Serves 2

2 cups butternut squash purée, frozen in ice cube trays
1 cup unsweetened coconut milk, plus additional as needed
¼ cup tahini
¼ cup pure maple syrup
1 teaspoon cinnamon

1. Release the butternut squash cubes from the ice cube trays and put them in a blender.
2. Add the coconut milk, tahini, maple syrup, and cinnamon.
3. Blend until smooth. If the consistency is too thick, thin with water or more coconut milk to achieve the desired consistency.
4. Pour into two glasses and serve.

Per Serving

calories: 660 | fat: 48g | protein: 10g | carbs: 59g | fiber: 11g | sugar: 28g | sodium: 260mg

Breakfast Oat-Leafy Smoothie

Prep time: 10 minutes | Cook time: 0 minutes | Serves 1

2 Cauliflower florets
1 cup frozen mixed berries
½ cup cooked oatmeal, cooled
6 leaves Romaine lettuce
1 tablespoon hemp seeds
1 tablespoon walnuts, roughly chopped
½ cup fresh pomegranate juice

1. To make pomegranate juice, get the pomegranate arils and place in a steel mesh.
2. Place a clean bowl beneath mesh and with back of spoon press down on arils until you have enough fresh juice.
3. In blender, crush into fine powder hemp seeds and walnuts. Add oatmeal and puree until smooth.
4. Add broccoli and lettuce, puree well until smooth and creamy.
5. Add remaining ingredients, puree once more until smooth and creamy. Serve and enjoy.

Per Serving

calories: 383 | fat: 13g | protein: 10g | carbs: 65g | fiber: 12g | sugar: 36g | sodium: 137mg

Tart Cherry and Greens Smoothie

Prep time: 5 minutes | Cook time: 0 minutes | Serves 1

1 cup fresh frozen tart cherry, pitted
½ cup broccoli florets
½ cup packed kale, stems removed and chopped
½ cup freshly squeezed orange juice
½ cup ice cold water

1. In a blender, puree cherries, broccoli, kale and orange juice until smooth and creamy.
2. Add remaining ingredients, puree until well blended and smooth.
3. Transfer to a glass and enjoy.

Per Serving

calories: 157 | fat: 0.6g | protein: 4g | carbs: 37g | fiber: 4g | sugar: 29g | sodium: 32mg

Anti-inflammatory Smoothie

Prep time: 10 minutes | Cook time: 0 minutes | Serves 2

1 medium banana, halved and frozen
¼ cup macadamia nuts
1 teaspoon chia seeds
1-inch slice of ginger, peeled
½ teaspoon turmeric powder
2 cups cold green tea
1 cup sweet ripe pineapple

1. In a blender, add all ingredients.
2. Puree until smooth and creamy.
3. Transfer to a glass, serve and enjoy.

Per Serving

calories: 227 | fat: 13g | protein: 3g | carbs: 28g | fiber: 5g | sugar: 17g | sodium: 5mg

Green Tea and Raspberry Smoothie

Prep time: 5 minutes | Cook time: 0 minutes | Serves 2

¼ cup protein powder
1 tablespoon honey
1 banana
2 cups frozen unsweetened raspberries
1 ½ cups chilled green tea

1. In a blender or food processor, mix protein powder, honey, banana, raspberries and green tea.
2. Puree until you have a smooth consistency.
3. Pour into two glasses, serve and enjoy.

Per Serving

calories: 241 | fat: 5g | protein: 12.5g | carbs: 41g | fiber: 11g | sugar: 23g | sodium: 76mg

Detoxifying Super Green Smoothie

Prep time: 10 minutes | Cook time: 0 minutes | Serves 2

¼ cup chopped fresh mint leaves
¼ cup chopped flat leaf parsley
1 cup chilled orange or tangerine juice
2 medium ribs celery, chopped
1 ¼ cups mango, frozen cubes
1 ¼ cup Kale, stems and ribs removed
1 medium cucumber, peeled
6 ice cubes
2 to 3 dates for sweetness (optional)

1. Add all ingredients in a blender and puree until smooth and creamy.
2. Serve and enjoy.

Per Serving

calories: 160 | fat: 0g | protein: 3g | carbs: 39g | fiber: 5g | sugar: 6g | sodium: 56mg

Turmeric Cinnamon Tea

Prep time: 5 minutes | Cook time: 5 minutes | Serves 1

½ teaspoon turmeric
½ teaspoon cinnamon
1-inch ginger root, quartered
1 cup boiling water

1. Add all ingredients in a cup and allow to steep for 5 minutes.
2. Discard ginger root and allow to cool for 5 minutes more.
3. Serve and enjoy.

Per Serving

calories: 10 | fat: 0g | protein: 0.2g | carbs: 2.4g | fiber: 1.1g | sugar: 0.1g | sodium: 6mg

Cucumber Pineapple Juice

Prep time: 5 minutes | Cook time: 0 minutes | Serves 2

2 cups pineapple chunks
1 whole cucumber, peeled and quartered
1 jalapeno deseeded
1 tablespoon mint leaves

1. Add ingredients into your juiced.
2. Serve and enjoy in a glass with ice.

Per Serving

calories: 94 | fat: 0g | protein: 1g | carbs: 23g | fiber: 3g | sugar: 17g | sodium: 3mg

Golden Milk Recipe

Prep time: 5 minutes | Cook time: 0 minutes | Serves 1

1 cup almond milk, heated
½ teaspoon turmeric
A dash of pepper

1. Add all ingredients in a cup.
2. Nuke in microwave.
3. Serve and enjoy.

Per Serving

calories: 154 | fat: 8g | protein: 8g | carbs: 13g | fiber: 0.4g | sugar: 12g | sodium: 105mg

Ginger-Pear Smoothie

Prep time: 10 minutes | Cook time: 0 minutes | Serves 1

1 large ripe pear, cored and quartered
2 cups baby spinach
1 tablespoon peeled, chopped ginger
1 tablespoon fresh lemon juice
¼ cup whole almonds
¾ cup cold water
1 cup ice

1. Add all ingredients in a blender.
2. Blend until smooth and creamy.
3. Serve and enjoy.

Per Serving

calories: 334 | fat: 0g | protein: 10g | carbs: 37g | fiber: 11g | sugar: 19g | sodium: 115mg

Cucumber-Pineapple Spice

Prep time: 5 minutes | Cook time: 0 minutes | Serves 1

1 cucumbers
1 cup pineapple
1 teaspoon pieces turmeric
1 teaspoon of cinnamon
8 ice cubes

1. Add all ingredients in a blender.
2. Blend until smooth and creamy.
3. Serve and enjoy.

Per Serving

calories: 189 | fat: 0.6g | protein: 1g | carbs: 48g | fiber: 5.5g | sugar: 39g | sodium: 8mg

Beans, Peaches and Greens Smoothie

Prep time: 10 minutes | Cook time: 0 minutes | Serves 1

Pinch of nutmeg
⅛ teaspoon cinnamon
¼ can white beans (Great Northern or Cannellini)
1 cup frozen peaches
½ cup unsweetened almond milk
¼ cup almonds
¼ cup quick cooking oats
1 cup packed lettuce (any kind)
¼ cup Italian parsley
6 cubes of ice

1. Add all ingredients in a blender.
2. Blend until smooth and creamy.
3. Serve and enjoy.

Per Serving

calories: 346 | fat: 11g | protein: 12g | carbs: 55g | fiber: 9.5g | sugar: 26g | sodium: 261mg

Banana and Peanut Butter Detox

Prep time: 10 minutes | Cook time: 0 minutes | Serves 1

6 ice cubes
½ cup plus 2 tablespoons unsweetened almond milk
½ of banana, frozen or fresh
¼ cup dandelion greens
1 cup beet greens

1. Add all ingredients in a blender.
2. Blend until smooth and creamy.
3. Serve and enjoy.

Per Serving

calories: 366 | fat: 20g | protein: 10g | carbs: 44g | fiber: 9g | sugar: 28g | sodium: 415mg

Protein, Green and Fruity Smoothie

Prep time: 10 minutes | Cook time: 1½ minutes | Serves 1

1 cup spinach, packed
1 cup ice cold water
½ banana
½ avocado
1 tablespoon unsweetened almond milk
¼ cup packed kale, stem removed and chopped
1 cup frozen broccoli florets

1. In a microwave safe cup, add almond milk and quick cooking oats. Microwave for 1½ minutes. Once done, mix first before adding two ice cubes and mixing again.
2. Then, in a blender, add almonds and blend until you form a powdery substance.
3. Then. Pour in all ingredients along with the cooked oats and blend until you have a smooth and uniform mixture.
4. Tip: As you get accustomed to leafy veggies in your smoothie, you can increase lettuce servings up to 3 cups without too much change in the taste of the smoothie.

Per Serving

calories: 361 | fat: 24g | protein: 11g | carbs: 34g | fiber: 15g | sugar: 11g | sodium: 76mg

Escarole, Pineapple and Apple Smoothie

Prep time: 5 minutes | Cook time: 0 minutes | Serves 1

1 head escarole lettuce
1 stalk celery
2 cups pineapple, cubed
2 apples, cored
8 ounces (227 g) unsweetened almond milk

1. Add all ingredients in a blender.
2. Blend until smooth and creamy.
3. Serve and enjoy.

Per Serving

calories: 466 | fat: 8g | protein: 8g | carbs: 103g | fiber: 18g | sugar: 75g | sodium: 40mg

Green and Leafy Ginger-Apple Drink

Prep time: 5 minutes | Cook time: 0 minutes | Serves 1

8 ounces (227 g) filtered water
1 tablespoon freshly grated ginger root
2 large handfuls baby spinach
1 medium apple, cored
2 medium carrots, chopped

1. Add all ingredients in a blender.
2. Blend until smooth and creamy.
3. Serve and enjoy.

Per Serving

calories: 163 | fat: 1g | protein: 3g | carbs: 40g | fiber: 9g | sugar: 25g | sodium: 139mg

Berry Green and Leafy

Prep time: 10 minutes | Cook time: 0 minutes | Serves 2

8 ounces (227 g) filtered water
1 tablespoon ground flax seeds
1 head of green leaf lettuce
3 cups chopped dandelion greens
8 large strawberries
1 large mango, peeled and pitted
3 bananas, peeled

1. Add all ingredients in a blender.
2. Blend until smooth and creamy.
3. Serve and enjoy.

Per Serving

calories: 361 | fat: 3g | protein: 9g | carbs: 85g | fiber: 14g | sugar: 50g | sodium: 120mg

Cran-banana Smoothie

Prep time: 10 minutes | Cook time: 0 minutes | Serves 1

8 ounces (227 g) filtered water
3 dates
1 stalk organic celery
2 cups baby spinach
1 banana
½ cup cranberries

1. Add all ingredients in a blender.
2. Blend until smooth and creamy.
3. Serve and enjoy.

Per Serving

calories: 205 | fat: 0.8g | protein: 1g | carbs: 52g | fiber: 9g | sugar: 30g | sodium: 68mg

Pomegranate and Cactus Pear Smoothie

Prep time: 10 minutes | Cook time: 0 minutes | Serves 1

2 ounces (57 g) filtered water
2½ tablespoons goji berries
¼ cup raw almonds
2 bananas, peeled
1 cup frozen blueberries
2 cactus pears, juice and flesh, strain out seeds and peel
½ cup fresh pomegranate juice

1. Add all ingredients in a blender.
2. Blend until smooth and creamy.
3. Serve and enjoy.

Per Serving

calories: 598 | fat: 3g | protein: 5g | carbs: 147g | fiber: 22g | sugar: 95g | sodium: 20mg

Nutty Pina Colada

Prep time: 10 minutes | Cook time: 0 minutes | Serves 1

5 to 6 ice cubes
¼ teaspoon coconut extract
½ cup diced fresh pineapple
½ banana
1 (6 ounces / 170 g) container Greek yogurt
¼ cup quick cooking oats
1 cup unsweetened almond milk
1 cup Swiss chard
¼ cup dandelion greens

1. Add all ingredients in a blender.
2. Blend until smooth and creamy.
3. Serve and enjoy.

Per Serving

calories: 321 | fat: 6g | protein: 15g | carbs: 55g | fiber: 39g | sugar: 39g | sodium: 218mg

Banana-Spinach Smoothie

Prep time: 10 minutes | Cook time: 0 minutes | Serves 1

1 huge handful spinach
¼ packed cup kale, torn and stems removed
¾ cup water
½ banana
⅔ cup Greek yogurt
1 tablespoon unsweetened almond milk

1. Add all ingredients in a blender.
2. Blend until smooth and creamy.
3. Serve and enjoy.

Per Serving

calories: 263 | fat: 17g | protein: 7g | carbs: 23g | fiber: 2g | sugar: 15g | sodium: 1.2mg

Berry-Banana Yogurt

Prep time: 10 minutes | Cook time: 2½ minutes | Serves 1

5 to 6 ice cubes
½ cup blueberries, fresh or frozen
½ banana, frozen fresh
1 container 5³⁄₁₀-ounce (150-g) non-fat Greek yogurt
¼ cup quick cooking oats
1 cup unsweetened almond milk
¼ cup of chopped collard greens, middle stem removed and discarded

1. In a microwave safe cup, microwave on high for 2½ minutes the 1 cup almond milk and ¼ cup oats.
2. Once oats are cooked, add 2 ice cubes to cool it down quick and mix.
3. Add all ingredients in a blender.
4. Blend until smooth and creamy.
5. Serve and enjoy.

Per Serving

calories: 379 | fat: 10g | protein: 13g | carbs: 63g | fiber: 5g | sugar: 48g | sodium: 123mg

Green Detox Queen

Prep time: 10 minutes | Cook time: 0 minutes | Serves 1

1 Lemon Wedge
1 slice of ginger
1 cup of grapes
1 cup kale, chopped
3 ice cubes
1 cup green tea, cooled

1. Add all ingredients in a blender.
2. Blend until smooth and creamy.
3. Serve and enjoy.

Per Serving

calories:152 | fat: 1g | protein: 4g | carbs: 38g | fiber: 4g | sugar: 26g | sodium: 36mg

Lemon Fennel Detox

Prep time: 10 minutes | Cook time: 0 minutes | Serves 1

Half a lemon
1 bulb of fennel
2 apples
1 cucumber
1 bunch of mint
10 ounces (283 g) of spinach
6 ice cubes

1. Add all ingredients in a blender.
2. Blend until smooth and creamy.
3. Serve and enjoy.

Per Serving

calories: 362 | fat: 2.6g | protein: 13g | carbs: 85g | fiber: 24g | sugar: 52g | sodium: 351mg

Chai Tea Drink

Prep time: 5 minutes | Cook time: 0 minutes | Serves 1

1 cup boiling hot water
1 green tea bag
¼ teaspoon cacao powder
1 tablespoon honey
1 cup unsweetened almond milk

1. In a large mug, add hot water and tea bag. Let it steep for 5 minutes.
2. Discard tea bag. Stir in cacao powder and honey. Mix well.
3. Stir in cold almond milk.
4. Serve and enjoy.

Per Serving

calories: 216 | fat: 8g | protein: 8g | carbs: 29g | fiber: 0.2g | sugar: 30g | sodium: 113mg

Lemon-Mint Green Tea

Prep time: 5 minutes | Cook time: 0 minutes | Serves 1

3 mint leaves
2 cups boiling water
1 green tea bag
2 lemon slices
1 tablespoon honey

1. In a large mug, add hot water, lemon slices and tea bag. Let it steep for 10 minutes.
2. Discard tea bag. Stir in honey and squish lemon slices. Mix well.
3. Stir in mint leaves.
4. Serve and enjoy.

Per Serving

calories: 87 | fat: 0.2g | protein: 0.8g | carbs: 24g | fiber: 0.3g | sugar: 20g | sodium: 14mg

Choco Loco Tea Drink

Prep time: 10 minutes | Cook time: 0 minutes | Serves 1

1½ cups boiling water
1 green tea bag
1 tablespoon cacao powder
1 tablespoon honey
¼ teaspoon cinnamon
½ cup unsweetened almond milk

1. In a large mug, add hot water and tea bag. Let it steep for 10 minutes.
2. Discard tea bag. Stir in honey, cinnamon and cacao powder. Mix well.
3. Stir in mint almond milk.
4. Serve and enjoy.

Per Serving

calories: 152 | fat: 2g | protein: 2g | carbs: 35g | fiber: 2g | sugar: 28g | sodium: 101mg

Iced Matcha

Prep time: 5 minutes | Cook time: 0 minutes | Serves 1

½ cup hot water
1 teaspoon matcha tea powder
½ cup unsweetened coconut milk
1 teaspoon raw organic honey
Ice cubes

1. In a large mug, add hot water and dissolve matcha powder. Mix well.
2. Mix in rest of ingredients.
3. Serve and enjoy.

Per Serving

calories: 298 | fat: 29g | protein: 3g | carbs: 13g | fiber: 3g | sugar: 10g | sodium: 21mg

Turmeric-Spiced Coconut Milk Shake

Prep time: 10 minutes | Cook time: 0 minutes | Serves 1

½ teaspoon Turmeric Powder
¼ teaspoon ginger powder
¼ teaspoon cinnamon powder
2 tablespoons flaxseed, ground
1 cup water
1 cup unsweetened coconut milk

1. Add all ingredients in a blender.
2. Blend until smooth and creamy.
3. Serve and enjoy.

Per Serving

calories: 266 | fat: 17g | protein: 12g | carbs: 10g | fiber: 6g | sugar: 13g | sodium: 116mg

Oats, Flaxseeds and Banana Smoothie

Prep time: 10 minutes | Cook time: 0 minutes | Serves 1

½ cup of ice
1 teaspoon honey
2 teaspoons flaxseeds
¼ cup 100% whole grain rolled oats
½ cup Greek Yogurt, plain
½ cup unsweetened almond milk
½ banana, peeled
¼ cup kale, shredded and stems discarded

1. Add all ingredients in a blender.
2. Blend until smooth and creamy.
3. Serve and enjoy.

Per Serving

calories: 305 | fat: 10g | protein: 11g | carbs: 54g | fiber: 8g | sugar: 30g | sodium: 147mg

Berry Red Smoothie

Prep time: 10 minutes | Cook time: 0 minutes | Serves 1

2 tablespoons cocoa powder
2 dried and pitted dates, sliced
1 cup unsweetened almond milk
1 frozen banana
4 medium hulled strawberries
¾ cup raw red beets

1. Add all ingredients in a blender.
2. Blend until smooth and creamy.
3. Serve and enjoy.

Per Serving
calories: 377 | fat: 10g | protein: 13g | carbs: 69g | fiber: 11g | sugar: 45g | sodium: 188mg

Pineapple Banana-Oat Smoothie

Prep time: 10 minutes | Cook time: 2½ minutes | Serves 1

5 to 6 ice cubes
¼ teaspoon coconut extract
½ cup diced pineapple, fresh frozen
½ banana, frozen
1 container of 5³⁄₁₀-ounce (150-g) nonfat Greek yogurt
¼ cup quick cooking oats
1 cup unsweetened almond milk

1. In a microwave safe cup, microwave on high for 2½ minutes the 1 cup almond milk and ¼ cup oats.
2. Once oats are cooked, add 2 ice cubes to cool it down quick and mix.
3. Then pour the rest of the ingredients in a blender and puree until mixture is smooth and creamy along with the slightly cold cooked oats.

Per Serving
calories: 255 | fat: 4g | protein: 14g | carbs: 45g | fiber: 4g | sugar: 29g | sodium: 123mg

Pineapple-Lettuce Smoothie

Prep time: 10 minutes | Cook time: 0 minutes | Serves 2

¼ teaspoon ground cinnamon
3 dates
1 banana, peeled and frozen
2½ cups fresh orange juice
2½ cups pineapple juice
½ apple
¼ cup red leaf lettuce
½ cup Romaine lettuce

1. Add all ingredients in a blender.
2. Blend until smooth and creamy.
3. Serve and enjoy.

Per Serving
calories: 352 | fat: 1.2g | protein: 4.5g | carbs: 88g | fiber: 7g | sugar: 65g | sodium: 7mg

Spiced Carrot Smoothie

Prep time: 10 minutes | Cook time: 0 minutes | Serves 1

½ teaspoon ground cinnamon
½ teaspoon vanilla extract
1 banana, frozen
1 cup carrot, peeled and halved
1 cup unsweetened almond milk
3 tablespoons raisins
1 cup spinach (optional)

1. Add all ingredients in a blender.
2. Blend until smooth and creamy.
3. Serve and enjoy.

Per Serving
calories: 274 | fat: 3g | protein: 11g | carbs: 53g | fiber: 8g | sugar: 34g | sodium: 209mg

Mango, Cucumber and Spinach Smoothie

Prep time: 10 minutes | Cook time: 0 minutes | Serves 1

1 cup water
1 cup orange juice, fresh
3 cups baby spinach
1 cup frozen mango, cubed and deseeded
2 apples, cored and chopped roughly
1 cucumber, ends removed and chopped roughly

1. Add all ingredients in a blender.
2. Blend until smooth and creamy.
3. Serve and enjoy.

Per Serving
calories: 455 | fat: 2g | protein: 8g | carbs: 111g | fiber: 15g | sugar: 84g | sodium: 90mg

Grape-Avocado Smoothie

Prep time: 10 minutes | Cook time: 0 minutes | Serves 1

1 tablespoon lime juice, fresh
2 tablespoons avocado
6 ounces (170 g) Greek yogurt, plain
15 pieces red or green grapes
1 pear, peeled, cored and chopped
2 cups packed spinach leaves

1. Add all ingredients in a blender.
2. Blend until smooth and creamy.
3. Serve and enjoy.

Per Serving
calories: 243 | fat: 3g | protein: 20g | carbs: 37g | fiber: 7g | sugar: 26g | sodium: 111mg

Spiced Pumpkin Smoothie

Prep time: 10 minutes | Cook time: 0 minutes | Serves 1

Ice (optional)
Pinch of nutmeg
½ teaspoon ginger
1 teaspoon cinnamon
1 small frozen banana
½ cup pureed pumpkin
1 tablespoon chia seeds
¼ cup rolled oats
1 cup unsweetened almond milk

1. Overnight or for an hour, soak chia seeds and oats in almond milk. This will give your smoothie a finer consistency.
2. Then, place all the ingredients in your food processor and blend ingredients until you get a smooth consistency.

Per Serving
calories: 348 | fat: 11g | protein: 15g | carbs: 61g | fiber: 9g | sugar: 28g | sodium: 109mg

Almond and Pear Smoothie

Prep time: 5 minutes | Cook time: 0 minutes | Serves 1

2 to 3 dates (optional)
¼ teaspoon ground cinnamon
½ cup plus 1 tablespoon unsweetened almond milk
½ pear, deseeded
1 banana, frozen

1. Add all ingredients in a blender.
2. Blend until smooth and creamy.
3. Serve and enjoy.

Per Serving
calories: 341 | fat: 11g | protein: 6g | carbs: 62g | fiber: 9g | sugar: 41g | sodium: 88mg

Berry Nutty Smoothie

Prep time: 10 minutes | Cook time: 0 minutes | Serves 1

1 cup frozen mix berries
½ cup unsweetened almond milk
¼ cup raw cashews
¼ cup quick cooking oats
1 cup packed Romaine lettuce
¼ cup packed Swiss chard, packed, chopped and stems discarded
Ice cubes or cold water (optional)

1. Add all ingredients in a blender.
2. Blend until smooth and creamy.
3. Serve and enjoy.

Per Serving
calories: 269 | fat: 10g | protein: 6g | carbs: 43g | fiber: 7g | sugar: 25g | sodium: 114mg

Pomegranate-Avocado Smoothie

Prep time: 10 minutes | Cook time: 0 minutes | Serves 1

½ cup spinach
½ cup ice
½ teaspoon vanilla extract
½ tablespoon. honey
½ cup Pomegranate Juice
¼ cup Greek Yogurt
½ Avocado, peeled

1. Add all ingredients in a blender.
2. Blend until smooth and creamy.
3. Serve and enjoy.

Per Serving
calories: 295 | fat: 15g | protein: 7g | carbs: 36g | fiber: 7g | sugar: 27g | sodium: 906mg

Spinach, Lettuce and Pear Smoothie

Prep time: 10 minutes | Cook time: 0 minutes | Serves 1

¾ to 1 cup water
1 cup lightly packed spinach leaves
2 kale leaves, thoroughly washed
2 romaine lettuce leaves
½ avocado
1 pear, stemmed, cored, and chopped

1. In a blender, combine the water, spinach, kale, romaine lettuce, avocado, and pear.
2. Blend until smooth and serve.

Per Serving
calories: 180 | fat: 10g | protein: 4g | carbs: 23g | fiber: 7g | sugar: 7g | sodium: 45mg

Buttery Mixed Berry Smoothie

Prep time: 5 minutes | Cook time: 0 minutes | Serves 1

¾ to 1 cup water
½ cup frozen raspberries
½ cup frozen strawberries
¼ cup frozen blackberries
2 tablespoons nut butter or seed butter, such as almond butter, sunflower seed butter, or tahini

1. In a blender, combine the water, raspberries, strawberries, blackberries, and nut butter.
2. Blend until smooth and serve.

Per Serving
calories: 186 | fat: 9g | protein: 4g | carbs: 24g | fiber: 5g | sugar: 17g | sodium: 1mg

Banana and Kale Smoothie

Prep time: 10 minutes | Cook time: 0 minutes | Serves 2

2 cups unsweetened almond milk
2 cups kale, stemmed, leaves chopped
2 bananas, peeled
1 to 2 packets stevia, or to taste
1 teaspoon ground cinnamon
1 cup crushed ice

1. In a blender, combine the almond milk, kale, bananas, stevia, cinnamon, and ice.
2. Blend until smooth.

Per Serving

calories: 181 | fat: 4g | protein: 4g | carbs: 37g | fiber: 6g | sugar: 15g | sodium: 210mg

Turmeric, Matcha and Mango Smoothie

Prep time: 10 minutes | Cook time: 0 minutes | Serves 2

2 cups cubed mango
2 teaspoons turmeric powder
2 tablespoons matcha (green tea) powder
2 cups unsweetened almond milk
2 tablespoons honey
1 cup crushed ice

1. In a blender, combine the mango, turmeric, matcha, almond milk, honey, and ice.
2. Blend until smooth.

Per Serving

calories: 285 | fat: 3g | protein: 4g | carbs: 68g | fiber: 6g | sugar: 63g | sodium: 94mg

Pear and Spinach Smoothie

Prep time: 10 minutes | Cook time: 0 minutes | Serves 1

1 pear, cored and quartered
½ fennel bulb
1 thin slice fresh ginger
1 cup packed spinach
½ cucumber, peeled
½ cup water
Ice (optional)

1. In a blender, combine the pear, fennel, ginger, spinach, cucumber, water, and ice (if using).
2. Blend until smooth.

Per Serving

calories: 147 | fat: 1g | protein: 4g | carbs: 37g | fiber: 9g | sugar: 6g | sodium: 89mg

Cherry and Raspberry Smoothie

Prep time: 10 minutes | Cook time: 0 minutes | Serves 1

1 cup frozen no-added-sugar pitted cherries
¼ cup fresh or frozen raspberries
¾ cup coconut water
1 tablespoon raw honey or pure maple syrup
1 teaspoon chia seeds
1 teaspoon hemp seeds
Drop vanilla extract
Ice (optional)

1. In a blender, combine the cherries, raspberries, coconut water, honey, chia seeds, hemp seeds, vanilla, and ice (if using).
2. Blend until smooth.

Per Serving

calories: 266 | fat: 2g | protein: 3g | carbs: 52g | fiber: 6g | sugar: 48g | sodium: 122mg

Green Apple and Spinach Smoothie

Prep time: 10 minutes | Cook time: 0 minutes | Serves 1

½ cup coconut water
1 green apple, cored, seeded, and quartered
1 cup spinach
¼ lemon, seeded
½ cucumber, peeled and seeded
2 teaspoons raw honey or pure maple syrup
Ice (optional)

1. In a blender, combine the coconut water, apple, spinach, lemon, cucumber, honey, and ice (if using).
2. Blend until smooth.

Per Serving

calories: 176 | fat: 1g | protein: 2g | carbs: 41g | fiber: 6g | sugar: 34g | sodium: 110mg

Banana and Blueberry Smoothie

Prep time: 5 minutes | Cook time: 0 minutes | Serves 1

1 cup packed spinach
½ cup fresh blueberries
½ banana
1 cup unsweetened coconut milk
½ teaspoon vanilla extract

1. In a blender, combine the spinach, blueberries, banana, coconut milk, and vanilla.
2. Blend until smooth.

Per Serving

calories: 152 | fat: 5g | protein: 2g | carbs: 27g | fiber: 5g | sugar: 15g | sodium: 90mg

Mango and Green Grape Smoothie

Prep time: 10 minutes | Cook time: 0 minutes | Serves 1

1 cup fresh or frozen mango chunks
½ cup fresh seedless green grapes
¼ fennel bulb
½ cup unsweetened almond milk
½ teaspoon fresh thyme leaves
Pinch sea salt
Pinch freshly ground black pepper
Ice (optional)

1. In a blender, combine the mango, grapes, fennel, almond milk, thyme leaves, sea salt, pepper, and ice (if using).
2. Blend until smooth.

Per Serving

calories: 274 | fat: 4g | protein: 3g | carbs: 65g | fiber: 7g | sugar: 54g | sodium: 125mg

Banana Chai Smoothie

Prep time: 10 minutes | Cook time: 0 minutes | Serves 1

1 cup unsweetened almond milk
1 date, pitted and chopped
¼ teaspoon vanilla extract
½ teaspoon chai spice blend
Pinch salt
1 banana, sliced into ¼-inch rounds
Ice cubes

1. In a blender, combine the almond milk, date, vanilla, chai spice blend, salt, banana, and ice.
2. Blend until smooth.

Per Serving

calories: 171 | fat: 4g | protein: 3g | carbs: 35g | fiber: 5g | sugar: 20g | sodium: 336mg

Pear and Spinach Smoothie

Prep time: 10 minutes | Cook time: 0 minutes | Serves 2

2 pears, peeled, cored, and chopped
¼ cup cilantro leaves
3 cups baby spinach
1 tablespoon grated ginger
3 cups unsweetened apple juice
1 cup crushed ice

1. Pour all the ingredients in a food processor. Pulse to purée until creamy and smooth.
2. Serve immediately.

Per Serving

calories: 307 | fat: 1g | protein: 2g | carbs: 77g | fiber: 8g | sugar: 61g | sodium: 51mg

Blueberry and Turmeric Chocolate Smoothie

Prep time: 10 minutes | Cook time: 0 minutes | Serves 2

1 cup frozen wild blueberries
1 (1-inch) fresh turmeric, peeled
2 tablespoons cocoa powder
2 cups unsweetened almond milk
1 to 2 packets stevia, or to taste
1 cup crushed ice

1. Pour all the ingredients in a food processor. Pulse to purée until creamy and smooth.
2. Serve immediately.

Per Serving

calories: 96 | fat: 5g | protein: 3g | carbs: 16g | fiber: 5g | sugar: 7g | sodium: 183mg

Pear and Green Tea Smoothie

Prep time: 10 minutes | Cook time: 0 minutes | Serves 2

2 pears, peeled, cored, and chopped
2 cups strongly brewed green tea
1 (1-inch) fresh ginger, peeled and roughly chopped, or 1 teaspoon ground ginger
2 tablespoons raw honey
1 cup unsweetened almond milk
1 cup crushed ice

1. Pour all the ingredients in a food processor. Pulse to purée until creamy and smooth.
2. Serve immediately.

Per Serving

calories: 207 | fat: 2g | protein: 1g | carbs: 51g | fiber: 7g | sugar: 38g | sodium: 95mg

Sunshine Smoothie

Prep time: 10 minutes | Cook time: 0 minutes | Serves 2

2½ cups frozen strawberries
2 cups spinach
⅛ to ¼ teaspoon ground turmeric
½ teaspoon ground cinnamon
1¼ cups coconut milk
1 cup crushed ice

1. Pour all the ingredients in a food processor. Pulse to purée until creamy and smooth.
2. Serve immediately.

Per Serving

calories: 418 | fat: 36g | protein: 4g | carbs: 26g | fiber: 8g | sugar:16g | sodium: 45mg

Tropical Smoothie

Prep time: 10 minutes | Cook time: 0 minutes | Serves 2

1 cup frozen pineapple
1 cup frozen mango
2½ cups spinach
¼ cup hemp seeds
1 teaspoon grated fresh ginger
1½ cups water
1 cup crushed ice

1. Pour all the ingredients in a food processor. Pulse to purée until creamy and smooth.
2. Serve immediately.

Per Serving

calories: 197 | fat: 7g | protein: 7g | carbs: 29g | fiber: 5g | sugar: 24g | sodium: 29mg

Carrot and Celery Smoothie

Prep time: 10 minutes | Cook time: 0 minutes | Serves 1

1 carrot, trimmed
1 small beet, scrubbed and quartered
1 celery stalk
½ cup fresh raspberries
1 cup coconut water
1 teaspoon balsamic vinegar
Ice (optional)

1. In a blender, combine the carrot, beet, celery, raspberries, coconut water, balsamic vinegar, and ice (if using).
2. Blend until smooth.

Per Serving

calories: 140 | fat: 1g | protein: 3g | carbs: 24g | fiber: 8g | sugar: 23g | sodium: 293mg

Kale and Grape Smoothie

Prep time: 10 minutes | Cook time: 0 minutes | Serves 1

1 cup packed kale leaves, thoroughly washed
¼ avocado
1 cup fresh grapes
¼ cup cashews (optional)
1 tablespoon hemp seed
1 or 2 mint leaves
1 cup unsweetened coconut milk
Ice (optional)

1. In a blender, combine the kale, avocado, grapes, cashews (if using), hemp seed, mint leaves, coconut milk, and ice (if using).
2. Blend until smooth.

Per Serving

calories: 500 | fat: 32g | protein: 13g | carbs: 47g | fiber: 7g | sugar: 34g | sodium: 199mg

CHAPTER 10:
SNACKS, SIDES AND APPETIZERS

Vegetable Crackers with Flaxseed

Prep time: 5 minutes | Cook time: 1½ hours | Makes 20 to 24 crackers

½ small green cabbage head, chopped
1 zucchini, grated
1 carrot, grated
¾ cup ground flaxseed
¼ cup water, plus additional as needed
2 tablespoons extra-virgin olive oil
¾ teaspoon salt

1. Preheat the oven to 275°F (135°C).
2. Line a baking sheet with parchment paper.
3. In a food processor, combine the cabbage, zucchini, carrot, flaxseed, water, olive oil, and salt. Process until mostly smooth. If the mixture seems dry, add more water, 1 tablespoon at a time.
4. With a spatula, spread the cracker mixture evenly over the prepared sheet.
5. Place the sheet in the preheated oven and bake for 1½ hours, checking every 30 minutes to see how the crackers are drying. They're done when they are completely dry and crispy.
6. Remove from the oven and cool completely.
7. Break into pieces and store in a sealed container.

Per Serving (4 crackers)

calories: 163 | fat: 11g | protein: 5g | carbs: 11g | fiber: 7g | sugar: 3g | sodium: 377mg

Turmeric Bars

Prep time: 10 minutes | Cook time: 0 minutes | Serves 6

1 cup shredded coconut
10 dates, pitted
1 tablespoon coconut oil
1 teaspoon cinnamon
1 ¼ cup coconut butter
1 ½ teaspoon turmeric powder
2 teaspoons honey
⅛ teaspoon black pepper

1. Prepare a baking pan and line with parchment paper.
2. Place the coconut and dates in a food processor and pulse until well combined. Add in the coconut oil and cinnamon.
3. Press the dough at the bottom of the pan and allow to set in the fridge for 2 hours.
4. Make the filling by melting the coconut butter in a double boiler. Stir in turmeric powder and honey.
5. Pour in the mixture into the pan with the crust.
6. Allow to set in the fridge for at least 2 hours.

Per Serving

calories: 410 | fat: 41g | protein: 1g | carbs: 13g | fiber: 2g | sugar: 11g | sodium: 208mg

Anti-Inflammatory Turmeric Gummies

Prep time: 5 minutes | Cook time: 5 minutes | Serves 8

1 teaspoon ground turmeric
6 tablespoons pure maple syrup
8 tablespoons unflavored gelatin powder
3½ cups water

1. In a pot, combine the water, turmeric, and maple syrup.
2. Bring to a boil for 5 minutes.
3. Remove from the heat and sprinkle with gelatin powder. Mix to hydrate the gelatin.
4. Turn on the heat and bring to a boil until the gelatin is completely dissolved.
5. Pour the mixture in a dish and chill the mixture in the fridge for at least 4 hours.
6. Once set, slice into small squares.

Per Serving

calories: 68 | fat: 0g | protein: 0.2g | carbs: 17g | fiber: 0.1g | sugar: 15g | sodium: 19mg

Ginger Spiced Mixed Nuts

Prep time: 5 minutes | Cook time: 40 minutes | Serves 4

2 large egg whites, pasture-raised
2 cups mixed nuts (raw almond, pumpkin seeds, cashew, etc.)
1 teaspoon grated ginger
½ teaspoon salt

1. Preheat the oven to 250°F (121°C).
2. Whip the egg whites until frothy. Add in ginger and salt.
3. Add in the mixed nuts into the egg mixture. Stir to coat everything.
4. Place parchment paper in a baking tray and spread the nuts evenly on to the sheet.
5. Bake for 40 minutes.
6. Allow the mixture to cool and harden.
7. Break into pieces and store in the fridge until ready to consume

Per Serving

calories: 423 | fat: 36g | protein: 17g | carbs: 16g | fiber: 9g | sugar: 3g | sodium: 28mg

Spicy Tuna Rolls

Prep time: 5 minutes | Cook time: 0 minutes | Serves 6

1 medium cucumber
1 can yellowfin tuna, wild-caught
2 slices avocado, diced
⅛ teaspoon salt
⅛ teaspoon pepper

1. Use a mandolin to thinly slice the cucumber lengthwise.
2. In a mixing bowl, combine the tuna and avocado. Season with salt and pepper to taste.
3. Spoon the tuna and avocado mixture and spread evenly on cucumber slices.
4. Roll the cucumber slices and secure the ends with toothpicks.
5. Allow to chill in the fridge before serving.

Per Serving

calories: 135 | fat: 10g | protein: 7g | carbs: 6g | fiber: 5g | sugar: 0.9g | sodium: 73mg

Veggie Burrito

Prep time: 10 minutes | Cook time: 1 minutes | Serves 2

4 medium collard greens, stalks trimmed
1 teaspoon avocado oil
⅓ cup bell pepper, julienned
⅓ cup chopped tomatoes
⅓ cup red onions, sliced thinly
¼ cup avocado meat
1 cup cooked quinoa
¼ cup cilantro leaves, chopped
¼ teaspoon salt

1. Bring water to a boil and blanch the collard greens. Set aside.
2. In a skillet, heat the avocado oil over medium flame and sauté the bell pepper for 1 minute. Set aside.
3. Assemble the burrito by placing the blanched collard greens on a flat surface.
4. Place the bell pepper, tomatoes, onions, avocado meat, and quinoa in the center. Add in the cilantro leaves.
5. Roll the collard greens to create a burrito.

Per Serving

calories: 175 | fat: 7g | protein: 5g | carbs: 25g | fiber: 5 | sugar: 3g | sodium: 11mg

Spicy Kale Chips

Prep time: 5 minutes | Cook time: 20 minutes | Serves 4

1 bunch curly kale, rinsed
¼ teaspoon ground cayenne pepper
⅛ teaspoon garlic powder
spray oil for greasing
¼ teaspoon salt
⅛ teaspoon black pepper

1. Preheat the oven to 300ºF (150ºC).
2. Pat dry the kale to remove water.
3. Tear the kale leaves into bite-sized pieces and place on a baking sheet lined with foil.
4. Spray with cooking oil and season with garlic powder, season, and black pepper.
5. Bake in the oven for 20 minutes or until crunchy.

Per Serving

calories: 5 | fat: 0g | protein: 0.4g | carbs: 1g | fiber: 0.3g | sugar: 0.3g | sodium: 3mg

Ginger Date Bars

Prep time: 5 minutes | Cook time: 20 minutes | Serves 8

1 ½ cups almond, soaked in water overnight then drained
¾ cup dates, pitted
¼ cup unsweetened almond milk
1 teaspoon ground ginger

1. Preheat the oven to 350ºF (180ºC).
2. Place the almond in a food processor. Pulse a thick dough is formed.
3. Press the dough in a baking dish lined with parchment paper. Set aside.
4. Make the date mix by combining the rest of the ingredients in a food processor. Pulse until smooth.
5. Pour the date mixture on to the almond crust.
6. Bake for 20 minutes.
7. Allow to cool before slicing.

Per Serving

calories: 45 | fat: 0.3g | protein: 0.5g | carbs: 11g | fiber: 1g | sugar: 9g | sodium: 6mg

Vanilla Turmeric Orange Juice

Prep time: 10 minutes | Cook time: 0 minutes | Serves 2

3 oranges, peeled and quartered
1 cup unsweetened almond milk
1 teaspoon vanilla extract
½ teaspoon cinnamon
¼ teaspoon turmeric
1 pinch of pepper

1. Place all ingredients in a blender.
2. Pulse until smooth.
3. Pour into glasses and allow to chill in the fridge before serving.

Per Serving

calories: 188 | fat: 5g | protein: 5g | carbs: 33g | fiber: 6g | sugar: 27g | sodium: 53mg

Spicy Taro Crunch

Prep time: 5 minutes | Cook time: 20 minutes | Serves 8

2 cups taro, sliced thinly
1 teaspoon cayenne pepper powder
1 tablespoon olive oil
1 pinch of salt

1. Preheat the oven to 350°F (180°C).
2. In a bowl, combine all ingredients. Toss to coat the taro with the spices and seasoning.
3. Place the taro slices on a baking rack.
4. Bake for 20 minutes or until the taro becomes crispy.

Per Serving

calories: 179 | fat: 7g | protein: 2g | carbs: 28g | fiber: 5g | sugar: 0.5g | sodium: 12mg

Turmeric Nuggets

Prep time: 10 minutes | Cook time: 25 minutes | Serves 4

2 cups cauliflower florets
2 cups broccoli florets
1 cup carrots, chopped
1 teaspoon garlic, minced
½ teaspoon ground turmeric
½ cup almond meal
2 egg, pasture-raised
¼ teaspoon salt
¼ teaspoon black pepper

1. Preheat the oven to 400°F (205°C) and line a baking sheet with parchment paper.
2. In a food processor, combine all ingredients and pulse until smooth.
3. Scoop a tablespoon of mixture and place on the baking sheet.
4. Bake for 25 minutes.

Per Serving

calories: 97 | fat: 5g | protein: 7g | carbs: 7g | fiber: 3g | sugar: 3g | sodium: 93mg

Coconut Flour Muffins

Prep time: 10 minutes | Cook time: 25 minutes | Serves 6

6 large eggs, pasture raised
½ cup unsweetened coconut milk
⅓ cup pure maple syrup
1 teaspoon vanilla extract
14 tablespoons coconut flour
½ teaspoon baking soda
2 teaspoons turmeric powder
½ teaspoon ginger powder
Salt and pepper, to taste

1. Preheat the oven to 350°F (180°C).
2. Prepare a muffin tin and line with muffin liners.
3. In a mixing bowl, combine the eggs, milk, maple syrup, and vanilla.
4. In another bowl, sift the coconut flour, baking soda, turmeric, and ginger powder. Season with salt and pepper to taste.
5. Gradually pour the wet ingredients into the dry ingredients until well combined.
6. Pour into the prepared muffin tins.
7. Bake for 25 minutes or until a toothpick inserted in the middle comes out clean.

Per Serving

calories: 157 | fat: 9g | protein: 3g | carbs: 15g | fiber: 1g | sugar: 12g | sodium: 150mg

No Bake Golden Energy Bites

Prep time: 5 minutes | Cook time: 0 minutes | Serves 6

1 cup unsweetened almond milk
¾ cup coconut flakes, unsweetened
6 tablespoons protein powder
1 teaspoon coconut oil
½ teaspoon pure maple syrup
2 teaspoons turmeric

1. In a bowl, combine all ingredients until a thick dough is formed.
2. Place dough in a pan lined with parchment paper and spread evenly.
3. Place in the refrigerator for at least an hour to set.
4. Remove the bars from the pan and slice to 16 pieces.

Per Serving

calories: 376 | fat: 36g | protein: 6g | carbs: 9g | fiber: 2g | sugar: 5g | sodium: 194mg

Banana Ginger Bars

Prep time: 10 minutes | Cook time: 40 minutes | Serves 5

2 large ripe bananas, peeled and mashed
1 cup coconut flour
⅓ cup coconut oil
⅓ cup raw honey
6 eggs, pasture-raised
1 tablespoon grated fresh ginger
2 teaspoons cinnamon powder
1 teaspoon ground cardamom powder
1 teaspoon baking soda
2 teaspoons apples cider vinegar

1. Preheat the oven to 350°F (180°C).
2. Grease a baking dish or line with parchment paper.
3. In a food processor, combine the bananas, coconut flour, coconut oil, honey, eggs, ginger, cinnamon, and cardamom. Pulse until smooth.
4. Add the baking soda and apple cider vinegar last and quickly blend.
5. Pour into the prepared pan.
6. Bake in the oven for 40 minutes or until a toothpick inserted in the middle comes out clean.
7. Allow to cool before slicing.

Per Serving

calories: 364 | fat: 26g | protein: 12g | carbs: 23g | fiber: 1g | sugar: 20g | sodium: 187mg

Kombucha Gummies

Prep time: 10 minutes | Cook time: 5 minutes | Serves 8

1 teaspoon grated ginger
1½ cups plain kombucha
½ cup grapefruit juice
1 tablespoon grapefruit zest
6 tablespoons honey
⅓ cup gelatin powder

1. Line the bottom of a glass pan with plastic wrap. Set aside.
2. In a pot, add the ginger and a cup of water. Bring to a boil for 5 minutes. Drain and save the grated ginger.
3. In another saucepan, combine the kombucha, grapefruit juice, zest, and honey. Sprinkle with the gelatin powder and allow to hydrate for 5 minutes.
4. Turn on the heat and bring to a boil until the gelatin dissolves. Add in the grated ginger.
5. Pour into the mixture the prepared glass and chill for 3 hours until the gelatin has set.
6. Slice into small squares.

Per Serving

calories: 99 | fat: 0g | protein: 0.4g | carbs: 26g | fiber: 0.1g | sugar: 26g | sodium: 15mg

Cacao Coffee Protein Bars

Prep time: 10 minutes | Cook time: 0 minutes | Serves 6

2 cups mixed nuts (almond, pecans, cashew and walnuts)
1 cup egg white protein powder
¼ cup cacao powder
3 tablespoons powdered coffee
18 large medjool dates, pitted
¼ cup raw cacao nibs
5 tablespoons water

1. Line a baking pan with parchment paper. Set aside
2. In a food processor, pulse the nuts, protein powder, cacao powder, and powdered coffee.
3. Add in the pitted dates and process until fine crumbs form. If dry, add a tablespoon of water until a sticky dough is formed.
4. Place in a bowl and stir in the cacao nibs.
5. Transfer the mixture into the pan and spread evenly.
6. Place inside the fridge and allow to set for 30 minutes before slicing.

Per Serving

calories: 493 | fat: 25g | protein: 12g | carbs: 67g | fiber: 12g | sugar:50g | sodium: 2mg

Hibiscus Ginger Gelatin

Prep time: 5 minutes | Cook time: 5 minutes | Serves 5

3 tablespoons dried hibiscus flower
1 ½ tablespoons honey
1 teaspoon ginger juice
2 tablespoons gelatin powder
1 cup water

1. Bring water to a boil.
2. Once the water boils, remove from the heat and add the hibiscus flowers.
3. Allow to infuse for 5 minutes.
4. Remove the flowers and discard.
5. Heat the liquid and add the honey, ginger, and gelatin.
6. Allow the gelatin to dissolve.
7. Pour the mixture into a baking sheet.
8. Place in the fridge and allow to set.
9. Slice the gelatin once it hardens.

Per Serving

calories: 27 | fat: 0g | protein: 0.2g | carbs: 7g | fiber: 0g | sugar: 7g | sodium: 6mg

White Beans Hummus

Prep time: 10 minutes | Cook time: 0 minutes | Serves 7

¼ cup olive oil
1 teaspoon fresh rosemary, chopped
2 cups cooked white beans
¼ cup unsweetened almond milk
1 garlic clove, minced
1 tablespoon lemon juice
¼ cup hot water
¼ teaspoon salt

1. Heat oil in a skillet over medium heat and fry the rosemary for a few minutes. Remove from heat and allow to cool before removing the rosemary leaves. Set aside.
2. In a food processor, combine the white beans, almond milk, garlic, and lemon juice. Season with salt, to taste.
3. Pulse until smooth. Gradually drizzle with oil and water to adjust the consistency. Save a quarter of the oil.
4. Place in a bowl and drizzle the remaining olive oil on top.
5. Serve with vegetable sticks.

Per Serving

calories: 195 | fat: 13g | protein: 7g | carbs: 15g | fiber: 4g | sugar: 0.8g | sodium: 28mg

Mushroom Pizza

Prep time: 5 minutes | Cook time: 15 minutes | Serves 4

2 tablespoons olive oil
¾ pound (340 g) portobello mushrooms, stems removed
½ cup tomato puree
2 garlic cloves, minced
½ cup mozzarella cheese, shredded
Salt and pepper, to taste

1. Preheat the oven to 350°F (180°C).
2. Brush oil on the inverted side of the mushrooms.
3. Brush with tomato puree and sprinkle with garlic and mozzarella cheese on top.
4. Place on a baking pan and bake for 15 minutes.

Per Serving

calories: 112 | fat: 7g | protein: 7g | carbs: 7g | fiber: 2g | sugar: 4g | sodium: 122mg

Quinoa and Beet Kale Dolmades

Prep time: 10 minutes | Cook time: 55 minutes | Serves 1

¼ cup uncooked quinoa
4 leaves dinosaur kale
½ cup beets, grated
1 tablespoons lemon juice
1 teaspoon balsamic vinegar
½ teaspoon orange zest
1 tablespoons olive oil
½ cup water

1. Bring water to a boil over medium flame and cook the quinoa according to package instruction. Drain and allow to cool. Save the warm water.
2. Place the kale leaves in warm water and blanch for 10 minutes. Set aside and allow water to drain.
3. In a bowl, combine the quinoa, beets, lemon juice, balsamic vinegar and orange zest.
4. Place the kale leaves stem side up and add 2 tablespoons of the quinoa mixture. Fold the edges as you would a burrito or spring roll.
5. Place them in a pan with olive oil and pour ½ cup water.
6. Cover and bring to a gentle boil over medium low heat. Cook for 45 minutes.
7. Once the leaves have darkened, remove from the pan and transfer to a plate.
8. Serve with hummus.

Per Serving

calories: 490 | fat: 19g | protein: 18g | carbs: 71g | fiber: 16g | sugar: 23g | sodium: 406mg

Salted Raw Caramel Dip

Prep time: 5 minutes | Cook time: 0 minutes | Serves 2

1 cup soft medjool dates, pitted
1 teaspoon fresh lemon juice
¼ cup unsweetened almond milk
1 teaspoon vanilla extract
1 tablespoon coconut oil
¼ teaspoon salt

1. Combine all ingredients in a blender or food processor.
2. Pulse until smooth.
3. Place in a container and allow to chill before serving.

Per Serving

calories: 113 | fat: 7.2g | protein: 0.4g | carbs: 12g | fiber: 0.9g | sugar: 11g | sodium: 22mg

Red Pepper Hummus with Garlic

Prep time: 5 minutes | Cook time: 0 minutes | Serves 4

1 cup chickpea, cooked
2 whole roasted red pepper, seeded and peeled
2 teaspoons minced garlic
4 tablespoons lemon juice
3 tablespoons olive oil
1 teaspoon salt
1 teaspoon black pepper

1. Place all ingredients in a food processor and pulse until smooth.
2. Place in a bowl and serve with grain-free chips or vegetable chips.

Per Serving
calories: 293 | fat: 12g | protein: 11g | carbs: 35g | fiber: 7g | sugar: 7g | sodium: 91mg

Greek Yogurt with Fresh Toppings

Prep time: 5 minutes | Cook time: 0 minutes | Serves 1

1 cup plain Greek yogurt
¼ cup fresh strawberries
1 teaspoon organic raw hone
¼ teaspoon cinnamon

1. Combine all ingredients in a bowl.
2. Chill in the fridge before serving.

Per Serving
calories: 164 | fat: 8g | protein: 9g | carbs: 15g | fiber: 1g | sugar: 14g | sodium: 150mg

Simple Guacamole

Prep time: 5 minutes | Cook time: 0 minutes | Serves 2

2 tablespoons chopped onion
2 tablespoons chopped cilantro
1 medium chopped avocado
⅛ teaspoon salt

1. Place all ingredients in a food processor.
2. Pulse until smooth.

Per Serving
calories: 165 | fat: 15g | protein: 2g | carbs: 10g | fiber: 7g | sugar: 1g | sodium: 8mg

Cranberry Pistachio Energy Bars

Prep time: 10 minutes | Cook time: 23 minutes | Serves 5

1 cup uncooked rolled oat
¾ cup cooked quinoa
¾ cup dried cranberries, chopped
½ cup dry roasted pistachios
⅓ cup unsweetened coconut flakes
2 tablespoons flaxseed meal
1-ounce bittersweet chocolate, chopped
½ cup creamy almond milk
6 tablespoons honey
1 tablespoon olive oil
¼ teaspoon salt

1. Preheat the oven to 350°F (180°C).
2. Spread the oats and quinoa on a baking sheet and bake for 8 minutes until lightly browned.
3. Place the mixture in a bowl and add in the cranberries, pistachios, coconut flakes, flaxseed, and chocolate.
4. In a saucepan, combine the almond milk, honey, and olive oil. Mix over low heat for one minute.
5. Pour the milk mixture into the dry ingredients. Toss to coat.
6. Press the mixture into a baking dish.
7. Place the oven and bake for 15 minutes until lightly browned.

Per Serving
calories: 487 | fat: 27g | protein: 13g | carbs: 60g | fiber: 9g | sugar: 33g | sodium: 135mg

Zucchini and Black Beans Enchiladas

Prep time: 10 minutes | Cook time: 20 minutes | Serves 6

3 large zucchini, diced
3 teaspoons extra-virgin olive oil
1¼ teaspoons salt
½ small red onion, chopped
1 cup black beans, cooked
¼ cup goat cheese, diced
1 cup tomatoes, diced
A handful of coriander, chopped
Salt and pepper, to taste

1. Preheat the oven to 375°F (190°C).
2. Place zucchini in a baking tray and drizzle with olive oil. Season with salt.
3. Bake for 20 minutes or until the edges have browned.
4. Allow to cool.
5. Mix all ingredients in a bowl and toss to coat everything.
6. Serve with vegetable chips.

Per Serving
calories: 225 | fat: 9g | protein: 14g | carbs: 22g | fiber: 5g | sugar: 2g | sodium: 121mg

Thai Sesame Edamame

Prep time: 5 minutes | Cook time: 1¹⁄₁₀ hours | Serves 6

4 cups edamame pods
1 tablespoon dark sesame oil
1 tablespoon rice vinegar
1 teaspoon toasted sesame seeds
3 tablespoons water
½ teaspoon salt
½ teaspoon ground black pepper

1. Preheat the oven to 300°F (150°C).
2. Line a baking sheet with aluminum foil. Set aside.
3. Place all ingredients in a bowl and toss to coat the edamame pods with the seasoning.
4. Arrange the seasoned edamame pods in the baking sheet.
5. Bake for 1 hour and 10 minutes until the pods are crispy.

Per Serving

calories: 149 | fat: 8g | protein: 11g | carbs: 10g | fiber: 5g | sugar: 2g | sodium: 9mg

Sweet Potato Anti-Inflammatory Muffins

Prep time: 15 minutes | Cook time: 35 minutes | Serves 6

1 small sweet potato, cooked
1 egg, pasture-raised
¾ cup unsweetened coconut milk
2 tablespoons olive oil
½ cup pure maple syrup
1 cup brown rice flour
¼ cup coconut flour
1 tablespoon baking powder
1 tablespoon ground cinnamon
1 teaspoon ground ginger
1 teaspoon ground turmeric
⅛ teaspoon ground cloves
⅛ teaspoon ground nutmeg
½ teaspoon salt

1. Preheat the oven to 400°F (205°C).
2. Peel the cooked potato and place in a bowl. Mash gently with fork or masher.
3. Add in the eggs, coconut milk, olive oil, and maple syrup. Mix until well combined.
4. In a separate bowl, mix the rice flour, coconut flour, baking powder, cinnamon, ginger, turmeric, cloves, and nutmeg.
5. Gradually add the milk mixture into the flour mixture. Fold until well combined.
6. Grease muffin cups then pour batter into the pan until ¾ full.
7. Bake in the oven for 35 minutes.

Per Serving

calories: 311 | fat: 14g | protein: 5g | carbs: 43g | fiber: 3g | sugar: 18g | sodium: 41mg

Beet Chips

Prep time: 5 minutes | Cook time: 1½ minutes | Serves 2

3 medium beets, peeled and sliced thinly
1 tablespoon olive oil
Salt, to taste

1. Preheat the oven to 350°F (180°C).
2. Place all ingredients in a bowl and toss to coat.
3. Arrange the seasoned beet slices on a baking tray lined with aluminum foil.
4. Bake in the oven for 1 hour and 30 minutes.
5. Make sure to flip the beets halfway through the cooking time.

Per Serving

calories: 120 | fat: 7g | protein: 2g | carbs: 12g | fiber: 3g | sugar: 8g | sodium: 210mg

Granola Bars with Chocolate Chips

Prep time: 10 minutes | Cook time: 5 minutes | Makes 10 bars

1½ cups pecans
⅓ cup unsweetened shredded coconut flakes
¼ cup dairy-free chocolate chips
⅓ cup sunflower seed butter
⅓ cup pure maple syrup or raw honey
3 tablespoons coconut oil

1. Line a loaf pan with parchment paper.
2. In a food processor, grind the pecans into a coarse flour. Transfer to a medium bowl.
3. Add the coconut flakes and chocolate chips.
4. In a small pot over low heat, gently melt the sunflower seed butter, maple syrup, and coconut oil together until smooth, about 5 minutes.
5. Pour the wet mixture over the dry ingredients. Stir well to ensure everything is incorporated.
6. Press the granola mixture into the prepared pan.
7. Refrigerate for 2 hours and then slice into bars. Cover and keep refrigerated until ready to serve.

Per Serving

calories: 305 | fat: 25g | protein: 4g | carbs: 21g | fiber: 4g | sugar: 14g | sodium: 60mg

Simple Quinoa Flatbread

Prep time: 5 minutes | Cook time: 25 to 30 minutes | Serves 8 to 10

1½ cups dry quinoa
2¼ cups water
¼ cup extra-virgin olive oil
1 teaspoon salt

1. Preheat the oven to 350°F (180°C).
2. Line a 9-by-13-inch baking pan (or a baking sheet with 1-inch sides) with parchment paper.
3. Using a spice grinder or high-speed blender, pulverize the quinoa into a fine meal. Transfer to a medium bowl.
4. Add the water, olive oil, and salt. Whisk well, so there are no lumps.
5. Pour the batter into the prepared pan and smooth it. The batter will be quite wet.
6. Place the pan in the preheated oven and bake for 25 to 30 minutes, or until the flatbread is dry and lightly golden on top.
7. Cut into desired sizes and serve.

Per Serving
calories: 171 | fat: 8g | protein: 5g | carbs: 21g | fiber: 2g | sugar: 0g | sodium: 292mg

Garlic Roasted Chickpeas

Prep time: 5 minutes | Cook time: 1½ hours | Serves 8

1 cup dried chickpeas, soaked in water for 8 hours
2 teaspoons extra-virgin olive oil
1 tablespoon garlic powder, plus additional as needed
1 teaspoon onion powder, plus additional as needed
¾ teaspoon salt, plus additional as needed

1. Drain the chickpeas and rinse well. Place them in a large pot and cover with a few inches of water. Bring to a boil over medium-high heat. Cook for about 45 minutes, or until tender. Drain again.
2. Preheat the oven to 325°F (163°C).
3. Line a large baking sheet with aluminum foil.
4. In a large bowl, toss together the chickpeas, olive oil, garlic powder, onion powder, and salt.
5. Taste and adjust the seasoning if necessary. Remember that the flavors intensify as the chickpeas bake.
6. Spread the chickpeas onto the prepared sheet. Depending on the size of your sheet, you may need two (don't crowd the chickpeas).
7. Carefully place the sheet(s) in the preheated oven and bake for about 45 minutes, stirring and turning the chickpeas every 15 minutes, or until golden and crunchy. The chickpeas will also crisp as they cool.

Per Serving
calories: 106 | fat: 3g | protein: 5g | carbs: 16g | fiber: 5g | sugar: 3g | sodium: 223mg

Cumin Cauliflower Bites

Prep time: 5 minutes | Cook time: 25 minutes | Serves 6

2 medium cauliflower heads, broken into florets (about 8 cups)
3 tablespoons melted coconut oil
2 tablespoons ground cumin
1 teaspoon ground coriander
1 teaspoon salt

1. Preheat the oven to 400°F (205°C).
2. In a large bowl, combine the cauliflower, coconut oil, cumin, coriander, and salt. Toss to coat.
3. Transfer the florets to a large roasting tray, or two baking sheets.
4. Place the tray in the preheated oven and bake for 25 minutes, or until the cauliflower is tender and beginning to brown on the edges.

Per Serving
calories: 114 | fat: 7g | protein: 4g | carbs: 11g | fiber: 5g | sugar: 5g | sodium: 448mg

Smashed Peas with Mint and Dill

Prep time: 5 minutes | Cook time: 8 minutes | Serves 4

4 cups frozen peas, thawed
¼ cup extra-virgin olive oil
¼ cup chopped fresh mint
¼ cup chopped fresh dill
1 teaspoon salt, plus additional as needed

1. Fill a pot with 2 inches of water and insert a steamer basket. Place it over high heat and bring to a boil.
2. Add the peas. Cover and cook for 8 to 10 minutes, or until the peas are bright green and tender. Drain and transfer to a food processor.
3. Add the olive oil, mint, dill, and salt.
4. Process until completely smooth, or pulse a few times and leave some texture.
5. Taste and adjust the seasoning if necessary.

Per Serving
calories: 243 | fat: 13g | protein: 9g | carbs: 25g | fiber: 10g | sugar: 7g | sodium: 705mg

Steamed Brown Rice with Herbs

Prep time: 5 minutes | Cook time: 45 minutes | Serves 6 to 8

2 cups short-grain brown rice
4 cups water
1½ teaspoons salt
1 bunch fresh basil, washed, stemmed, and finely chopped
1 bunch fresh dill, washed, stemmed, and finely chopped
1 bunch parsley, washed, stemmed, and finely chopped

1. In a fine-mesh strainer, rinse the rice well and transfer to a large pot set over medium-high heat. Add the water and salt. Bring to a boil. Cover and simmer for 30 minutes.
2. Add the herbs to the pot and stir well.
3. Cook for 15 minutes more, or until the rice is tender and chewy.

Per Serving
calories: 241 | fat: 2g | protein: 5g | carbs: 54g | fiber: 5g | sugar: 1g | sodium: 595mg

Authentic Guacamole

Prep time: 5 minutes | Cook time: 0 minutes | Makes 3 cups

4 medium, ripe avocados, halved, and pitted
1 teaspoon garlic powder
½ teaspoon salt

1. Scoop out the avocado flesh and put it in a medium bowl.
2. Add the garlic powder and the salt. With a fork, mash the avocados until creamy.
3. Serve immediately, or cover and refrigerate for up to 2 days.

Per Serving

calories: 358 | fat: 32g | protein: 7g | carbs: 13g | fiber: 6g | sugar: 0g | sodium: 407mg

Vinegary Honey Two-Bean Dip

Prep time: 15 minutes | Cook time: 0 minutes | Makes 3½ cups

1 (14-ounce / 397-g) can black beans, drained and rinsed well
1 (14-ounce / 397-g) can kidney beans, drained and rinsed well
2 garlic cloves
2 cherry tomatoes
2 tablespoons filtered water
1 tablespoon apple cider vinegar
2 teaspoons raw honey
1 teaspoon freshly squeezed lime juice
¼ teaspoon ground cumin
¼ teaspoon salt
Pinch cayenne pepper
Freshly ground black pepper, to taste

1. In a food processor (or blender), combine the black beans, kidney beans, garlic, tomatoes, water, vinegar, honey, lime juice, cumin, salt, and cayenne pepper, and season with black pepper.
2. Blend until smooth. Use a silicone spatula to scrape the sides of the processor bowl as needed.
3. Cover and refrigerate before serving, if desired, or refrigerate for up to 5 days.

Per Serving (½ cup)

calories: 166 | fat: 0g | protein: 9g | carbs: 34g | fiber: 8g | sugar: 7g | sodium: 378mg

Cumin-Lime Roasted Cauliflower

Prep time: 10 minutes | Cook time: 15 minutes | Serves 4

1½ teaspoons ground cumin
1 teaspoon salt
½ teaspoon chili powder
½ teaspoon freshly ground black pepper
½ teaspoon garlic powder
1 head cauliflower, roughly chopped into bite-size pieces
3 tablespoons freshly squeezed lime juice
3 tablespoons ghee, melted

1. Preheat the oven to 450°F (235°C).
2. In a small bowl, mix the cumin, salt, chili powder, pepper, and garlic powder.
3. Spread the cauliflower in a baking pan.
4. Drizzle with the lime juice and ghee. Sprinkle with the spice mixture and toss to coat.
5. Bake for 15 minutes.

Per Serving

calories: 138 | fat: 11g | protein: 3g | carbs: 9g | fiber: 3g | sugar: 3g | sodium: 639mg

Baked Beets in Cider Vinegar

Prep time: 10 minutes | Cook time: 25 minutes | Serves 6

4 medium golden beets, peeled and diced into 1-inch pieces
4 medium red beets, peeled and diced into 1-inch pieces
½ yellow onion, diced into 1-inch pieces
½ cup apple cider vinegar
½ cup extra-virgin olive oil
2 tablespoons coconut sugar
¼ teaspoon salt
Freshly ground black pepper, to taste

1. Preheat the oven to 450°F (235°C).
2. Line a baking sheet with aluminum foil.
3. Spread the beets and onion into the prepared pan and drizzle with the vinegar and olive oil.
4. Sprinkle the coconut sugar and the salt onto the vegetables. Season with pepper and toss to coat.
5. Bake for 25 minutes, or until the beets caramelize around the edges and are fork-tender.

Per Serving

calories: 233 | fat: 19g | protein: 2g | carbs: 18g | fiber: 2g | sugar: 12g | sodium: 184mg

Brussels Sprout and Apple Kebabs

Prep time: 15 minutes | Cook time: 20 minutes | Makes 12 kebabs

1 pound (454 g) Brussels sprouts, discolored exterior leaves removed and discarded
2 apples, diced into 1-inch pieces
2 small red onions, diced into 1-inch pieces
1 tablespoon avocado oil
⅓ cup fish sauce
¼ cup filtered water
3 tablespoons rice vinegar
2 tablespoons freshly squeezed lime juice
2 roughly chopped pitted dates
2 garlic cloves, minced
Dash red pepper flakes
Dash ground ginger

1. Preheat the oven to 400°F (205°C).
2. Carefully press a skewer through 1 Brussels sprout, 1 apple piece, and 1 onion piece, leaving ½ inch between each piece. Repeat until 12 skewers are evenly filled. Place the kebabs on a rimmed baking sheet. Roast for 20 minutes, or until thoroughly roasted, turning the skewers halfway through.
3. While the vegetables roast, in a blender, combine the fish sauce, water, vinegar, lime juice, dates, garlic, red pepper flakes, and ginger. Pulse until smooth.
4. Remove the kebabs from the oven and drizzle with half the sauce. Serve immediately, with the remaining sauce as a dip.

Per Serving (2 kebabs)
calories: 132 | fat: 3g | protein: 3g | carbs: 25g | fiber: 5g | sugar: 12g | sodium: 1052mg

Roasted Vegetables with Garlic

Prep time: 10 minutes | Cook time: 25 minutes | Serves 4

2 zucchini, diced into 1-inch pieces
1 red bell pepper, diced into 1-inch pieces
1 yellow bell pepper, diced into 1-inch pieces
1 red onion, diced into 1-inch pieces
1 sweet potato, diced into 1-inch pieces
4 garlic cloves
¼ cup extra-virgin olive oil
1 teaspoon salt

1. Preheat the oven to 450°F (235°C).
2. Line a baking sheet with aluminum foil.
3. In a large bowl, toss together the zucchini, red bell pepper, yellow bell pepper, onion, sweet potato, garlic, olive oil, and salt. Spread the vegetables evenly on the prepared sheet.
4. Bake for 25 minutes, stirring halfway through.

Per Serving
calories: 184 | fat: 14g | protein: 2g | carbs: 15g | fiber: 2g | sugar: 4g | sodium: 608mg

Garlic Baked Cherry Tomatoes

Prep time: 5 minutes | Cook time: 15 minutes | Serves 6

1 pound (454 g) cherry tomatoes, halved
4 garlic cloves, minced
1 teaspoon dried basil (optional)
2 tablespoons extra-virgin olive oil
Salt, to taste

1. Preheat the oven to 400°F (205°C).
2. Line a baking sheet with aluminum foil.
3. In a large bowl, mix the tomatoes, garlic, and basil (if using). Drizzle with the olive oil and toss to coat. Season generously with salt. Transfer to the prepared pan.
4. Bake for 15 to 20 minutes, or until the tomatoes collapse.

Per Serving
calories: 46 | fat: 4g | protein: 0g | carbs: 3g | fiber: 1g | sugar: 2g | sodium: 4mg

Hummus-Stuffed Bell Peppers

Prep time: 5 minutes | Cook time: 0 minutes | Makes 12 peppers

2 cups hummus
2 tablespoons chopped fresh basil leaves (optional)
12 mini bell peppers, stemmed

1. In a small bowl, mix the hummus and basil (if using). Transfer to a small plastic bag, squeezing it down into one of the bottom corners.
2. Trim off the same bottom corner of the bag and squeeze the hummus into each pepper, filling it to the top.

Per Serving (2 peppers)
calories: 168 | fat: 9g | protein: 6g | carbs: 18g | fiber: 9g | sugar: 4g | sodium: 205mg

Zucchini Fries

Prep time: 5 minutes | Cook time: 20 minutes | Makes 12 fries

½ cup almond flour
½ teaspoon salt
½ teaspoon garlic powder
½ teaspoon freshly ground black pepper
1 medium zucchini, trimmed and halved widthwise
1 tablespoon avocado oil

1. Preheat the oven to 425°F (220°C).
2. Line a baking sheet with aluminum foil.
3. In a small bowl, mix the almond flour, salt, garlic powder, and pepper.
4. Cut each zucchini half into about 6 strips that resemble fries. Brush the strips with the avocado oil, and roll in the almond flour mixture until well coated. Evenly space the fries on the prepared pan.
5. Bake for 20 minutes, or until crispy.

Per Serving (6 fries)
calories: 230 | fat: 21g | protein: 6g | carbs: 7g | fiber: 4g | sugar: 0g | sodium: 582mg

Sesame Broccoli Stir-Fry

Prep time: 5 minutes | Cook time: 5½ minutes | Serves 4

2 tablespoons extra-virgin olive oil
1 teaspoon sesame oil
4 cups broccoli florets
1 tablespoon grated fresh ginger
¼ teaspoon sea salt
2 garlic cloves, minced
2 tablespoons toasted sesame seeds

1. In a large nonstick skillet over medium-high heat, heat the olive oil and sesame oil until they shimmer.
2. Add the broccoli, ginger, and salt. Cook for 5 to 7 minutes, stirring frequently, until the broccoli begins to brown.
3. Add the garlic. Cook for 30 seconds, stirring constantly.
4. Remove from the heat and stir in the sesame seeds.

Per Serving
calories: 134 | fat: 11g | protein: 4g | carbs: 9g | fiber: 3g | sugar: 2g | sodium: 148mg

Ginger Apple Stir-Fry

Prep time: 5 minutes | Cook time: 7 minutes | Serves 4

2 tablespoons coconut oil
3 apples, peeled, cored, and sliced
1 tablespoon grated fresh ginger
1 teaspoon ground cinnamon
1 packet stevia
Pinch sea salt

1. In a large nonstick skillet over medium-high heat, heat the coconut oil until it shimmers.
2. Add the apples, ginger, cinnamon, stevia, and salt. Cook for 7 to 10 minutes, stirring occasionally, until the apples are soft.

Per Serving
calories: 152 | fat: 7g | protein: 1g | carbs: 24g | fiber: 5g | sugar: 18g | sodium: 60mg

Garlic Spinach with Orange

Prep time: 5 minutes | Cook time: 5½ minutes | Serves 4

2 tablespoons extra-virgin olive oil
4 cups fresh baby spinach
2 garlic cloves, minced
Juice of ½ orange
Zest of ½ orange
½ teaspoon sea salt
⅛ teaspoon freshly ground black pepper

1. In a large skillet over medium-high heat, heat the olive oil until it shimmers.
2. Add the spinach and cook for 3 minutes, stirring occasionally.
3. Add the garlic. Cook for 30 seconds, stirring constantly.
4. Add the orange juice, orange zest, salt, and pepper. Cook for about 2 minutes, stirring constantly, until the juice evaporates.

Per Serving
calories: 80 | fat: 7g | protein: 1g | carbs: 4g | fiber: 1g | sugar: 2g | sodium: 258mg

Garlic-Rosemary Sweet Potatoes

Prep time: 5 minutes | Cook time: 10½ minutes | Serves 4

2 tablespoons extra-virgin olive oil
2 sweet potatoes (skin left on), cut into ½-inch cubes
1 tablespoon chopped fresh rosemary leaves
½ teaspoon sea salt
3 garlic cloves, minced
¼ teaspoon freshly ground black pepper

1. In a large nonstick skillet over medium-high heat, heat the olive oil until it shimmers.
2. Add the sweet potatoes, rosemary, and salt. Cook for 10 to 15 minutes, stirring occasionally, until the sweet potatoes begin to brown.
3. Add the garlic and pepper. Cook for 30 seconds, stirring constantly.

Per Serving
calories: 199 | fat: 7g | protein: 2g | carbs: 33g | fiber: 5g | sugar: 1g | sodium: 245mg

Brown Rice Bowl with Bell Peppers

Prep time: 5 minutes | Cook time: 10 minutes | Serves 4

2 tablespoons extra-virgin olive oil
1 red bell pepper, chopped
1 green bell pepper, chopped
1 onion, chopped
2 cups cooked brown rice
2 tablespoons low-sodium soy sauce

1. In a large nonstick skillet over medium-high heat, heat the olive oil until it shimmers.
2. Add the red and green bell peppers and onion. Cook for about 7 minutes, stirring frequently, until the vegetables start to brown.
3. Add the rice and the soy sauce. Cook for about 3 minutes, stirring constantly, until the rice warms through.

Per Serving
calories: 266 | fat: 8g | protein: 5g | carbs: 44g | fiber: 3g | sugar: 4g | sodium: 455mg

Almond and Blueberry Trail Mix

Prep time: 5 minutes | Cook time: 2 minutes | Serves 4

1 tablespoon extra-virgin olive oil
1 cup almonds
Pinch salt
½ teaspoon Chinese five-spice powder
½ cup dried blueberries

1. In a large nonstick skillet over medium-high heat, heat the olive oil until it shimmers.
2. Add the almonds, -salt, and Chinese five-spice and cook for 2 minutes, stirring constantly.
3. Remove from the heat and cool. Stir in the blueberries.

Per Serving
calories: 179 | fat: 16g | protein: 5g | carbs: 8g | fiber: 3g | sugar: 3g | sodium: 39mg

THE ULTIMATE ANTI-INFLAMMATORY DIET COOKBOOK

Cumin-Paprika Sweet Potato Fries

Prep time: 5 minutes | Cook time: 30 minutes | Serves 2

2 large sweet potatoes, cut into thin strips
1 teaspoon cumin
1 tablespoon extra-virgin olive oil
½ teaspoon black pepper
½ teaspoon paprika
Dash of cayenne pepper

1. Preheat the oven to 375ºF (190ºC).
2. Add the sweet potato strips into a large bowl.
3. Drizzle with some olive oil.
4. Sprinkle the rest of the ingredients over the top.
5. Toss together gently to evenly and fully coat the potatoes.
6. Get a baking sheet and arrange the coated potatoes into a thin layer.
7. Bake for around 30 minutes or until cooked through.

Per Serving

calories: 179 | fat: 7g | protein: 2g | carbs: 27g | fiber: 4g | sugar: 5g | sodium: 74mg

Sautéd Vegetables with Cayenne

Prep time: 15 minutes | Cook time: 32 minutes | Serves 4

1 can black beans
1 can cannellini beans
2 sweet potatoes, peeled and chopped
2 medium carrots, sliced
2 garlic cloves, minced
½ onion, diced
1 can chopped tomatoes
1 cup vegetable broth
1 tablespoon chili powder
½ teaspoon garlic powder
2 tablespoons extra-virgin olive oil
1 teaspoon cumin
½ teaspoon cayenne
½ teaspoon salt
½ teaspoon black pepper

1. Heat olive oil in a pan over medium heat.
2. Sauté garlic and onions for 1 to 2 minutes.
3. Add carrots and sweet potatoes for about 6 minutes or until the onions are soft.
4. Lower heat setting to medium-low, then add the rest of the ingredients.
5. Cover partially, and simmer for around 25 minutes, occasionally stirring to prevent sticking.
6. Serve.

Per Serving

calories: 196 | fat: 8g | protein: 4g | carbs: 27g | fiber: 7g | sugar: 7g | sodium: 552mg

Spicy Quinoa with Cilantro

Prep time: 10 minutes | Cook time: 24 minutes | Serves 2

1 teaspoon olive oil
1 can diced tomatoes
1 chili pepper, diced
1 cup rinsed quinoa
1 lime, juiced
1 onion, chopped
2 garlic cloves, minced
1 tablespoon paprika
2 cups low-sodium chicken broth
1 jalapeño, chopped
½ cup cilantro

1. Put the oil in a skillet and cook the quinoa and onion in the oil until the onion becomes translucent, about 5 minutes.
2. Add the garlic and pepper and then cook for 4 to 5 minutes until the garlic is fragrant.
3. Mix the undrained can of tomatoes with the paprika, and the chicken broth into the garlic and pepper.
4. Turn up heat to allow to boil, then turn heat down and allow to simmer for about 15 to 20 minutes, until the liquid reduces.
5. Stir in the cilantro and serve.

Per Serving

calories: 79 | fat: 3g | protein: 2g | carbs: 11g | fiber: 3g | sugar: 5g | sodium: 51mg

Carrot and Swede Mash with Tarragon

Prep time: 10 minutes | Cook time: 12 minutes | Serves 4

4 carrots, chopped
½ swede, chopped
3 garlic cloves, chopped
¼ cup finely chopped tarragon
1 tablespoon extra-virgin olive oil
Pinch of black pepper
1 tablespoon low-fat Greek yogurt

1. Put the carrots, swede and garlic in a large pan of salted water, bring to the boil, and cook for 12 minutes. Drain.
2. Add the tarragon and olive oil and season with pepper and mash with a potato masher.
3. Stir in a dollop of low-fat Greek yogurt if desired.
4. Serve and enjoy!

Per Serving

calories: 449 | fat: 9g | protein: 19g | carbs: 73g | fiber: 10g | sugar: 7g | sodium: 95mg

Rutabaga and Turnip Chips

Prep time: 10 minutes | Cook time: 40 minutes | Serves 4

1 rutabaga, peeled and finely sliced
1 turnip, peeled and finely sliced
1 tablespoon extra-virgin olive oil
1 onion, chopped
1 garlic clove, minced
1 teaspoon black pepper
1 teaspoon oregano
1 teaspoon paprika

1. Preheat the oven to 375°F (190°C).
2. Grease a baking tray with the olive oil.
3. Add turnip and rutabaga in a thin layer.
4. Dust over herbs and spices with an extra drizzle of olive oil.
5. Bake for 40 to 50 minutes (turning halfway through to ensure even crispiness!)
6. Serve with your choice of low-fat Greek yogurt, tomato sauce, or mustard.

Per Serving

calories: 100 | fat: 4g | protein: 2g | carbs: 14g | fiber: 4g | sugar: 6g | sodium: 34mg

Breaded Kale and Spinach Balls

Prep time: 15 minutes | Cook time: 30 minutes | Serves 4

2 cups frozen or fresh spinach, thawed and chopped
1 cup frozen or fresh kale, thawed and drained
½ cup finely chopped onion
1 garlic clove, finely chopped
3 tablespoons extra-virgin olive oil
2 free-range eggs, beaten
½ teaspoon ground thyme
½ teaspoon rubbed dried oregano
½ teaspoon dried rosemary
1 cup dry 100% whole-grain bread crumbs
½ teaspoon dried oregano
1 teaspoon ground black pepper

1. Preheat the oven to 350°F (180°C).
2. Line a baking sheet with parchment paper.
3. In a bowl, mix the olive oil and eggs, adding in the spinach, garlic and onions and tossing to coat.
4. Add the rest of the ingredients, mixing to blend.
5. Use the palms of your hands to roll into 1-inch balls and arrange them onto the baking sheet.
6. Bake for 15 minutes and then flip the balls over.
7. Continue to bake for another 15 minutes or until they're golden brown.
8. Serve with low-fat Greek yogurt or on their own.

Per Serving

calories: 233 | fat: 13g | protein: 7g | carbs: 22g | fiber: 2g | sugar: 2g | sodium: 243mg

Farro, Tomato and Mushroom Pilaf

Prep time: 10 minutes | Cook time: 35 minutes | Serves 4

1 cup pearled farro, rinsed
2 cups water
1 cup chopped tomatoes
1 package fresh mushrooms, sliced
1 teaspoon cumin
1 teaspoon chili powder
1 teaspoon turmeric
1 tablespoon cilantro
½ yellow squash, cubed

1. Add the farro and water to a saucepan and boil over high heat until boiling.
2. Reduce the heat, cover and simmer for 20 minutes or until the farro is tender, and the liquid is absorbed.
3. Meanwhile, in a separate pan over medium heat, cook the tomatoes and mushrooms with the cilantro and spices until the mushrooms are soft, 5 minutes.
4. Add the squash and sauté for 10 minutes, or until all the vegetables are tender.
5. Drain and stir the farro into the squash mix until heated through.
6. Serve alone as lunch or on the side of your favorite dish.

Per Serving

calories: 249 | fat: 1g | protein: 8g | carbs: 52g | fiber: 11g | sugar: 7g | sodium: 66mg

White Fish Ceviche with Avocado

Prep time: 20 minutes | Cook time: 0 minutes | Serves 6

Juice of 5 limes
Juice of 8 lemons
1 pound (454 g) fresh wild white fish, cut into ½-inch cubes
1 teaspoon minced fresh ginger
3 garlic cloves, minced
1 cup minced red onions
½ cup minced fresh cilantro
1 teaspoon Himalayan salt
1 teaspoon ground black pepper
½ medium Hass avocado, peeled, pitted, and diced

1. Combine the lime juice and lemon juice in a large bowl, then dunk the fish cubes in the mixture, press so the fish is submerged in the juice.
2. Cover the bowl in plastic and refrigerate for at least 40 minutes.
3. Meanwhile, combine the ginger, garlic, onions, cilantro, salt, and ground black pepper in a small bowl. Stir to mix well.
4. Remove the fish bowl from the refrigerator, then sprinkle with the powder mixture. Toss to coat well.
5. Spread the diced avocado over the ceviche and serve immediately.

Per Serving

calories: 159 | fat: 5g | protein: 19g | carbs: 12g | fiber: 2g | sugar: 3g | sodium: 677mg

Honey Granola Trail Mix

Prep time: 5 minutes | Cook time: 15 minutes | Serves 2

1 cup toasted almonds
1 tablespoon raw honey
½ cup cherries
1 cup granola

1. Preheat the oven to 350°F (180°C).
2. Spread the almonds across a baking sheet.
3. Bake for 5 minutes and then add cherries and granola and toss.
4. Drizzle honey on top and toss again to coat before baking in the oven for 10 to 15 minutes.
5. Remove to cool.
6. Serve alone or with your choice of milk as a cereal.

Per Serving

calories: 705 | fat: 45g | protein: 17g | carbs: 58g | fiber: 9g | sugar: 29g | sodium: 117mg

Golden Cauliflower with Almond Sauce

Prep time: 10 minutes | Cook time: 20 minutes | Serves 4

1 head cauliflower, cut into florets
2 tablespoons extra-virgin olive oil
1½ teaspoons sea salt, divided
½ teaspoon ground turmeric
½ teaspoon freshly ground black pepper, divided
Almond Sauce:
1 cup plain unsweetened almond yogurt
1 scallion, sliced
1 tablespoon chopped fresh parsley
¼ cup almond butter
1 garlic clove, minced
1 tablespoon freshly squeezed lemon juice
1 tablespoon pure maple syrup

1. Preheat the oven to 400°F (205°C).
2. Put the cauliflower in a large bowl, then drizzle with olive oil and sprinkle with 1 teaspoon of salt, turmeric, and ¼ teaspoon of ground black pepper.
3. Arrange the well-coated cauliflower in the single layer on a baking sheet. Put the sheet in the preheated oven and roast for 20 minutes or until golden brown.
4. Meanwhile, put the yogurt, scallion, parsley, almond butter, garlic, lemon juice, maple syrup, and remaining salt and pepper in a blender. Pulse to purée until smooth.
5. Transfer the roasted cauliflower on a plate, then baste with the almond sauce and serve immediately.

Per Serving

calories: 277 | fat: 23g | protein: 7g | carbs: 15g | fiber: 4g | sugars: 6g | sodium: 945mg

Easy Sautéed Spinach

Prep time: 5 minutes | Cook time: 5 minutes | Serves 4

1 tablespoons extra-virgin olive oil
1 (10-ounce / 284-g) package frozen chopped spinach, thawed and drained
1 garlic clove, minced
1 teaspoon sea salt
¼ teaspoon freshly ground black pepper
1 tablespoon fresh lemon juice

1. Heat the olive oil in a nonstick skillet over high heat until shimmering.
2. Add the spinach and garlic to the skillet, then sprinkle with salt and pepper. Sauté for 5 minutes or until the spinach is tender.
3. Transfer the sautéed spinach on a plate, then drizzle with lemon juice. Toss to combine well before serving.

Per Serving

calories: 49 | fat: 4g | protein: 2g | carbs: 3g | fiber: 3g | sugar: 0g | sodium: 631mg

Green Beans with Shallots

Prep time: 5 minutes | Cook time: 8 minutes | Serves 4

1 pound (454 g) green beans, trimmed
1 teaspoon sea salt, plus additional for seasoning
2 tablespoons extra-virgin olive oil
1 large shallot, sliced thin
1 tablespoon chopped fresh tarragon
Freshly ground black pepper, to taste

1. Put the green beans in a pot, then pour in enough water to cover. Sprinkle with 1 teaspoon of salt. Bring to a boil.
2. Reduce the heat to low and simmer for 5 minutes or until the beans are tender.
3. Pat the beans dry and place them on a plate. Set aside.
4. Heat the olive oil in a nonstick skillet over medium heat until shimmering.
5. Add the shallots and sauté for 3 minutes or until lightly browned.
6. Top the green beans with the cooked shallots, then sprinkle with tarragon, salt, and black pepper. Serve immediately.

Per Serving

calories: 146 | fat: 13g | protein: 2g | carbs: 9g | fiber: 4g | sugars: 2g | sodium: 475mg

Cardamom Roasted Apricots

Prep time: 5 minutes | Cook time: 25 minutes | Serves 4

20 fresh apricots, pitted and quartered
2 tablespoons coconut oil
⅛ teaspoon cardamom (optional)

1. Preheat the oven to 350°F (180°C).
2. Toss the apricots with the coconut oil and cardamom (if desired) in a baking dish until well coated.
3. Roast in the preheated oven for 25 to 30 minutes, stirring once or twice during cooking, or until the apricots are beginning to caramelize.
4. Let the apricots cool for 5 to 10 minutes before serving.

Per Serving

calories: 141 | fat: 8g | protein: 2g | carbs: 19g | fiber: 3g | sugar: 16g | sodium: 2mg

Garlic Cashew Hummus

Prep time: 10 minutes | Cook time: 0 minutes | Makes 1 cup

1 cup raw cashews, soaked in filtered water for 15 minutes and drained
¼ cup filtered water
2 garlic cloves
1 tablespoon extra-virgin olive oil
1 teaspoon freshly squeezed lemon juice
2 teaspoons coconut aminos
½ teaspoon ground ginger
¼ teaspoon sea salt
Pinch cayenne pepper

1. Place all the ingredients in a blender and blend until completely mixed. You'll need to stop the blender occasionally to scrape down the sides.
2. Serve immediately or refrigerate to chill for at least 2 hours for best flavor.

Per Serving (2½ tablespoons)
calories: 111 | fat: 9g | protein: 3g | carbs: 5g | fiber: 1g | sugar: 6g | sodium: 367mg

Crunchy Roasted Chickpeas

Prep time: 5 minutes | Cook time: 20 minutes | Makes 4 cups

4 cups cooked (or canned) chickpeas, rinsed, drained, and dried well
2 tablespoons extra-virgin olive oil
1 teaspoon garlic powder
1 teaspoon salt
Freshly ground black pepper, to taste

1. Preheat the oven to 400°F (205°C).
2. Spread the chickpeas out in an even layer on a rimmed baking sheet. Drizzle with the olive oil and toss to coat well.
3. Bake in the preheated oven for 20 minutes, stirring the chickpeas halfway through the cooking time, until browned and crunchy.
4. Remove from the oven to a large bowl. Season with garlic powder, salt, and pepper, then serve.

Per Serving (¼ cup)
calories: 151 | fat: 5g | protein: 6g | carbs: 21g | fiber: 6g | sugar: 4g | sodium: 327mg

Easy Trail Mix

Prep time: 10 minutes | Cook time: 0 minutes | Serves 12

1 cup sunflower seeds
1 cup pumpkin seeds
1 cup large coconut flakes
1 cup dried cranberries
1 cup raisins
½ cup cacao nibs

1. Combine the sunflower seeds, pumpkin seeds, coconut flakes, cranberries, raisins, and cacao nibs in a large bowl.
2. Serve immediately or store covered in a cool, dry place.

Per Serving
calories: 182 | fat: 11g | protein: 5g | carbs: 19g | fiber: 3g | sugar: 12g | sodium: 25mg

Butternut Squash Fries

Prep time: 20 minutes | Cook time: 40 minutes | Serves 4

1 large butternut squash, peeled, deseeded, and cut into fry-size pieces, about 3 inches long and ½ inch thick
2 tablespoons coconut oil
¾ teaspoon sea salt
3 fresh rosemary sprigs, stemmed and chopped (about 1½ tablespoons)

1. Preheat the oven to 375°F (190°C). Line a baking sheet with parchment paper.
2. Put the butternut squash in a large bowl, then drizzle with coconut oil and sprinkle with salt. Toss to coat well.
3. Arrange the butternut squash pieces in the single layer on the prepared baking sheet.
4. Bake in the preheated oven for 40 minutes or until golden brown and crunchy. Flip the zucchini fries at least three times during the cooking and top the fries with rosemary sprigs halfway through.
5. Transfer the fries on a cooling rack and allow to cool for a few minutes. Serve warm.

Per Serving
calories: 191 | fat: 7g | protein: 3g | carbs: 34g | fiber: 7g | sugar: 6g | sodium: 451mg

Sweet Potato and Celery Root Mash

Prep time: 5 minutes | Cook time: 20 minutes | Serves 4

2 cups chopped sweet potatoes
2 cups chopped celery root, scrubbed, trimmed, and peeled
2 tablespoons almond butter
1 teaspoon freshly squeezed lemon juice
½ teaspoon salt
Pinch cayenne pepper

1. Place a steamer basket in a large saucepan with 1 to 2 inches of filtered water. Put the sweet potatoes and celery root in the steamer basket.
2. Cover and steam over medium heat for about 20 to 25 minutes until fork-tender.
3. Transfer them to a blender or food processor, along with the almond butter, lemon juice, sea salt, and cayenne pepper. Blend until completely smooth. Serve immediately.

Per Serving
calories: 109 | fat: 5g | protein: 2g | carbs: 15g | fiber: 3g | sugar: 1g | sodium: 333mg

Homemade Guacamole

Prep time: 10 minutes | Cook time: 0 minutes | Serves 4

2 ripe avocados, peeled, pitted, and cubed
2 garlic cloves, finely minced
Juice of 1 lime
½ red onion, minced
2 tablespoons chopped fresh cilantro leaves
½ teaspoon sea salt

1. Place the avocados, garlic, lime juice, red onion, cilantro, and sea salt in a medium bowl. Mash them lightly with the back of a fork until a uniform consistency is achieved.
2. Serve chilled.

Per Serving

calories: 214 | fat: 20g | protein: 2g | carbs: 11g | fiber: 7g | sugar: 1g | sodium: 242mg

Pumpkin Spiced Apple Chips

Prep time: 5 minutes | Cook time: 1½ hours | Serves 3

2 tablespoons ground cinnamon
1 tablespoons ground ginger
1½ teaspoons ground nutmeg
1½ teaspoons ground cloves
3 apples, cored and sliced thinly

1. Preheat the oven to 200ºF.
2. Line a baking sheet with parchment paper.
3. In a bowl, toss all ingredients together to coat the apples.
4. Arrange the seasoned apple slices on the baking sheet.
5. Place in the oven and bake for 1½ hours until the apples are crispy.

Per Serving

calories: 119 | fat: 0.9g | protein: 0.9g | carbs: 31g | fiber: 8g | sugar: 19g | sodium: 3mg

Frozen Blueberry Yogurt Bites

Prep time: 5 minutes | Cook time: 0 minutes | Makes 50 bites

2 cups plain whole-milk yogurt
1 banana
½ cup fresh blueberries
1 tablespoon raw honey

1. Line a baking sheet with a piece of wax paper.
2. Pulse the banana, yogurt, blueberries, and honey in a blender until smooth and creamy.
3. Transfer the smooth mixture to a large resealable plastic bag with the corner snipped off. Squeeze the mixture into quarter-sized dots onto the prepared baking sheet. Transfer to the freezer to freeze until solid.
4. Store leftovers in an airtight container in the freezer.

Per Serving (8 bites)

calories: 91 | fat: 3g | protein: 3g | carbs: 13g | fiber: 1g | sugar: 10g | sodium: 29mg

Carrot and Pumpkin Seed Crackers

Prep time: 10 minutes | Cook time: 15 minutes | Makes 40 crackers

1⅓ cups pumpkin seeds
½ cup packed shredded carrot (about 1 carrot)
3 tablespoons chopped fresh dill
¼ teaspoon sea salt
2 tablespoons extra-virgin olive oil

1. Preheat the oven to 350ºF (180ºC). Line a baking sheet with parchment paper.
2. Ground the pumpkin seeds in a food processor, then add the carrot, dill, salt, and olive oil to the food processor and pulse to combine well.
3. Pour them in the prepared baking sheet, then shape the mixture into a rectangle with a spatula.
4. Line a sheet of parchment paper over the rectangle, then flatten the rectangle to about ⅛ inch thick with a rolling pin.
5. Remove the parchment paper lined over the rectangle, then score it into 40 small rectangles with a sharp knife.
6. Arrange the baking sheet in the preheated oven and bake for 15 minutes or until golden browned and crispy.
7. Transfer the crackers on a large plate and allow to cool for a few minutes before serving.

Per Serving (4 crackers)

calories: 130 | fat: 12g | protein: 5g | carbs: 4g | fiber: 1g | sugar: 0g | sodium: 66mg

Zucchini Chips

Prep time: 15 minutes | Cook time: 2 hours | Serves 6

2 medium zucchini, sliced thin with a mandoline or sharp knife
2 tablespoons extra-virgin olive oil
1½ teaspoons dried rosemary
1½ teaspoons dried oregano
1½ teaspoons dried basil
½ teaspoon sea salt

1. Preheat the oven to 200ºF (93ºC). Line a baking sheet with parchment paper.
2. Combine the zucchini slices with olive oil in a large bowl, then toss to coat well.
3. Combine the remaining ingredients in a separate bowl. Stir to mix well.
4. Pour the mixture in the bowl of zucchini, then toss to coat well.
5. Arrange the zucchini slices in the single layer on the prepared baking sheet.
6. Bake in the preheated oven for 2 hours or until golden brown and crispy.
7. Transfer the zucchini chips on a cooling rack and allow to cool for a few minutes. Serve warm.

Per Serving

calories: 52 | fat: 5g | protein: 1g | carbs: 3g | fiber: 1g | sugar: 1g | sodium: 202mg

Ginger Broccoli Stir-Fry

Prep time: 5 minutes | Cook time: 23 minutes | Serves 2

2 cups tender stem broccoli or purple sprouting broccoli
1 thumb-sized piece of ginger, peeled and minced
1 tablespoon extra-virgin olive oil

1. Boil water in a medium-sized pan and steam the broccoli for about 5 minutes or until tender and crisp.
2. Drain and transfer to ice cold water to preserve the nutrients.
3. In a skillet, heat the oil for 30 seconds and then stir-fry the ginger for 15 seconds, mixing in the broccoli, and sautéing for 3 minutes until hot throughout.
4. Serve as a delicious snack or on the side of your favorite meal.

Per Serving

calories: 95 | fat: 7g | protein: 2g | carbs: 6g | fiber: 2g | sugar: 1g | sodium: 30mg

Massaged Kale Chips

Prep time: 5 minutes | Cook time: 20 minutes | Makes 2 cups

4 cups kale, stemmed, rinsed, drained, torn into 2-inch pieces
2 tablespoons extra-virgin olive oil
1 teaspoon sea salt
2 tablespoons apple cider vinegar

1. Preheat the oven to 350°F (180°C).
2. Combine all the ingredients in a large bowl. Stir to mix well.
3. Gently massage the kale leaves in the bowl for 5 minutes or until wilted and bright.
4. Place the kale on a baking sheet. Bake in the preheated oven for 20 minutes or until crispy. Toss the kale halfway through.
5. Remove the kale from the oven and serve immediately.

Per Serving (1 cup)

calories: 138 | fat: 14g | protein: 1g | carbs: 3g | fiber: 1g | sugar: 1g | sodium: 1176mg

Lemony Berry Gummies

Prep time: 5 minutes | Cook time: 5 minutes | Makes 24 gummies

1 cup fresh or frozen berries of choice
½ cup freshly squeezed lemon juice
3 tablespoons raw honey
¼ cup filtered water
¼ cup gelatin powder

1. Purée the berries, lemon juice, honey, and water in a blender.
2. Transfer the purée to a small saucepan and heat over medium heat until it warms.
3. Add the gelatin powder and continue whisking for 5 minutes until well combined.
4. Pour the mixture into a mini muffin tin and freeze until the mixture gels, about 15 minutes.
5. Serve immediately or refrigerate for up to 1 week.

Per Serving (4 gummies)

calories: 67 | fat: 0g | protein: 4g | carbs: 13g | fiber: 1g | sugar: 17g | sodium: 2mg

Oat and Sweet Potato Muffins

Prep time: 10 minutes | Cook time: 20 minutes | Makes 12 muffins

1½ cups rolled oats
1 cup cooked sweet potato chunks or purée
1 cup nut milk of choice
⅓ cup coconut sugar
¼ cup almond butter
1 egg
2 tablespoons extra-virgin olive oil
1 teaspoon vanilla extract
1 teaspoon ground cinnamon
1 teaspoon baking powder
½ teaspoon baking soda
¼ teaspoon salt

1. Preheat the oven to 375°F (190°C).
2. Line a muffin tin with cupcake liners.
3. In a food processor (or blender), pulse the oats until a coarse flour is formed. Transfer the flour to a small bowl and set aside.
4. To the food processor (or blender), add the sweet potato, nut milk, coconut sugar, almond butter, egg, olive oil, vanilla, cinnamon, baking powder, baking soda, and salt. Pulse until smooth.
5. Slowly add the oat flour, pulsing until all ingredients are well incorporated.
6. Divide the batter among the 12 cupcake liners.
7. Bake for 20 to 25 minutes. Cool for 5 minutes.

Per Serving (1 muffin)

calories: 143 | fat: 7g | protein: 4g | carbs: 12g | fiber: 2g | sugar: 5g | sodium: 119mg

Spiced Nuts

Prep time: 10 minutes | Cook time: 10 minutes | Makes 2 cups

1 cup almonds
½ cup walnuts
¼ cup pumpkin seeds
¼ cup sunflower seeds
½ teaspoon ground cumin
1 teaspoon ground turmeric
¼ teaspoon red pepper flakes
¼ teaspoon garlic powder

1. Preheat the oven to 350°F (180°C).
2. In a medium bowl, stir together all the ingredients until well combined.
3. Spread the nuts out onto a rimmed baking sheet and bake for 10 to 15 minutes, stirring once or twice halfway through, or until the nuts are lightly browned and fragrant.
4. Let the nuts cool for 5 to 10 minutes before serving.

Per Serving (¼ cup)

calories: 179 | fat: 16g | protein: 6g | carbs: 7g | fiber: 3g | sugar: 1g | sodium: 5mg

CHAPTER 11:
DESSERTS

Avocado-Chocolate Mousse

Prep time: 5 minutes | Cook time: 2 minutes | Serves 4 to 6

8 ounces (227 g) bittersweet chocolate, chopped
¼ cup unsweetened coconut milk
2 tablespoons coconut oil
2 ripe avocados
¼ cup raw honey or pure maple syrup
Pinch sea salt

1. In a small heavy saucepan over low heat, combine the chocolate, coconut milk, and coconut oil. Cook for 2 to 3 minutes, stirring constantly, or until the chocolate melts.
2. In a food processor, combine the avocado and honey. Add the melted chocolate and process until smooth.
3. Spoon the mousse into serving bowls and top each with a sprinkle of sea salt. Chill for at least 30 minutes before serving.

Per Serving

calories: 653 | fat: 47g | protein: 7g | carbs: 56g | fiber: 9g | sugar: 42g | sodium: 113mg

Oat-Crusted Coconut Bars

Prep time: 10 minutes | Cook time: 0 minutes | Serves 8

Crust:
¾ cup almond flour
¾ cup rolled oats
¼ cup coconut oil, melted
2 tablespoons coconut sugar
1 teaspoon ground cinnamon
½ teaspoon vanilla extract
Dash salt
Filtered water, for mixing
Filling:
2 cups coconut cream, chilled
¼ cup freshly squeezed lime juice
1 tablespoon fresh lime zest
3 tablespoons raw honey, or pure maple syrup

Make the Crust
1. Line the bottom of a baking pan with parchment paper.
2. In a food processor or blender, add the almond flour, oats, coconut oil, coconut sugar, cinnamon, vanilla, and salt. Pulse until a sticky dough forms, adding 1 tablespoon of filtered water, if necessary, to help the ingredients combine fully.
3. Press the crust mixture evenly on the bottom of the prepared pan.
Make the Filling
1. In a medium bowl, whip the coconut cream with an electric hand mixer until it resembles whipped cream.
2. Add the lime juice, lime zest, and honey. Continue to mix until the ingredients are well incorporated. Spread the filling evenly over the crust.
3. Cover and place the baking dish in the freezer for up to 2 hours.
4. Slightly thaw and slice the bars before serving.

Per Serving

calories: 309 | fat: 24g | protein: 5g | carbs: 15g | fiber: 2g | sugar: 9g

| sodium: 24mg

Vanilla Coconut Ice Cream Sandwiches

Prep time: 15 minutes | Cook time: 15 minutes | Serves 6

Coconut Ice Cream:
4 cups full-fat coconut milk
¾ cup coconut sugar
2 teaspoons vanilla extract
Cookies:
2 cups almond flour
3 tablespoons coconut sugar
1 teaspoon salt
½ teaspoon baking soda
¼ teaspoon ground cardamom
6 tablespoons coconut oil, melted and cooled slightly
¼ cup pure maple syrup
1 tablespoon unsweetened almond milk
1 teaspoon vanilla extract
Finished Ice Cream Sandwiches:
½ cup shredded coconut

Make the Coconut Ice Cream
1. In a large saucepan over medium heat, combine the coconut milk and coconut sugar. Cook for about 5 minutes, stirring constantly, or until the sugar dissolves. Remove the pan from the heat and stir in the vanilla.
2. Chill the mixture for at least 4 hours, or overnight.
3. Make the ice cream according to the manufacturer's instructions for your ice cream maker.
4. Freeze the ice cream in an airtight container.
Make the Cookies
1. Preheat the oven to 325°F (163°C).
2. Line two baking sheets with parchment paper.
3. In a medium bowl, combine the almond flour, coconut sugar, salt, baking soda, and cardamom.
4. Add the coconut oil, maple syrup, almond milk, and vanilla. Mix until a thick dough forms.
5. Using a spoon, place scoops of dough on the prepared sheets, leaving about 2 inches between each cookie. There should be enough dough for 12 cookies.
6. Gently flatten the cookies with your hand or the back of the spoon.
7. Place the sheets in the preheated oven and bake for 10 to 12 minutes, or until golden brown. Cool the cookies thoroughly before making the ice cream sandwiches.
Assemble the Ice Cream Sandwiches:
1. Place a generous scoop of coconut ice cream on the bottom of one cookie and top it with a second cookie, pressing together gently. Individually wrap the cookies and freeze until ready to eat.
2. When ready to serve, press shredded coconut into the ice cream along the edges of each sandwich.

Per Serving

calories: 673 | fat: 53g | protein: 5g | carbs: 48g | fiber: 2g | sugar: 42g | sodium: 538mg

Blueberry Crumble with Nut Topping

Prep time: 10 minutes | Cook time: 15 minutes | Serves 6

Topping:
1 cup coarsely chopped walnuts
¼ cup coarsely chopped hazelnuts
1 tablespoon ghee or melted coconut oil
1 teaspoon ground cinnamon
Pinch salt
Filling:
1 cup fresh blueberries
6 fresh figs, quartered
2 nectarines, pitted and sliced
½ cup coconut sugar, raw honey, or pure maple syrup
2 teaspoons lemon zest
1 teaspoon vanilla extract

Make the Topping
1. In a small bowl, mix together the walnuts, hazelnuts, ghee, cinnamon, and salt. Set aside.
Make the Filling
2. Preheat the oven to 375°F (190°C).
3. In a medium bowl, combine the blueberries, figs, nectarines, coconut sugar, lemon zest, and vanilla.
4. Divide the fruit among six oven-proof single-serving bowls or ramekins.
5. Spoon equal amounts of the nut topping over each serving.
6. Place the bowls in the preheated oven and bake for 15 to 20 minutes, or until the nuts brown and the fruit is bubbly.

Per Serving
calories: 335 | fat: 19g | protein: 6g | carbs: 42g | fiber: 6g | sugar: 32g | sodium: 32mg

Almond-Cherry Chocolate Clusters

Prep time: 5 minutes | Cook time: 0 minutes | Makes 10 clusters

1 cup dark chocolate (60% cocoa or higher), chopped
1 tablespoon coconut oil
1 cup roasted salted almonds
½ cup dried cherries

1. Line a rimmed baking sheet with wax paper.
2. Over a double boiler, stir together the chocolate and coconut oil until melted and smooth.
3. Remove the pan from the heat and stir in the almonds and cherries.
4. By spoonfuls, drop clusters onto the wax paper. Refrigerate until hardened.
5. Transfer to an airtight container and refrigerate.

Per Serving
calories: 198 | fat: 13g | protein: 4g | carbs: 18g | fiber: 4g | sugar: 12g | sodium: 58mg

Banana and Oat Bars

Prep time: 15 minutes | Cook time: 40 minutes | Makes 16 bars

Cooking spray
½ cup pure maple syrup
½ cup almond or sunflower butter
2 medium ripe bananas, mashed
⅓ cup dried cranberries
1½ cups old-fashioned rolled oats
½ cup shredded coconut
¼ cup oat flour
¼ cup ground flaxseed
1 teaspoon vanilla extract
½ teaspoon ground cinnamon
¼ teaspoon ground cloves

1. Preheat the oven to 400°F (205°C).
2. Line a square pan with parchment paper or aluminum foil, and coat the lined pan with cooking spray.
3. In a medium bowl, combine the maple syrup, almond butter, and bananas. Mix until well blended.
4. Add the cranberries, oats, coconut, oat flour, flaxseed, vanilla, cinnamon, and cloves. Mix well.
5. Spoon the mixture into the prepared pan; the mixture will be thick and sticky. Use an oiled spatula to spread the mixture evenly.
6. Place the pan in the preheated oven and bake for 40 to 45 minutes, or until the top is dry and a toothpick inserted in the middle comes out clean. Cool completely before cutting into bars.

Per Serving
calories: 144 | fat: 7g | protein: 3g | carbs: 19g | fiber: 2g | sugar: 8g | sodium: 3mg

Quinoa and Almond Crisp

Prep time: 5 minutes | Cook time: 2 minutes | Serves 8

Coconut oil, for greasing the baking dish
½ cup almond butter
¼ cup raw honey
¼ cup carob powder
4 cups puffed quinoa
¼ cup chopped almonds

1. Lightly grease a baking dish with coconut oil and set it aside.
2. In a small saucepan over low heat, add the almond butter, honey, and carob powder, and stir until the ingredients are thoroughly mixed, smooth, and melted, for about 2 minutes. Remove the saucepan from the heat.
3. In a large bowl, toss together the quinoa and almonds.
4. Add the almond butter mixture. Stir everything together until well mixed and the cereal and nuts are completely coated. Press the mixture into the prepared dish and refrigerate for about 1 hour until firm.
5. Cut the bars into 16 pieces and serve.

Per Serving (2 pieces)
calories: 268 | fat: 13g | protein: 8g | carbs: 35g | fiber: 6g | sugar: 12g | sodium: 9mg

Honey-Ginger Banana Pudding

Prep time: 10 minutes | Cook time: 50 minutes | Serves 8

½ cup coconut oil, at room temperature, plus more for greasing the baking dish
½ cup raw honey
1 banana
1 egg
2 teaspoons grated fresh ginger
1 teaspoon pure vanilla extract
2 cups almond flour
1 teaspoon baking soda
Pinch sea salt

1. Preheat the oven to 350°F (180°C).
2. Lightly grease a baking dish with coconut oil and set it aside.
3. In a large bowl, beat the coconut oil, honey, banana, egg, ginger, and vanilla with a hand beater until well mixed, scraping down the sides of the bowl at least once.
4. Beat in the almond flour, baking soda, and sea salt. Spoon the batter into the prepared dish.
5. Bake for about 50 minutes, or until it is just set and lightly browned. Serve warm.

Per Serving

calories: 343 | fat: 26g | protein: 6g | carbs: 26g | fiber: 4g | sugar: 19g | sodium: 186mg

Clove Pears in Honey-Apple Juice

Prep time: 10 minutes | Cook time: 15 minutes | Serves 4

4 cups water
2 cups unsweetened apple juice
¼ cup raw honey
1 teaspoon whole cloves
½ teaspoon whole cardamom seeds
1 teaspoon pure vanilla extract
4 pears, carefully peeled, halved lengthwise, leaving the stem on one side, core removed

1. In a large saucepan over medium heat, combine the water, apple juice, honey, cloves, cardamom, and vanilla. Bring the mixture to a boil. Reduce the heat to low and simmer for 5 minutes.
2. Add the pear halves to the simmering liquid and cover the saucepan. Simmer the pears for about 10 minutes, turning several times until they are very tender.
3. With a slotted spoon, carefully remove the pears from the liquid and serve warm or cooled.

Per Serving

calories: 242 | fat: 0g | protein: 1g | carbs: 63g | fiber: 7g | sugar: 47g | sodium: 12mg

Honey Lemon Mousse

Prep time: 10 minutes | Cook time: 4 minutes | Serves 4

¼ cup water
2 teaspoons powdered gelatin
2 cups canned lite coconut milk
½ cup freshly squeezed lemon juice
¼ cup raw honey
2 tablespoons freshly grated lemon zest

1. Put the water in a small saucepan. Sprinkle the gelatin over the water and set it aside for 10 minutes to soften.
2. In a medium bowl, whisk the coconut milk, lemon juice, honey, and lemon zest until well combined.
3. Place the saucepan with the gelatin over low heat. Gently heat the gelatin for about 4 minutes, or until just dissolved.
4. Whisk the gelatin mixture into the coconut milk mixture and refrigerate for about 2 hours until set.
5. Scoop the lemon mousse into serving bowls.

Per Serving

calories: 348 | fat: 29g | protein: 3g | carbs: 25g | fiber: 3g | sugar: 22g | sodium: 22mg

Lemon-Honey Blackberry Granita

Prep time: 5 minutes | Cook time: 0 minutes | Serves 4

1 pound (454 g) fresh blackberries
½ cup water
½ cup raw honey
¼ cup freshly squeezed lemon juice
1 teaspoon chopped fresh thyme

1. In a food processor, combine the blackberries, water, honey, lemon juice, and thyme. Pulse until puréed.
2. Pour the purée through a fine-mesh sieve into a metal baking dish. Discard the seeds. Place the baking dish in the freezer for 2 hours. Remove the dish and stir the granita to break up any frozen sections, scraping along the sides. Return to the freezer for 1 hour. Stir and scrape again. Return the mixture to the freezer until completely frozen, about 4 hours total.
3. Cover the granita until you serve it. Use a fork to scrape off portions to serve.

Per Serving

calories: 182 | fat: 1g | protein: 2g | carbs: 46g | fiber: 6g | sugar: 40g | sodium: 4mg

Blueberry and Fig Pie

Prep time: 10 minutes | Cook time: 30 minutes | Serves 8

Crust:
1¼ cups gluten-free flour
Pinch sea salt
⅓ cup chilled coconut oil, cut into ½-inch chunks
¼ cup ice water, or more as needed
Filling:
2 cups fresh blueberries
1 cup chopped fresh figs
¼ cup raw honey
1 tablespoon arrowroot powder
¼ teaspoon ground nutmeg
1 egg, beaten

Make the Crust
1. In a medium bowl, stir together the flour and sea salt.
2. Add the cold coconut oil. With a pastry blender or a fork, work the ingredients together until they form coarse crumbs.
3. Add the ice water, 1 tablespoon at a time, and stir with a fork until the dough just comes together. Transfer the dough to a sheet of plastic wrap and use your hands to firmly press the dough into a disk about ½ inch thick.
4. Wrap the dough tightly in plastic wrap and refrigerate for 1 hour until firm.
Make the Filling
1. Preheat the oven to 350°F (180°C).
2. Line a baking sheet with parchment paper and set it aside.
3. In a large bowl, toss together the blueberries, figs, honey, arrowroot powder, and nutmeg. Set it aside.
4. Place a sheet of wax paper on a work surface, and place the unwrapped dough in the center. Cover the dough with another sheet of wax paper and gently roll it into a circle about 12 inches in diameter. Transfer the crust to the parchment-lined sheet.
5. Pour the berry mixture into the center of the crust. Spread out the berries, leaving about 1½ inches of empty crust around the edges.
6. Brush the empty crust with the beaten egg. Fold the edges of the crust over a bit of the filling, pressing lightly so the overlapping pieces of pastry stick together. Don't worry if it breaks; just patch it back together.
7. Bake the pie for about 30 minutes, or until the crust is golden and crisp and the filling is bubbling.

Per Serving
calories: 237 | fat: 9g | protein: 2g | carbs: 38g | fiber: 2g | sugar: 14g | sodium: 29mg

Rhubarb and Berry Cobbler

Prep time: 15 minutes | Cook time: 35 minutes | Serves 8

Cobbler:
Coconut oil, for greasing the baking dish
2 cups fresh blueberries
1 cup fresh raspberries
1 cup sliced (½-inch) rhubarb pieces
¼ cup unsweetened apple juice
¼ cup raw honey
1 tablespoon arrowroot powder
Topping:
1 cup almond flour
½ cup shredded unsweetened coconut
1 tablespoon arrowroot powder
½ cup coconut oil
¼ cup raw honey

Make the Cobbler
1. Preheat the oven to 350°F (180°C).
2. Lightly grease a baking dish with coconut oil and set it aside.
3. In a large bowl, toss together the blueberries, raspberries, rhubarb, apple juice, honey, and arrowroot powder until combined. Transfer the fruit mixture to the prepared dish and spread it out evenly.
Make the Topping
1. In a small bowl, stir together the almond flour, coconut, and arrowroot powder until well mixed.
2. Add the coconut oil and honey. With a fork, mix until coarse crumbs form. Spread the topping on top of the fruit in the baking dish.
3. Bake the crumble for about 35 minutes, or until bubbly and golden.

Per Serving
calories: 304 | fat: 22g | protein: 3g | carbs: 30g | fiber: 4g | sugar: 23g | sodium: 4mg

Banana Missouri Cookies

Prep time: 10 minutes | Cook time: 1½ hours | Makes 24 cookies

½ cup coconut oil
½ cup unsweetened almond milk
1 overripe banana, mashed well
½ cup coconut sugar
¼ cup cacao powder
1 teaspoon vanilla extract
¼ teaspoon sea salt
3 cups rolled oats
½ cup almond butter

1. In a medium bowl, stir together the coconut oil, almond milk, mashed banana, coconut sugar, cacao powder, vanilla, and salt. Pour the mixture into the slow cooker.
2. Pour the oats on top without stirring.
3. Put the almond butter on top of the oats without stirring.
4. Cover the cooker and set to high. Cook for 1½ hours.
5. Stir the mixture well. As it cools, scoop tablespoon-size balls out and press onto a baking sheet to continue to cool. Serve when hardened. Keep leftovers refrigerated in an airtight container for up to 1 week.

Per Serving
calories: 140 | fat: 9g | protein: 2g | carbs: 14g | fiber: 2g | sugar: 5g | sodium: 29mg

Vanilla Coconut Cake

Prep time: 10 minutes | Cook time: 45 minutes | Serves 8

½ cup coconut oil, melted, plus more for greasing the baking dish
2 cups egg whites (about 12), at room temperature
Pinch sea salt
1 cup unsweetened almond milk
6 tablespoons raw honey
2 teaspoons pure vanilla extract
1 cup coconut flour
½ cup shredded unsweetened coconut
2 teaspoons baking powder

1. Preheat the oven to 350°F (180°C).
2. Lightly grease a baking dish with coconut oil and set it aside.
3. In a large bowl, beat the egg whites and sea salt with an electric mixer until soft peaks form. Set them aside.
4. In another large bowl, whisk the almond milk, honey, remaining ½ cup of coconut oil, and the vanilla.
5. Whisk in the coconut flour, coconut, and baking powder until well combined.
6. Fold the beaten egg whites into the batter, keeping as much volume as possible, until just blended. Spoon the batter into the prepared dish and smooth the top.
7. Bake the cake for about 45 minutes, or until cooked through and lightly browned.
8. Cool the cake completely on a wire rack.
9. Serve with fresh fruit, if desired.

Per Serving
calories: 237 | fat: 17g | protein: 7g | carbs: 16g | fiber: 1g | sugar: 15g | sodium: 136mg

Cinnamon-Vanilla Pecans

Prep time: 10 minutes | Cook time: 3 hours | Makes 3½ cups

1 tablespoon coconut oil
1 large egg white
2 tablespoons ground cinnamon
2 teaspoons vanilla extract
¼ cup maple syrup
2 tablespoons coconut sugar
¼ teaspoon sea salt
3 cups pecan halves

1. Coat the slow cooker with the coconut oil.
2. In a medium bowl, whisk the egg white.
3. Add the cinnamon, vanilla, maple syrup, coconut sugar, and salt. Whisk well to combine.
4. Add the pecans and stir to coat. Pour the pecans into the slow cooker.
5. Cover the cooker and set to low. Cook for 3 to 4 hours.
6. Remove the pecans from the slow cooker and spread them on a baking sheet or other cooling surface. Let cool for 5 to 10 minutes before serving. Store in an airtight container at room temperature for up to 2 weeks.

Per Serving (¼ cup)
calories: 195 | fat: 18g | protein: 2g | carbs: 9g | fiber: 3g | sugar: 6g | sodium: 46mg

Maple-Vanilla Carob Sheet Cake

Prep time: 10 minutes | Cook time: 40 minutes | Serves 12

1 cup melted coconut oil, plus more for greasing the baking dish
10 eggs
1 cup pure maple syrup
2 teaspoons pure vanilla extract
¾ cup coconut flour
½ cup carob powder
1 teaspoon baking soda
⅛ teaspoon sea salt

1. Preheat the oven to 350°F (180°C).
2. Lightly grease a baking dish with coconut oil and set it aside.
3. In a large bowl, beat or whisk the eggs until frothy.
4. Add the remaining 1 cup of coconut oil, the maple syrup, and vanilla. Beat or whisk until well blended.
5. In a small bowl, stir together the coconut flour, carob powder, baking soda, and sea salt. Add the dry ingredients to the wet ingredients and blend until smooth. Pour the batter into the prepared dish.
6. Bake for about 40 minutes, or until a knife inserted in the center comes out clean.
7. Remove the cake from the oven and let it cool on a wire rack.
8. Serve with fruit or topped with whipped coconut cream, if desired.

Per Serving
calories: 312 | fat: 25g | protein: 6g | carbs: 21g | fiber: 2g | sugar: 18g | sodium: 188mg

Maple Carrot Cake with Pecans

Prep time: 10 minutes | Cook time: 45 minutes | Serves 12

½ cup coconut oil, at room temperature, plus more for greasing the baking dish
¼ cup pure maple syrup
2 teaspoons pure vanilla extract
6 eggs
½ cup coconut flour
1 teaspoon baking soda
1 teaspoon baking powder
1 teaspoon ground cinnamon
½ teaspoon ground nutmeg
⅛ teaspoon sea salt
3 cups finely grated carrots
½ cup chopped pecans

1. Preheat the oven to 350°F (180°C).
2. Lightly grease a baking dish with coconut oil and set it aside.
3. In a large bowl, whisk the ½ cup of coconut oil, maple syrup, and vanilla until blended.
4. One at a time, whisk in the eggs, beating well after each addition.
5. In a medium bowl, stir together the coconut flour, baking soda, baking powder, cinnamon, nutmeg, and sea salt. Add the dry ingredients to the wet ingredients and stir until just combined.
6. Stir in the carrots and pecans until mixed. Spoon the batter into the prepared dish.
7. Bake for about 45 minutes, or until a toothpick inserted in the center comes out clean.
8. Cool the cake on a wire rack and serve.

Per Serving
calories: 254 | fat: 21g | protein: 5g | carbs: 12g | fiber: 2g | sugar: 6g | sodium: 182mg

Vanilla Coconut Yogurt

Prep time: 5 minutes | Cook time: 1 hour | Makes 3½ cups

3 (13½-ounce / 383-g) cans full-fat coconut milk
5 probiotic capsules (not pills)
1 teaspoon raw honey
½ teaspoon vanilla extract

1. Pour the coconut milk into the slow cooker.
2. Cover the cooker and set to high. Cook for 1 to 2 hours, until the temperature of the milk reaches 180°F (82°C) measured with a candy thermometer.
3. Turn off the slow cooker and allow the temperature of the milk to come down close to 100°F (38°C).
4. Open the probiotic capsules and pour in the contents, along with the honey and vanilla. Stir well to combine.
5. Re-cover the slow cooker, turn it off and unplug it, and wrap it in an insulating towel to keep warm overnight as it ferments.
6. Pour the yogurt into sterilized jars and refrigerate. The yogurt should thicken slightly in the refrigerator where it will keep for up to 1 week.

Per Serving (½ cup)

calories: 305 | fat: 30g | protein: 2g | carbs: 7g | fiber: 0g | sugar: 3g | sodium: 43mg

Turmeric-Cinnamon Almond Milk

Prep time: 5 minutes | Cook time: 3 hours | Serves 4

4 cups unsweetened almond milk
4 cinnamon sticks
2 tablespoons coconut oil
1 (4-inch) piece turmeric root, roughly chopped
1 (2-inch) piece fresh ginger, roughly chopped
1 teaspoon raw honey, plus more to taste

1. In your slow cooker, combine the almond milk, cinnamon sticks, coconut oil, turmeric, and ginger.
2. Cover the cooker and set to low. Cook for 3 to 4 hours.
3. Pour the contents of the cooker through a fine-mesh sieve into a clean container; discard the solids.
4. Starting with just 1 teaspoon, add raw honey to taste.

Per Serving

calories: 133 | fat: 11g | protein: 1g | carbs: 10g | fiber: 1g | sugar: 7g | sodium: 152mg

Cinnamon Dark Drinking Chocolate

Prep time: 10 minutes | Cook time: 3 hours | Serves 4

5 cups unsweetened almond milk
2½ tablespoons coconut oil
5 tablespoons cacao powder
5 cinnamon sticks
3 to 4 teaspoons coconut sugar or raw honey
1 tablespoon vanilla extract
1 (3-inch) piece fresh ginger
1 (2-inch) piece turmeric root
3 tablespoons collagen peptides
½ to ¾ teaspoon sea salt, divided

1. In your slow cooker, combine the almond milk, coconut oil, cacao powder, cinnamon sticks, coconut sugar or honey, vanilla, ginger, and turmeric.
2. Cover the cooker and set to low. Cook for 3 to 4 hours.
3. Pour the contents of the cooker through a fine-mesh sieve into a clean container; discard the solids.
4. Stir in the collagen peptides until well combined.
5. Pour the chocolate into mugs and gently sprinkle ⅛ teaspoon of sea salt on top of each beverage. Serve hot.

Per Serving

calories: 235 | fat: 14g | protein: 7g | carbs: 20g | fiber: 4g | sugar: 12g | sodium: 512mg

Whipped Goat Cheese with Berries

Prep time: 10 minutes | Cook time: 0 minutes | Serves 4

5 ounces (142 g) goat cheese, at room temperature
1½ tablespoons honey, plus more for serving
1 tablespoon lemon juice
½ teaspoon grated orange zest
Kosher salt
2 cups blueberries
2 cups blackberries
¼ cup pistachios, chopped

1. Place the goat cheese, honey, lemon juice, orange zest, and 1 pinch of salt in a medium bowl. Whisk until the goat cheese is fluffy and smooth.
2. Divide the goat cheese mixture among bowls or wineglasses, reserving about four spoons.
3. Top each portion with berries, pistachios, and a spoonful of the whipped goat cheese. Drizzle with additional honey. Serve immediately.

Per Serving

calories: 270 | fat: 15g | protein: 11g | carbs: 27g | fiber: 6g | sugar: 18g | sodium: 188mg

Simple Lime Sorbet

Prep time: 5 minutes | Cook time: 0 minutes | Serves 4

1 cup water
½ cup raw cane sugar
1 cup lime juice, plus grated zest from ½ lime

1. Fill a medium bowl with ice water. Combine the 1 cup water and sugar in a small saucepan. Warm over low heat until the sugar is dissolved.
2. Remove the simple syrup from the heat, place the pan in the ice-water bath, and stir to chill rapidly. Alternatively, refrigerate the syrup until chilled, about 3 hours. (Store in an airtight container in the refrigerator for up to 2 weeks.)
3. Combine the lime juice with 1 cup of the simple syrup in a medium bowl. Whisk in the lime zest. Freeze the sorbet in an ice-cream maker according to the manufacturer's instructions.
4. Transfer the ice cream to a freezer-safe container and place in the freezer for 3 hours to set, or store for up to 2 weeks.

Per Serving

calories: 79 | fat: 0g | protein: 0g | carbs: 21g | fiber: 0g | sugar: 16g | sodium: 4mg

Cinnamon-Nutmeg Pecans

Prep time: 5 minutes | Cook time: 15minutes | Serves 4

1 cup pecan halves
¼ cup packed coconut sugar
3 tablespoons ghee, melted
1 teaspoon ground cinnamon
½ teaspoon ground nutmeg
¼ teaspoon sea salt

1. Preheat the oven to 350°F (180°C).
2. Line a rimmed baking sheet with parchment paper.
3. In a medium bowl, toss together the pecans, coconut sugar, ghee, cinnamon, nutmeg, and salt to combine. Spread the nuts in a single layer on the prepared sheet.
4. Bake for 15 to 17 minutes until the nuts are fragrant.

Per Serving

calories: 303 | fat: 27g | protein: 2g | carbs: 18g | fiber: 3g | sugar: 14g | sodium: 150mg

Coconut-Blueberry Rice

Prep time: 5 minutes | Cook time: 10 minutes | Serves 4

1 (14-ounce / 397-g) can full-fat coconut milk
1 cup fresh blueberries
¼ cup honey
1 teaspoon ground ginger
Pinch sea salt
2 cups cooked brown rice

1. In a large pot over medium-high heat, combine the coconut milk, blueberries, honey, ginger, and salt. Cook for about 7 minutes, stirring constantly, until the blueberries soften.
2. Stir in the rice. Cook for about 3 minutes, stirring, until the rice is heated through.

Per Serving

calories: 437 | fat: 26g | protein: 5g | carbs: 51g | fiber: 5g | sugar: 25g | sodium: 61mg

Greek Yogurt with Nuts and Blueberries

Prep time: 5 minutes | Cook time: 0 minutes | Serves 4

3 cups unsweetened plain Greek yogurt
1½ cups blueberries
¾ cup chopped mixed nuts
½ cup honey

1. Spoon the yogurt into four bowls.
2. Sprinkle with the blueberries and nuts and drizzle with the honey.

Per Serving

calories: 457 | fat: 18g | protein: 15g | carbs: 62g | fiber: 3g | sugar: 54g | sodium: 213mg

Berry Pops

Prep time: 10 minutes | Cook time: 0 minutes | Makes 4 medium ice pops

1 cup blueberries, fresh or frozen
1 cup strawberries, fresh or frozen
2 tablespoons raw honey
2 cups plain whole-milk yogurt
1 teaspoon freshly squeezed lemon juice
¼ cup filtered water

1. Put all the ingredients in a blender, then pulse to combine well until creamy and smooth.
2. Pour the mixture in the ice pop molds, then place in the freezer to free for at least 3 hours. Serve chilled.

Per Serving

calories: 140 | fat: 4g | protein: 5g | carbs: 23g | fiber: 2g | sugar: 20g | sodium: 58mg

Peach and Nectarine Cobbler

Prep time: 10 minutes | Cook time: 20 minutes | Serves 8

1 teaspoon coconut oil plus ¼ cup, melted
2 cups sliced fresh nectarines
2 cups sliced fresh peaches
2 tablespoons freshly squeezed lemon juice
¾ cup almond flour
¼ cup coconut sugar
¾ cup rolled oats
1 teaspoon ground cinnamon
½ teaspoon vanilla extract
Sea salt, to taste
Filtered water, for mixing

1. Preheat the oven to 425°F (220°C). Grease a baking sheet with 1 teaspoon of coconut oil.
2. Combine the nectarines, peaches, and lemon juice in the sheet. Stir to mix well. Set aside.
3. Put the almond flour, coconut sugar, oats, cinnamon, vanilla, salt, and remaining coconut oil in a food processor. Pulse until a dry dough forms. Add a tablespoon of water if the dough is too dry.
4. Transfer the dough in a large bowl, then break the dough into chunks with your hands. Top the fruit in the baking sheet with the dough chunks.
5. Place the baking sheet in the preheated oven and bake for 20 minutes or until golden brown. Serve warm.

Per Serving
calories: 182 | fat: 9g | protein: 4g | carbs: 29g | fiber: 4g | sugar: 12g | sodium: 293mg

Blueberry Parfait

Prep time: 5 minutes | Cook time: 2 minutes | Serves 4

Cream:
2 (14-ounce / 397-g) cans coconut cream, chilled
1 tablespoon pure maple syrup
1 tablespoon fresh lemon zest
½ teaspoon vanilla extract
Sea salt, to taste
Parfait:
2½ cups fresh blueberries

Make the Cream
1. Whip the coconut cream in a large bowl with a hand mixer for 2 minutes or until the peaks form.
2. Then add the lemon zest, vanilla, maple syrup, and salt. Whip to combine well.
Make the Parfait
3. Pour half of the cream mixture in the bottom of a serving glass, then top with 1 cup of blueberries.
4. Spread the cream mixture on top of the blueberries, then top the cream with remaining blueberries.
5. Serve immediately.

Per Serving
calories: 458 | fat: 43g | protein: 5g | carbs: 23g | fiber: 2g | sugar: 12g | sodium: 609mg

Hot Coconut Chocolate

Prep time: 10 minutes | Cook time: 7 minutes | Serves 2

1 tablespoon coconut oil
2 cups coconut milk
1 tablespoon collagen protein powder
2 tablespoons cocoa powder
2 teaspoons coconut sugar
½ teaspoon ground turmeric
1 teaspoon ground ginger
1 teaspoon vanilla extract
1 teaspoon ground cinnamon
Sea salt, to taste
Cayenne pepper, to taste

1. Heat the coconut oil and almond milk in a saucepan over medium heat for 7 minutes. Stir constantly.
2. Mix in the collagen protein powder, then fold in the cocoa powder and coconut sugar. Stir to mix well.
3. Pour the mixture in a blender, then add the remaining ingredients. Pulse until the mixture is creamy and bubbly.
4. Serve immediately.

Per Serving
calories: 570 | fat: 57g | protein: 8g | carbs: 17g | fiber: 3g | sugar: 5g | sodium: 50mg

Almond Butter Fudge with Chocolate-Honey Sauce

Prep time: 5 minutes | Cook time: 5 minutes | Makes 9 pieces

Chocolate-Honey Sauce:
3 tablespoons cocoa powder
1½ tablespoons raw honey
3 tablespoons coconut oil
Sea salt, to taste
Fudge:
¼ cup coconut oil
2 tablespoons coconut sugar
½ teaspoon vanilla extract
1 cup natural almond butter
½ teaspoon salt

For the Chocolate-Honey Sauce
1. Put the ingredients for the chocolate sauce in a saucepan and heat over medium heat for 5 minutes or until the sauce is lightly thickened. Keep stirring during the heating.
2. Turn off the heat and let sit in a small bowl until ready to use.
For the Fudge
3. Line a loaf pan with parchment paper.
4. Melted the coconut oil in the cleaned saucepan over medium heat.
5. Turn off the heat and mix in the coconut sugar. Pour them in a separate bowl.
6. Add the remaining ingredients and stir to combine well.
7. Pour the mixture in the loaf pan, then put in the freezer to freeze for 15 minutes or until solid.
8. Remove the fudge from the freezer, then cut into 9 pieces and baste with sauce to serve.

Per Serving (1 piece)
calories: 284 | fat: 26g | protein: 6g | carbs: 11g | fiber: 3g | sugar: 6g | sodium: 132mg

Chocolate and Almond Butter Mini Muffins

Prep time: 5 minutes | Cook time: 0 minutes | Makes 9 muffins

6 ounces (170 g) dark chocolate, chopped
½ cup natural almond butter
2 tablespoons raw honey
½ teaspoon vanilla extract
Sea salt, to taste

1. Line a 9-cup muffin tin with paper muffin cups.
2. Melt the chocolate in a saucepan over low heat, then divide half of the chocolate in the muffin cups. Set the remaining half aside.
3. Combine the almond butter, vanilla, and honey in a bowl. Stir to mix well. Divide and shape the mixture into 9 balls, then drop each ball in each muffin cup.
4. Top the balls with remaining melted chocolate, then sprinkle with salt.
5. Place the muffin tin in the refrigerator for at least 3 hours or until solid.
6. Serve chilled.

Per Serving (1 muffin)

calories: 213 | fat: 16g | protein: 5g | carbs: 14g | fiber: 4g | sugar: 9g | sodium: 22mg

Blueberry and Peach Cobbler

Prep time: 10 minutes | Cook time: 2 hours | Serves 4 to 6

3 tablespoons coconut oil, divided
2 cups frozen blueberries
3 large peaches, peeled and sliced
1 cup rolled oats
1 cup almond flour
1 tablespoon coconut sugar
½ teaspoon vanilla extract
1 tablespoon pure maple syrup
1 teaspoon ground cinnamon
Pinch ground nutmeg

1. Grease the slow cooker with 1 tablespoon of coconut oil.
2. Put the blueberries and peaches in the single layer in the slow cooker.
3. Combine the remaining ingredients in a large bowl, then stir to mix well. Break the mixture into chunks with your hands, then spread the chunks on top of the blueberries and peaches in the slow cooker.
4. Cover the slow cooker lid and cook on high for 2 hours or until golden brown.
5. Allow to cool for 15 minutes, then serve warm.

Per Serving

calories: 515 | fat: 34g | protein: 10g | carbs: 49g | fiber: 10g | sugar:

24g | sodium: 1mg

Pecan and Spice Stuffed Apple Bake

Prep time: 10 minutes | Cook time: 2 hours | Makes 5 apples

5 apples, cored
½ cup water
½ cup crushed pecans
¼ teaspoon ground cloves
1 teaspoon ground cinnamon
¼ teaspoon ground cardamom
½ teaspoon ground ginger
¼ cup melted coconut oil

1. Peel a thin strip off the top of each apple.
2. Pour the water in the slow cooker, then arrange the apples in the slow cooker, upright.
3. Combine the remaining ingredients in a small bowl. Stir to mix well.
4. Spread the mixture on tops of the apples, then put the slow cooker lid on and cook on high for 2 hours or until the apples are tender.
5. Allow to cool for 15 minutes, then remove the apples from the slow cooker gently and serve warm.

Per Serving (1 apple)

calories: 216 | fat: 12g | protein: 0g | carbs: 30g | fiber: 6g | sugar: 22g | sodium: 0mg

Banana Cacao Brownies

Prep time: 10 minutes | Cook time: 3 hours | Serves 4 to 6

3 tablespoons coconut oil, divided
2 ripe bananas, mashed
1 cup unsweetened cacao powder
1 cup almond butter
2 large eggs
½ cup coconut sugar
2 teaspoons vanilla extract
1 teaspoon baking soda
½ teaspoon sea salt

1. Grease the slow cooker with 1 tablespoon of coconut oil.
2. Combine the remaining ingredients in a large bowl. Stir to mix well until a batter forms.
3. Pour the batter in the greased slow cooker. Cover and cook on low for 3 hours or until lightly firmed and a toothpick inserted in the center comes out clean.
4. Remove the brownies from the slow cooker and slice to serve.

Per Serving

calories: 778 | fat: 51g | protein: 18g | carbs: 68g | fiber: 15g | sugar: 35g | sodium: 666mg

Glazed Pears with Hazelnuts

Prep time: 5 minutes | Cook time: 15 minutes | Serves 4

4 pears, peeled, cored, and quartered lengthwise
1 cup apple juice
1 tablespoon grated fresh ginger
½ cup pure maple syrup
¼ cup chopped hazelnuts

1. Put the pears in a large pot, then pour the apple juice over. Bring to a boil over medium-high heat.
2. Reduce the heat to medium-low, then cover and simmer for 15 minutes or until the pears are tender.
3. Meanwhile, put the ginger and maple syrup in a saucepan. Bring to a boil over medium-high heat. Stir constantly. Turn off the heat and let stand until ready to use.
4. Transfer the simmered pears onto a large plate, then glaze with the gingered maple syrup. Spread the hazelnuts on top and serve warm.

Per Serving

calories: 285 | fat: 3g | protein: 2g | carbs: 67g | fiber: 7g | sugar: 50g | sodium: 9mg

Blueberry Muffins

Prep time: 10 minutes | Cook time: 15 minutes | Serves 4

½ cup fresh blueberries
3 free range egg whites
1 tablespoon coconut flour
1 cup chickpea flour
1 tablespoon nutmeg, grated
1 teaspoon baking powder
1 teaspoon vanilla extract
1 teaspoon stevia

1. Preheat the oven to 325°F (160°C). Line a 4-cup muffin tin with paper muffin cups.
2. Combine all the ingredients in a large bowl. Stir to mix well.
3. Divide the batter into the muffin cups, then place the muffin tin in the preheated oven.
4. Bake for 15 minutes or until a toothpick inserted in the center comes out clean.
5. Transfer the muffins on a cooling rack to cool for a few minutes before serving.

Per Serving

calories: 133 | fat: 2g | protein: 8g | carbs: 20g | fiber: 3g | sugar: 5g | sodium: 58mg

Banana Brownies with Strawberry Sauce

Prep time: 15 minutes | Cook time: 18 minutes | Makes 9 brownies

Strawberry Sauce:
1 cup mashed fresh strawberries
2 teaspoons coconut sugar
1 tablespoon filtered water
Banana Brownies:
Coconut oil, for greasing the pan
½ cup cocoa powder
¼ cup coconut sugar
¾ cup almond butter
1 egg yolk, whisked
1 teaspoon vanilla extract
½ teaspoon baking soda
1 ripe banana, mashed
¼ teaspoon sea salt

Make the Strawberry Sauce
1. Put the ingredients for the strawberry sauce in a saucepan.
2. Cook for 6 minutes or until thickened and well combined. Keep stirring during the cooking.
3. Turn off the heat and set aside until ready to use.
Make the Banana Brownies
4. Preheat the oven to 350°F (180°C). Grease a baking pan with coconut oil.
5. Combine the cocoa powder, coconut sugar, and almond butter in a bowl. Stir to mix well.
6. Combine the egg yolk, vanilla, baking soda, banana, and salt in a separate bowl. Stir to mix well.
7. Make a will in the center of the cocoa powder mixture, then pour the egg mixture in the well. Stir to mix well until a batter forms.
8. Pour the batter in the prepared baking pan, then level with a spatula.
9. Bake in the preheated oven for 12 minutes or until a toothpick inserted in the center comes out clean.
10. Remove the brownies from the oven and allow to cool for 5 minutes.
11. Glaze the brownies with strawberry sauce and slice to serve.

Per Serving (1 brownie)

calories: 193 | fat: 14g | protein: 6g | carbs: 15g | fiber: 5g | sugar: 7g | sodium: 139mg

Easy Cranberry Compote

Prep time: 5 minutes | Cook time: 10 minutes | Serves 4

4 cups fresh cranberries
1 tablespoon grated fresh ginger
Juice of 2 oranges
¼ cup raw honey
Zest of 1 orange

1. Combine all the ingredients in a large pot. Stir to mix well.
2. Bring to a boil over medium-high heat, then cook for 10 more minutes or until it thickens and the cranberries pop.
3. Turn off the heat and allow to cool for a few minutes.
4. Pour them in a large bowl and serve warm.

Per Serving

calories: 171 | fat: 1g | protein: 1g | carbs: 39g | fiber: 6g | sugar: 30g | sodium: 1mg

Blueberry Crisp with Oats and Pecans

Prep time: 10 minutes | Cook time: 20 minutes | Serves 4

½ cup coconut oil, melted, plus additional for brushing
1 quart fresh blueberries
¼ cup pure maple syrup
Juice of ½ lemon
2 teaspoons lemon zest
1 cup gluten-free rolled oats
½ teaspoon ground cinnamon
½ cup chopped pecans
Pinch salt

1. Preheat the oven to 350°F (180°C).
2. Brush a shallow baking dish with melted coconut oil. Stir together the blueberries, maple syrup, lemon juice, and lemon zest in the dish.
3. In a small bowl, combine the oats, ½ cup of melted coconut oil, cinnamon, pecans, and salt. Mix the ingredients well to evenly distribute the coconut oil. Sprinkle the oat mixture over the berries.
4. Place the dish in the preheated oven and bake for 20 minutes, or until the oats are lightly browned.

Per Serving
calories: 497 | fat: 33g | protein: 5g | carbs: 51g | fiber: 7g | sugar: 26g | sodium: 42mg

Almond Ice Cream with Cherries

Prep time: 5 minutes | Cook time: 0 minutes | Serves 4 to 6

1 (10-ounce / 284-g) package frozen no-added-sugar cherries
3 cups unsweetened almond milk
1 teaspoon vanilla extract
½ teaspoon almond extract

1. In a blender or food processor, combine the cherries, almond milk, vanilla extract, and almond extract. Process until mostly smooth; a few chunks of cherries are fine.
2. Pour the mixture into a container with an airtight lid. Freeze thoroughly before serving.

Per Serving
calories: 82 | fat: 2g | protein: 1g | carbs: 14g | fiber: 2g | sugar: 12g | sodium: 121mg

Ritzy Compote

Prep time: 10 minutes | Cook time: 5 minutes | Serves 8

4 cups apples, peeled and sliced
2 cups dried apricots, finely chopped
2 cups black figs, finely chopped
2 cups peaches, finely chopped
2 cups dates, finely chopped
Juice of 1 lemon

1. Put all the fruits in a large pot, then pour in enough water to cover.
2. Soak for an hour, then turn on the heat and bring to a boil.
3. Reduce the heat to low and simmer for 5 minutes.
4. Turn off the heat and drizzle with lemon juice.
5. Transfer them in a large bowl and serve immediately.

Per Serving
calories: 319 | fat: 1g | protein: 4g | carbs: 83g | fiber: 11g | sugar: 68g | sodium: 8mg

Rosemary Pineapple with Chocolate Ganache

Prep time: 5 minutes | Cook time: 1 minutes | Serves 6

Ganache:
½ cup unsweetened coconut milk
1½ cups semi-sweet or bittersweet chocolate morsels
Pineapple:
1 pineapple, peeled, cored, and cut into 16 wedges
1 tablespoon coconut oil, melted
1 tablespoon coconut sugar
1 teaspoon chopped fresh rosemary

Make the Ganache
1. In a medium saucepan over medium-high heat, add the coconut milk. Heat the milk until it just begins to scald (little bubbles or foam will begin to collect around the perimeter of the pan).
2. Remove the pan from the heat and add the chocolate. Let stand for 1 minute.
3. Whisk the mixture until it's smooth and satiny.
Make the Pineapple
4. Preheat an indoor stove-top grill until very hot.
5. Brush the pineapple wedges with melted coconut oil.
6. Grill the wedges for 1 to 2 minutes per side, or until grill marks appear.
7. Arrange the pineapple on a serving platter and sprinkle with the coconut sugar and rosemary.
8. Serve with the ganache.

Per Serving
calories: 462 | fat: 23g | protein: 5g | carbs: 61g | fiber: 2g | sugar: 48g | sodium: 5mg

Almond Butter Chocolate Cups

Prep time: 5 minutes | Cook time: 0 minutes | Makes 9 cups

6 ounces (170 g) dark chocolate, chopped
½ cup natural almond butter
2 tablespoons raw honey
½ teaspoon vanilla extract
Dash salt

1. Line 9 cups of a mini muffin tin with mini paper liners.
2. In a small saucepan over low heat, slowly melt the chocolate. Use half of the chocolate among the mini muffin cups. Set the rest of the chocolate aside.
3. In a small bowl, stir together the almond butter, honey, and vanilla. Divide the mixture into 9 portions and roll each into a small ball. Drop 1 ball into each muffin cup.
4. Drizzle the remaining chocolate into each cup, covering the almond butter balls.
5. Sprinkle each lightly with the salt.
6. Refrigerate until solid.

Per Serving (1 cup)
calories: 193 | fat: 16g | protein: 5g | carbs: 14g | fiber: 0g | sugar: 9g | sodium: 22mg

Pumpkin Pudding with Pecans

Prep time: 10 minutes | Cook time: 0 minutes | Serves 6

2 cups canned full-fat coconut milk
1 cup pure pumpkin purée
¼ cup pure maple syrup
1 teaspoon ground cinnamon
½ teaspoon ground ginger
¼ teaspoon ground nutmeg
Pinch cloves
2 tablespoons chopped pecans, for garnish

1. In a large bowl, whisk the coconut milk, pumpkin, maple syrup, cinnamon, ginger, nutmeg, and cloves. Cover the bowl and refrigerator it for about 2 hours until chilled.
2. Serve topped with the pecans.

Per Serving
calories: 250 | fat: 21g | protein: 3g | carbs: 17g | fiber: 3g | sugar: 9g | sodium: 12mg

Vanilla Cookies with Chocolate Chips

Prep time: 10 minutes | Cook time: 9 minutes | Makes 12 cookies

¾ cup creamy almond butter
½ cup coconut sugar
¼ cup cocoa powder
2 teaspoons vanilla extract
1 egg
1 egg yolk
1 teaspoon baking soda
¼ teaspoon salt
½ cup semi-sweet chocolate chips
Dash sea salt (optional)

1. Preheat the oven to 350°F (180°C).
2. Line 2 baking sheets with parchment paper.
3. In a medium bowl, cream together the almond butter, coconut sugar, cocoa powder, and vanilla.
4. In a small bowl, whisk the egg and egg yolk. Add the eggs to the almond butter mixture and stir to combine.
5. Stir in the baking soda, salt, and chocolate chips until well mixed. Divide the dough into 12 pieces. Roll the dough into balls and put 6 on each prepared pan.
6. Bake for 9 to 10 minutes. Let the cookies rest on the pans for 5 minutes, where they'll continue to cook. Sprinkle each with a dash of sea salt (if using). Remove to a cooling rack.

Per Serving (2 cookies)
calories: 307 | fat: 20g | protein: 9g | carbs: 28g | fiber: 4g | sugar: 20g | sodium: 364mg

Honey-Cinnamon Apple Compote

Prep time: 5 minutes | Cook time: 10 minutes | Serves 4

6 apples, peeled, cored, and chopped
¼ cup apple juice
¼ cup honey
1 teaspoon ground cinnamon
Pinch sea salt

1. In a large pot over medium-high heat, combine the apples, apple juice, honey, cinnamon, and salt.
2. Simmer for about 10 minutes, stirring occasionally, until the apples are still quite chunky but also saucy.

Per Serving
calories: 247 | fat: 1g | protein: 1g | carbs: 66g | fiber: 9g | sugar: 54g | sodium: 63mg

APPENDIX 1: MEASUREMENT CONVERSION CHART

VOLUME EQUIVALENTS(DRY)

US STANDARD	METRIC (APPROXIMATE)
1/8 teaspoon	0.5 mL
1/4 teaspoon	1 mL
1/2 teaspoon	2 mL
3/4 teaspoon	4 mL
1 teaspoon	5 mL
1 tablespoon	15 mL
1/4 cup	59 mL
1/2 cup	118 mL
3/4 cup	177 mL
1 cup	235 mL
2 cups	475 mL
3 cups	700 mL
4 cups	1 L

VOLUME EQUIVALENTS(LIQUID)

US STANDARD	US STANDARD (OUNCES)	METRIC (APPROXIMATE)
2 tablespoons	1 fl.oz.	30 mL
1/4 cup	2 fl.oz.	60 mL
1/2 cup	4 fl.oz.	120 mL
1 cup	8 fl.oz.	240 mL
1 1/2 cup	12 fl.oz.	355 mL
2 cups or 1 pint	16 fl.oz.	475 mL
4 cups or 1 quart	32 fl.oz.	1 L
1 gallon	128 fl.oz.	4 L

TEMPERATURES EQUIVALENTS

FAHRENHEIT(F)	CELSIUS(C) (APPROXIMATE)
225 °F	107 °C
250 °F	120 °C
275 °F	135 °C
300 °F	150 °C
325 °F	160 °C
350 °F	180 °C
375 °F	190 °C
400 °F	205 °C
425 °F	220 °C
450 °F	235 °C
475 °F	245 °C
500 °F	260 °C

WEIGHT EQUIVALENTS

US STANDARD	METRIC (APPROXIMATE)
1 ounce	28 g
2 ounces	57 g
5 ounces	142 g
10 ounces	284 g
15 ounces	425 g
16 ounces (1 pound)	455 g
1.5 pounds	680 g
2 pounds	907 g

APPENDIX 2: INDEX

Made in the USA
Monee, IL
08 September 2021